Further Praise for *Joy Enough*

"[*Joy Enough*] is a book about an extraordinary figure who was a housewife, mother and divorcée. . . . The word 'mother' doesn't entirely do her justice, and yet that's what this memoir does: does her justice, in more than a summarizing word."

—Rachel Khong, *New York Times Book Review*

"*Joy Enough* resonates with the immediacy of a love letter and the dark wonder of a dream. A tender, candid, force field of an elegy, compressed and expansive at once."

—Paul Lisicky, author of *The Narrow Door: A Memoir of Friendship*

"[Sarah] McColl's gift is in distilling a lifetime—the relationships, hopes nurtured then dashed, joys still sought, even at life's end—into vignettes of great beauty, ordinary moments held up for loving examination. . . . The book begins, slyly enough, with a literary question: 'I loved my mother, and she died. Is that a story?' It turns out that the answer is yes, and if the mother is anything like Allison, you will want to read it, and to know her."

—Kate Tuttle, *Los Angeles Times*

"*Joy Enough* is so compelling that I stayed up most of the night while traveling by train in a sleeper car. Sarah McColl's exquisite memoir is the perfect balm for anyone who has experienced the sharp sting of loneliness or inhabited the liminal space between grief and happiness." —Michele Filgate, writer and contributing editor at *Literary Hub*

"Written with enough beauty to stop clocks ticking and hearts beating. . . . McColl's resonant first book is resplendent with love, and the hope she finds in discovering that her unfathomable grief also carved a space for more profound joy."

—*Booklist*, starred review

"Oh, my heart. *Joy Enough* is a stunningly beautiful and meditative map of loss—a mother, a marriage, an idea of what life is supposed to be. . . . I will carry this book with me for the rest of my goddamn life: a manual, a friend, an inspiration."

—Megan Stielstra, author of *The Wrong Way to Save Your Life*

"What if the greatest love you ever had was your mother? In sensuous and elliptical prose, Sarah McColl takes us into the small spaces that contain a life, revealing both the emptiness left by the loss of her mother and the joy that endures. I was intoxicated by this book from start to finish. McColl has a superfan now."

—Sarah Hepola, author of *Blackout*

"Pitch-perfect . . . the kind of book that will remain your dear friend, that will be there for you, long after you've finished the last page." —Piper Weiss, author of *You All Grow Up and Leave Me*

"Already drawing comparisons to C. S. Lewis's *A Grief Observed*, Sarah McColl asks her readers to join her as she navigates both grief and the parentless world she faces following her mother's death. . . . The memoir results in a brilliant portrayal of two women: McColl's mother, a fierce protector who sprinkled joy wherever she went, and McColl herself, a woman full of love who must go on despite losing everything she thought to be a constant."

—Samantha Grindell, *Romper*

"Beautifully tender; a deceptively delicate slow-burn story of grief and love and the desire to hold close those we love."

—Sophie Mackintosh, Booker-longlisted author of *The Water Cure*

"In beautiful, spare prose, Sarah McColl offers an elegant and deeply felt meditation on loss that is steeped in the pleasures of this life: in good bread and soft sweaters, friendship, flirtation, and especially love. *Joy Enough* is a memoir about the death of a mother and a marriage, yes, but more than that, it's about the new life that can spring from those empty spaces. A gorgeous, painful, exhilarating debut."

—Kirstin Valdez Quade, author of *Night at the Fiestas*

"A touching, beautifully written memoir that looks back on both losses with love." —Elizabeth Entenman, *Hello Giggles*

"*Joy Enough* is a diamond in book form, a beauty forged by the weight of loss and learning. It stunned me with its taut clarity, with the way it probes. . . . McColl has a rare talent, and it shines."

—Molly Wizenberg, author of *A Homemade Life* and *Delancey*

"Through sparse yet shimmering prose, readers will come to know McColl's own mother as well. . . . Even though McColl's story fits neatly into the genre of 'grief memoir,' it is utterly hopeful. An unforgettable debut." —*Library Journal*, starred review

JOY

enough

SARAH McCOLL

JOY enough

A Memoir

LIVERIGHT PUBLISHING CORPORATION

A Division of W. W. Norton & Company

Independent Publishers Since 1923

Excerpt from "Amy Hempel, The Art of Fiction No. 176" interview by Paul Winner, originally published in *The Paris Review*, Issue 166, Summer 2003. Copyright © 2003 The Paris Review, used by permission of The Wylie Agency LLC.

For information about permission to reproduce selections from this book, write to Permissions, Liveright Publishing Corporation, a division of W. W. Norton & Company, Inc., 500 Fifth Avenue, New York, NY 10110

For information about special discounts for bulk purchases, please contact W. W. Norton Special Sales at specialsales@wwnorton.com or 800-233-4830

Manufacturing by LSC Communications, Harrisonburg
Book design by Ellen Cipriano
Production manager: Anna Oler

Library of Congress Cataloging-in-Publication Data

Names: McColl, Sarah, author.
Title: Joy enough : a memoir / Sarah McColl.
Description: First edition. | New York : Liveright Publishing Corporation, a division of W. W. Norton & Company, [2019]
Identifiers: LCCN 2018026979 | ISBN 9781631494703 (hardcover)
Subjects: LCSH: McColl, Sarah—Health. | Children of cancer patients—Biography. | Mothers and daughters. | Divorce.
Classification: LCC RC265.6.M39 A3 2019 | DDC 618.92/9940092 [B]—dc23
LC record available at https://lccn.loc.gov/2018026979

ISBN 978-1-63149-663-9 pbk.

Liveright Publishing Corporation, 500 Fifth Avenue, New York, N.Y. 10110
www.wwnorton.com

W. W. Norton & Company Ltd., 15 Carlisle Street, London W1D 3BS

1 2 3 4 5 6 7 8 9 0

For Duncan, Katy, and Bliss

Some writers have a more defined sense of cause and effect. Plot. My sense of life is more moment, moment, and moment. Looking back, they accrue and occur to you at a certain time and maybe you don't know why, but you trust that they are coming back to you now for a reason. And you make a leap of faith. You trust you can put these moments together and create story.

—Amy Hempel

Finally, the lessons of impermanence taught me this: loss constitutes an odd kind of fullness; despair empties out into an unquenchable appetite for life.

—Gretel Ehrlich

The mere sense of living is joy enough.

—Emily Dickinson

winter

LOVED MY MOTHER, and she died. Is that a story?

Story is giving a character a tangible desire, then putting things in her way. A writer I was falling in love with told me that. My desire is for my mother to live. *More tangible*, he says. My desire is not to forget. *More tangible*, he says.

Then my desire is for her to meet the next man I love, the one I keep now that I know a thing or two. My desire is for her to see my round silhouette in a summer dress, then to hold my baby in the delivery room. In winter, my desire is to make chili with the mixture of garden tomatoes and hot peppers she calls *hell* that I've kept in the back of my freezer. Our desires are equally impossible: to freeze hell, to thaw it; to reverse time, to stop it. My desire is to have more of what I do not need, seconds of what has been my fair share: a fight, a car ride, a cup of coffee, ignored advice straight from the mouth of a grade A know-it-all.

Or none of this. My desire is preservation, to carry her lodged beneath my breast like a bone.

More tangible, he says.

H ER NAME WAS Allison, but her father called her Tune. My little petunia, he said.

It was like living in a green bowl, she said, the way the valley curved out a hollow at the foot of Mt. Greylock, and another ridge rose behind the barn and silo, enclosing their loneliness. The sphere at the end of the banister was the size of a boy's face and about the right height. She leaned in with eyes closed to practice. Ridgeview Farm was in Western Massachusetts, five long, hilly miles outside of Williamstown along the cold Green River. She let the screen door bang on her way out to the pasture.

The air was manure and hay. It smelled of warm earth, of growing things. How do you round up cows? They are docile but slow moving, recalcitrant, with calves at their sides like small shadows. Maybe she called them by name or had the help of a dog, but somehow she herded those somnolent beasts into the barn where there were quiet stalls lined with stiff straw, and birds sat overhead in the eaves of the aluminum roof. Somehow she convinced them that was where they wanted to be.

It was not where she wanted to be. She felt the ache at every age, when she played house with a family of her own imagined children and performed from a rock to an audience of dumb day-lilies. Her father shook the ice in his bourbon-and-gingers while he told jokes at a dinner table tight with seven plates of spaghetti. But the neighborhood was empty of anyone who wasn't a relative or slow-talking farmer. Just as her mother escaped to town each morning to swivel around an office, Tune rode a bike into thick woods. Under a slow-waving canopy, the light came through in patches. Mother and daughter's longing was shared but unspoken.

When Tune was an adult and her own mother died, the parked cars overflowed onto the road's grassy shoulder, and four college presidents stood in the back of the church. Tune didn't cry. She had lost her mother a long time ago, she said, when she understood her mother was not the kind she had needed. This is one kind of mother and daughter.

She and I are another.

WHEN PEOPLE SAY, tell me about your mother, which they never do, I say she was my spiritual home.

So to say I miss her—which I often did in the months following her death, because I did not have the language to express my roiling grief—was a polite way of calling myself a cosmic orphan, like a moon whose planet has fallen out of orbit.

My physical home: Sixth Avenue in Brooklyn, where I mark time by the trees, one in particular. The willow at Fifteenth Street is lush with long, falling maiden hair, its boughs rustling in the thawed breeze like underskirts across a polished wood dance floor. My husband moved out three months before my mother died, when the snow was still on the ground. Since then, I live alone.

But in the first weeks of spring, a heavy perfume hangs in the air on the corner of Fourteenth Street, and I stop on the sidewalk outside the Italian restaurant. Honeysuckle. The thick fragrance is unmistakable, but I cannot see the blooms, as if someone is calling my name who has not yet stepped into view.

WE REHEARSE OUR adult lives from the beginning. Mine was a game in the front yard. Into a bucket go sharp holly leaves, cedar chips from the flower beds, errant sticks, fistfuls of clover—never can find the lucky ones—rippled pink blooms from the crape myrtles, and pale yellow honeysuckle blossoms. The bush forms a lush border between our house and the neighbors next door. One for me to eat; the stamen like a slide whistle and tongue touched to the drop of nectar. One for the bucket, and the blossom drifts to join the lawn detritus. The afternoon is a quiet expanse, the house emptied of my older brother and sister at school, my younger brother not yet born. I pause to watch doodlebugs dawdle along the pebbled surface of our front porch. Then into the kitchen, where my mother smears peanut butter on white bread, drips honey, and sinks a knife to cut fours. It is just the two of us, and I am out to make something, too. My bucket slides under the tap, there is a rush of hot water, and I stand as if at a cauldron with my witch's brew, stirring with a wooden spoon until there is a fierce swirl at the center. *Lunch*, she says, and my sandwich is on a blue and white plate. *Stew!* I announce, vainglorious at my own creation.

HER FIRST MEMORY is of ants, of watching a single-file parade inside the trumpet of a daylily. Theirs is a bicentennial farm. For two hundred years a single family has pushed orchard apples through a food mill and lined the cellar shelves with canned pole beans, slipped from the barn roof, and died in labor. When my mother is older, she will bring her own diapered children to the top of the same hill and slide daylilies behind our ears, and many years after that, I will sneak away with my husband from a barbecue and lie down with him in the shadow of a tractor. But the first thing she remembers, she tells me, is the ants, their fluid line like pen ink, a whole city inside a bloom. It is June, and the sheets are snapping dry on the clothesline.

This is a memory of a memory, an image of my mother's childhood inside an image of my own, like nesting *matryoshkas*. When I hear about the ants, my mother is dropping me off at school. I am in fifth grade and fat, and Anne Murray's *Greatest Hits* is in the tape deck of her white Ford Taurus. I have a lavender backpack with neon zippers on my lap, and even I know it looks cheap. It's raining, and I am nearly late for the second bell, the drop-off traffic snaking around the block, and my mother won't stop talking.

Your first memory, she goes on, is significant. She's getting her masters in social work and spends the evenings hammering away at her typewriter, smoking cigarettes. I don't ask what she thinks her ants mean. This is how she and I talk, about what things mean, but today I'm distracted—by the time, by the distance to the side door if I get out of the car and run, and mostly by the rain, which will soak my white t-shirt, under which I am not wearing a bra because no one but me has yet noticed I need one.

The adults in my life are themselves distracted. My father drives a Cadillac as long and silver as a shark. But last week he picked me up for Wednesday night Hamburger Helper at his apartment wearing pants I'd never seen with a hole in the crotch.

He talked about money, why Christmas would be different this year, and asked why my mother keeps writing hot checks at the grocery store. I don't know what a hot check is.

The morning in the car my mother asks what my first memory is and waits for the answer like it matters, the windshield wipers like a metronome. How is a memory different from a photograph or a story you've been told about yourself? I am nine going on ten and beginning to get angry, not just at the rain that morning or the delay, but at a growing sense of life's unfairness. Our house is filled with moving boxes, and letters from my father's law office arrive by courier at the front door. I am more interested in visions of on and on, like this: I imagine sitting in front of a television. On the screen is a person watching television of another person, seated on a couch, watching television. And so on. I tell my mother I would like to minor in philosophy. She thinks this is funny, but I find it all very deep.

WE ONLY EVER WRITE one story, the writer I was beginning to love told me. Several months after my mother's death, looking through stacks of paper in her sewing room, I found a yellow folder. "The Life of Allison Marie Young," she wrote in felt-tipped calligraphy pen, "by her daughter, Sarah." This was my third-grade project. *Tell me what you were like when you were my age*, I asked, then neatly wrote the most interesting parts on ruled notebook paper beside crayon illustrations. She sank a homemade raft in the Green River and sat astride her cousin Bonnie's pony.

Bonnie looked good in cheap clothes, my mother always said, and that's all I know about Bonnie.

Tell me what you were like when you were my age, I asked in high school. We did most of our talking in the warmth of the car, waiting for a school bus that stopped a distance from our house. My mother wore her nightgown beneath a down parka and spilled tea on the floorboards. On the first hot day, the scent of sour milk haunted the car. She babysat, she said, and when the kids went to sleep, she ate leftovers from the fridge, didn't wash the dishes though she had a feeling she was supposed to, and thumbed the parents' copy of *Tropic of Cancer* for the sex parts.

Ice crystals scattered on the windows like field-borne burrs. I had woken that morning from a dream, I told her, in which I stood in a tunnel, my arms wrapped inside the peacoat of a boy as a train barreled toward us. "Well, that's obviously about sex," she said. And then, "Here comes the bus." I slumped on and into the first seat, perturbed. She could decode my subconscious, so why did hers seem so opaque? I wrote a poem, which is what sixteen-year-olds do, and left it at her place at the kitchen table one night before bed.

"Dear Sarah," she wrote in a letter she slid under my bedroom door. "If it seems that I am vague about my childhood, forgive me. It's only that there is not much to tell. I was dreamy and lonely and liked to read magazines and ride my bike."

I did not know how to ask a question impossible to answer. Can you explain what people mean when they say, *You are just like your mother*?

Now she is dead, and unable to answer, and still I cannot stop. There is comfort in asking. The possibility of discovery seems, at once, as real as the night sky and as difficult to measure as love.

Another surprise sewing room find, the motherlode: beside the plush camel chair she dozed in at the end, her head tipped back into the afternoon sun, a bag from Stop and Shop. It was overstuffed and heavy, filled with knitting needles, leather-bound journals, drafts of letters to doctors, friends, her therapist, my father. There were five copies of her divorce papers, and two day planners from the 1980s. Neon Post-its popped from the pages like flags.

"Hope now?" she wrote on a small piece of lined, mono-grammed notepaper in her thirties. "That I won't just die and become fertilizer—that I won't be forgotten as if I had never lived. That I'll give good people to the world. That things will become clearer to me, that I'll understand better. It really bugs me that I don't understand everything already."

It bugs me, too.

S HE TOLD THE STORY the same way each time, with the fresh-ness of someone relaying details the next morning from a dormitory hall phone. Now seems as good a time as any to men-tion she was an unreliable narrator, but here we go.

Heat blasted through the vents in the dashboard and the win-dows fogged with their girl talk, headlights blunted by a vortex of snowflakes. Someone reapplied lipstick while someone else announced street names as the signs came into view. My mother buttoned her purple maxi coat. The heavy dorm door creaked open, and my father stood in the stony hallway with a thick red beard.

I could feel his hot breath on my cold cheeks as he said, "Would you like a cup of coffee?"

When my father was on chapel duty, they sat in the back pew, cookies inside their coat pockets. He was so handsome, one of my mother's classmates said later, she wanted to put his head on her mantle.

This was one of my mother's truisms: A person will reveal everything you need to know about them within the first twenty minutes. The trick is whether or not you're paying attention.

After coffee, my mother grabbed a toothbrush and toothpaste from her purse.

Don't you want the flavor to linger in your mouth? my father asked.

On she went to the bathroom, maybe noticing a moment where pleasure locked horns with practicality, but maybe not.

And so it was the same for me, a daughter like a rerun.

"It's weird, Allison," one of her classmates said at a reunion, when I was my mother's date, flipping through magazines on a dorm room floor and swinging my legs in the air. "It's like it's you thirty years ago there on the floor."

F OR TEN YEARS, I was crazy about one man. He becomes my husband. I go wild for his hands, the way he ties a square knot, and how, when he holds a drink, he smiles at me slyly from the side of his mouth.

Just like my parents, dumb with infatuation and blind to early evidence of their failed future, my husband and I can't see what's clearly coming: that he will spend more time writing code at his computer than in my company, that I am relatively unambitious, and, not Chinese.

When we're in the dark of it I say, "Let's do something fun." And because we are so far down, I don't even know what that might mean. So I ask him, "What's fun?"

"Fun is noodles," he answers, his Chinese mother's phrase. Chow fun, mei fun. The only way to have it is to eat it. A month later he has emptied his closet, and two months after that he pushes a thick manila envelope under the door of our apartment. Inside, divorce papers and a bar of dark chocolate. Not fun.

Each morning, I slip a silk blouse over my head and ride the subway to an office in midtown. I am the editor in chief of a website about food, and I cannot eat. In the office bathroom, I sink to my feet. At my desk, I lean my head toward my knees. My mother says my body is processing the pain.

And then one day, because I cannot bear masking my personal mess at the office again, I get off the D train at Grand Street by the stinky fish vendors and walk across Nolita to a coffee shop on Mott Street. When I swing the door open, I look up into the face of a man.

"Hi," I say. I am breathless from the cold.

"Hi," he answers, and he bares his teeth like a friendly wolf.

I think I can feel his hot breath on my cheeks.

We do not fall in love. Or we do, and it doesn't last. What matters is this: I've been slapped by white sun, and for weeks my mind is blank-frantic, whirling like an empty spin cycle. Yet what I feel is full.

Call this boy-crazy, as I usually do, and it's a bone-deep embarrassment. Call it the life force, as my mother did, and it's elemental—proof I am alive, that the heart beating inside this chest is a woman's.

HERE'S SOMETHING a woman can do: birth boy, girl, girl, boy. I am that second girl. She let the first three of us unfurl with random assignment of Xs and Ys. For the fourth, she got serious. She wanted us lined up like von Trapps, longed for two more sons but would settle for one. Her old-timer gynecologist had strategies to determine sex, and so my mother nodded, sitting in a cotton gown on his examining table, the opening in front. He mailed instructions, the letter stamped at the post office on June 27, 1986. Postage was twenty-two cents.

"To favor conception of a male: (1) Intercourse at or as close to ovulation as possible with prior abstinence during the cycle, immediately preceded by an alkaline douche of water and baking soda. (2) Intercourse with female orgasm. (3) Deep penetration at the time of emission."

Now for the fun part. It must have been the following January when my mother placed a call to my father's law office saying he was needed at home. He was due in court, so when he hung up, he placed a call of his own. *Your Honor*, he said, and told the truth. More remarkable still, it worked. That is the story of how we got my little brother, Bliss, and how we became a complete set.

We made our home in glitzy Dallas, where only maids waited at bus stops, though we did not call them maids, we called them housekeepers. In our neighborhood, sixteen-year-olds woke to luxury cars in the driveway, the hoods festooned with giant red bows. My mother enlivened errands with a new bumper sticker: NUCLEAR WASTE IS FOREVER. At night, my parents fantasized about returning to San Antonio or Austin, where they had been young and poor and happy. We stay.

Ours was a monkey house. Someone was naked or dropping the fire ladder from a third floor window to escape. There was dog shit on the Oriental rug and an empty roll of paper towels. My mother weaved herself in with husband and kids in a water-tight web. We hollered down the hallway, shoved. She said, *Give your sister a hug and say you're sorry*, and we rolled our eyes. When the country station was on in the kitchen after dinner, my parents danced the push. My father's loafers shuffled across the black and white tile floor. The soles sounded like leaves rustling along a riverside. Farm lore says when the silver undersides turn face up, it's going to rain.

Problems: a husband who flexed in the mirror each morning after swimming laps, a tony town of Joneses she didn't care to keep up with, and even with all those kids, that same dogged loneliness followed. There was a longing still. If the farm of her youth was cloaked in a kind of quiet separateness, at least the family she made felt different, loud, and braided like a lasso.

My older brother says our parents' bedroom door was locked for most of his childhood. "I thought it was because they were Democrats," he said.

"Your mother must *love* being pregnant," my Brownies troop

leader said when my mother pulled up in our red Suburban, the other three already in the car.

My sister came home for college vacation and announced on the way to buy spring dresses that the vagina was a hole. She'd read something. I was fifteen and in the backseat.

"The vagina is not a hole," my mother said. "The vagina is a vessel."

She sewed wrap skirts she could wear at any size waist, chose colors for the baby's room, supervised sleepovers. There's a photograph of her pregnant at a picnic. She has one hand on her belly, another holding a glass of iced tea, the red curls at her temples damp with sweat. My sister is inside, my brother at her feet, still in diapers.

Introduced at a cocktail party or turning to a fellow dinner guest, she could see the boredom in their eyes when she said she was a mother. But hers was the real work, she thought, the kind that defines a civilization. Her materials were empty toilet paper rolls smeared in peanut butter, rolled in birdseed, and hung from the honeysuckle bush outside the dining room window.

"The thought of life after my children are grown depresses me. I will probably read some and drink a whole lot," she wrote. She thought there might be a novel in this about a thirty-nine-year-old woman who doesn't want to stop having children. "But I don't know where the plot would take her."

Husband and wife are both blue, really. They see a marriage counselor. The early diagnosis is that she is grieving the end of childbearing. "But I wonder if I really want more children, or if I just want to be sure I remember all the joyfulness I've felt."

To remember all the joy.

TWICE A WEEK she takes her two-year-old to swimming lessons. Bliss is ready to spring from the edge, shouts *8–9–2–3–4–JUMP!* Voice and splash bounce off the cool tiled walls, and the sun is bright on the turquoise water. The class sings the "Hokey Pokey" and the "Wheels on the Bus," and when they are done with those he says, *More song, Mommy.* But class is over, and they must emerge from the pool. Mothers and children file off, their wet feet slapping the deck. In the echoing locker room, everyone showers in an open room, the easy roaming bodies of naked women and children together. Women lean their heads under the blare of hand dryers. They button oxford shirts and slip into leather penny loafers and hand their children snacks of saltines and bags of granola. The parking lot thrums with heat, and their cooled skin is still faint with chlorine. Click into the car seat, and on the way home, waiting at a stoplight, she sees in the rearview mirror her son has flopped his head into sleep.

SHE DIDN'T LOOK at anyone the way she looked at my brothers. She deemed kindergarten Duncan the kindest person she has had the luck to meet. Grown, he will send her money to supplement her social security checks, she predicts, and she is right. Her girls are studious and wound tight, like her. I begin to set an alarm clock with crayon hands in elementary school, and Katy, the night before first grade, not trusting even that fail-safe, sleeps in her first-day outfit. But the boys fascinate her with their difference. Bliss only yawns when my mother calls him by name each morning, and later still, after she has climbed the stairs to his room, stirs sleepily under the sheets when she shakes his shoulder to wake him. She shops for their size fourteen shoes, leans girlishly into their six-foot-plus frames. They are physically big and emotionally kind, and she had made them so, though she didn't entirely understand how.

She loved my father and my stepfather and some men in between, and I watched her love all of them bravely, without fear or restraint.

But after the divorce, I also watched from a magnolia tree while a family friend delivered sacks of groceries to our front door. Aside from a stint in a jewelry store while my father was in law school, my mother had never had a paid job in her adult life. This is also what comes from loving a man without fear or restraint.

I do not want to be made a fool of, I repeated in one romance after another, as if anyone were capable of assuring that but me.

"Oh, Sarah," my mother explained once I was married. "I wasn't a fool. That is a little girl's understanding of a grown woman's problem," she said. And: "I would do it all again."

What is a grown woman's understanding of a grown woman's problem?

That if I, too, am quick to fall in love, and I am, it is because of her. See: guileless; also: open, unguarded. It occurs to me loving this way may not be smart for a grown woman. Romantic love so often seems at odds with seriousness, and it does not endure. But what does? Why should duration equal significance? Besides, I know no other way. She would say there is no shame in relationship—in deep feeling, a surge of hormones, the pleasures of the body, she would say. Nor is there in its end.

"I never understood the term 'codependent,'" she said. "Isn't that the nature of being human, to depend on each other?"

OTHER FAMILIES we knew sent Christmas cards of a particular type—a studio portrait, each parent and child in coordinating ivory cashmere sweaters, a teenager with a wedge haircut, a hand positioned on a sister's shoulder to suggest love. Or a full-denim portrait, chambray shirts and 501s in the great outdoors, a tree swing for the youngest and everyone else's shiny boots and loafers buried in the colored leaves.

When our Christmas tree was decorated with miniature birds, strings of wooden red beads, classroom-crafted paper chains, and bubbling, multicolored lights, a photographer arrived for our own season's greetings. We sat on the burgundy velvet couch in the living room.

It started civil enough. Parents in the center with baby Bliss on our mother's lap, and the rest of us crowded around. I am in a six-year-old's perfect outfit: pigtails and pink tights bunched at my ankles above patent leather Mary Janes. Then Katy, already regal at eleven, her hair glossy and smile beguiling. Duncan's eyes look naughty beneath his thick wave of hair, but he is thirteen, and that is his job. Everyone in this picture has a different shade of red hair.

We can only hold it together for so long. Duncan cracks a joke and calls a kid rebellion. Then I'm splayed across my parents' laps screaming with laughter, my hands cupped around Bliss's smiling face, as if to remind him he's one of us, he's on our side. Katy sticks her tongue out at the camera, puts her thumbs in her ears. Duncan's legs spill off the couch. He cocks his head; the white collar of his striped polo shirt goes from flat and folded to rumpled. He is the leader of our loudmouthed mutiny. The photographer keeps snapping.

In the first of these photographs, my parents are laughing. These crazy kids. Then their faces become obscured by our mayhem, visible only from their laps down. The kids take control of the couch, the photo shoot, the picture's frame. We are cracking one another up, spurring one another on. It is four against two, and we are winning. This is us at our best, a wild and raucous team, stirred into a joyous mania. Peace on earth, good will to men.

I do not know if my mother mailed one of these pictures as our Christmas card that year. It would have been like her to see the charm of our madhouse and take pride in her delightful, expressive children—a mother's description. I cannot say for sure. But I do know she preserved what others may have called outtakes, that the series hung in the hallway in a large, poster-sized frame, and that the photos tell two stories unfolding alongside each other. Read from left to right and down the page, it is both a portrait of sibling unity and a prescient view of a family's unraveling.

THIS WAS THEIR recurring argument.

I would like you to defer to my judgment in most matters, he says.

I have only one precious life to live, she says, *and I shall make my own decisions*. She tries, at least.

Away from home, outside the domestic sphere, she liked the dynamic better. In Santa Fe for the weekend, both sick, they stayed in their room reading aloud from a best seller and gossiping about the characters. "Our noses were so runny that neither of us could be on top. It was very funny. It was very romantic."

IT IS THE BEGINNING of the end for their marriage, and the Brownie leader is at it again. When my mother pulls up to the curb, she learns I have entertained the troop during circle share with details of her latest marital dispute. The troop leader leans against the driver's side door and speaks to my mother through the open window. *I liked the part where you said he had been a jerk the entire year he turned forty,* she said, *and now it is your turn.*

THE HOUSEKEEPER has been gone six weeks. Economy move. Someone is always home sick: chicken pox, strep throat, another chicken pox, stomach flu. The pharmacist greets her by name when she places the telephone orders for lice shampoo, Kaopectate, orange Triaminic. She puts on the *Dirty Dancing* CD when she vacuums and pops a chocolate cake in the oven to cheer everyone up. A father arrives to pick up his daughter who has come over to play, and he and my mother stand in the front hall amid wet bathing suits, a rocking horse, and a month's worth of unopened mail. This man is also a pediatrician. He says it looks like she'll be needing a penicillin shot soon. But she doesn't get sick, and when she next sees him, she is wearing blue jeans, the mail is still in stacks, and baby Bliss sits on her hip. He says she reminds him of something he learned early in his practice. *God didn't make mothers*, he says, *He made women. Whatever that means*, she thinks, annoyed. It is only later that week, perhaps, when the house is finally quiet, the dishwasher humming in the downstairs dark, her husband not yet home, and upstairs the kids are asleep or at least pretending. When she is finally in the soft light of her own bedroom with her hair brushed and her face clean, sinking into the down pillows with something to read, she arrives in a moment that is her own and not in relation to anything else—not a carpool, a nursing infant, nor a man she loves. She is self-contained, not only a woman but the sole measure of her own life.

ER HUSBAND SAYS he has an ulcer. He says he is so worried about money he cannot sleep. He says they cannot afford a trip to London to celebrate her birthday.

His doctor tells him to get a hobby. He chooses calf roping and barrel racing and buys a $250,000 farm with a five-bedroom Victorian farmhouse in unsettled country far out of town. He cannot afford it, but he cannot resist. The house, he says, is his private getaway. He says she gave him the ulcer. She says, *I certainly am powerful, aren't I?*

He spends all of his time within the barbed-wire fencing of his new farm. It is a neglected place. The previous owners left behind a pony whose hooves have begun to curl up in the shape of elves' shoes. The terrain is rolling but treeless, the landscape an ill yellow. He forgets to come home for Christmas dinner.

She struggles through the ticktock of the lonely weeks just to make it to Friday mornings, when the kids are at school, and she leaves baby Bliss at the church nursery and goes to see the marriage counselor by herself. He is kind with his fragrant pipe and soft cognac leather chair, and he tells her he looks forward to their hour all week. He is her bright spot, too, so patient as she wonders aloud what is going on with her husband. Why she had to spend so much time wondering, I do not know, except that certain dreams are harder to wake from than others. She had nursed a desire for this family for more than twenty years, and that hope had rocked her into willful slumber.

SHE IS PROFOUNDLY uninterested in sex and thinks it a separate issue that she is very angry at her husband. Their bed has been their reliable return to each other, and without it, they must find other ways to communicate. They take a walk on the gray November sidewalks to sort themselves, and she begins to describe her inner life. Feeling is living, to her, she says. She has only just begun to speak. Can't they talk about literature or art instead, he asks. She has no idea why she married this man.

SOMETIMES HE WOULD come home late at night and in the dark tell her she did not know how to be a woman. The culprit in their marriage, he told her, was her mother. There are games men like to play, he said, and her mother had failed to teach them. I don't know what games he was talking about, since I didn't learn them either, but I do know some things about my grandmother. That she spent her adult life flirting through offices in pink lipstick and shift dresses. That when my brother-in-law met her, he told my sister he now understood oversexed to be a family trait on my mother's side. And that long before that, when my grandmother's beau went off to serve in the Air Force in his tailored green uniform, she gave him one last good time for the road and something to remember her by: a wallet-sized leather book filled with photographs of her own tame pinup poses. A skimming rayon dress, saddle shoes, a wide and knowing smile. *Hurry home, lover*, she wrote on the back of one; *Remember these lips* . . . on another, stamped with the red outline of her mouth. When he returned, they married, and when he died, she discovered the photographs still tucked inside the sleeve of the wallet he carried in his back pocket every day, and every night placed in the top drawer of his bureau as he undressed for bed.

SORTING THE LAUNDRY, my mother finds condoms in the pocket of my father's jeans. It is becoming difficult to find a good book to read when her own life has become such cliché-ridden trash.

WHEN SHE STOPPED nursing her final child, her breasts disappeared. The fullness she craved was draining from her life. Was it then, or long before, when her husband ceased to moan when she unbuttoned her blouse each evening? Was it then, or not long after, when she knew she would not have another child with him? She makes an appointment with a plastic surgeon and voices a vague concern about no longer feeling sexy. He gets it, he says, he is losing his hair. His hair doesn't matter, she says, and he says her breasts don't matter, either. They laugh at their lot, and he sends her home. Yet the facts remain: One year her husband boasts he knows how to make her come like a pet monkey, and the next he has left her alone in the soft evening light, aching with the embarrassment of her own unmet desire. The only pet monkey she knows is Curious George, who never does as his owner expects.

IT IS A RAINY SUNDAY afternoon, the first day in a long time her husband has stayed home from the office. It is the domestic witching hour. Nearly dinnertime, she has mashed potatoes on the stove, wet lettuce leaves in the sink, a chicken sputtering in the oven. They argue about a plastic video cassette holder my father has purchased at Woolworth's for the living room and which my mother deems hideous. (It is never about what it's about, a friend's mother will tell a group of us girls in college.) As he storms out, she is seized by a feral, vicious impulse. She follows him to the porch, and throws her hot tea on his starched shirt. She grabs his arm, and snaps her jaw shut on the wide bone. There is the sour, metallic taste of blood in her mouth. *Miss Sunday supper*, she snarls at him, *and never come back*. We do not regularly attend any church, so the ritual of this meal, in particular, matters. But he is already down the steps, and when his engine roars she is wilder still, racing through the house, ripping artwork she never liked from the walls. She gathers dirty socks and expensive, unused sports equipment, hauls his case files from the hallway, and dumps the whole heap of it on the wet porch. The oven timer beeps and beeps again. The phone rings. *Hey, baby*, he says. She cannot abide her own threat, and now she must race again: She collects his belongings from the porch and stuffs them in the hall closet. He takes his place at one end of the table, and she at hers. We bow our heads and say grace. Typically, the most reliable source of joy in her life is right here, when the glass salad bowl is passed around the table, and the children are loud and pouring milk from the cat-shaped jug, and either she or her husband—they take turns—winks down the length of the table at the other. That night we all eat dinner in miserable, utensil-scraping silence. She would say she acted childishly, but even her own children have never bitten someone in their rage.

WE HAD A STEREO with speakers the size of my Barbie Dream-house, and I remember Willie Nelson's plaintive timbre fill-ing the house as my father carried me up the staircase to bed one night, softly singing "The Party's Over" into the shell of my ear.

She returned to the gynecologist when she felt her uterus was slipping out of her. The gynecologist said it was. A harder problem to solve: Her husband complained it was impossible to get enough attention from a woman with four children. The doctor told her she didn't have four children but five. Divorce him, he told her, and you'll have men climbing in your window at night. He blushed when he said this, and my mother thanked him for blushing.

The divorce didn't happen that way, but it did happen.

I LEARNED THE WORD "cunt" the night my mother ran into the street to scream at my father. They argued in the red taillights of his Cadillac, his girlfriend's hair hot-roller curly and blonde through the car window. David Koresh and the Branch David-ians were under siege in Waco. On the news and at school, people talked about "cults." The words sounded the same to me.

YOU ARE JUST LIKE your mother, people say. They mean long-winded and loud mouthed, wide faced, charming in finer moments, obnoxious in others. Actually, I don't know what they mean, so one day I asked her.

"I'm sorry," she said. "I *hate* when people say I'm like my mother."

But the night after she died, it came up again. "You look just like your mother," her friend told me at the dinner table.

For a long time before she died, she no longer looked like herself. Late one night, I found her distraught in the living room, flipping through old photo albums.

"I wish there were more pictures of me," she said, crying.

When her friend says this, I know he is not only talking about our faces, but of something inexact and iterative—my echoed laugh, how my lipsticks also curl into the shape of a shepherd's hook, or the way I absentmindedly stand with my hands on my hips like an angry teacher.

"It's like she's still here," he said, putting his hand on my shoulder, looking as if he wanted to kiss me.

N OUR HOUSE growing up, my mother's bathroom had a wall of mirrors outlined by globe lights like a movie star's dressing room. She seemed to take her time getting ready to go out. She might slick her lashes with mascara, then lean back, read a few pages of a novel, and smoke a cigarette in her long ivory robe. It had a ruffle at the neckline. Hot rollers, lipstick, the crossing and uncrossing of her legs. There were purple spots on them, small ones like starbursts, and thick, raised veins that looked like knotted shoelaces trapped beneath the skin.

The morning after a party. "I looked so beautiful last night," she said.

I was six, eating cereal. "How did you know?"

She looked pleased as she lifted the kettle off the burner and poured boiling water over a tea bag. "I could see it in the mirror, and in other people's eyes," she said.

THE MOTHER-APPROVED facts as she reported them to me, the ones her mother had not told her:

You are so beautiful, so intelligent, and so talented.

And: *Someone will always be more beautiful, more intelligent, more talented.*

And: *Someone will always be less so, too.*

"I think the healthily vain woman looks at her bare, God-given physical self, accepts it, shows her love for herself by making the most of her best features, and then gets on with living."

So let's get on with it—the rest of the story, every tangible desire these two women can have.

THE U-HAUL STOOD in the morning shadows cast by the twin trees outside our house. My mother's ring had been pawned. The expensive rugs, the green felt-covered pool table, the Irish wake table with a slab down the center as wide as a casket—all sold. Inside the moving truck were the basics: beds, sofas covered in blue and white ticking with spare white slipcovers, the Crock-Pot, our clothes.

A stranger stood bowlegged in our driveway, squinting in the June sun and chewing tobacco. Doyle owed my mother's friend a favor. It must have been a big one, since paying up required driving a forty-three-year-old woman and two children, five and ten, from Texas to Massachusetts. My mother let Duncan and Katy, both teenagers, stay in Dallas for the summer. Doyle could be trusted with what valuables remained.

He was a painter but moved art for money. He wore a stiff white cowboy hat. From the iron-creased legs of his Wranglers emerged the pointed toes of snakeskin boots. My father said *Howdy, pardner* in the country and to certain folks downtown, but I had never seen a real cowboy, and the only adult I knew who called herself an artist was Lindsey Russell's mom. Everything about Doyle was an enigma.

He pulled the sliding metal door at the back of the truck down like he was closing up shop. The four of us slid onto the seat of the cab, Bliss and me in the middle, my mother by the window. We pulled away from the curb with the nose of the truck pointed north, and behind us, my mother's white Ford Taurus dangling from the back hitch like a figure standing at the railing of a caboose.

Doyle switched the radio on, traveling the analog dial from one end to another. Country music, static, off again. I asked if we could turn the air conditioner up. When the windows were down, the humidity was like another body crowding us. Bliss slid off the hot black plastic bench seat into the roomy dark of the floorboards. By my mother's sandaled feet and red-painted toenails, his Power Rangers argued heatedly back and forth before crashing into each other until someone toppled. Bliss made an explosive sound.

We reached the state line. Texarkana is perhaps best known for a 1946 serial killer who struck couples parked on lovers lanes. But I knew "Texarkana" as a word I heard my father use on the telephone when he talked about his cases—the literalness of the place caught in my ear like a dumb tune. Where are we? Half here, half there, and nowhere soon.

When we passed the birthplace of our new president, my mother and Doyle got to talking. Three hours in she still looked fresh, leaning her elbow next to the window of the sunbaked door, her red lipstick polished and the collar popped on her lavender polo shirt. She, for one, didn't see Clinton's sex appeal, she said. She'd met him at a campaign fund-raiser and found him red and sweaty. It was Al who was the real charmer, she said.

Doyle laughed and pushed the gearshift forward, as long and black as a fire poker. The muscles in his forearms twitched. I had a yellow sports Walkman in my lap and the gray foam-lined headphones nestled on my ears. It looked like I was listening to REM's *Out of Time*, but I had not hit play.

In Tennessee, stopped at a gas station, the papers in the wire racks by the cash registers all said Conway Twitty had died. His hair was stiff and tall, as out of fashion as his name, I thought, with Elvis's pomp but not at all handsome. Still, I was curious. I asked my mother to buy a copy.

Doyle stood at the open driver's side door with the creased map spread on his seat. His finger traced a line along the bottom of the state as he suggested something to my mother. *That sounds good*, she said, smiling. He refolded the map the right way, and my mother said I could have the window seat. They talked about the man who died and a woman he sang duets with. It was as if I'd entered a room to find people cleaning up after a party I wasn't invited to.

I had never seen a state like Tennessee. Even the long, flat stretches of interstate did not bore me, the medians flooded with yellow wildflowers. Texas in summer dries up like an insect husk, but Tennessee sighed its green warmth into the cab. I was quiet and daydreaming. One day I would be grown and decide things for myself. Tennessee was my favorite state so far.

Late that afternoon, stopped at a brown, sun-bleak motel set in long afternoon shadows, my mother made tea in our room with her electric kettle while I sat alone on the edge of the tur-quoise pool, my feet dangling in. I so seldom felt weightless. The cement radiated the day's heat through the seat of my shorts and on the backs of my legs. The tabloid was open beside me, and I was rapt with Conway Twitty and Loretta Lynn. Events of love and death were to me still sensation.

It did not seem worth the trouble to change into my bathing suit only to swim alone. As much as I longed for solo girlhood adventures—I wanted to feel for myself the same independent pride I had for my favorite storybook heroines—at that time, I knew "alone" as an expression mostly of "forgotten" and also sometimes of "fear."

My mother and Doyle must have decided we weren't in much of a hurry. We took the scenic route through the Smokys, the truck chugging up curvy roads that hugged the mountainsides. Clouds draped over the soft peaks, and we barreled in like children pushing through the back of a wardrobe.

We stopped at McDonald's.

"I want a chef's salad," I said. My mother looked into my face, disapproving.

"It's too much," she said. I didn't know if she was talking about money or the amount of food.

We sat in a booth by a window that looked out onto an empty parking lot. Bliss wore his Batman cape and handed my mother the toy from his Happy Meal. She opened the pouch and passed back the Joker and his purple roadster and kept talking with Doyle about *Lonesome Dove*. There was never an arc of quiet between the last word of her sentence and the first of his. I squeezed a packet of ranch dressing across the top of my salad in a zigzag. I thought this was how to get thin. Walking home at the end of the school year in my favorite lavender shorts, a boy I liked yelled "redwood thighs" up the street at me so everyone could hear. I loved trees, but I did not love that. Lunch seemed to last a long time. I ate each stick of ham, each piece of cheese, the gray-yolked hard-boiled egg.

Each night we stopped at a single-story highway motel standing in the shadow of an overpass, the kind of place that cost thirty-nine dollars a night. The door to our room would spill into a parking lot. Did we only ever get one room? If the other bed was for Doyle, I never saw him in it. Mom, Bliss, and I lined up in one bed. I slept in a t-shirt that hung to my knees, and my mother wore her vanilla robe. Each night, she leaned against the headboard and raked an orange-paddled brush across her scalp. It pulled her loose curls into highlighted waves in the lamplight. The television hummed until sleep, laugh tracks and sitcom families seated close around a kitchen table. In the mornings, I opened my eyes to see Doyle silhouetted before the slats of the plastic blinds. The whole room was blue, his legs lean inside his starched jeans. His boots were already on.

Virginia, Maryland, Pennsylvania, New York. They discussed one book after another. *Sophie's Choice, A Bed by the Window, Anna Karenina, Beyond the Bedroom Wall.* On I-95, *The Prince of Tides* sounded dark and thrilling. "What happened?" I asked. My mother shooed me out of the conversation. "It's not age appropriate," she said. Doyle looked at me with *Sorry, kid* sympathy, then continued with my mother. He had a red mustache, thick as a shortbread cookie.

I stared back out the window, pretending I wasn't watching myself in the side-view mirror. My face was round and ruddy, with a bob that fell to my chin and along my soft jawline. But my lips had a dark natural stain, noticeable enough that a teacher hissed at me in assembly to wipe off my lipstick. Along with red hair, it was what I had going for me. It wasn't much.

I counted billboards. Dollywood, divorce lawyers, injury lawyers, reminders from God, adoption hotlines, caverns ahead, country buffets now with salad bar. I hadn't seen an armadillo since Arkansas but at night I loved the way the sharp smell of skunk entered through the air vents, shaking my senses awake like smelling salts. I didn't want to miss anything. I saw a Volks-

wagen Beetle and punched Bliss in the arm. *Slug bug red*, I said.
Slug bug white. The interstate traveled alongside oak forests and
hardwood pine, black fences and paddocks with horses swishing
their tails at glossy hindquarters. Branches of flowering dogwood
reached toward the truck like an outstretched hand.

In five days we crossed the country and arrived in another world.
It was cool in the valley when we pulled into the driveway of my
grandmother's farm. Though the house was large, there was little
room for us. Nanny had her hair done once a week on Spring
Street, went to the Stop and Shop on Tuesdays, and said to keep
our showers to three minutes. My uncle, who was brown from
the haying, looked as if it pained the muscles in his face to smile
at us. Doyle stacked our belongings in the fragrant barn, filling
an empty stall where milk cows once slept. My grandmother
cooked Italian sausages, tomatoes, and green peppers in a skillet,
and we ate together at the kitchen table. The downstairs windows
were open, and I wished I knew where my sweatshirt was packed.
The air smelled mellow and green. We finished dinner in time
for Nanny to watch *Dr. Quinn, Medicine Woman*. I lay on the deep
carpet, sneaking one foil-wrapped chocolate after another out of
a covered glass dish and reading *People*. On the cover, Shannen
Doherty stared me down in stonewashed jeans and a black bra,
a heavy cross hanging between her breasts. Her fiancé had filed
papers with a judge saying she was so violent he feared for his life.
That night, I slept with my mother in her childhood bedroom.
Her senior portrait still hung on the wall.

The next day my mother was driving Doyle to Boston, and

because his return flight to Texas did not leave until the following day, he would stay overnight in a hotel. *The round trip is really too long for a single day*, my mother said. I saw her soft robe folded at the mouth of her unzipped bag. She would spend the night in Boston, too, she said.

I sat on the stairs and watched the familiar parade of my mother walking from the kitchen to the car and back again. In our house, I had stayed in front of the television while Duncan left for pool halls. He returned with his jean pockets filled with rumpled twenty-dollar bills. When a car horn blared, Katy rushed out to a silver LeSabre driven by a senior girl with the top down, the words to "Roxanne" or "Red Red Wine" audible from inside. Each time the door slammed shut, I stayed home. Now Doyle had a knapsack over his shoulder, his hat on, and a thick hardcover book in his hand.

"I dog-eared it," he whispered, pushing the book across the step like he was passing me a note in class. "Don't tell your mom." I wrapped my arms around his neck. His whiskers were rough on my cheek.

The car engine turned over, and I watched from the window as my mother and Doyle pulled onto the smooth blacktop of Sloan Road, edged in cattails and Queen Anne's lace and black-eyed Susans. At the foot of the stairs, I split the book open on my lap to the single marked page of *The Prince of Tides*. The plastic library cover made a cellophane crinkle. Reading, I felt hot, panicked. My Barbie was having sex with Ken, but this was different. My eyes couldn't follow the lines fast enough, and when I finished the scene, I read it again. Did I want it to stop or to go on? I wasn't sure. All summer sounds—the low metallic rumble of my uncle's tractor in the field, the gentle movement of the curtains, their pompoms bumping softly against the windowsill in the breeze, George Jones's coaxing voice spilling out of the clock radio above the kitchen sink—all seemed suddenly vacuumed from the world. I was in on a secret I had wanted to know, and now I wanted to unknow it. That there was sex and then there was something else, and a man could wreck me in ways I hadn't even known. A man could wreck anyone. I wanted to be noticed, but I didn't want this.

My mother returned from Boston the next day, breezy.

T HE JOB INTERVIEW parade required a costume for someplace darker, colder, fancier than home: sheer black stockings, low-heeled patent leather pumps, and a purple blazer with gold buttons. She returned in the evenings without the optimistic smile. I would live on white rice for a year, I said, if we could just move out of Nanny's. We were both determined.

With her first paycheck, we rented a little yellow house in town on Sabin Drive. It was a triumph. I slept in my own bedroom and liked to sit outside under the shady tree boughs that edged the property, brittle brown pine needles poking through my jeans.

Then a boy dropped me off after the movies. We were "going out," or "going," as we had said in Texas. "This looks like a serial killer's house," he said, when his mother pulled into our driveway. That was the end of that sixth-grade romance.

Yet I couldn't unsee the paint peeling back from the white

stucco in thin curls like pencil shavings; the ragged weeds that edged the front walk and driveway; the garage that stood agape, serving the neighborhood an unmerciful view of paint cans, bicycles, homeless furniture we couldn't fit inside. The house itself was shaped like a trailer that had aspired to something more. Shame crept into our lives like algae bloom on a bay. The neighbors hated us, Nanny reported, and wondered whether they should call the police when Katy and I screamed at each other. Somehow I had only noticed the crab apple tree in the front yard with a rough, weathered rope swing, and how I could ride my bike to the library on Main Street, or walk to the end of our dead-end street, cut across a field, and arrive in the rear of the art museum. Free admission.

My mother was less free to roam. Her long commute crossed a mountain range and was even slower in the snow. She counseled troubled kids, and then in the evenings, there we were: the TV on, the spaghetti pot in the sink, the bottle of Wild Turkey missing. Duncan's cutting out pages from lingerie catalogs in the basement, and Katy's running up the phone bill in her room. Bliss plays video games, Sarah chronicles prepubescence in a pastel diary with lock and key. My mother slides out of her shoes and sleeps on a bed tucked into the uninsulated landing of the back stairs. We are crowded, and we are lonely.

She made lists for reassurance. Here's all we needed: a table with a chair for each family member, a bed for each of us, too. Bicycles for those who wanted them, library cards. Her signature extras: red geraniums on the windowsills, a blue and white teapot. A tiny, framed watercolor landscape arrived in the mail painted by Doyle. By this count, we were doing all right.

But by less material measure, I think if she had not had us, she would have laid down on that bed and never gotten up. I don't remember her eating or laughing or smiling during this time—I don't remember her much at all. Her presence moved through the house like a fog, appearing on Sunday nights in plastic containers filled with chicken Rice-A-Roni and steamed broccoli for us to reheat for dinner during the week, and in the unopened pack of toilet paper placed under the bathroom sink.

*P*OOR RICK, Nanny said. *Marrying a woman with four children.* He didn't see it that way, so I think that reveals something about Nanny.

My mother's first love, a man with the bearing of a country veterinarian, was about to become her second husband. It snowed so wildly the night before the wedding, guests traveling from across the state were unsure they would arrive in time for the morning ceremony. We woke to a world shimmering and white, the streets blanketed and still.

Her wedding suit was damask paisley in peacock blues and black with a soft velvet collar. Beneath the nip of her waist, the jacket flared into a peplum. She looked like a queen in her winter robes. I had wondered about her first wedding dress. She said it was green, but there were no photographs from the day she and my father eloped, and moths ravaged the gown until it was nothing but a fishing net.

She stood in the upstairs bathroom, fastening the clasp of her necklace. By this time, two years later, we had moved to a cheap, paper-thin house on Linden Street, but it had a staircase. *Women Who Run with the Wolves* lay on the linoleum floor between her low-heeled pumps and the toilet. The contents of other rooms were already packed inside brown moving boxes. After the wedding, we would drive south to Rick's farm in New Jersey. I could count four new schools in the past three years. "You ready?" my mother called to me across the hallway.

My future stepfather drove us to the South Williamstown Second Congregational Church, the place where he had met my mother thirty years before. He put down the visor to block the sun, and she leaned toward me in the backseat holding a wide gold band between her fingers.

Would I hand this to her when it was time to exchange the rings, she asked.

I inherited my father's sweaty hands, palms so wet they left damp spots on my notebook paper when I wrote. I was afraid the ring would slip from my fingers. I was also trying on preteen prickliness.

Why couldn't she ask Katy to do it, I said.

"Because I want you to," she said.

She didn't ask for much. She didn't ask me to stop skipping so many days of eighth grade or to wash the spaghetti pot or burn through less International Tasters Choice while I watched call-in romantic advice shows. She asked me to stop watching *Melrose Place*, to move with her again to another state, and to give her this ring so she could wed a man she loved, one who loved her almost as much as she loved us. A man eager to love all four of us to prove it.

I'm sure I sighed. But I slipped the band over my thumb and wrapped my slick fingers around it in a fist.

"Thank you," she said in triumph, as she twisted forward in her seat again and readjusted her seat belt.

We went to the chapel, we got married.

SPENT THE school day turning pages of *The Bell Jar* under my desk in algebra and feigning stomachaches so I could lie on the black vinyl bed in the nurse's office during lunch. She asked questions with answers that seemed self-evident, like how was I adjusting to my new school. My English teacher handed back my poetry, "I'm here for you!" written in cheerful, rounded script.

After school, my mother drove me home on Ferry Road, past the blind fork. The overcast March sky hung heavy overhead. She was chattering on, wearing a cobalt blue turtleneck with moth holes at the ribbed trim of the waistband. Her face was inside a double frame: the dark line of her high-necked sweater beneath her jaw, and the black rubber edging of the driver's side window outlining her profile like a Renaissance portrait. She had pink cheeks with large pores and teeth stained from nicotine and tea. Curls sprang loose around her face. At the time, I thought this was a moment in which I realized my mother was beautiful. I no longer think it is only that.

She had once told me my father said she was the kind of woman who tied her hair back with the rubber band from the morning newspaper. If that is true, I think it one of the keenest observations my father has ever made. In the car that day on the ride home from school, I looked at my mother, and she was in love again, like a teenager, like I would be in a few years with the boyfriend we would call Rattail at the dinner table. She was forty-six. She was planning her vegetable garden and ordering fruit trees for the area of the lawn she'd started calling her orchard and peony bulbs for the ditch by the septic tank. For the first time I saw: My mother was a girl, too.

spring

*T*ELL ME WHAT *you were like at my age*, I asked in college. When I called home, I could hear the television in the background. Every night, my mother and stepfather watched hours of news. He was a Republican and she was a Democrat, and they flipped between Fox News and MSNBC until he began to snore with the remote in his hand. I wanted to know if she'd been in love with the first person she slept with.

She found this a dumb question. "Of course," she said.

"What about the second person," I asked.

"Sarah," she said, weary of explaining the obvious. "Of *course* not."

First: a stone mason I met on my twenty-first birthday. There were some red flags. He was tangled up in a vague lawsuit with a former girlfriend, and had lost his sense of smell after an accident—I hesitated to call it brain damage—leading him to call and ask whether I would come over to smell his milk. Not a euphemism. But when he stood behind me in line at the movies, he rested his chin on the crown of my head and wrapped his body around me, draped and protective like a layer of chain mail. I introduced him to my mother when she visited in the spring. He was late to the coffee shop, and I thought he might not arrive. Then he burst in from the sunshine, and she saw the bright smile and blue collar body, too. I had omitted the questionable details. "He's very sexy," she said, nodding at me.

Before him there had been an almost first: a cowboy who worked the door at the bar. One night he led me from the white wicker loveseat on his front porch inside across creaky floors. He turned on no lamps, flipped no switches, and so it must have been the light from the streetlights or the neighbors or the moon, because our bodies cast shadows around the windowed room. The light navy. Tall and sleepy, he put one hand on each of my shoulders and turned me toward the mirror hanging from the linen closet door. *Look*, he said. I saw his face over my shoulder. Is this what a man is? He wanted to give me something, show me something. *Look*, he said again, and I did. My hair fell in waves past my shoulders, my skin pale as the ocean in the moonlight, feet bare on the moaning dark wood floors. I reached toward the hem of my dress, pulled it over my head, dropped it at my feet as if planting a flag.

The man I married was so like my father, everyone said. But that night, as I pulled my face away from the cowboy, I was so struck by surprise that I couldn't begin to entertain an insight. What does it mean if, in the dark, the shape of a man's face reminds you of your mother?

WHEN I WAS NINETEEN, the man who would become my husband sent three dozen roses to my dorm room with a card. "One dozen for your beauty, two for your charm, and three because they're late," it said. My birthday had been the day before, and the arrangement occupied half the floor between my room-mate's bed and mine. I called my sister. "What does it mean?" I asked, and we both scratched our heads, if not genuinely confused, then disbelieving.

He was my stepfather's nephew, a story I found romantic and he found humiliating. He begged me not to tell it at parties, preferring a cagey, *We met through family friends*. Maybe I loved the story too much. How my stepfather had attended college in the town where my mother was a girl, how he was her aching high school crush, and years later, her first boyfriend. Had my mother not left a note on the meet-up bulletin board during his reunion weekend, *Rick: Call Allison*, how would my husband and I have met? Inside her happy ending was my own.

"I'm in love with your daughter," he told my mother when we began dating in earnest years after Rick's arrival.

"Which one?" she asked.

He was eight years older but believed in another generation's kind of manhood: to open doors and hold umbrellas, pick up checks, and order another round. In Paris we stood on a bridge, and he offered me a ring. What we had, he said, made him believe in God. I thought it was holy, too. For the first eight years, I took his arm and followed. It is little wonder he admitted at the end he preferred me at twenty-two.

REMEMBER THE BEGINNING, driving to a movie theater across a state line on a flat stretch of highway. The day was overcast with hot July haze. He leaned back into his seat with one hand on the wheel and the other firm on the gear shift. I thought that was silly; it was an automatic transmission. I also thought, as our silent car passed the Chevron station on the left and overgrown farmland on the right, that this trip would unfold in quiet. Around this time, I began asking with semiregularity, *What if we run out of things to talk about?* He found this question kind of cute, I think. Didn't it show how much I was trying? For me, the idea arrived in the car like a bill in the mailbox, the sort you stuff in a drawer and decide to deal with later.

But I cannot omit another memory, likely from the same week, sweeter and as significant in my mind, the one that made more impact at the time, the one that allowed everything to follow. Independence Day. We walked in the early evening, and because we were new lovers, could not travel far beyond the first intersection before we stopped to embrace. There were no cars on the road and the hem of my skirt fluttered at my knees in the humid breeze. The sound of fireworks in the distance. Here, fireflies. I wanted to tie myself up in his arms and he wanted to be the rope.

We decided to walk on.

ONCE HEARD an anthropologist on the radio explain our brains awash in the hormones of sexual attraction. "Love is madness," she said. "You're *literally* insane."

So there's that excuse.

ONCE, MY HUSBAND helped me carry sixteen volumes of the Time-Life *Foods of the World* series from a church jumble sale on the Upper East Side home to our apartment in Brooklyn. He was very romantic.

At my first job in New York, I stood at a photocopier for hours, staring blankly at the gray cubicle walls of a morgue-quiet academic press. I moved manuscripts from one pile to another, sent the same letter. Congratulations so-and-so, herewith find a contract, a very small check, your modest dreams coming true.

After bills each month, $160. If I called my mother crying from a bench in Madison Square Park, which was not uncommon, she told me I needed more vitamin D. "Go outside and stare directly into the sun," she urged, advice I regretfully followed.

Things were better at home when a chicken roasted in the oven or eggs cooked in a hot buttered pan, even better when my job became food editor. Cooking was a meditation, I thought. It anchored me in my body—here was my hand, holding a knife, slicing through celery. Here I was, standing on the black and white kitchen tile of my first apartment in Brooklyn, listening to records, making dinner. Here I was, I thought, *living*.

It is a lot of meaning for a meal to bear, a habit I would not break.

WE WERE ALREADY falling out of love when my husband and I met downtown for a friend's book party. She stood on stage in a tight black dress and read from her memoir, and my husband and I drank champagne at the bar with her fiancé, listening. He turned to us as the room began to clap. "She is the most amazing person I know," he said, his face bright with admiration. I sipped my drink.

Later that evening, my husband and I stood on the dark Thompson Street sidewalk, waiting for a table at a sushi restaurant he'd wanted to take me to since we first started dating. We were finally getting around to some things, and still not getting around to others.

"Who is the most amazing person you know?" I asked. At the time, I did not realize it was a test. His face, which I never stopped finding so handsome, was illuminated in a streetlight.

"Your mother," he answered. "Who is the most amazing person you know?"

"Same," I said. That was not one of our irreconcilable differences.

ASKED MY MOTHER if she believed in God.

"People are my church," she said.

summer

BUDDHISTS SAY when someone close to us is dying, the veil that separates the living from the dead is lifted. We exist in full awareness of the end. Some experience this as pressure, like a deadline. *Now is the time to start living!* In later months, I would sense an urgency, but I felt it first as a space, like a window thrown open and then a breeze through the bedroom.

"It's very clarifying," my mother said.

My soon-husband was fond of the yearlong increment. On the other side of that period of limbo our real lives would start, next year, when everything would be different, most certainly better. By then he would be rich, he said, and we could begin our lives in earnest. We kept a cartoon he had drawn on a sheet of printer paper affixed to our refrigerator with a magnet. Drawn in black marker, there was a house with a kitchen island, a cock-eared dog in the yard, a nearby main street with a yoga studio, and at the foot of a staircase a basket, out of which peeped two tiny feet. Why such modest desires required millions of dollars wasn't entirely clear. It did not occur to me the holdup on our hands was not a matter of money or of time but of willingness.

What I understand now is that I was very young, that time was still to me a resource that was abundant, heaped around me like playground sand piles to scale, slide down, and conquer again.

That is why I could then still have more conviction in someone else's dreams than my own.

When my mother was sick, I began to realize the future would never arrive. There was no golden door we stepped through into serene forever. Time swept by us, more sinkhole than ascension; meanwhile, we never arrived there. We were always only ever *here*.

This was our ongoing argument:

Happiness tomorrow requires suffering today, he said.

But all we ever have is today, I said.

Somewhere in the middle was someone who was right.

"Don't take anything for granted," my mother said, and I groaned. "That's so *hard*."

"Enjoy," she said. "It's the same thing."

I WAS TWENTY the year my mother taught me how to roast a chicken. It was the deep dark of January, and we cut celery side by side on soapstone counters. She softened stale bread with warm chicken broth, gathered the torn cubes up by the handful and stuffed the cavity. I stood next to her taking notes, wrote *Bell's Seasoning*. I was about to move into my first apartment twelve hundred miles away and four blocks from my Saint Paul college campus, and this was my home economics crash course.

We baked a loaf of whole wheat bread that night from a stained page of the spiral-bound *More-with-Less Cookbook*, written by Mennonite missionaries in the 1970s. It was filled with her backward checkmarks and a note to add buttermilk to the refrigerator bran muffins. She gave me its lessons in shorthand.

This is how to rub two pennies together and eat for a week. Serve some of the chicken hot from the oven with steamed broccoli and a spoonful of stuffing. Pull the meat from the bones and chop. Tomorrow, pile chicken on slices of homemade bread with mayonnaise, salt, and pepper. Cover the carcass with water, and boil the bones for soup. She took the bread from the oven, knocked the top crusts, and told me to listen for a hollow sound.

We sliced two slabs of bread from the loaf, buttered them, and ate the chicken and the soft, herby stuffing at the kitchen table beside the bay window blooming with tall amaryllis and paperwhite bulbs. She wrote a grocery list. Here's what to keep in your pantry. She wrote *Bell's Seasoning*, too. Here's how to soften brown sugar. Here's how to make a cheap chocolate cake in a sheet pan, and here's how to cover it with walnuts so no one sees its uneven surface. She ripped the list from a pad, folded it, and sent me back to Minnesota for the spring semester feeling equipped as a pioneer.

Once there, in my sunny kitchen, I followed her instructions and hatched herb seedlings in empty eggshells on the sill of the kitchen window next to the table where I read *Richard III*. My roommates entered the kitchen, sniffing. Something rotting, they said.

WE TREATED HER first illness as a blip. It was fall, and my siblings and I took turns joining our mother at a New Jersey hospital every other Friday. Under a mobile of one thousand paper cranes, we sat in a ring of recliners we called the "chemo corral." We had jokes for everything. The nurses handed her tea in paper cups while Tamoxifen entered her body through a port beneath her collarbone. She wore a short strand of gold beads, dented from teething babies and taken, she claimed, off the body of a dead relative. I sat beside her with a laptop scrolling through china patterns. My wedding would be the following October. We laughed too loudly about things I can't remember, until the nurses returned, their hands tea-less this time. *Some people here are really sick*, they scolded.

But we were not them. Her children love chemotherapy, she joked to the staff. It was the only time we could claim her undivided attention. None of us realized how bad she looked until we saw the photographs after Thanksgiving. In the kitchen, reaching toward a guest's newborn, her expression is joyous but her skin colorless. Her body was vanishing as if in a film dissolve. I missed her eyebrows. She missed them, too.

After the holidays was radiation, and after radiation was remission. By the time her peonies bloomed in June, she and my stepdad were planning a trip to Scotland. It's so nice to take you for granted again, I joked on the phone. In October, wearing a red silk shantung suit, she hooked her arm through my left elbow and walked me down the aisle.

NEARLY FIVE YEARS later, we were not granted the same luxury of disbelief. She had been dragging her right leg around for months, complaining of a yoga injury. By the time she entered the chemo corral just before the holiday season, she was one of the really sick ones. This cancer was not excisable; it was embedded in her bones, had burrowed its way into the marrow, nested in her soft organs. We didn't have as many jokes, so we embraced understatement. She was *sick*, we said.

I don't remember her losing her hair, only when it was suddenly gone. She wore scarves tied loosely around her bare scalp: botanical block prints on Indian cotton, batiks, and large silk squares she'd worn at her waist and neck in the 1980s. She wasn't very good at tying them. They were always gathered loosely, slipping off, and she'd tug them lower on her forehead. "At least I haven't lost my eyebrows this time," she'd say at the downstairs mirror, putting on lipstick.

She lost other things instead. Twenty-two pounds, her toenails, taste buds, nerve endings. My childhood had been measured in the width of her back. When we hugged, I'd run my hands inside the deep channel of her spine, her bones flanked on either side by dense muscle. She had rowed crew and run after four kids, arms loaded with laundry and plastic bags from Tom Thumb. Now, her body was a stranger's. Unable to stand upright, she curled over a walker. But I recognized her hands. Her fingers were long for the size of her palm, with freckles beneath the knots of her knuckles. They're the same as mine. She gripped the steering wheel at ten and two.

Driving, she said, was the only thing that made her feel normal, but even quick trips were disrupted by nausea. She would feel a wave rise in her throat, keep one hand on the wheel, and extend the other toward me. That was my signal. I reached for the roll of paper towels she kept on the floorboards, ripped off a wad of rough sheets, and thrust them toward her. It was like a gym class relay race. *Here!* She held them to her mouth like an oxygen mask, then clenched the wheel, staying straight. She looked down the double lines of the road like a gangplank and took deep, deliberate breaths. *I just, need, to relax.* Once, after she returned home from a meeting, I found her in the driveway wiping streaks of yellow vomit from the inside of the driver's-side door.

It was like science fiction. First, she shrank. Wearing new black corduroys in a size formerly unknown to her, her concave thighs left dead air between legs thin as a fashion model's. More jokes.

Then she grew, expanding in all the wrong places. She unbuttoned the new pants to accommodate the swell, and my sister and I, stopped under a traffic light, wondered aloud what was growing inside. Her blood vessels began to leak into the tissue, so that her upper arms swelled like Popeye. Then her calves, ankles, and feet. Sometimes the pressure of the fluid was so great it would burst the skin. She sat at a luncheon, her feet in a pool of herself.

Try not to lose any weight, the oncologist said. Not dying seemed like a matter of meals. To lose weight was to move into an unseen space, the way headlights round the walls of a room at night, illuminating it a final time before a car turns the corner.

Here's what I heard: If she eats, she'll live. My older brother had gotten into the habit of depositing protein shakes on the bottom shelf of her refrigerator. They accumulated there, untouched. I could do better, I thought.

I was thirty-one the June Saturday a friend drove me out to my mother's farm. I left my husband and the china we had finally settled on—paper-thin and plain white—in our Brooklyn apartment for the summer. It did not occur to me that what I did looked like leaving; I would return for meetings at work and for date nights, I said, and my stepfather could use the break. I packed a suitcase of summer dresses, a sharp knife, and my good sea salt. When we turned into my mother's driveway, the weeds in the garden were waist high, and the redbud in front of the house was split in half, pulled apart by the weight of its two heaviest branches. It did not occur to me I might fail at any of what I attempted to save. I arrived in my mother's blue and white farmhouse kitchen. I thought if I could cook, I could cure.

WROTE A NEW grocery list. No peanut butter, she told me, unless it's with saltines. Potato skins sounded good and those sticks of cheddar cheese wrapped in plastic she could stick in her purse. Hamburgers, devil's food cake, creamy potato soup made with real cream. Crisp toast with salty butter, Greek yogurt, guacamole. She liked fish still, she said, and steak, and grease-stained sacks of fried chicken from the grocery store. Salads—big piles of ribby romaine, bright with vinegar. She had dressed one most nights for the past forty years. Now it was my turn.

We shopped together when she felt well enough, but when

her feet ached from neuropathy, and shoes seemed only to make it worse, she walked into the Amish market wearing thick wool socks. Waiting in line for a pretzel-wrapped sausage to share, another woman, about my age and tight with propriety, stared at my mother's feet as if a barnyard animal had clod into her dining room. My mother didn't notice; she was watching the bonneted women braid dough before dropping the pretzels into fryers of hot oil. The woman standing with us in line had a child with her, one who kicked his chubby legs from the top shelf of the shopping cart. She was ordering a platter for a party, sighing and shifting from one foot to another, impatient with the wait, and annoyed that a bald woman and her bitchy daughter were now standing in the way, foreshortening her view.

My rage was stealth. Its arrival never surprised me since I could feel it there, quiet but ever present in my body, like the steady machinations of menstruation. Still, it was startling when it ruptured the surface of an ordinary day. Women riled me— generations of them who walked together arm in arm through the parking lot of the zoo, who posted photos from a bright hospital room where there were more eager arms than could hold a swaddled new baby. Or a woman like this one, one who I had deemed insufficiently pleased with her precious little life and the littler one she had made, one with so much ahead that she could blithely waste what was being wrenched from my fingers, one who I knew nothing about, and yet had seen enough of. She could feel my glare.

"Am I in your way or something?" she asked.

"Not at all," I said, my mouth lifting into the kind of smile I had learned watching women in Texas. "But I believe we were next."

N DALLAS, I had accompanied my mother on mornings of end-less errands. JoAnn Fabrics, Weir's Furniture, Snider Plaza. This was the only bearable time to be outside in high summer—before the heat of the day gathered thickness and the sun burned, relent-less. East of the skyscrapers, where shotgun houses sat behind parched lawns and hanging laundry, five aluminum structures similar in dimensions to a football field rose from the color-less landscape. On their short sides, under the triangle of their pitched roofs, each was painted with a number. I remember 4 and 5. Inside, parked pickups, flatbeds facing in, filled with watermel-ons, with cantaloupes, with honeydew, trucked in from anony-mous tracts of land in east Texas off I-35. This was the farmer's market in the mid-1980s. No bluegrass band, no cooking demos, no heritage pork.

The vendors were men. Tan and ropey thin, they tucked soft packs of cigarettes into the chest pockets of their worn cot-ton shirts. They were polite but terse, wore mesh-backed base-ball caps and mirrored sunglasses. My mother strode the length of the buildings in blue jeans and square sunglasses with lenses that faded to the palest purple. Her hot-roller curls were brushed loose, her perfume deep as ripe melons. She pointed at quarts of peaches and red plums, and the men tumped green cardboard containers of fruit into plastic grocery sacks. She said something, and they laughed. She hooked the bags over her forearm, took her change, and we walked to the back of another man's truck to buy tomatoes and corn. If there was a breeze that day, and my hair were gathered into a ponytail, I could feel the air move at the nape of my neck.

We began to run errands together again. A few rolling miles from her home with my stepfather, at the Dvoor dairy farmer's market on the Route 12 circle, my mother leaned on her walker, stooped like Nanny before she died. She was only sixty-three, but she moved like an old woman. I followed her around the circle of vendors. We bought sweet potatoes from a young farmer with short sleeves and a tan, easy smile. His looked great, she told him, what was his secret? His face brightened, and he explained the conditions were right this year, and how to keep them over the winter in a cool garage. He handed her change, and she pushed it in her pocket, raising her shoulder like a girl. She hooked the bags on the handles of her walker. We moved on, and she sighed. "I used to be cute," she said.

On our way to the car, a little boy ran up to my mother with a coffee can. "Would you like to give to the Hunterdon Land Trust?" he asked. She pulled a dollar from her pocket and slipped it in his can. The boy looked back at his own mother, who handed him a roll of stickers. "Say 'thank you,'" she urged. "Thank you!" he chanted, then peeled off a sticker and placed it on my mother's extended forefinger. She put it above her breast. "I give," it said.

She was tired, so I drove us home, stopping at the Texaco just as the gas light turned on. The attendant was young, and we smiled at each other. When he turned his back to lift the nozzle from the pump, my mother looked ahead through the windshield, delighted by something unseen.

"What?" I said.

"Only a beautiful young woman could buy ten dollars worth of gas at a full-service station," she said. "Enjoy it."

M Y HUSBAND CALLED to say he'd been staying up all night writing code for his iPhone app and eating cold pizza for dinner. "That sounds grim," I said. "Life without my wife is grim," he said. On the weekends, he worked from bed with the curtains drawn. He thought he had Lyme disease, lupus, Celiac, a stomach parasite, cancer. The doctor told him to stop googling symptoms. I told him I could not hold all our joy.

I BUILT FOUR raised beds inside the fence of my mother's large garden. Some things, neglected, were still kicking: the apricot, apple, and plum trees; the raspberry bush. I ran the mower through the overgrown grass to cut a path, and then my mother rolled her walker out to talk me through the next steps before heading back to the porch to read the newspaper.

Inside the four-foot square beds, I made layers according to her instructions: newspapers and collapsed cardboard first to block weeds; then rotted sheep manure, shoveled from the heap as big as a jungle gym behind the barn; a six-inch crown of dark and fragrant soil.

We had ordered the seeds before the snow melted from catalogs with pen-and-ink illustrations, and my mother had drawn the beds to scale on graph paper. Now, I pushed the seeds into the soil with an unsure index finger. Basil, a mix of bitter Asian greens, Brandywine and Big Boy tomatoes, Cashflow summer squash and zebra-striped zucchini, bright French breakfast radishes, two kinds of kale. We had decided to devote an entire bed to flowers, for beauty and for the bees. The envelope of cosmos was called the Sensation Mix. The winter squash were space hogs, so my mother suggested piling the manure between the walls of two separate beds and planting them there, free-form.

It was too late in the season for any of this, and in my panic, I treated it more as science than art. I cut back and forth across the lawn to the porch to ask follow-up questions. My mother sat on the chipped wicker furniture repainted white each year before this one. I stood in front of her, sweaty and concerned about seed spacing. She was nearly subsumed by the slipcovered cushions and the sections of the paper on her lap, but she was calm in the hot, insect buzz of the afternoon.

"There's no way to screw this up," she said. "What's the worst thing that could happen?"

Within days the green tops of the radishes sprang right out of the dirt, and I dug them in wide-eyed marvel, before slicing them into salads I handed to her at lunch. I was amazed at how simple it was to grow something from seed.

I give.

HER YOUNGER BROTHER, Quennie, hosted a picnic at his dairy farm in Westminster, Vermont, pitching a party tent beside the driveway so we could linger for the afternoon out of the sun eating hamburgers and potato salad. One of my younger cousins had returned home with her newborn. Together with my sister's daughter, the babies rolled and toppled on a yellow blanket spread at my mother's feet. The skin hung loosely from her bony jaw, slipping from her face like a landslide. She wore a black daisy-print bucket hat someone had given her.

"I feel so happy, and so stimulated!" she said. She looked terrible.

I paced the rows of my aunt's gardens, then stepped out of sight into a shed. It smelled like hay and bicycle tires. I could hear my mother's laugh as the babies played with the Hungry Caterpillar, an orange rubber ball, a toy Hess truck.

I wanted to be pregnant, and I needed my husband's help. But the baby I wanted was not with him, it was with her. For her. Birth was the logical continuation of a circle, the reassurance to both of us that as she died, something of us grew. It was the closest I could come to knowing my mother from inside the vessel of my own skin, to understand how she loved, and to pass it on. This was my inheritance. These were the only riches I had ever cared about. *I give.*

But before I went to care for my mother, and again after I returned home, each month, timed perfectly to ovulation, my husband and I argued about something small, then walked into our bedroom stony and lay in the dark, silent and awake with our backs to each other, the way you do when there is a big thing no one is yet ready to say.

COOKED WHOLE sides of salmon with thick, fennel-flecked yogurt sauce. Outside, over charcoal's gray ash, I grilled butterflied chicken and then pounded parsley and basil in a mortar before adding a stream of green olive oil. I carried glass jugs of full-fat chocolate milk home from a local dairy. I made a peach crumble and burned the top, then scooped ice cream to cover it. I assembled tomato sandwiches with thick layers of mayonnaise on gold-toasted sourdough, and criss-crossed slices of crisp, hot bacon on top. Every meat had a sauce, every meal a dessert.

My mother insisted she didn't care about food. In fact, she never had cared, would have happily sustained herself on buttered toast and tea were it not for the hungry mouths of a family and the required ritual of a meal.

"Don't get your ego involved with cooking for me," she warned. But sometimes she requested seconds, and those nights sent me upstairs, fist-pumping in triumph. I would lie awake in bed under the glow-in-the-dark stars I had affixed to the ceiling in high school, brainstorming extra calories. Soft pats of butter into her bowls of rice, more olive oil poured onto the salad. I sent progress reports to my sister in Massachusetts. "I will be very, very surprised if she loses weight this week," I wrote.

ME, I ATE peanut butter and jelly sandwiches. Popcorn. Or I did not eat at all, strangely comforted by my stomach's savage growling. It was one of three times in my life I have lost my appetite, increasingly disinterested in my own meals as I focused on my cooking project for her.

For my mother, I turned on the stove. For my mother, I set the table. For my mother, I took the wineglasses from the cabinet, struck a match, lit the candles, cut zinnias and cosmos and collected them in an empty marmalade jar. My stepfather would leave us at the table to our talk. Those nights, neither of us must have cared about eating. Our desires were less tangible. There is one way to slow a story as it speeds toward its inevitable end, and that is to linger in the scene. There was no other purpose for a meal than this: for my mother and me to unfold our napkins in our laps and sit side by side until the sun sank behind the barn and I rose to clear our plates, empty or not, and switch on the overhead light so we could stay and stay and stay.

SOME DAYS, the medicine made her weird. She dozed sitting upright, out of it, and listened with her eyes closed. She was there—wearing a twin set, cup of milky tea in front of her on the coffee table—and also not there. She dipped in and out of conversation to smile at someone, and then, drugged and heavy-headed, rolled out again. She was like this one afternoon sitting next to me on the couch while I read a poem aloud, realizing too late what it was about. She blinked her eyes open. Our faces were very close, and we looked at each other—really *looked*, the way, I imagine, a portrait painter can see beyond the surface of a subject—the shape of an eye, the slope of a shoulder—to what is immaterial but plain. I was watching her body waste its way off the earth, a witness to the very simple process of disintegration. But the material world, the facts of its entropic systems, were complicated that day by what I saw. How could a thing be in the process of dying when I had never seen anything more alive? I know, from the way she looked back at me, she saw the same thing in me.

I T WAS NOT a reversal of roles. She did not become the child and I the parent. My care was her own mothering returned. I didn't fuss, wasn't precious. I made soup, mopped the floors.

"You are me," she said one night when I returned from a meeting in the city. "Taking out the garbage in your high heels."

"I can't make her comfortable the way you can," my sister told me on the telephone, and I felt I had been chosen.

I N THE EARLY evenings, I pushed the wheelbarrow and shoveled manure. One night in the bathroom, washing up before cooking, I saw sheep manure smeared on my cheekbone. I smiled hugely, proud. There was bright summer air in my chest, and my skin was salty with sweat.

But I felt, too, the reel of summer's speed and our slow progress in it. I didn't know the names for country things and forgot family stories. What was the tiny quick-headed bird with yellow tail feathers? How do I rotate the vegetables next year so they don't deplete the soil? Who was struck by lightning while driving a tractor, left witless with the teeth of his zippers fused? There were days when I felt thoroughly consumed by the work at hand, when picking wet strawberries and fetching the mail at the end of the long driveway and thinning the overgrown thicket of basil was enough to occupy my mind and body. Yet there was a sort of light in the early evenings, a kind I failed repeatedly to capture in photographs, that would bring my eye to the wider landscape. Its quality was by nature ephemeral and also sort of skittish, weaving its view out of my hands perhaps for my own good, as if the attempt to reduce splendor to a single small frame was to misinterpret its inherent scale. The faded hay wagon stood empty in the field across the road, and the sun illuminated the tree line until it dipped behind the green horizon. Our home here on the Delaware River sat on one hundred acres. There were another hundred acres and eight generations of stories on the farm my mother grew up on at the foot of Mt. Greylock. What I didn't learn would die with her.

The world was in such full bloom, we were wavering on the quick edge of a ripeness about to rot.

THE FARMHOUSE SLUMPED into the earth. I could manage the vegetable garden but not my mother's flower beds, too, now overgrown with weeds as tall as high school basketball players. Digging them up was a sweaty, cursing war. The downstairs toilet sank into the soft, warped wood floor. The garbage bin overflowed. Open, abandoned yogurt sat on the fridge shelf, overgrown with black spots. The ants were everywhere. I sprayed bleach on the countertops and threw out old jars of olives. I could not keep pace with the decay.

My mother had stayed in bed all day. I climbed the stairs to her room, which sat underneath the sharp, pitched angles of the roof, and stood in the doorway, not wanting to enter. The smell was sour and fetid. I was feeling mean.

"It smells bad in here," I said. She looked up from her magazine, stunned, embarrassment and surprise on her face.

"You're rude," she said. "Maybe it's because I've been sick for eight months," she added, as if we were talking about the flu. My heart beat hot with shame. And because she wanted me to leave, and because I wanted to, too, I turned back downstairs.

Ten months later, I looked for something in her bedroom. She was no longer stretched atop the floral sheets with *The New Yorker*, but the smell was still there. It was from the dog bed, I realized, the thick mat of hair and oily skin rubbed into the plaid fabric and the rag rug beneath it, hot canine breath hanging close in the air.

AT NIGHT, crickets sawed outside the windows of my childhood bedroom, and I read sixteen years of old journals, turning their pages into the early morning hours, as if I did not know what would happen next. There I was, same as ever, a linked paper chain of self-replication, continuously through time, the very same shorthand for a simple, happy life: muffin tins, cross-country skis, a desk by an open window. When had I made everything so complicated?

Downstairs my mother was at the sink, washing dishes in yellow rubber gloves. My feet were bare. She leaned her hands on the counter and turned to me at the kitchen table.

"Can't you see yourself teaching English and having babies and inviting people over on Saturday night for dinner and dancing in the living room to the ukulele?" She looked at me, the plastic gloves drippy with soap suds, as if I were to answer. "Can't you see it?"

The yellow porch light brightened the window over the sink. Bugs circled the brass fixture outside. I could see it, I said.

"It's not too late to start over," she said. "You don't always have to be a good girl."

We spent the rest of the summer driving the long-way places, and when we arrived, sat in parking spaces with our seat belts on.

Maybe I should apply to graduate school.

Great.

I'm afraid I'll meet a man, and he'll pay attention to me, and I'll like it.

That would be the most natural thing in the world.

Should I start recording these conversations?

We're not saying anything interesting.

In our talk, we were not faced with an end. We were present and entertaining the possibility of something beyond, as if we were crouched on a riverbank, dipping a toy boat into the current.

"What if I expect too much of life?" I asked.

She shrugged. "So what if you do?"

STOOD AT the kitchen sink rinsing a colander full of cherries, black-red and glossy. My stepfather's car pulled into the driveway, returning from chemotherapy. The car doors opened, and my mother watched her steps on the uneven flagstones, or hung her head, I couldn't tell. Sleigh bells, sewn to a leather strap and hooked on the front door, rang merrily as she pulled the door closed behind her. She had a thing for Santa Claus, she joked. Jim Morrison and Saint Nick.

She declined a cup of tea. She wheeled her walker straight into the TV room. I poured the wet cherries in a bowl and followed.

She sat on the couch, her bony knees pressed tight together and between her slim thighs a widening space of nothing. I eased beside her and placed the cherries on her lap. She was already crying, and she did not often do that.

It was as if she confessed, the way she said it. Three pounds. Going, going, gone.

The afternoon sun was bright on her collection of terra-cotta pots filled with leggy geraniums. The leaves smelled like dirt. Her writing desk stood in the window cluttered with recipes torn from magazines and letters that needed response.

"It's very simple, Sarah," she said. "I love you, and I don't want to die."

There was nothing else to say. We each ate a cherry, then spit the pits into the blue and white bowl.

SHE WANTED A burger at the Stockton Inn. We sat on the front porch with a view of the bridge across the Delaware River to Pennsylvania. The traffic was very close. Silver-haired men rolled by in red cars with the tops down. Each had a woman as a passenger, usually wearing what seemed like too much makeup for a hot day. Motorcycles passed through the small town inter-section with their guttural roar. I drank a gin and tonic. Did she have a drink, too? She'd sometimes order bourbon and ginger ale, which is what her father drank and her mother drank, too. The waitress seemed preoccupied and kept returning to our table to provide a forgotten menu, an omitted fork. Maybe she was new. Maybe she was heartbroken. I once absentmindedly wan-dered away from my shopping cart in the fabric section at Ikea to look at lamps. I returned to find the cart had stayed put but the purse inside it had not. I sat in the front of the store canceling credit cards and crying, because I was now not only heartbroken but also a fool. A man approached. "I've been looking all over for you," he said, "you walked off without your purse." I never got to tell my mother that story. She would have said, *See? There you go*, as if she'd known all along the outcome would include a good deed performed by a handsome stranger. This is one trick-iness of grief. How can I "mourn" the "loss" of someone I can still summon? We ate our burgers and kept talking. The waitress refilled our water glasses, and a group of Italian men arrived, sat at the table beside us, ordered wine. They made a comment to my mother, and everyone laughed. The appliance store across the street was closed and washing machines stood in the darkened front windows like undressed mannequins. It was August, and the sun was low and golden, so it must have been around seven or eight o'clock when my mother said, "Who knows how many more summer evenings like this we'll get?"

fall

HOW ABOUT A last-ditch vacation? I had been asked to cover a food event in Hawaii, and we could make the most of it, I suggested. On the plane, most people looked like my husband: relaxed, happy, at least half Asian. The flight attendants walked up and down the aisles in maxi dresses printed with island blooms like Luau Barbie, then one leaned close to hand him his chocolate-covered macadamia nuts, and a sheet of glossy black hair fell around her face. He shared with me, 23A and B. I fished my fingers inside the slit of the shiny silver pouch and looked down at brown Colorado, rugged as a cowboy's calloused hand. The view gave me hope, as if I might be able to sort my life from cloud distance and then on island time. *Hawaii*, my husband had said in the days leading up to our trip. *Hawaii*, like an incantation. I looked at him now in his seat, munching macadamias pleasantly, engrossed in a game on his phone.

We lowered our heads for the front desk clerk at the hotel who draped long, muted necklaces strung with brown shells the size and shape of small beetles around our necks. Our room was seashell pale and sounded just the same, filled with orchids and a basket of exotic fruit. We stood at the railing of our balcony above two pools and countless palms, hushed by the curling ocean waves below. Who were all these people, I thought, reclining below us on chaises, lazily turning magazine pages and sipping rum. A thin strip of white shoreline stretched to Diamond Head, rising like a promise.

"Hideous," I joked.

He had been to this island before with another woman and here's what I knew about her: She was rich from her father's line of convenience stores and accordingly difficult; she had orgasmed most reliably with the light tickling of a feather, which she kept in her bed-stand drawer. I entered stage left on a romantic set piece. Blooms nestled on the crushed ice of a *mai tai*, the crisp bed linens in boxy rooms with windows pushed open to the ocean, the idle slide of slack-key guitars. New character, same motivation. *Birds do it, bees do it. Let's fall in love.* That evening we transformed into the strangers we had observed from our balcony. We ate plates of tuna soaked in inky soy and pushed aside the paper umbrellas in our drinks for a sip. Three men with ukuleles sang in swaying harmony while two hula dancers moved beside them. The women swirled their hands like conjurers, playing the air close at their hips like stringed instruments and then twirled their hands up into the darkness, smiling at some skyward beneficence, as if they could harness it from the atmosphere and tuck it back in their pockets. Maybe they could. "You would make an excellent hula dancer," my husband whispered to me. Later, my heels dangling from one hand, we walked the stretch of sand in front of our hotel. I stumbled ankle deep into the salty waves. That night we went to bed together in the dark, the balcony door open to the ocean sounds.

The sun felt like a menace, the way it bore down on us all day with its unrelenting intensity. I smeared my skin with SPF 70, sweat it off, reapplied. Pimples emerged. One of us was a natural to this climate, but it was not me. Beyond the Hard Rock Cafe and California Pizza Kitchen, the streets of Honolulu did not seem designed for pedestrians. We waited at streetlights for traffic to subside, then rushed across intersections without striped painted lines. Platters of hamburger patties and pork, with slices of orange cheese on top, ice cream scoops of white rice, everything covered in thick brown gravy. I wanted a vegetable. My husband had self-diagnosed a gluten allergy, and having forgone the macaroni salad, chatted merrily about his improved digestion as we ate at a plastic picnic table lacquered bright red beside a sun-dull road.

It was not hiking food, but we hiked. Pedestrians on their way to the Diamond Head trailhead must pass single file through a dark, narrow two-lane tunnel toward oncoming traffic, then across a parking lot where a truck sold shaved ice painted with syrups.

"How is it different from a snow cone again?" I asked.

The ice was finer, shaved, soft, he said.

The sun pressed down on us like a sandwich griddle while we wound through ochre dust and scrub brush on a cement trail. We drained our little bottles of Poland Spring. Halfway up our ascent, a woman had scrambled off the trail. She sat on the bald face of a short hill between two large boulders. She leaned between her knees to vomit. Her face was tear streaked. We stood below her on the trail, and I hollered.

"Are you okay?"

"Can we get you some water?" my husband added.

She raised her head from between her knees and stared at us with narrowed eyes.

"Please leave me alone."

So we climbed. My t-shirt was wet at my lower back, and the elastic of my underwear rubbed the crease of my thigh. My mind was scorched blank as the crater we climbed. The sun had ablated my consciousness. What was left was the wet rind of my body and a will that seemed to exist without volition; this is what moved me toward the top of the volcanic cone. Up 74 steps, up 99 more, then out of the sun to the final 43, enclosed in the tight spiral staircase of an old military observation deck. The task at hand was my imperative, but I understood the pull to rest between rocks, to give up before the payoff of the final view.

Here is what you see after the 560-foot ascent. Dry blond grasses that arch in the breeze; mesquite with brittle branches called *kiawe*; the crisp, long pods of *haole koa*, hanging like cicada husks from a tree; a red lighthouse on the shoreline that looks like an impostor; an abandoned bunker from the Fort Ruger days, salt bleached and battered, its squared shoulders huddled against the dull landscape and wind. More commanding is the wide view: the rising silver city and winding stretch of Waikiki, slim as the penciled eyebrow of a wizened barmaid beneath a distant domed sky. It is not just the sun that is unrelenting but the view itself— its insistent, bald-faced pronouncement, swaggering and unsubtle as a beauty queen. *Let's do it. Let's fall in love.* For a long time, we stood together at the railing of an observation deck, looking out. I wondered why I was so unmoved.

Good morning. There was coffee on the night table for me, a forehead kiss. My husband carried a plastic bag from the gift shop across the street filled with floral purchases. A blue polyester Hawaiian shirt for him, a rust-colored, one-size-fits-all dress for me. It was sweet, I could see that, but the color of the dress made me sad. It looked funereal, like late-season chrysanthemums.

"Do you like it?" he asked.

"I do, thank you." I got up from the bed to brush my teeth and pulled a cotton sundress from my suitcase.

"No, wear your new dress," he said, holding it out to me, limp in his hands. "I'll wear my shirt, too," he urged.

We walked the bright sidewalks of Kalakaua Avenue looking like employees on our lunch break in amusement park-issued costumes. A camera dangled from my husband's shoulder, and he stopped in front of a kiosk with a paper sign handwritten in black marker: WAIKIKI'S OLDEST LEISTAND 1928. The first owner's name was Kapela, somehow mangled into Aunty Bella; she had strung the garlands of fresh, fragile orchids by hand. Then her daughter took over, then a granddaughter. Such ephemera seemed expensive to me, but he insisted. He selected a pale lei of flowers whose essence, crushed and contained, comprised my favorite perfume.

He draped the ring of plumeria, tuberose, and gardenia across my bare shoulders and we kissed there on the groomed sidewalk of the Royal Hawaiian Center. A Japanese tourist took our picture. In it, my husband needs a haircut and I need sunglasses. I am squinting at the camera.

We had married in a boxwood-trimmed garden. He had not lifted a veil, though I knew he would have liked the drama of it; I wore a net at the crown of my head that cascaded to my waist like

Rapunzel's hair. On my way down the aisle, I had stumbled over the uneven grass, and both my parents had gripped my elbows at either side. The photographer caught my laugh, my young shoulders shrugging, my eyes in a half roll at my own lack of grace. *Nobody's perfect*, my look says, though perhaps I expected others to be. It did not occur to me to kiss my parents when the three of us arrived before the groom standing between two large brass candelabras. When they dropped their arms, I stepped up to him like a woman about to win her carnival prize. In the picture of us leaving the reception later that night, a friend said my husband looked like the cat that ate the canary. Each of us thought we were the lucky one. *I do*, he said, and back then, I did, too.

On our honeymoon in Mexico, I trotted out seven nights of cheap polyester lingerie. Day three, emerging from the bathroom in the barest of all and bearing a beer. "Let's just watch TV," he said, putting an arm around me. I learned *mira* from dubbed Woody Allen that night. *Look!*

We spent a day at Chichen Itza, where I carried a large black umbrella to block the sun, like Mary Poppins on holiday. On the way back to the hotel, after passing the bright, swinging hammocks for sale by the side of the road woven by women and inmates, was a vast *cenote*, an Indiana Jones swimming hole secret. The ceiling of the cave arched over the opaque water like the dome of a cathedral with a light-flooded opening at its apex. Bats swooping. Someone took our photo there, too. In that one, my husband's hand on his tanned hip bone, me in a red swimsuit, we look happy.

But before climbing into the van for the final leg of the return trip to the hotel, he had slipped into a dry change of clothing. Decades of swim practice made him adept at the deck change, practiced perhaps more out of habit than modesty. Even at home, he wrapped a towel around his waist, stepped into his underwear and jeans, and then whipped the towel away to rub his hair dry, all without ever having revealed himself.

The windward side of the island was dense with water-thick rain forest foliage. In the rental car, my husband turned the radio to a pop station. I dangled my hand out the window on the highway, and examined my face in the side-view mirror. New pimples. We had three agenda items that day: visit a Buddhist temple; attend the Polynesian Cultural Center; and see the beach at Kailua, which he remembered from the last time he was on the island and in love with another woman.

We parked in a bleached, palm-lined lot, the sun-soaked pavement hot as a range, then walked a narrow sandy path past lush, low-growing sea lettuce and down to the waterline. I picked up a kalanchoe flower that had fallen onto the path and tucked it behind my ear.

The pale sand of Kailua Beach rings a turquoise bay, bookended between the high volcanic peaks of the Ko'olau Range. The sky arches to the water, the convex curve of blue meeting blue and then our bare feet sliding into the hot sand. I wore a black string bikini under a white linen dress, the skirt made of widening tiers like a cake, swirling fiercely around my legs. His hair stood on end in the wind, his eyes squinting in the brightness. We walked up and down the beach, its beauty like an impenetrable wall. We never seemed to arrive. I looked for a break in the landscape, for a loophole, something set askew. The sound of the wind at my ears was like traffic. I reached to rear-range the flower.

"Congratulations!" warbled through the wind to us. A man with a naked torso, as tan as a nut, his hulking hand holding a black ribbon leash that led to a perky Chihuahua, was beaming at us.

My husband shouted back, confused. "What's that?"

"I said, 'Congratulations!' You're in this long white dress, you got the flower behind your left ear like a wedding band. And you," he looked at my husband knowingly, as if they shared a secret lan-guage. "You're newlyweds, right?"

We looked down at our clothes, and then back to him, laughing.

"Look at that," my husband said. "You're right."

Was that all it took? A plane ride, frozen drinks, a wide white expanse of beach unspooling to the horizon? One of us thought it did, more present in paradise than in our days making the bed, clearing the table, rinsing the dishes in the sink. The other pre-ferred the ordinary hours, felt here in the tropical sunshine as empty as an abandoned shell.

The temple was set inside the deep shade at the foot of the Ko'olau Mountains. I rang a peace bell, watched sparrows dive past the lacquered Buddha, and then sat alone under a small red-roofed pavilion. I counted my breaths, then kept breathing but forgot to count. Then I started over.

People do not go to the Polynesian Cultural Center for the food. We wandered through a cavernous dining room—an authentic luau, someone boldly claimed—our brown plastic trays crowded with macaroni salad, roast pork, and tall red plastic cups with pellet ice and fruit punch. We sat across from each other. The long, communal tables were crowded with big groups of families. A kid spilled his milk and chairs scraped across the tile floors, echoing in a room loud with crying and benign talk.

Waiting for the big nighttime show, we sat in the grass near a tented pavilion that sold miniature ukuleles and magnets. It was getting dark. The tall lampposts lighting the cement pathways clicked on. Bugs swirled beneath them.

My husband began to tell me a story about the first time he'd been there. He pulled at the blades of grass while he talked. He was ten, he said. What he remembered was a couple sitting together on a bench. They had seemed hot and tired, but he watched them share a sexy glance, and then the woman shook her shoulders, side to side, he said, in a flirty little shimmy. He looked at me, sitting with my legs folded in the grass. "And now here I am, back here with my wife."

I was hot and tired, too, but I knew it was my cue. I grinned at him, then shimmied my shoulders in the pale lamplight. He smiled back at me widely.

But blackness seeped into the car on the way home, blowing in on the air off the ocean. The dark edges of roadside palms leaned over the highway like crouched, menacing animals. Salt and hibiscus through the windows. We named our favorite parts of the day. Me: lying on the stiff, shorn grass in my wet bathing suit after paddleboarding, the quiet of the temple. Him: postcard view at Kailua, fire dancers.

"It's funny," he said in the quiet. "Yours are so small."

"What do you think that means?" I asked.

"Isn't it obvious? You love the small moments, and I love the big ones."

"Yeah," I said. "But what do you think *that* means?" The dash of our tiny rental car gleamed blue in the dark, and the headlights only shone so far.

"I don't know," he said, kindly.

HOME AGAIN, Saturday morning, still wrapped in sheets. My husband placed a white paper cup of thick dark espresso and foamy milk in my hands. "Cappuccino," he said. I thought that the height of romance. My hair was a big red tumble, pink imprints of sheet creases on my skin and my eyes sleepy. "Thank you," I said, though my intention was to coo. He sat on the far side of the room by the window. I had asked my mother for a white slipcovered reading chair, but I never did read in it. The chair would be more at home in a nursery.

He asked if I'd had fun last night. It had been a late and boozy one with girlfriends. My head hurt. I suddenly remembered the bartender, the free drinks, his smiling, sidelong comments. I wanted my husband in bed beside me and considered the merest joke of competition might bring him close. At parties, I liked watching other women flirt with him at the punch bowl knowing he would come home with me. My efforts had the opposite effect.

"If you want to sleep with other people, it's okay with me," he said.

Maybe I should have brushed my teeth, my hair. That was our bed, the Tempur-Pedic we bought several winters ago when we had less money. In the gray showroom, we lay side by side on the mattress, our hands folded politely over our belly buttons. Then we deliberated the purchase at a French restaurant now long out of business. We decided to go for it, and I opened a store credit card that day. Zero percent interest.

What I was feeling from him now.

Later that day, walking home from yoga, I sat on a stoop and called my mother. Her voice wavered with rage through the phone, like hot air rising from a tarred road. It is so damaging to a woman's self-esteem, she said. If she wasn't crying yet, she sounded like she soon would. Her reaction surprised me, until I realized it was a remembered one. We were not talking about me, we were talking about her. The refusals, the late-night absence, the *Why-can't-you-be-more* criticism, the proverbial credit card receipt.

"No, no, no," I reassured her. "I don't think the problem is me." Maybe I should have.

I heard her surprise through the telephone.

"Oh," she said, and paused. "That's good."

THERE IS MORE to marriage than weekends and vacations, my mother said, and there was more to our marriage than that, too. But it was the time free from the numbing habits of our everyday—of commuting home, ordering Chinese, and then rinsing the plastic containers for the recycling bin—when the friction of our misalignments began to chafe.

He liked to argue in metaphor. After watching a miniseries on John Adams, he admired aloud the partnership of a woman like Abigail. Her endurance of long separations had been fortified, he said, by the knowledge her husband was achieving something great. I no longer thought my husband about to achieve anything great, and the part I remembered was the miscarriage Abigail suffered alone one summer.

We argued, recurringly and bizarrely, about a hypothetical road trip to the Grand Canyon. I longed for scenic byways and roadside slices of berry pie. Why stop at the world's largest ball of twine, he said, when we were on our way to one of the world's wonders. We should drive all night just to get there.

We were arguing about how to love. We were arguing about how to live. Then we were arguing about how to die, and in the end, not arguing in metaphor at all.

"You're in denial," my husband said. "You need to prepare for the fact that your mother is going to die."

I did not know how to prepare for her death other than to be witness to her life.

On Friday nights, when I boarded a bus at Port Authority and rode two hours into the Garden State, I watched strip malls thin into farmland. The evening sky changed over the countryside, streaked with clouds and color as the sun set. My mother and I sat at the table in her darkened kitchen.

She would not outlive her husband, she told me. She would not move into a condo by the ocean someday, or sew a slipcover for a loveseat in the tropical fabric she'd already selected. She would know only one grandchild. She would not, she said, grow old in the way she had imagined. She would not grow old at all.

"I need to be able to say these things to someone," she said, and so I listened.

I T WASN'T LIKE a plane going down. It was more like a car lurching forward, then stalling out. Each new chemotherapy drug brought a burst of wellness—deep reserves of energy, a renewed appetite. With it, she painted furniture, picked basil, whipped up a batch of pesto and froze it in ice cube trays. She knit baby blankets and hauled out the sewing machine. After she died, one of her friends mailed me two blue-and-white-striped Easter outfits. A seersucker dress and a seersucker onesie, both lined in plain white cotton. "Your mother sewed these for my kids," she wrote, "but I thought you should have them." She attended marathon board meetings and lunches with friends that stretched late into the afternoon. She would gain weight, take long drives, send long, chatty emails. We would all relax.

Each new drug also brought a spate of new side effects. Mouth sores, loss of appetite, nausea, peeling hands and feet, retained fluids, the full array of digestive problems.

There are only so many cancer drugs. The protocol was to try each drug for three months, then test to see whether there had been any change. There was a list we would soon exhaust.

"Rick and I were surprised to learn the results of my PET scan today," she wrote. We had been at this the better part of a year.

"I guess I should be impressed I feel so good when I have been pumped up with ineffective poisons for nine months."

Sometimes someone would tell me about a drug they thought was a "miracle," and I would send my mother a message. Was this on our list? Had she already tried it? And she would reply the next morning.

"It makes me very sad to think of my precious, luscious daughter reading about drug therapies. Pursue happiness, pleasure, and sensual delight! Cook, ride your bike, pick out your spring clothes. Just live harder! That is the medicine."

M Y BOSS ORGANIZED a dinner at an Italian restaurant in the East Village. In a private room behind heavy wood doors, my coworkers and I sat at a long table set under dim chandeliers. The cost of one night's privacy was one thousand dollars. Most of our tab was wine.

That night at the table, after the plates of squid ink risotto and sausage orecchiette had been cleared, when people began to escape outside to smoke cigarettes, when we were leaning back in our chairs having enjoyed ourselves and still draining the last of the wine, I remember someone began talking about wanting to lose weight. She pinched a handful of flesh above her waistband. There was murmured commiseration about thighs.

I had watched my mother age twenty years in the past six months, I said. We should enjoy our bodies. It's only downhill from here, and fast.

I must have been tedious company.

I N MANY RELIGIONS and philosophical traditions, the body is an obstacle, a liability. It must be controlled or overcome, and to reach enlightenment, it must be transcended.

For years I practiced a form of yoga based on Tantric philosophy. I am not a scholar of Tantra, but here is what I understand. On Tantric paths, everything is sacred. Rocks, tonsils, an octopus. The human body itself can be a gateway to the divine. If it happens here in earthly life, it's called *jivanmukti*.

I cannot conceive of an enlightenment as a sustained state, static once achieved. But I have had moments of illumination as bright and flashing as a fish. They arrive unannounced, without fanfare—say, stepping off the Sixth Avenue bus or walking the foothills of the Blue Ridge Mountains. The sky turns lavender in the evening. Is that divine? I know it is the beauty of the material world, that I feel it in my body, and that it means something to me—that my breath will catch in my throat, that it fades almost as soon as it arrives, that I will be stunned again at its sudden reappearance.

T HAT FALL I developed a new habit. Two blocks from our apartment was a storefront offering *qigong tui na*, a style of acupressure massage. Fifty dollars for sixty minutes. It was nothing fancy, but every week or two I returned to see a man who told me to call him Peter. He wore flowing black track pants, had broad shoulders and a wide, welcoming face. Sometimes when I swung the door open he was scooping rice out of a cooker under the low drop ceiling, but he would smile wordlessly, gesture toward one of the curtain doors, press play on the stereo, and I would undress in a bare room. It was always painful, the way he manipulated the tender knots tucked beneath my scapula with his elbow, or sunk his knuckles into the soft arch of my foot. I would allow myself to whimper, the face cradle growing damp, and he would whisper *Shhh*. When I returned to the waiting room, buttoned up again but also somehow undone, he would hand me a thin plastic cup of water and tilt his head with sympathy. I sat and slowly sipped, studying the charts near the register. They illustrated the meridian lines running through the body, how every area corresponded to another, and I would wonder about the original sources of all the hard places in me. When the cup was empty, I would sign the credit card slip and put on my coat. He would always stop me before I stepped back outside and give me one last adjustment. Pull my coat zipper higher beneath my chin or put both his hands on my upper arms and pat, as if warming me for the journey. And then, after several visits, he began to hug me, to fold me into his arms just as I was about to leave, and I would rest my head against him for a long, long moment. *Bye bye, thank you*, he said, and I would say thank you, too.

ONE OPTION FOR earliest memory: We have spent the day at the Highland Park Pool, where I lay my towel in the shade by the snack bar. Snow cones drenched in red and blue syrups, snack-sized bags of Fritos, hot dogs, the menu spelled out in black letters slid across rails like an abacus. My mother held on to the side of the pool, dutifully scissor kicking her legs and chatting with other mothers. Loud sounds of Marco Polo, the spring of the high board, the quiet pause, the punctuating splash.

In the hot late afternoon my mother drives us home on the tree-shaded streets by Turtle Creek in our red Suburban. I am sun weary, sinking into the scratchy gray upholstery, my limbs exhausted and the core of me cool from the water. It may be my favorite feeling in the world—the physical exhaustion after swimming that leads to a particular kind of hunger. It's when I most want fried chicken.

At home, I wriggle out of my wet swimsuit and pull a dry cotton t-shirt over my head. It hangs to my knees for sleeping. That evening, I sit on one of the two wide windowsills in my bedroom. They are painted white. It is the hour when the sun bathes the redbrick houses on our street gold. My window looks out over the top of the honeysuckle bush in our front yard. I watch as cars pull up to the stop sign at our corner and turn right or left toward home, toward Bubba's for biscuits and gravy, toward the Texaco around the corner to have their windshields washed, toward the evening bells ringing in the tower of the gray Methodist church. This is our neighborhood: Drexel Drive, Hillcrest Avenue, Mockingbird Lane. My mom has brought me chicken noodle soup, the kind from a red and white can, and because it was unusual to eat in my bedroom, this must be why I remember—how I ate it from frosted-opaque Tupperware, the noodles soft, the oil-splatched surface of the salty broth. It is the first time I can recall, with a certainty as indelible as bedrock, being within the envelope of my own skin. My senses surrounded my consciousness, vibrating like an electric fence. Outside my window, the whole world.

T HE KINDS OF people who prefer to be naked, to stand at the kitchen counter fixing a sandwich in the nude, are still not dressed at their desk later, phoning the cable company. "I need to reeroticize my body," a friend told me on the telephone after her partner had grown accustomed to the sight of her long legs, bare and languid, draped about their apartment.

When the time finally came at the end of college, and I began to lie beside another body all night long, I was surprised at my own sexual ease. It was not because I believed my worth seated there, though I felt worthy of fun, desire, playfulness. What I cared about was meaning, and the pleasure of sex was another place it lived. It is mysterious to me, in the way faith can be. It seemed such a simple expression of self and an all-consuming act of presence, like a prayer, but one said in tandem.

I HAD NO male friends, no male coworkers. "You need more men in your life," my mother said. "They offer a different perspective." Maybe I would call up my old college roommate and ask if he wanted to get a beer.

"And you should try to smile at a man in the street every day," she added, like homework. This had never occurred to me. I had only ever been interested in the man whom I married, his hairline launching at me like an arrow.

In crosswalks and on the sidewalk, I let my eyes wander to bald heads and tattooed biceps. They were everywhere, and they looked back. I began to smile.

IF YOU WANT to understand partnership, take a dance class or go canoeing. *Hold me tighter*, I said on the dance floor. *Paddle when I say or just stop*, my husband instructed from the stern.

Sitting at a karaoke bar after Friday night swing, we once had a conversation we forgot to have before exchanging vows.

"Let's each write what our definition of marriage is," I said, handing him a stubby pencil and a song request slip.

I wrote: Marriage is physical and emotional intimacy.

He wrote: Life is a boxing ring, and marriage is my coach, wiping the blood from my face and squeezing cold water into my mouth.

Whatever that means.

THE POLICE OFFICERS in line before me at 7-Eleven were buying a day's worth of car snacks. Cellophane pouches and drinks were piled on the counter by the cash register, and one of the officers was still racked with indecision.

"Cheez-Its or Goldfish?" the one asked the other, who then looked at me.

"Go ahead," his partner said, waving me toward the cashier. "Slurpee's on me."

A week later, walking in Prospect Park, a squad car pulled beside me and rolled down the window. I worried I was in trouble, and then I recognized the face.

"How was the Slurpee," he asked.

It had been a very hot day, and it was great, and that was so nice, and thank you.

"I didn't know if you were married or what," he said, trailing off.

I wore a diamond ring and a gold band, but I don't think they ever look. Before stating what I thought the jewelry made obvious, I enjoyed the simple fun of that brief moment. A girl in a pair of wide 1940s-style shorts that fluttered in the hot breeze, a man in uniform, a summer day.

"Well, you have a beautiful smile," he said.

A FRIEND HOSTED a rooftop party. Guests wore feathers and eyeshadow and caftans. We drank dentist cups of whiskey, and my dear old friend introduced me to his new friends. After a toast, I called one of them a gorgeous man.

"Minnie, here, is a lady," my friend clarified.

Later, sitting on a low brick wall, a photographer touched my shoulder. He was a man. He asked if he could get me a beer from the ice chest, then told stories about midnight bourbons in Southern juke joints, about the pagans who pilgrimage to Stonehenge in spring and dance with wreaths of flowers, about a woman he once met at a trailhead who offered him a blow job when they reached a peak. I wondered how these stories usually went over. I wondered how it would feel to kiss him. But more so, especially in the days that followed, when I began to imagine myself at the end of a dark bar on a red stool, aglow in the light of a Wurlitzer, alone in another state, I wondered what it would feel like not to meet a man like this but to be him.

When he finally asked, I said I worked as a food editor at a big company.

"Oh," he said, looking at me as if I had just come into focus. "You're *corporate*."

I wish my friend had been on hand to intervene. "Sarah, here, is an artist."

All the terms were up for redefinition.

N THE LATE FALL, on mornings when frozen dew still covered car windows, my husband and I rode together in taxis five long avenues to a basement office. For fifty minutes, before we each reported to work in midtown, we sat on a loveseat opposite a woman with close-clipped hair and long silken scarves, and talked about our feelings. *Permanent Partners* and *Goddesses in Everywoman* stood on her bookshelf.

The diagnosis was that we had very different levels of emotional fluency. After each session, we stood on the icy sidewalk with our arms around each other. Wasn't this trying? And if it was working, why didn't it feel better?

On the subway, I sealed myself up again, cordoned off the brief opening I'd allowed. At editorial meetings, when I was pitched stories about what rising lime prices would do to the cocktail and guacamole industries ("We'll call it 'Limepocalypse!'"), I did not want to look as though I had been crying.

"It will take fewer than ten sessions," my mother said. "Either way, you'll know."

It was exhausting, waiting for the final outcome of these two diagnoses.

That was when I began to fantasize about road trips, plotting giant circular routes around the perimeter of the United States. My escape was powered by one recurring daydream: My back on hard-packed sand beside a dying campfire under black cover of night, the fabric of desert sky pricked with white stars like cross-stitch. I would need a month; I would need a car.

"I get it," my brother, Bliss, said. "I ran all the way to China."

"Take two weeks," my boss said over vodka tonics. Then a few days later in the kitchenette, she suggested I could do it in one.

I applied to graduate school instead. I rented a hippie farmhouse upstate for a weekend to finish my applications. There was a portrait of JFK hanging on the porch next to a stack of firewood and a disco ball in the living room. The house was obstinately cold despite the fires I built in the wood stove. On the sheepskin rug, I read the love letter my husband had pressed into my hand at my departure. It was all too late. In the morning, I sat at the long kitchen table in fingerless gloves. I wrote about my mother. She was affecting my sense of time, and everything was beginning to seem urgent. Then I ran hilly country roads past Jewish summer camps for city kids, mixed myself a Manhattan, and cooked a dry-aged steak for dinner. When the fire died down, I threw on another log.

winter

GOOD ROAD TRIPS with a carful of friends begin with Diet Dr Pepper and beef jerky and an ironic Metallica lighter to replace what TSA took away. It was three days before New Year's Eve. While Laurie watched Chicago shrink in the rearview mirror, Jenny poured Sour Patch Kids into her open hand and cued up the lesbian soundtrack we've harmonized to since college. I sat on the backseat hump with one snow boot in each wheel bed and leaned forward between the front seats; I took the low parts. My husband was snug against his window reading the news on his phone.

Wisconsin welcomed us—a couple freshly in love and a couple falling out.

But we all loved the alien landscape. When the last glacier moved through the Upper Midwest, it scraped off mountaintops and rounded topographical edges, leaving green hill states that gently roll and unfold. The wedge of land where Wisconsin, Minnesota, Illinois, and Iowa lean their backs against each other was bypassed, so what remains is the Driftless—an area that is bony shouldered and dramatic with craggy rock faces and blind valleys. Insoluble limestone mountain ranges rise suddenly from grassy prairies, dark on the near horizon like a declaration that takes everyone by surprise.

The roads were snow streaked through the thinning towns.

Gays Mills got a laugh and was followed by Soldiers Grove, where all the lights were off. We turned left at the bend in County Road x-marked by a red mailbox and an old outhouse and slowly traveled an unmarked road past a snowed-over creek bed. It seemed like we were lost, like we had turned too soon and now overcommitted to our error. The car slid as we took a sharp turn and then, there it was on the left: a white farmhouse with a plume of wood smoke and every window bright. That was Annie's.

My husband lifted his bag from the trunk and cursed the cold under his breath. He brought his laptop but forgot to pack the long underwear I bought for our trip to Denmark the year before.

"There's no bad weather," I said, dragging my suitcase up the snowy drive. "Only bad clothing." I inherited know-it-all from my mother. He inherited long-suffering from his father.

That trip to Copenhagen had felt different, where we sat side by side at café tables with daytime candlelight and silver pots of winter heather. We drank strong, milky coffee until it was time to drink beer. First thing in the morning we were already off to a good start: I piled thick blankets over us in the dark hotel room and pretended we were prehistoric, bedding down under pelts of fur in the belly of a cave. Behind the closed door of the bathroom each day, I removed ovulation tests from my toiletries case. Walking the gray streets shopping for candlesticks and ceramics for our home, or on trains to see a cathedral out of town, I remembered what a good man my husband was. He bought presents for each of his coworkers, gave up his seat for women on the metro. I was very sorry I had forgotten. "What's your favorite part of vacation?" I asked, and he answered, "Seeing my wife so happy."

And now he had forgotten his long underwear.

"I made split pea soup," Annie said, while pointing to our bedrooms up steep, creaky stairs. She wore a plaid flannel nightgown, waved her hand at the stove, and said help yourself. Jenny met Annie singing in a square dance band in Chicago. In the city, Annie owned her own business and wore lipstick. Then four hours away, she lived a country life with a cherry orchard and shaggy white horses in the paddock. She dug swimming holes and painted her face with mud. The sign above the old toilet in her bathroom read WHEN IT'S YELLOW, LET IT MELLOW. The simple things we dreamed about, Annie made real.

She dropped the needle onto a Loretta Lynn record, and sat back on the couch in the red glow of the Christmas tree. On the Oriental rug, old beagle Betty crossed her paws like a lady, rested her head on top, and sighed. There was a fire in the woodstove.

I was the first to climb the stairs to bed. Lying under wool blankets, I heard my husband in the living room tell the story of how we fell in love. It was the long version, the one he didn't tend to tell, the one that begins with my mother. His voice traveled up through the metal heating grate in the floor like a genie from a bottle. It sounded like a fable from so long ago.

Jenny was wearing glasses and a topknot and meant business frying bacon and sausage patties. She pointed the spatula toward the ceiling as she considered the larder, waiting like a teacher at the chalkboard.

"We'll need black-eyed peas," she said, and I added that to the grocery list, along with four dozen eggs, lemons for hot toddies, tortilla chips. Laurie was out for a walk, but wanted to make her egg-and-green chile casserole for breakfast and Jenny's favorite spinach dip; I added those ingredients, too. My husband was on the couch in the next room with his laptop. I brought him a cup of coffee.

"Do you want to go into town with us to get groceries?"

"No, thanks," he answered with a brusque smile. He stroked Betty with his bare foot. We were taking turns being optimistic.

The front door opened and Tommy stamped his snowy boots on the mat. He is as red bearded as a sea captain, and his cheeks were pink with cold from working in the high pasture. He knows everything Annie knows how to do, only now they do it together: curry burrs out of the horses' manes, repair the floor in the pole barn, shepherd the goats, build a one-room cabin. But Annie knows how to do things Tommy doesn't, like call a square dance and close real estate deals. *Who's that*, he asked of the woman leading a band of bolo ties in a tight dress at the lip of a Chicago stage, and that's how they fell in love.

"That smells really good, Jenny," Tommy said, and hung his snow-wet Carhartt overalls on a hook by the door. He sat at the kitchen table with a satisfied exhaustion. "Tonight might be a good night to fire up the sauna," he said, unfolding the paper, and Jenny and I agreed that it was.

After breakfast, Tommy headed back up to the pasture, and Jenny and I sat at the kitchen table drinking our coffee. We planned the day. After errands, there were country songs to sing, hills to ramble, tarot cards to read, dulcimers to pick at, beans to soak. We drank coffee until cocktail hour and bourbon until bedtime.

"Why are we so happy here?" I asked, as if there were more to

it than the free expanse of vacation. It was sunny and bitter outside, and there were three swallows hopping on and off the bird
feeder near the window.

"It's all our favorite things," she answered. "Maybe the question is Why do we insist on making our lives in the city?"

After a while, I asked if she thought they needed a new coffee
shop in the nearby town, though I was tired of the sentence before
it had finished leaving my mouth.

"Probably not," she said.

"How does anyone ever make any money without selling
their soul?" I asked. She didn't have an answer for that, so we sat
quietly for a few minutes, listening to the man in the next room,
tapping at his keyboard, writing code.

In the evenings, Jenny and I took turns cooking. We kneaded
dough for sheet-pan pizzas and heated old cast iron skillets until
they shone. I showered coarse salt on thick ribeye steaks that
hissed as I laid them in the pan. Annie sat at the table with her guitar and the three of us sang while we cooked. Stews simmered,
root vegetables roasted, and breads rose. We sliced venison sausage from a local hunter, arranged crumbly cheeses on a platter,
mixed simple drinks.

At the dinner table, we drank too much wine and passed the
salad for the second time. My husband sat mute at the head, staring at his empty plate. His hands were folded in his lap, his legs
crossed at the knee, fork and knife at a forty-five degree angle.

"Are you having fun?" I asked later when we pulled back the
sheets. We slid in side by side, and I kicked my legs to get warm.

Sociologists have studied eyes at the dinner table, he told me. The people we look at even when they are not talking—when they are shaking the salt or wiping sauce from their lips—reveals who we love.

"So who do I look at?" I asked.

"You look at Jenny," he said. "You all look at Jenny."

"Because Jenny talks the most," I started to say defensively, but he was already switching off the lamp and rolling over.

Before he was my husband, before he sent me roses, Jenny and I were hanging around each other's dorm rooms, flipping through hulking CD catalogs and approving of each other's bookshelves. I noted the black-and-white photograph of Anne Sexton on her bulletin board and photographs of her friends back home in a park, wearing black sack dresses and huge sunglasses.

There was a snapshot on that same bulletin board of Jenny in a grand and voluminous taffeta plaid skirt, nipped at the waist. It had belonged to her great Aunt Pat, she said. I was always asking Jenny to tell more stories about Pat. We'd sit on the steps of our dorm, where we drank coffee and looked out at a wide, leafy boulevard lined with turn-of-the-century mansions, and she would. How Pat fled midwest heartbreak in the 1930s by sailing steerage to Europe—the apocryphal version that she was a stowaway. How she pursued painting instead of men, though men still pursued her. How Japanese diplomats sent her boxes carved from jade and ivory, how a famous novelist wooed her with a watercolor. How she was a great beauty, cruel and brilliant. We could never understand why art and all those lovers hadn't given her more pleasure, how she had died so angry and so bitter and so alone. Hadn't she chosen? What makes someone turn so sour, we wondered. We thought it had something to do with risk taking and with resilience.

Over the years, as Jenny's parents sorted through belongings in their garage and attic, I would sometimes receive care packages filled with silk scarves printed with scenes of Venezia, white horsehair clutches, black suede gloves edged in gold lamé, a robin's egg bathing costume, a green silk cumberbund-style belt with folds deep enough for stashing lipstick or a spare twenty-dollar bill. I loved the glamour of the items, and how they functioned in my wardrobe as both calling and warning. "We're unloading more of Pat's things," Jenny would write in the enclosed note. "And you're the only one who appreciates this stuff."

The afternoons were quiet. Laurie strummed a ukulele, Tommy was up in the high pasture again hammering nails on the one-room cabin, and Annie had exchanged guitar lessons for pottery classes from a neighbor. It was zero degrees in Soldiers Grove, but every day I left the house for a long jog. The runs were hard, the weather and terrain extreme. That landscape is an anachronism, a loophole in the surrounding topography, and as I ran, I imagined that I entered a portal to a frontier, one that would be more difficult to traverse but potentially more beautiful. I wore an ivory fisherman's sweater over my workout clothes and ascended a steep hill to a ridge with an old dairy farm. I slid on the ice, and at the base of a hill, a dog snarled madly until I passed from his view. I returned to Annie's feeling triumphant, my eyelashes frozen and legs numb. Upstairs, Jenny was reading in bed. I took off my wet sneakers and slid in beside her. Maybe it was the sudden change in temperature, or the exertion, but my feelings were right at the surface, like a leaf trapped under the thinnest morning frost.

"I had no idea life would be so disappointing," I said, and wiped my face on the pillow. She put her book down on the quilt.

"Seems to me you're only disappointed about one thing," she said.

"Then I guess I'm confused," I suggested. She turned on her side so we were facing each other and put a hand beneath her cheek.

"I don't think you're confused. I think you know how you feel."

The sociologists are right. I love Jenny's flat wide fingernails, the calm and assured way she navigates traffic, her untouchable *don't fuck with me* attitude at parties, and I love the Southern timbre of her voice, even when it gets slow and honeyed, which is what it does when she's about to deliver what's hardest to hear.

"How do I feel?" I asked.

"You're over it."

New Year's Eve morning. It's the best time of year for someone who likes imagining a better future, and my husband was sunny and warm. He poured me a cup of coffee and pulled me close.

"I know what my New Year's resolutions are," he said with a grin like he'd been up to no good. It had been so long since he had flirted with me, it felt sudden and inappropriate, like an uncle kissing me on the lips.

"Oh yeah?" I wanted to soften into his arms. There he was, finally. I was there, too. I leaned into him, felt supported by the muscles of his chest, the bones. He put his lips to my ear.

"I want to have a baby," he whispered, "and anal sex."

Before dinner, Tommy carried logs to the barrel-shaped wood-fired sauna so that its hot maw would welcome our naked bodies once we were full of black-eyed peas cooked with bacon and Annie's homegrown onions. Only the women ever made the pilgrimage up the snowy hill. We carried glass vials of chakra-clearing potions to dab on our damp skin and mason jars of cocktails. Inside, it was like a gypsy's caravan. Sweat beaded on our breasts like jeweled necklaces, and we told secrets in the dark. When we emerged, I plunged into the snow, and arced my arms and legs until there was an angel.

When my husband and I were on that happy Scandinavian vacation, we traveled to a nineteenth-century sauna built at the end of a wooden pier. He waited for me in the snack bar, and I pushed through the door marked DAMER. As I sat in a sauna with a square window that faced the Øresund strait, it began to snow. A swan glided past the picture window view, no joke. I liked being among the bodies on the teak benches. We were old and young, some folded with skin and age and others languorous, starlet-stretched.

I sat there as long as I could, skin scorched. The cold plunge was straight into the sound. I pretended to be brave and jumped. Just seconds of splash in the water, then hauling my body out on the ladder, my skin electric and burning, my mind slapped right into present tense.

ENOUGH TALK. To become the kind of woman you want to be, my mother said, you have to take the kind of actions that woman would take.

I LOVED MY HUSBAND, and then I didn't. Is that a story?

Story is giving a character a tangible desire, then putting things in her way. I wanted my husband to "be there" for me as my mother died. *What does that mean?* he asked for months. *To "be there"?* More tangible, he said.

Then my desire was for him to acknowledge my body, to hook an arm at my waist on the street, and in our bed, to press his torso against my back in the dark. Be there like that. We, at least, were still alive. Please, I said.

His desire was to not be told what to do. I began to cry beside him on the loveseat in our therapist's office.

"Is there something you could do now to comfort Sarah?" the

therapist asked. He looked at her like a student eager to have the right answer. He graduated summa cum laude, but I thought I'd had the better education. "I don't know," he said. I pulled another Kleenex from a box on the side table. "Hold her?" he asked.

"That's a great idea," she nodded, with gentle encouragement. He moved closer to me, draped his arm around my shoulders, and we looked at each other with proud embarrassment at this modest, remedial breakthrough. The awkwardness underscored— this was not practice, it was performance.

T WAS AN ACTION, but it was not the action of the woman I wanted to be.

He sat at the end of the bar in a Klos Nomi t-shirt and a leather jacket. It was late. That winter, I often stayed out late, telling my friends to go home, that I would just have one more alone.

What is it like to be a man, I asked, and when he answered, I replied that maybe I would like to be one. We ate free popcorn and white flecks settled in his beard. He paid such close attention when I talked, he forgot to close his mouth while he listened. A person will tell you everything within the first twenty minutes of meeting them, my mother had said. The trick is whether or not you're paying attention.

He said, Fish or cut bait.

He had kind eyes, and people have gone on less before.

You haven't made any promises, my mother would say to excuse any behavior in a relationship that was not a marriage. Only now I had promised. In our own selfish ways, neither husband nor wife had upheld their vows.

What if a man pays attention to me, and I like it, I had asked my mother.

And she had said: That would be the most natural thing in the world.

The wind tunneled down Third Avenue, icy from the waves of New York Harbor. He said, Let me walk you home. We made it three blocks up the hill toward my house before I stopped on the cold, dark sidewalk. I no longer wanted my own life, did not want to return to its quiet rooms and blank walls. We had never framed a single wedding photo.

His studio was filled with Walter Benjamin books and DVDs of dark Scandinavian police procedurals, a guitar, an easel, and paintings I didn't like. He spread a sleeping bag on the floor like a picnic blanket. With the lights off, he played the trumpet. Then we laid side by side like train rails. I felt blisteringly alive, and relieved I could still feel that way.

"It is so nice to look at someone else's face up close," I said.

I knew, at how true the words felt in my mouth, that it was my cruelest betrayal.

M Y MOTHER CALLED it the end of puppy love. My husband agreed but struck a word. It was the end of love, he said.

Once named, our terms defined, at least he could be honest. I kept my secret.

I consider it our last date, the night we sat in a dim neighborhood wine bar. It was the same place we'd celebrated Valentine's years before. I had given him a handwritten card, poorly but painstakingly designed. After he moved out, I found it among electronics manuals and a stack of junk mail. But that night long ago, he had arrived at our table with a bouquet of orange tulips. We drank in low candlelight that cast heavy shadows. An elixir of bourbon and admiration traveled the distance between us.

Now it was truth serum. "What would you look for in your next partner?" he asked, and the question took me by surprise, though my answer was as ready as his, both of them knee jerk and reactionary and mean.

"Sexual enthusiasm and someone really, really fun," I said. "What about you?"

He looked at me hard, level, dead-eyed.

"Loyal," he said. "Someone loyal."

WE BOTH SEEMED more buoyant on the walk home, unburdened from our postures of hope, from being on our best behavior. When I emerged from the bathroom, drying my face with a towel, he already had a black bag in his hand. For years, his signature fighting stance was a sudden, wordless departure.

I didn't mind the leaving so much as the silence. *Just say you need some time*, I'd ask, *or a walk. Don't just go.*

This time, he remembered my request.

"I want to leave," he said.

"I don't love you," he added. "I don't even like you."

SAT WITH my mother one winter afternoon in her kitchen. The snow was banked under the bay window by the table. It was easy to spot birds from our seats there, their colors vivid against a white canvas and the thin dark lines of tree branches. We saw a cardinal that day, and a blue jay. Blue jays are the bullies of the bird world, she said.

"You need to make a list of what you learned from your marriage," she said. "That way, when you meet the next guy and your mind goes blank, you'll know what to look out for." A magnet held an index card on the refrigerator. "Good judgment is based on experience," she'd written in black Sharpie. "Experience is based on bad judgment."

At the time, I wrote a list of vague qualities. Sense of humor, it said. Someone who is present and not postponing joy, it said. But what did I learn?

Events occur in time and space, singular alignments of a moment, a choice, a chance. To search for a lesson in the timeline is to pretend it is, in fact, a line—that life progresses in linear fashion, with its subjects gathering an accumulation of knowledge and wisdom applicable from one occurrence to the next. That is the effort to moralize our lives, as if they were folktales. I'm not convinced. She and I had always been more interested in meaning than plot, but a lesson is the merest articulation of significance.

"What happened," a man too young for me asked. And when I said, Same vision for the future, different ideas of how to get there, he looked disappointed. "I thought one of you might have stepped out," he said. He was asking for a story.

Condoms in jeans pockets are tangible but not the whole story. They signify all of the sex and none of the despair. The longer version, had I told it to him, would have gone like this: When I stepped in from stepping out, and shook the cold out of my coat and scarf and slumped into the bathtub, I still had bourbon on my breath and the memory of another man inside me. I sat beneath the shower and cried for the mess I had made, at the cowardice of the only rebellion I could muster. Sometimes I'd fall asleep on the enamel and wake when the hot water had turned cold.

Now my life was the cliché-ridden trash.

AFTER HE LEFT the hangers in his closet swinging, I pushed all the living room furniture to the center of the room and covered it with a rough taupe drop cloth. I wanted to paint.

In years of photographs from our dinner parties, the orange color on the walls had seemed warm, and with the low candlelight, our faces glowed as if we sat not around a dinner table but a campfire. But in summer, the color had always struck me as too hot—close and oppressive like a stranger's breath.

I chose a stark, matte hospital white. Night after night, I returned from work to the room that looked like a home long vacated, the furniture draped in white sheets. I painted by the light of a bare bulb, then sat on the ladder, exhausted, overwhelmed, scanning my eyes across the patchy walls. It was all taking so long.

Three girlfriends arrived unannounced on Sunday afternoon. "You hold her," Laureen said, handing me her one-year-old daughter. Katie looked at my last near-empty gallon. "You need more paint," she said. "Eggshell?" She left for the hardware store around the corner.

Jessica climbed the ladder and with her long arms carefully painted the seam where the ceiling met the wall. Laureen suggested painting the ugly closet door. I nodded, bobbing up and down with the baby. Katie returned, cracked open the can, and poured it into a pan on the floor. Before the hour was up, they pulled the drop cloth off the couch and pushed it nearer to the wall, then scanned the room, pleased.

"It looks good," Jessica said. "This is a cool single-girl apartment." The blank white walls reminded me of the Parisian apartments in Godard films, the emptiness a kind of shabby bohemian glamour. I could start to see it: I would lean my bicycle against the wall. I would keep oranges in a blue and white bowl on the table.

Jessica's husband arrived to pick her up, and jiggled my front door handle. "Do you have any tools?" he asked. Those had been my husband's, I said. He turned around and left, then returned with a screwdriver, crouched before the knob, and tightened screws.

I looked at my friends. Katie was checking her phone, Jessica had her hand on her husband's shoulder, and Laureen was suggesting how I might arrange art on the expanse of white wall now behind my couch. Her baby gurgled at my ear.

"Thank you guys," I said, and my voice buckled. "Thank you so much."

"Well, don't cry about it," Katie said, typing with her thumbs. I said that I would not.

THE LETTERS ARRIVED. They said, Congratulations.
But maybe I should stay at my job, I thought, save more money, buy a cottage upstate. I was beginning to understand how people could hide from their lives inside the ceaseless demands of work. Yet it was becoming increasingly difficult to summon daily devotion for what had once been at its worst benign, and more often truly fun, and now seemed almost offensively inane. I consulted another food editor over fourteen-dollar cocktails. Maybe there's more to life than traffic goals, I said. Do we really care what the new quinoa is?

"Oh," she said, as if I'd revealed an adorable hobby. "You want to make the world a better place."

"Well, I'm from poor people," I said, since I thought that explained it.

"Not me," she replied, "I'm from money." I wondered how I should reply to this.

"I can't talk to other women like I can talk to you," she said. "We really should be friends."

On the walk home across the Gowanus Canal, telling my mother the story, I couldn't stop laughing. The dark water swirled with rainbows of shiny oil, the moon mirrored on its surface. I was as clear-eyed as a cat.

I HAVE ALWAYS wanted a sense of self as immutable as a diamond, a fixed thing that refracts light regardless of outside attention or indifference. I'm not even sure this is how ego works, but I do know parents play a part in it, that a generous one can help give form to the inchoate shapes they see in their kids. Maybe this is why, in the months following my divorce, my mother kept repeating the story of my flying past her on the sidewalk the day I learned to ride a bike. She remembered I called over my shoulder, my long red hair streaming behind me. *Isn't it interesting? I taught myself!*

"You're turning into one of those New York women who knows how to do everything herself," my mother said that last winter. All I had done was driven us through snow to an Indian restaurant and suggest *saag paneer*. We listened to Joni Mitchell's *Blue* on the ride home. My mother nodded off, her head toward the foggy window, and woke to me singing. *I want to make you feel better, I want to make you feel free.* Her laugh was a mix of relief and pride, as much for herself as it was for me.

"See, you don't need me," she said. "You're going to be okay."

SOME OF HER FLAWS: She was helpless and avoidant. *Oh, I didn't get your message*, she'd say, when what she meant was she hadn't listened to it. She thought her tax bill a personal attack. She was both a know-it-all and an unreliable source, a dramatic arc more important than fact. *Oh, I don't know anything!* she'd demure if challenged. She whined. She was so practical she could be tone deaf. *But I love him*, I might say over a heartbreak, and she became a deli counter employee. *Next!* she said. And though she called my stepfather "pathologically optimistic," she must have also seen brighter things ahead. Days before she died, boxes of peony bulbs and rhubarb plants arrived in the mail. *I do not know if I have the energy to plant them*, she said. On Mother's Day, I dug holes for the peonies at the edge of the lawn, but they never bloomed.

SOMEONE THOUGHT there was an information blockage. That we weren't learning new details about my mother's condition there were to be learned. Someone called the oncologist, and all of us awoke to a group email the next morning.

"Anyone who calls the doctor will be permanently on my shit list," she wrote. "Do you think he will give you a secret prognosis that you can handle, and I cannot?"

Prognosis is an average. Prognosis, according to one opinion, said she should have been dead six months after diagnosis. I have never had the guts to call my mother's oncologist. I still don't want to be permanently on her shit list. There are questions I have about the end that will go unanswered. They have been supplanted by a belief as fixed as my DNA, inscribed perhaps with its own genetic doom. I think I know what he would say on the phone, his voice tender. It would not be about how she died but about how she lived.

I T WAS A crowded Friday night at a strip mall steakhouse after chemotherapy. A black hockey puck flashed to tell us our table was ready. My brother and I softened our edges with alcohol.

My mother ordered filet mignon and a baked potato. Growing up, she encouraged us to eat the skins. That's where the vitamins are, she had said. Now I noted she left hers on the plate.

"I'd like to be buried in a plain pine box like Johnny Olesen," she announced. "With a honeysuckle planted on top."

I sat opposite her in the booth, the beaded lampshade between us like the ones on horseshoe tables in an old movie big band supper club. Next to the salt shaker there was a laminated dessert menu with photographs of multilayered, whipped-cream-topped cakes and blue cocktails. This life is filled with so many distracting and crude details. I put down my silverware and looked at her across the table.

"I think honeysuckles are invasive," I said.

"Good," she answered, cutting a bite of steak.

spring
again

WE WERE ALL pulling away from one another by early spring, the veil between the living and the dead already falling. Why summon Bliss from China, my mother asked, when each of her children off living their lives was what made her happiest? We visited my sister for Easter. My mother slept in a hotel with my stepfather, where she stayed in bed, dozing, while Katy and I went to junk shops, took a yoga class. Saturday, we hid plastic eggs for my niece: in hotel room drawers, on windowsills, balanced on a roll of toilet paper. Violet searched, and my mother laughed.

My memory of the next day is vivid with color. My aunt had decorated the table with egg-shaped chocolates wrapped in pink and purple foil. My mother ate ham and green beans. Violet wore a yellow cardigan and a striped blue dress, both too long. Duncan practiced his Texas two-step with me across the pale maple kitchen floor. I drank espresso with whipped cream on top. It really was a beautiful day.

My mother and stepfather drove me to the train station after lunch. Everyone in the family was piggybacking on my Amazon Prime account, and it was up for renewal in August. Would she split the cost with me this year? Sure, she said noncommittally. I was flipping through a survivalist's homesteading guide someone had left in the backseat.

"Talk to me," she said, when what she meant was, *I have some things to say.*

This conversation I remember. It was when she told me marriage was Sunday morning and Tuesday night. That she was so proud I was going to graduate school. That I have only one life, and it is mine alone.

At the train station, I opened her passenger-side door, leaned in, and burrowed my face in her chest. I often felt afraid to touch her in the normal ways. I didn't know where it hurt and thought it might be everywhere. But that last time, I held her so tight. She wrapped her arms around me, I was subsumed. Her sweater was very soft.

As I waited on the platform for the train to arrive, I saw my stepfather watching from the station house. He stayed until the train came, and my mother sent me a text message.

"We want you to feel loved but not smothered. It is a delicate balance!"

AND THEN THE veil fell completely. The phone at the farm rang with no answer, and she replied infrequently to text messages and to email.

"I am going to see *Alice Doesn't Live Here Anymore* with Jane," I texted on the way to the movies.

"That is exactly what you should be doing," she replied, meaning she was glad I hadn't come home for the weekend. When the movie let out, I wrote again. "Update: Kris Kristofferson is my dream man." She reminded me of the time we saw a handsome farmer in a hunter green MG, his dog's tongue flapping in the top-down Vermont wind.

"I'm worried about Mom," I told Duncan.

He sounded annoyed. He continued to bring her dinner, but he noticed with increasing frequency that our stepfather was the only one who ate. Has anything changed, he asked. But nothing really had.

What I didn't yet know but sensed, was the latest news her doctor had reported the previous week: she had months, maybe weeks, and certainly not years. This should not have even qualified as news to us, but it did. She told her book club in an email as they planned the next meeting, but she did not tell me.

"It is hard to express how much I love my life," she wrote them on Monday. "Please just make your plans, and I will endeavor to be there."

Don't be angry with her, one of her friends told me later. It is a mother's nature to protect her children.

On Tuesday she said I might consider taking medical leave from work to be with her. I was at home with a sprained ankle, learning how to use crutches. You just say when, I told her. Yet wasn't she saying it?

I did not recognize the event as it arrived; I did not take the action of the woman I wanted to be. I waited for a more urgent request. *Come to me now, baby*, I thought she would say.

But on Thursday morning, I woke to the voicemails Duncan had left throughout the night while I tossed and turned, unable to sleep.

"Sarah, Sarah," he said in one message after another, "please call me when you get this."

I N THE NIGHT, my stepfather offered her a sip of water through a green straw, the kind wide enough for bubble tea. She began to cough, and what came up, based on the darkened pillow that lingered in their bedroom for days, did not appear to be blood but necrotic tissue. Her body was already dead inside. She coughed and coughed and she must have been very scared, and my stepfather, holding the cup with the green straw as her eyes widened must have been very scared, too. By the time the ambulance arrived, the event was long over. My stepfather says his two black Labradors, usually ill behaved and in the way, lay quiet and obedient as the men from the funeral home carried her down the stairs, holding her body in delicate balance down the winding staircase. My stepfather stood in the bedroom holding her gold rings in his palm.

H E WAS FORGETFUL with grief. He didn't remember anything she wanted, and when the funeral home asked about embalmment, he said that was fine, go ahead. It changed her. It made her smell sharp, like a biology classroom. "Can I see her?" I asked. "She doesn't have any clothes on," the men at the funeral home warned. "She hasn't been made up. She's just under a sheet." As if that were not exactly what I wanted. This was the better time, when she felt more like she had been. But still it wasn't her. I knew that as I bent down to hold her. She wasn't there. Her body was hard and cold, and I nuzzled against her cheek and squinted

my eyes to make the picture of her face a little fuzzier, because
the face was wrong. It wasn't right. I don't know how else to say
it. And I don't know if it was the fluid they filled her veins with or
if it was just that all the animation was gone. And when I'd close
my eyes at night, that's what I would see, that wrong face, that
cold body. I tried so hard to remember the way she touched me,
what it felt like when she was tucking the tag of my sweater inside
the neckline or leaning down to kiss me good night. *I love you*, I'd
say. *I love you more*, she'd answer, like it was a game I'd never win.

THE CLICHÉS ARE always embarrassing.
     Like when I was sixteen and crazy about a boy who drove
me to the seashore on our second date, then let my head nod onto
his shoulder on the long drive home. I stood in the cafeteria the
next day unable to sit at a table, my stomach too filled with flutter-
ing to eat a sandwich. Butterflies. That boy is now a girl, I recently
learned, and felt happy for her.
     Grief is a mirror image of love.
     At the funeral home, a man in a black suit told us where to
send the obituary, and as he outlined the logistics, I wrote notes on
a yellow legal pad taken from my stepfather's office. I was proud
to be so competent in a crisis. When the man in the black suit
began to list nondenomination cemeteries, my stepfather interrupted, as if there were important information he needed to contribute to this conversation. He began to tell stories: how he met
my mother in the Williamstown Second Congregational Church

basement, how they found each other again at a college reunion, and their second, second date in Paris—four days in a two-star hotel during which they rarely left the room. "If I had my choice," he finally said, "I'd keep her right here with my arm around her." The man listened patiently with soft eyes. "Thank you," I said about the cemeteries, "we'll check them out."

But as my stepfather and I left the building, I found I could not travel the distance to the sidewalk. My muscles went slack, and the scaffolding of my bones collapsed at the knee joint. On the front walk of the funeral home the afternoon my mother died, my stepfather held me until I could stand. I went weak in the knees, as they say.

N THE CAR to scout our list of cemeteries, my stepfather said maybe we should put the funeral off for a month, maybe two. Dancing is Duncan's romantic side, but he is the most practical among us. He works in insurance and is able to say things no one else will. "There will never be a good time," he said. "Better to get it over with."

My husband wanted to pay the rush fees for our divorce.

"It is a cliché that the man wants a quick divorce," my mother had told me on the phone, "and then after it is said and done reconsiders."

But now I could understand: I did not want my mother's body hanging around for a month or two.

My husband and I split the cost, and I wrote him a check for four hundred dollars. He did not reconsider.

Lower Amwell Cemetery was windswept, with an empty, unlocked one-room shed with a broken window. This isn't right, my stepfather said. He lifted his chin to the grass on the far side of a low stone wall. A lawyer he wasn't crazy about owned the adjacent field. We opened the car doors, closed them again. My brother drove. The sky was ash gray.

When we turned into Sandy Ridge Cemetery, the car pointed straight toward a tall, upturned conifer. This wouldn't do either.

"Your mother hated red cedars," my stepfather said. The announcement was like a love letter to intimacy and to knowing, and it made me laugh. "Well, that won't do," I said. My brother rolled on between the headstones and out toward the exit.

One thing she didn't hate: Mexican barrel chairs. I knew that. Years before, when I was moving into my first Brooklyn apartment, we found a disintegrated pair at a garage sale on Kingwood-Stockton Road, directly across the street from Rosemont Cemetery. I bought a wrought iron fireplace screen to hang above my bed as a makeshift headboard and two glass decanters etched SCOTCH and GIN. She did not buy the chairs. They would have worked in Texas, she explained, but that was her old life. They no longer suited the style of her house now. It was my turn. I would waste sunny Saturdays with the man who would become my husband, gripping my fingers around the wrought iron scrolls.

"That's a marvelous redbud tree," my stepfather said at the third cemetery. It was in full bloom, the same electric fuchsia as the branches outside their bedroom windows. He sat on a bench dedicated to the memory of someone else. "I can sit here," he said, patting the empty wood slats beside him. He took two plots, side by side.

F AMILIAR COUNTRY SIGHTS: mice skittering across the pantry floor, snakes silent and sleepy in the garden, and silverfish leggy against the bathroom tile. Yet there was an unfamiliar country sound as I went to sleep that first night at the farm. The ruckus in my childhood bedroom was a trapped bird, beating wings and feathers. It was so out of place, so unexpected, like a clown waiting at the bus stop. I shut the door, though part of me knew this was cruel, and slept in my little brother's empty room. I was tired of thinking about others. I had never been so tired.

By morning, I choked awake with the memory of a body beneath a white quilt. Then my husband on the telephone. We hadn't spoken since the night he stuffed shirts and underwear in his laptop bag. It had been another season. "I thought she was getting better," he said, his voice blank with shock.

Time to deal with the bird. It would have been months since anyone had ventured beyond the sick rooms of the house: master bedroom for sleep, TV room for couch naps, kitchen for cups of tea. However long it had been trapped, this bird had managed to shit everywhere. On the blue and white Laura Ashley duvet cover, on the antique folding desk, on the changing table my mother had seen by the side of the road while driving home with my stepfather after lunch years before. *Stop!* she said, as soon as white spindle legs and a cardboard sign that read FREE came into view. She threw it in the backseat for a grandchild who had yet to be conceived.

While the bird flew from one corner of the room to the other, landing atop the tall bookshelves stacked with watercolor palettes and a hand-painted Japanese tea set, I threw open the window above the changing table. My two-year-old niece's unworn diapers were now splattered gray-green. And then—after all that furious flapping and wing beating, of crumpling collision into the ceiling and walls—this bird found its way out. It sailed through the open window with the purposeful ease of a button slipping through its hole. The room was suddenly still, and the panicked pace of my heart slowed in the quiet. It was time to mop.

"I still think Murphy Oil Soap is one of the finest smells in the world," my mother wrote at the end of an email that spring, apropos of nothing. Her houses had always been a wreck; Murphy Oil Soap was the fragrance of making things right. So I pushed and pulled the perfumed mop across the wide-planked wood floor with alternating fury and exhaustion. I dragged the bucket around the room, its water turning opaque as it filled with long, stray hairs from my sister's head and mine and dust puffs like season's-end dandelions. And then I found it. On the waxed floorboards beneath a west-facing window, another bird's body, stiff as a Christmas ornament.

This was country life. But that morning, it felt like something else—an uncanny death pileup, a haunting. The wooden mop handle slapped the floor. I went downstairs and returned with a white tea towel from a kitchen drawer. I wrapped the body and carried it down the long driveway, past my mother's order of peony bulbs and rhubarb plants collected on the porch, still in their brown packages. On the far side of the road, I opened the cotton bundle to drop the bird in its open grave and—who knows, maybe from blood or the stiff catch of its feathers or dried, brittle feet—the bird stuck to the towel. I stood on the side of the road, the one that led to the sloping graveyard where my mother would soon be buried, shaking the cotton fabric. The bird wouldn't fall free from its shroud or my hands, until finally, it did. It landed with the ceremony of another day's newspaper tossed onto the front step.

THEY ARRIVED WITH mops and buckets, yellow rubber gloves, vacuum cleaners, plastic caddies filled with cleaning products. My mother had been reading, and not reading, in a book club for more than a decade. Actually, she had been a member of two book clubs, each group discovering the other at the funeral like a secret family. That sunny morning, they walked toward me standing on the porch.

"Your mother would have wanted you to be comfortable in the house," one of her friends said. She had tried to send a cleaning lady over in the last months, but my mother had demurred, either embarrassed by the state of things or simply not wanting a stranger to rearrange what was, at least to her, the familiar order of her own chaos. "It was important to her the house be ready for you kids."

My mother had used that phrase a lot in the last year of her life, that she wanted to "get the house ready," that she wanted it to be "finished." She searched Craigslist for furniture and drove an hour to pick up free chairs upholstered in a dusty-red fabric she liked. When Bliss came home for six weeks between teaching jobs, she asked him to refinish the kitchen floors. He spent hot days on all fours, sanding small, hard-to-reach places by hand, and painted three different stains in side-by-side stripes for her to select the best shade. When she peeked into the kitchen to survey his progress, he wrapped his arms around her shoulders. They swayed back and forth while they talked, as if in the gym of a middle school dance.

The book club stayed for hours, the music of their caretaking filling the house: the rhythmic motions of the vacuum back and forth over the rugs, their feet up and down the stairs, the opening and closing of closet doors, the laundry room rumbling with what would soon be clean sheets on each bed. Murphy Oil Soap perfumed each room. When their work was finished, they gathered together in the living room and bowed their heads. *Allison*, they said.

THE FUNERAL HOME asked me to return with a bag of clothes for her to wear. The forever outfit. I chose the pink crocheted dress she wore to both my brother's and sister's weddings. "Crotch-et-ed," she had called it, imitating the saleswoman. Pompoms hung from the sleeves and the hem of the skirt, and she would shimmy whenever she wore it, shake her hips to show how the pink pompoms could bounce and bop. This span of time is liminal and uncanny: A person is dead but their body is present, and so we relate to it in the ways we always have. My stepfather said pack a pair of underwear for her to wear, too. "But she never wears underwear with hose," I said, and he said pack them anyway, it seemed like the right thing to do. When I told my sister what I'd done, she must have also thought of our mother's body as if it were alive, the comfort we still wanted to give it, how she would go into the ground wearing underwear she never would have worn in this life. "Poor girl," my sister said. I packed shoes, too: leopard flats with pink trim.

She left no instructions, just the snippets of things she'd mentioned in passing. I remembered the plain pine box and the honeysuckle bush. All the other choices were for us, not her. That I wanted her to wear a swipe of her favorite lipstick and to spray her with Ralph Lauren's Safari one more time, that Rick wanted her to wear underwear. And when I was upset about the embalming, which she didn't want, Jenny reminded me what my mother would have said in her high-pitched singsong. After that, every decision got easier. *Sarah, I don't care. I'm dead!*

One of those afternoons between death and funeral, when my sister had arrived and was changing her daughter's diaper by a bedroom window, a bee buzzed up to the panes of glass and hovered there. "Mom used to call Violet her little bumble bee," Katy told me. When I was in the bathroom that same day, I said, splashing water on my red swollen eyes and already wet cheeks, the lights wouldn't stop flickering. "Okay," I said, "*okay*," nodding at the light so hard, soapsuds still on my face. They are nonsense coincidences; they are messages from beyond. Both true.

My sister was very concerned about what the funeral directors would do to her face. "Call them," she said, "you *have* to." I called from a PNC Bank parking lot. She didn't wear makeup except lipstick and mascara, I told them, so please don't use anything else. They told me about how her skin color would start to change. Maybe a little bit of blush then, I said. Sometimes you find yourself saying things you never imagined you'd have to say.

It took Bliss several days to fly home from China, which made the embalming seem sort of okay in the end. You put four kids in a car, and it feels like a party, even when you are going to see your mother one last time before she is dropped into the earth. Duncan drove. He is very left brained and logical, the savior of the unsayable again. He said, "Okay, who has seen a body in this state before?" I think he and I were the only ones who raised our hands. I loved him for asking that question.

The funeral home dressed her. I don't like to think about that. I brought her perfume and sprayed under the ugly blanket they covered her with and behind her ears, so that when each of us hugged her, it would feel more familiar. "Her perfume was a good idea," my sister said. "That was the realest part for me." My little brother stood over her body and read her a letter. Then he collapsed on her chest. I'd never seen him like that. Or my older brother, who, when he walked away from her body, doubled over and pressed his fingers to his eyes. My stepfather kissed her face again and again. My two brothers and my stepbrother and my sister and my stepfather and I stood in a tacky room while morose music played. I sprayed more of her perfume.

My sister turned to me. "I prefer the bumble bee," she said.

GATHERED BLOOMING BRANCHES of lilac and white dogwood from the fence at the edge of the farm and carried them to the cemetery. *It's good to wear red shoes on important days*, my mother had said. The heels I'd worn to college commencement sank into the soft May soil. I had worn a different pair on my wedding day.

The day was clearbright, cloudless and blue, and my family stood circling a deep pit on a hillside. A pine box was suspended over the hole, and I thought about her bones blunted against the wood. Against the dark earth, the pine was pale and pretty in the sunlight, like the white of an ocean wave.

When my niece began to cry, my sister gathered her into her lap and began to breast feed. I stood alone in the sun, only blossoms in my arms to hold. The minister read Edna St. Vincent Millay. My mother had carried a paperback of her poems to college. *How incredible, the coincidence*, I had thought. Now, I pity that girl on the hillside. She is so desperate for signs. Who doesn't read the sonnet that begins "I am not resigned to the shutting away of loving hearts in the hard ground"?

The talking finished, and there was not much, my family members took the lilac and dogwood branches from me one at a time and placed them on the lid of the casket. One blew off in the breeze. Someone picked it up and placed it gingerly again. The second time it fell off, they didn't bother. I laid my branches and grabbed a handful of dirt and placed it on top of the pale casket. That looked pretty to me, too, the black rubble of earth against the bare sanded surface.

THE PLAN WAS to sing Anne Murray, but Bliss warned me he would not be able to harmonize, despite our practice. My voice cracked at the first line. *People smile and tell me I'm the lucky one.* He joined in. My niece spilled her Cheerios on the creaky oak floor. *Even though we ain't got money, I'm so in love with you honey.* The full-throated voice of a woman surprised me. It was me and not me. It reverberated on the wood pews.

I cried in the white wooden church, and later, eating a ham sandwich.

"I am realizing," I told one of my mother's friends, whom I had never met, "that having a mother who loves you is a lucky stroke, like being born beautiful or rich."

"Arguably," she said, "a mother who loves you is the best advantage."

TO MYSELF I called it a "roiling" grief. I knew no other word to describe how I heaved: at the steering wheel, lying sleepless in bed at night, in the arms of anyone who paused long enough to offer a sympathetic look. The emotions were a testament and comfort. *Feeling is living to me*, to me, too. When the fit would end, I was hollowed out, scooped clean. Ready again to be full.

My therapist suggested group grief counseling, but I shook my head at the idea. Someone else might know loss, but no one could understand mine. My grief was special, singular, as all are, unknowable by anyone who had not also belonged to my mother by birth. Even among my siblings, we each had our separate ways.

Six months after her death, a relative by marriage approached me at a party and began to cry. I knew him as the man who used to sit with my mother in the kitchen after Thanksgiving dinner when he'd had too much to drink. Once, as I cut a second slice of pecan pie, I saw him lean close and whisper how much he loved sex, how he loved to get sweaty.

She had made him feel so understood, he said.

"You think you're special?" I asked.

A NOTHER FRIEND WROTE another book and hosted an event in a Brooklyn bookstore. The tables were crowded with her hardbacks, cupcakes, and Champagne flutes. My friend wore a stylish dress with an architectural detail at the neckline that seemed to say *I am a serious literary author.* Her hair had been blown out, and there were no empty seats. "It's so amazing to see all these people from different times in my life in one place," she said from the podium. She looked around the full room and leaned into the slim microphone. "Hi, former boss. Hi, ex-boyfriend," she joked. Her face was bright. I felt so proud of her and so happy. One day my name would be written on the chalkboard propped outside on the sidewalk. *Tonight, 7 p.m.!* My dress would have some kind of cool neckline, too. Then she stopped scanning the room, and her eyes settled on a face. From the back, I could see a sleek gray bob, the stiff collar of a starched shirt, a red silk scarf. It was her biggest smile yet. "Hi, mom." I was glad I could not see her face. I was glad my friend could not see mine. "You guys, she came all the way from Ohio."

FLIRTING FILLED ME up again. It pulled me from the edge of a deep pit on a cemetery hill and brought me back among the living.

"I think it's a blessing," my friend Jane said. "What are you going to do, sit home alone and feel the full weight of your sadness?"

Instead I felt the full weight of a man's body. David left oily sardine cans on the counter and fell asleep to a 12-hour YouTube recording called "Rain on a Tent." He sang "If I Were a Carpenter," and looked like he wanted me to harmonize, or answer. When he watered the neglected orchid on my windowsill, its green buds cracked into five-petaled blooms, their insides washed watercolor-violet, edges pale as a celery heart.

When I spilled bourbon in the grass and couldn't remember the words to the songs I love, he led me from one body of water to another. Down a wooded path to a creek bed swimming hole, to the ocean. We sat on a sun-bleached slab of driftwood, slipped out of our clothes, and tiptoed across the uneven stones pressing into the soft arches of our feet, down to the lapping edge, then into the cold water, rocks ragged underfoot. The day was bright, and we bobbed underwater like corks. I tilted myself back, held on the water's surface like a hammock. The bay was filled with moored sailboats, and then suddenly I couldn't stop laughing—at the sun on my face, the cold water stinging my eyes, salty in my mouth; at the man who stood naked nearby, as tall and stately as a heron. We waded back to the shore and I said, "Thank you thank you thank you, that was such a good idea," and he shooed it away. "Of course." The seat belts clicked, our hair wet in the windows-down wind. He said, "Let's go for ice cream," and we did.

Night after night at Long Pond, we watched the sun sink below the pines. The water reflective lavender, the sky soft pink, like a fingertip. I felt a duty to experience each pleasure twice— once for my own sake and again for someone who could not. My mother would have liked the cool of a Berkshire evening, the Irish fisherman's sweater I had pulled over my sundress. She would have found this cocktail too strong and too sweet. David stoked the wood fire in the evenings, carrying in logs from the wood pile out front, and she would have liked that, too—going in once the fireflies came out, the clanging pots in the kitchen as they hit the burners. After dinner, he sat in the stern of a canoe and paddled us from end to end, the oar dipping into the dark water. I sat in the bow, relieved to let someone else steer.

But if he left me alone for the post office, or to buy orange juice, he returned to find me on the couch.

"Why are you crying?" he'd ask, and I'd answer, "I don't know," because the truth seemed too long to explain.

I think again of that anthropologist on the radio, the one who talked about our brains under the influence of attraction.

Who wouldn't want to crowd out grief with something that feels like hope?

WHEN THE SUN shone, I tilted my face up to it and closed my eyes. God was not everywhere, but she was.

PLEASURE BECAME THE escape hatch to my grief. One friend was impressed by the range of men to whom I was attracted. A captain of the Staten Island Ferry, a motorcyclist, a cocky magazine editor, a bad artist, another cocky magazine editor, a barista, a sci-fi novelist with a trust fund, a Canadian, a surfer, a waiter, a bartender, a silver-haired architect, the writer I began to love. I had never done this before. *This*, being what I understood my friends had been up to in our twenties when I was playing wife and roasting chickens. Meet-cute in the dark, sniff out fun with a bourbon nose, feel your way. I loosened the valve in me that had been turned right-tight, and skin became my sail, directing me toward an island of relief. Witness: my forearm, my foot sole, my fingertips; the bowl of my hip bones, an earlobe, lower lip. Grief introduced an unknown abyss, just as it revealed the inverse, like the black-and-white trick silhouette of an old woman. Seen just so, she is young, too. And so a scrim parted, and behind that was a vast expanse. It could be saturated with the sense of something other than pain; it could be flooded with joy.

T HE LIGHT OF early evening, driving a fast highway at rush hour. I remember: "It is hard to express how much I love my life." I had heard this as a kind of grateful prayer. "I have not accomplished much in this life," she decided on her fiftieth birthday. "But I have loved and been loved, raised four great kids, and I still wear the same size I did ten years ago. It just doesn't *look* the same." Suddenly I'm in the fast lane, and I see her reclining in bed. She can't sleep, and so she is up weeping, pushing the sticky buttons of an old cell phone to send this last note to the women she has read novels with for years, a last note about how much she loves her life, and this time, the words ring in my ears with panic. The sound goes sour, like an atonal turn to minor key. What if it were not gratitude but a lament? I hear it then as a cry, the sound of a life pulled from its vessel. *It is hard to express how much I love my life. Please do not make me leave it yet.*

I WAS COMFORTED by my own grief. I liked to sob until my breath couldn't keep up, like staying underwater too long and then returning to the surface, panicked, disoriented, and then awash with relief. I liked working myself to exhaustion this way, heaving until I was scraped clean. I liked feeling that total and complete emptiness. It felt factual to me, like irrefutable evidence. This was how much we loved, now turned inside out.

WHEN I RETURNED to work two weeks later, I thanked my boss for understanding I needed the full time allotted by our company bereavement policy.

"We all understand," she said. "Sometimes life gets in the way."

She had it all backward.

Shortly after that, I gave notice.

I WAS TEN years late to being alone and began to note its difficulties one by one. I could not reach the overhead kitchen light, for example, and had never before bothered to purchase a stepladder; my husband could reach it standing on a chair.

My car was a culprit. Whenever I awoke to the gray slate roof of the church out my bedroom window buried under snow, I felt the aloneness. I felt it stepping into my boots and pulling on my gloves, holding the shovel, and then outside in the storm, stooped beside my tires as I tried to clear myself a path.

Imagine my relief to learn a friend hired a neighbor boy to dig out her car. And when I discovered I could climb onto the kitchen counter and hold the top of the refrigerator with one hand and reach for the overhead lightbulb with the other, I felt an outsized sense of triumph. *How many divorcées does it take to change a lightbulb?*

Our marriage, in the end, had echoed with loneliness. How many times had we been restaurant silent, the couple that dines wordlessly, then beams up into the server's face at the offer of more water and dessert? To feel the absence of affection between us where once there had been so much, florid and overflowing—*that* was lonely. This was just being alone. Empty rooms, carrying the laundry, the bed so wide I began to sleep diagonally across it. I could begin to wrap my arms around each instance, one by one; I could get my sea legs on the ocean of aloneness. As a divorced person it was not terrible.

As a daughter, it was.

HAD GIVEN UP on dinner. Not the activity of eating in the evening, but the meal as a recognized daily event. It was not a ritual I was interested in partaking in at home or providing for myself, and so I ceased to turn on the stove, didn't even make my own coffee anymore. What I wanted was to be out in anonymous public places or safe, familiar ones—on other people's couches, at a bar with a strong drink and a sweet friend. My friends treated me to expensive wood-fired pizzas and assembled complicated snack plates piled with cured fatty salami, briny black olives, crumbling slices of aged cheddar. They ladled homemade chicken soup. My own kitchen had become a room to pass through after it was long dark outside, and only then on the way to the bathroom, where the smooth curves of the bathtub held me like a crib.

The cross-streets in my neighborhood slope down to a view of New York Harbor. On the walk home from the subway, between the rooflines of Sixteenth Street, the water is busy with the white wakes of speeding ferries, the creaking, high masts of histori-cal replicas; the Statue of Liberty stands at the center framed by cranes and low-slung barges. One evening in the spring, I arrived home before the sun had disappeared behind the milky folds of her massive robed figure. I tried to find a new way to name the sky's shade of old-fashioned sailor's delight. One thing I loved about my mother was her odd celestial observations. A certain moon was like a fingernail clipping, a sort of sunset like God winking. This sky was the saturated hot pink of a ripe fruit not found in nature.

When I stepped across my threshold that evening, I dropped my purse on the floor and found eggs in the fridge. Low heat, a knob of pale butter, and I stood for several minutes at the stove dragging the spatula in figure eights, tending to it, until I tipped the yellow eggs onto a white plate. That night, I sat on the floor of the hallway, my back against the wall, and I ate dinner. That night, I did not cry in the bathtub.

NOTE TO SELF, care of mom's Stop and Shop bag: "Sometimes I wonder that our six-year-old may be brittle," she worried about me. "But when I advise her to look into herself and feel her strength, she responds with jolly self-control and a temporary surge of self-reliance."

I sometimes wonder that I am brittle, too, that the ordinariness of the world that others seem to bear with such grace and forbearance is enough to break me. I feel joy today. I feel sad today. Ticktock, careening from frivolity to despair in the span of a week. Feeling may be living, but living like this is exhausting.

The evidence to the contrary is today. Or May 9, 2014. Or May 22, June 13, July 28, August 17. All of the days I awoke from the cool relief of sleep to the blunt force of my grief, or even a less acute awakening to the simple devastation of what had been lost. Predawn birdsong can break your heart. Still, I swung my bare legs out of bed, put the coffee on, moved through sorrow and joy as they came in waves. After a year had passed, my doctor praised me with a pronouncement that proved my mother wrong. We sat in a small office downtown, and he tapped at his computer keys under black-and-white photos of skyscrapers. "You are very resilient," he said. True: To bend to force and not shatter proves a kind of strength I did not know I possessed, and still, that surge, too, is temporary—all of this is.

THERE WERE DAYS when I thought my mother had given me a great gift by dying. Later, I was grateful for certain logistical conveniences, like one less household to negotiate at holidays or the freedom to move far away, but I do not mean that.

Here is a woman who fills her one small life. Not with milestones—birthdays, graduations, weddings she wasn't particularly good at. In fact, it wasn't until college, when people fussed over one another's birthdays with hand-drawn cards, a proffered doughnut, little treasures left like bird's nests outside dorm room doors, that I came to know the importance of celebrating those special days, too. For her, the anniversary was in the hour hand. Branches of bittersweet in the snow. The copper kettle on to boil. Beauty is the ticktock, and feeling it the pulse. There is no reward in the end, my mother said of parenting. The only reward, ever, is ongoing; it must be the day itself. *Would I like it?* she would ask of a movie, a restaurant. She is out for her own enjoyment and yours. Go ahead, wink with a stranger at the cash register. This is how to make the drone of a day come alive. You want something done, ask a busy person, they say. You want to know joy, ask a woman who swims against her own sadness. Opposites are most striking when held at once: bloom and rot, reverie and boredom, grief and joy. You are just like your mother, people say, and finally I know.

summers

JANE DROVE ME to the farm the morning my mother died, and Jane drove me to the ocean in August when I was still crying. She let me be her mute and deadened passenger while she kept busy.

It reminded me of the picture book my sister had loved as a girl, *We Help Mommy*. We help Mommy prune the rose bushes. We help Mommy fold the laundry. On the North Fork, I helped Jane buy raw milk from a kind old Welsh farmer who handed us a glass jug and six brown eggs. I helped Jane buy a paper sack of square ice. I helped Jane shell beans and shuck corn, and eating outside next to the blooming hibiscus as big as a dinner plate, the salt air waving our hair, of course it was Jane who helped me. We walked into the lapping water of Long Island Sound, our hairless legs prickling at the salt, and when it was dark, laid our backs flat on the benches of the picnic table, still and silent, watching for something to happen, and knowing it was already right there, happening.

Jane gestured at the wide galaxy with her hand. That's Mars and the Big Dipper.

"This is how you feel now," she said. "Soon, you will feel something else."

I had only known one other person who could relax into life like that, could so take it moment by moment.

Inside, she flipped the downstairs lights off and the ones in the upstairs bathroom on. She combed her fingers through my hair, painted Jolene bleach onto a stripe near my ear and wrapped it in aluminum foil.

We piled into her bed, her laptop between us, and watched a movie about two women who run away together, turn tough and wild as she wolves. The lush 1930s wallpaper was like hiding in a tower of cabbage roses. She peeked inside my foil.

"It's ready," she said.

I leaned my head under the faucet and washed out the white bleach. In the mirror, Jane standing behind me, the white strands were like a feather woven into the underside of my hair or an earned stripe of paint across a warrior's face. *Look*, she said. Is this what a woman is? It is the more interesting question to me now. We called it my coven streak.

"We need berries," she said in the morning, and we drove toward the town at the tip of the island. First, a stop: a shaded street dead-ends at the beach, covered not with sand but with white rocks as smooth and round as eggs. We spread our towels and raked our fingers through them. Smaller stones the color of citrine and cooked shrimp, wet-shiny as marbles at the shoreline. We collected a little pile to bring back home to anchor the pages we each kept on our desks. The water was Aegean green with three jagged boulders that broke the surface near the shore. We dove from them like mermaids, waded, fought the undertow.

I was laughing again. Water and white sun my most reliable sources of joy.

"Our great mother," Jane said, and she was laughing, too.

Our limbs dried in the sun, and we packed up to buy berries and three kirby cucumbers. The beach stones were heavy in
my bag. We drove with the windows down, hair whipping across
our faces.

"When I met you, you were a girl," Jane said. Three years
before, I was twenty-nine. It seemed another lifetime. "Isn't it great
being a woman?" she asked. She turned onto the road marked
NO TRESPASSING like she owned the place, and tree branches
scratched at the car like bony witches' fingers.

N THE FALL, I entered graduate school, driving an hour north
from my apartment twice a week. I wrote in a library carrel with
a view of the turning foliage and checked out stacks of books an
armful at a time. I called workshop the dead mother parade, since
I was not the only one who wrote obsessively about hers. There
were dead husbands, too, fathers, pets, siblings.

"Are you in graduate school?" Duncan asked me, "or a two-
year grief program?"

Both. I did frequently dissolve during meetings with professors, but my crying was as often about gratitude as it was about
grief. When we sat around a table discussing Virginia Woolf as
the first snow began to fall, I was acutely aware of what I was not
doing. I was not buttoning my emotions beneath a starched collar
or announcing myself on conference calls or analyzing click rates
or writing advertorial about the versatility of a butter-like food

product. I was no longer living my life in division. My heart, head, and body were in the same place at the same time, all pointed in the same direction.

I T WAS NEARLY Mother's Day again, and I stood in the cemetery under the afternoon sun. On the drive to New Jersey, I watched the vines of a yellow honeysuckle wave in my rearview mirror. It was the first time I'd been back, and it looked as it had that day—the sprawling purple redbud in bloom, the white dogwood at the base of the hill. It was a pretty spot, as far as death parks go. A man rode a mower up and down the hill. It was difficult to be maudlin in the drone.

When I arrived at the patch of lawn where I remembered we'd stood, there was no marker. I walked up and down the rows of dead, searching. There was no headstone with her name. We had not wanted to select one in haste before the funeral. The honeysuckle would do. Now it appeared this was an errand no one had wanted to resume or return to.

For most of the trip to the cemetery, my vision had been blurred from tears. The greatest comfort was imagining myself lying on the clipped grass above my mother's body. This spot seemed close—the angle of the sun and pitch of the slope. I split the difference between two spots that seemed like contenders, and tried to cover as much space as possible, sprawled like a snow angel. The mower buzzed in the distance, and a butterfly bobbed in the air. I wished I was the sort of person who believed that a butterfly was a sign, but since I couldn't, since I couldn't even be sure the bones beneath me were hers, since that quiet country graveyard was, at this very moment, loud with the sounds of upkeep, and of keeping on, I had to admit: It was all suddenly quite funny.

More likely *that* was her sign.

A FEW MONTHS later, between my first and second years of graduate school, I drove to visit my sister in Alabama where she had moved for a new job. "It was Mom's favorite magazine," Katy said, and it was true: I had found a copy on her bedside table, the recipes for coconut cake and black bean chili dog-eared. My niece had just turned three, and my sister drove us to the wooded grounds of her corporate office park to collect moss. We were going to make terrariums.

We had a spade, and Violet was very deft at separating the fluorescent green fur from the compacted, moist dirt by wriggling the trowel between the layers. She crouched thoughtfully in the same yellow cardigan she had worn at last year's funeral. It fit. My sister had cut Violet's blonde bangs straight across her forehead. "I got it!" she announced again, raising the trowel in the air with the moss in one large chunk like a green island. We gathered pinecones, and thin, spindly seedlings that looked like grown pine in miniature, like bonsai.

Violet is the first baby I have watched grow. It is like a little sister to say this, or perhaps like a mother, but she reminds me of me. It is her dramatic eyes, the way she widens them when she says, *You know what?* and the way she stirs up her listener before she delivers the payoff of her big news: that she can ride a scooter, or roll into a somersault, or has three best friends at school. It is also the way she can whir herself into a frenzy and is overcome, overwhelmed, by the intensity of her own emotions. Violet was spirited that day with the moss, and naughty, repeatedly careening near an edge of landscaping that dropped off onto a blacktop, far below. "Violet, stop," my sister said with a scary edge in her voice, and Violet screamed. She hated to get in trouble, to do anything wrong, and mostly she hated this voice from her mother. It was all familiar to me. *You are spirited*, my mother said, *and naughty*. Katy crouched and pushed Violet's bangs aside with a soft hand, her voice soothing again. "It is because I love you so much, Peanut," she said, "past the stars. I don't want you to get hurt."

Back at home, my sister gathered glass vessels from the lower kitchen cabinets. Inside each one we arranged a bed of moss, planted a thin, faint fern, and covered them. Sealed under glass, terrariums create their own gentle weather systems, pass time, and thrive in their own delicate atmospheres. It seemed an ideal model—that with the right conditions, they required little outside intervention to grow. We arranged the glass domes like emerald cities on the kitchen table. Violet and I rested our chins on our hands, folded on the marble table, and watched, amazed. Made small like that, anything seemed possible.

WHEN MY FATHER snapped the photos on the early evening South Padre beach, he didn't know the brackish Gulf of Mexico seawater had seeped inside the camera. It was my mother's discovery at the counter at Eckerd Pharmacy, flipping through a white envelope of blurred and out-of-focus photos, the dusk-warm shapes as fuzzy as a skein of mohair. In them, she stands on the low-tide sand with Bliss, then a toddler. She is long legged and leaning over him, wearing a t-shirt from the elementary school carnival where she worked the pie toss in the morning, the dunking booth in the afternoon. She is shaking her finger in a faux scold while he looks up at her with mischievous laughter. Earlier in the day, sitting cross-legged with her in the sand eating cold grapes, I saw delicate, dark hairs like spider's legs escape from inside her suit at the crease of her thigh. She loved the light of those photos, and the serendipitous streaks. She handed the envelope back to the developer and asked that they be blown up. Framed, they joined the other photos in the hallway outside her bedroom, including my little brother in a high chair, the bright slant of early morning sun spotlighting his sleep hair, his mouth full of ripe banana, eyes closed from laughing. Motherhood was the highest art in our house.

THE JULY HEAT in Florence, Alabama, is an oppressive menace. I am on my own cross-country adventure, nearly retracing

the route I saw from the cab of a moving truck as a kid. I am not
just like my mother. This time, I am at the wheel and eat Cheetos
and giant, expensive salads made of kale and sunflower sprouts,
take scenic routes of my own design, pick up grocery sacks of
used paperbacks in Southern cities. I stop at a junk store and purchase a white silk slip, a tire gauge, and a sugar bowl in her china
pattern with money I've earned.

I stop at a Residence Inn for a swim, where the view is of
Highway 2, a gas station with four rusted pumps, and a mobile
park across the street. Some trailers have plywood leaning where
windows should be. My swimsuit was once sexy, but no longer
fits. I tug at the top and slide into the water.

I dog-paddle, dip my head back, and then two young brothers
swim to me. The younger one wears inflatable wings. His accent
is so thick, I can't make out a word.

"Hi," the older one translates. He is the age of not being afraid.
His cheeks are red from a day in the sun. "What's your name?"

I tell him, and he gets to talking: he is five, his name is Davis.
We swim around each other and splash for a while, and then I say,
Well, nice to meet you, pull myself up the pool ladder, and drop into
the hot tub with my novel. Then splash, wet pages, and Davis is
suddenly beside me again.

"What's your book about?"

"Davis, leave her be." His mother, in short shorts and a t-shirt,
is sitting at a table under an umbrella. I smile, tell her it's fine. She
turns back to her phone.

"It's about Italy," I say. "Do you know where Italy is?" He
shakes his head no.

"Italy is in Europe, on the other side of the world." He looks at me blankly, interested but unsatisfied. "It's where macaroni comes from," I add, proud of myself for this orienting detail. "And spaghetti."

"Shells and cheese?" he asks.

His brother slips in the water on my other side and touches my arm to get my attention. He is not yet afraid of anything, either. I am beginning to acclimate to his molasses singsong. I gather his name is Owen, that he is three years old but will turn four on July 27, which is in ten days.

Davis wants his turn again and reaches for my other arm. They touch me in an absentminded, easy way, not caring that I am a stranger. Davis arranges himself in my lap, and Owen strokes my wet hair. Suddenly they are my puppies, scaling my body with playful care, as if I am theirs. They want something from me, and whatever it is, I want to give it to them. Is this what a mother is? It is the closest I can come for now. Freckles stretch across the bridge of Davis's nose, constellations among them. I do not want a bad thing to ever happen to him.

"Yes, shells and cheese," I say, and Davis looks up at my face, ready for the next thing.

"Wanna get back in the pool?" he asks, and I do.

Acknowledgments

I would like to express my profound gratitude to a lifetime of teachers and to my Sarah Lawrence family, in particular. Jo Ann Beard, Jake Slichter, Vijay Seshadri, Brian Morton, and Paige Ackerson-Kiely showed me what was possible, and generously offered their support and friendship.

My family has been admirably graceful and encouraging of a writer-daughter-sister-niece to whom nothing is too private. I'm especially grateful to Katy Lukens and Madelyn Young for multiple careful readings and corrections of chronology and fact and for understanding, as Tobias Wolff wrote, that memory has its own story to tell.

I can never fully express my gratitude to Sarah Weir and Peter Grossman, who offered not only creative feedback and friendship but food, clothing, shelter, and a place in their family when I was most in need of a home. Thank you to Megan Bayles, Jenny Walton-Wetzel, Piper Weiss, Sonia Evers, Laureen Ellison, Jessica Cannon, Katie Melone, and Shane O'Neill for their friendship, endless brainstorming, and encouragement. I am also grateful to

Sarah Hepola, Siobhan Adcock, Amy Shearn, and Jessica Hendry Nelson for their meaningful pep talks at critical junctures.

I cannot overstate my gratitude to the MacDowell Colony, Ucross Foundation, Vermont Studio Center, and Virginia Center for the Creative Arts for their generous gifts of time and space. These places taught me about magic. Thank you, also, to the artists at each of their dinner tables who helped me grapple with the work as it was making its way onto the page.

My profound thanks to Gráinne Fox for her steadfast belief in my writing, unflappable calm, and wicked sense of humor, as well as Veronica Goldstein. At Liveright, I am grateful to Gina Iaquinta, Cordelia Calvert, Steven Pace, and especially Katie Adams. I wish for all writers to work with such a sensitive and incisive editor.

And to Max Hart, for margaritas, and truly, more than I can name.

INTO GREAT SILENCE

into great silence

A MEMOIR OF DISCOVERY AND LOSS
AMONG VANISHING ORCAS

Eva Saulitis

Beacon Press, Boston

Beacon Press
25 Beacon Street
Boston, Massachusetts 02108-2892
www.beacon.org

Beacon Press books
are published under the auspices of
the Unitarian Universalist Association of Congregations.

16 15 14 13   8 7 6 5 4 3 2 1

This book is printed on acid-free paper that meets the uncoated paper
ANSI/NISO specifications for permanence as revised in 1992.

"Mother Tongue" was published in *Gnawed Bones*, Red Hen Press, 2010.
Excerpt used by permission of the author. Excerpts of song lyrics from the
album *Raven River* by David Lynn Grimes used with the artist's blessing.

Exxon Valdez photo on page 56 copyright © 1989 *Los Angeles Times*.
Reprinted with permission.

Text design by Wilsted & Taylor Publishing Services

Library of Congress Cataloging-in-Publication Data
Saulitis, Eva.
Into great silence : a memoir of discovery and   599.536
loss among vanishing orcas / Eva Saulitis.
   p. cm.
ISBN 978-0-8070-1435-6 (hardcover : alk. paper) 1. Killer whale—Alaska—
Prince William Sound. 2. Killer whale—Mortality—Alaska—Prince
William Sound. 3. Killer whale—Effect of oil spills on—Alaska—Prince
William Sound. 4. Whales—Alaska—Prince William Sound. 5. Oil spills—
Environmental aspects—Alaska—Prince William Sound. 6. Exxon Valdez
Oil Spill, Alaska, 1989—Environmental aspects. I. Title.
QL737.C432S37 2012
599.53'6—dc23   2012023722

For Eyak, for the last ones, and for Wilderness

Time held me green and dying
Though I sang in my chains like the sea.

DYLAN THOMAS

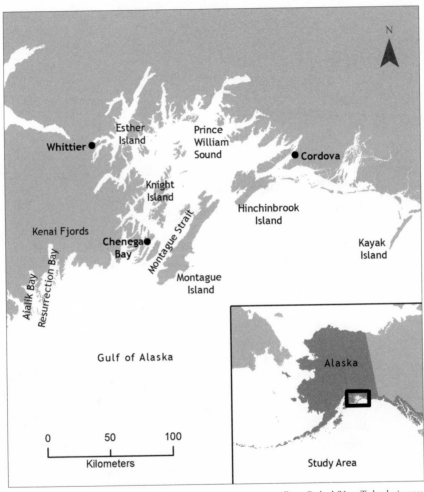

Contents

A Note about Names

Some names in this book have been changed to protect vulnerable habitats and human histories.

While the book is true to the data I collected, and conveys all that is known scientifically of the Chugach transients, it is principally a memoir, a work of contemplation, not science or reportage. It abides by naturalist William Beebe's call for "softening facts with quiet meditation, leavening science with thoughts of the sheer joy of existence," and in this case, the sheer pain of loss as well. My use of names reflects that intention. In the scientific literature, the Chugach transients are called the "AT1 transient population." My friend David Grimes pointed out that I might read their scientific moniker metaphysically as "At One," and yet I decided that for the purposes of this book, the whales needed a familiar name, a family name. They belong to a specific place once called Chugach Sound. They are linked to specific indigenous cultures—the Chugachmiut and the Eyak—through oral tradition. Hence, the Chugach transients. Hence, Eyak, a central whale in the narrative. Individual Chugach transients in our identification catalog, and in scientific papers, go by alphanumeric names (for example, Eyak is AT1; Chenega is AT9). As is common in long-term field studies, those names have, over the years, been supplanted by familiar names, and the latter are the ones I use here.

Finally, I use the common name "orca," at the risk of annoying my scientific colleagues, who prefer "killer whale." They argue that "orca" sugarcoats the predatory nature of the animal, invoking the captive hand-fed version, performing tricks in tanks for crowds. I see their point, but decided that the essence of the Chugach transients, which are no more, no less killers than any other carnivore, is better reflected by "orca," derived from the name of a Roman god of the underworld.

Prologue: The Last One

Like the others the last one fell into its shadow.
It fell into its shadow on the water.
They took it away its shadow stayed on the water.
—W.S. MERWIN, FROM "THE LAST ONE"

Before I knew there was such thing as species, much less one that was endangered, I understood extinction. When I was nine years old, I understood extinction not with my mind, but with my heart. Aptly, I received this instruction not at school, but after, on *The Last of the Curlews*, an ABC Afterschool Special episode based on a novel by Fred Bodsworth. I don't remember the film's plot. Only that at some point, there was one pair of curlews left. I vaguely remember a father and son who debated whether or not to shoot a curlew. I recall with clarity the last one, the last Eskimo curlew on earth, circling and calling above the tundra. In the bird's own memory, I imagined a sky darkened and drummed to life by bodies, wings and the *tr tr tr*-ing of flight song, an era when it migrated between the Canadian Arctic and Patagonia with millions of other Eskimo curlews. I can still summon my ache for that last curlew; almost forty years later, it throbs in my chest.

When I was twenty-three, I saw my first orca, a lone female. That day, I had no inkling that I would study her kin for my entire adult life, that she was already one of the last ones. Fresh out of college, I'd taken a job at a fish hatchery in Prince William Sound, Alaska. One blustery winter day, out for a skiff ride, I spotted a black fin amid gray waves. A few minutes later, a whoosh near the skiff startled me. I turned to see a wind-flattened blow, the fin rising, the arch of a flank emerging and sliding back under the water. Then she disappeared, as if the rough sea had swallowed her. I looked everywhere, but she was gone.

Twenty-five years later, I'm still searching for that whale, for what's left of her family. For me, watching *The Last of the Curlews* was what Susan Cerulean calls an "origin moment." That day, when I realized human beings could eliminate a kind of bird from the earth, my assumptions about the world overturned.

A lifetime of origin moments leads to this one. It's September 2011. I sit on our research boat, *Natoa*, scanning a familiar shoreline for orca blows. The tide is low. A raft of sea otters rests near Squire Point. For many seasons, I followed small groups of orcas called Chugach transients past this point as they hunted for harbor seals. Sometimes harbor seals hauled out on Squire Point to rest, or hunkered in the shallows alongside the rock to hide from passing orcas. Though I see no seals sprawled on the rock today, I know orcas might appear at any moment. They are like that, unpredictable in their appearances and disappearances.

And so are stories we tell about them. Take today. As we idle along the point, Craig, my partner in research and in life, recalls that thirty-five years ago, with a cadre of volunteer observers on the bluff top on Squire Island, he watched Chugach transients swim along this shoreline. A young field assistant, eye pressed to the lens of a spotting scope, shouted: "Look, the orcas are playing with a porpoise!" That evening, after hiking back down from the bluff to their tents on a beach we still call Whale Camp, they found the severed lungs, heart, and head of a porpoise calf washed up on shore. "I tried to preserve the skull, but the porpoise was so young, the bones just fell apart," Craig says. With Craig, I've studied orcas for twenty-five years, nearly half my life, and I've never heard that story before. What I know, after all this time, about the whale called orca, *arlluk, aglu*, blackfish, killer whale—is a lot like that.

Now our boat rounds the bend of Squire Island, and Whale Camp beach slides into view. Many times, Chugach transients swam past Whale Camp when I lived there. Often they startled my field assistant and me from our tasks. Some still pass this way. But it won't always be so. I force myself to write these words: the Chugach transients are going extinct. They are leaving the earth under my watch. There will, perhaps in my lifetime, be a last one. I type the words, and that old hurt I felt for the Eskimo curlew throbs. How do I accept the reality of the word "extinction"? Forty years later, do I understand with my heart, much less my head, what it means?

Last summer, from an unexpected angle, I got closer to understanding the concept when I edged up to—no, was shoved toward—the possibility of my own extinction. From a sickbed, my laptop open on my lap, cell phone on the coverlet beside me, I followed the movements of Chenega, one of the last Chugach transient matriarchs, on a computer screen. I stared as a digitized map of Prince William Sound drew itself, then displayed the points and lines of her nighttime travels. There. Off Point Helen. I clicked on the biggest dot, the most recent satellite hit: 4:30 a.m., heading south. The dots told me only that much, not whether she traveled alone. She had been with her companions, Iktua and Mike, when Craig had tagged her the night before.

A sea breeze blew in, and I looked up, past a couch and a coffee table piled with get-well cards, to the open window. There my eyes met not the Pacific, but the Atlantic; not Prince William Sound, but Cape Cod Bay, where wind clawed white marks on the indigo. For the first summer in twenty-four years, I was not on Prince William Sound studying orcas. I clicked on the link to the Iridium satellite phone website, typed a message to Craig and our friend Cy, who was filling in for me on the boat: *G'morning. AT9 off pt helen 0430 heading s, xo E.*

I shut the laptop, pushed it to the side of the bed, sank down into the pillows, closed my eyes, and put off confronting my current reality. The day before, in a Boston hospital, an IV had conveyed a toxic chemical into a vein on top of my left hand. I was being treated for breast cancer, and what awaited me was a regimen of anti-nausea meds to be swallowed with a few baby spoons of applesauce. I was not on Prince William Sound, where it was rainy and cool, far from it—Boston was humid and hot every day that summer, it seemed. Before I rose, mentally I placed myself there, in Knight Island Passage at dusk, off Squire Point, in the rain, on *Natoa* with Craig and Cy, and I tried to re-create the encounter Craig had described on the sat-phone the night before. How Chenega had been hunting with Iktua and Mike all afternoon, impossible to approach as transients so often are. How Craig and Cy had given up. How it had been late, the shelter of Sanctuary Bay beckoning. How they had been wet and cold and frustrated. How they had turned east, Craig taking the wheel inside the cabin, Cy enjoying a few minutes of solitude on the bridge, watching the hidden entrance to Sanctuary Bay reveal itself. How she, Chenega, had appeared beside the boat. How she had swum alongside the bow, lunging out of the water to keep up. How Cy had stamped his foot on the cabin roof to signal Craig. How Craig had poked his head out, heard Cy shout, "It's Chenega, right here, I think she wants you to tag her now." How Craig had easily tagged, with one shot, one of the last seven Chugach transients. That was why, from thousands of miles and a continent away, I could call Chenega each morning and see where she was. This is how I could track an animal that exemplified fidelity to place, fidelity against all odds, in sickness and in health, in peace and calamity.

I had been told by healers to visualize my immune system preying on cancer cells. I had been told that visualization could lessen chemotherapy's side effects and speed up healing. So I visualized. The animals, the place. I visualized kayaking into Sanctuary Bay, where Chenega, Mike, and Iktua milled, waiting. I drifted into their midst and placed my hand on Chenega's fin, placed my hand on the cold, rubbery skin, knowing hot, oxygen-rich blood flowed inside, and I imagined her red and white blood cells traveling up my arm, infusing my own blood with power.

The next time Craig called, he told me he had photographed all of the remaining seven Chugach transients: Chenega, Iktua, Egagutak, Mike, Marie, Ewan, Paddy.

All that hot, humid summer, I sat at a desk, or I sat in bed with the laptop propped open, and I wrote their stories. In doing so I understood, not just with my head, not just with my heart, but with my whole body, that certain places on this earth have healing power, and that the place where the Chugach transients live is one. I came to believe that the place and the whales played a part in rescuing me. Not in some mystical sense, but simply by existing, with or without me. They saved me, though I can't save them.

Now a year has passed. I'm back in Prince William Sound, back on *Natoa*, short-haired, my body altered, a strange new post-chemo ringing in my ears, one I hear only when it is quiet. As always in August, my fingertips are blueberry-stained. As always, resident orcas appear in the passages to feed on silver salmon. As always, salmon spawn and die by the millions in streams. Craig douses four silver salmon he caught off Whale Camp beach with bucketfuls of saltwater. As always, we search the shorelines for Chugach transients. Now the tide has risen and swallowed all but one of the Squire Point rocks. Now a pelagic cormorant and three glaucous-winged gulls cluster on that shrinking, kelp-skirted surface. A front has pulled a gray blanket over the Sound. I scan with binoculars the choppy water in front of familiar landmarks—Pleiades, Icy Bay, Iktua Passage, Brandt Island, Labyrinth—for a black fin that might at any moment appear amid those waves.

A close pass by resting orcas during an acoustic recording session. (Craig Matkin)

PART I

Place of First Permission

I

By Beaver, by Bear

JOURNAL, ESTHER ISLAND HATCHERY, JANUARY 1987
I dreamed it was night and I was at the ocean. I stepped onto a
long boardwalk. I walked and walked and close to me were black
waves and it was windy. Suddenly, I was surrounded by orcas.
They exhaled all around me and I sat down, stunned, blood
pounding in my ears. Paralyzed, I held my breath, but at the
same time, on the inside, I leapt up. It was silent, but inside
I understood the whales, and they, me.

Alaska. As a college student, a dream for me of blue-white tundra, wolves, caribou, moose, indigenous hunters: wilderness. A dream of emptiness, silence. Growing up south of Buffalo on the flat, populated, polluted Lake Erie floodplain, I knew nothing of silence in nature, nothing of the sea, nothing of wilderness, of predators besides raptors and owls. As a teenager, I developed an owl obsession. I painted them, wrote science papers about them, drew an owl cartoon strip, collected owls: carved, molded, printed, stuffed. I didn't imagine the stab of a beak into the meat of a vole's shoulder, blood spattered on a snow owl's breast. Predation didn't figure into my imagination. I loved all animals and birds, foxes, deer, rabbits, garter snakes, hawks; I didn't imagine how they killed to stay alive.

Fate placed the predator in my path. After graduating from Syracuse with a degree in fish and wildlife biology in 1986, I headed north and west by car with my boyfriend, RJ, to a fisheries job in a place I'd never heard of: a temperate rain forest archipelago called Prince William Sound. Hired as fish culture technicians, RJ and I spent that winter with seven other workers at a salmon hatchery on Esther Island, near the Sound's northern rim of snowy mountains. No road linked the hatchery

3

to the "outside" world. To get there you had to fly in a floatplane called a Beaver across a mountain pass littered with wrecks of floatplanes, a pass often closed by weather. Or you could get there on a train, by way of a tunnel boring through one of those mountains. On the other side, in the tiny port town of Whittier, you could hitch a ride twenty miles on a rusty barge called *Itswoot*, which means "bear" in the Chinook language, down Passage Canal, past the Blackstone Glacier, across Port Wells to Esther Island. Two ways to get there: by beaver, by bear.

My wilderness that winter was not one of tundra but of islands, inlets, forest, muskeg. My landscape was intimate, tucked away, shadowed by mountains, muffled by fog. It was sodden; nearly two hundred inches of precipitation fell in a year. My wilderness was populated not by wolves and moose and willow scrub but by moss-draped hemlock and spruce, blueberry brush, Sitka black-tailed deer, black bear, sea lion, seal, orca. My wilderness was complicated. A single-minded crow flying from Chenega Bay, the westernmost village in the Sound, to Cordova, the easternmost, would cover less than a hundred miles. A seal-hunting orca combing the Sound's convoluted coastline would cover thirty-five hundred.

My indifference to orcas (they were RJ's obsession) gave way one December day. RJ and I'd spent the morning in the hatchery's incubation room, in the dark, adjusting incubator flows by our headlamp beams. At lunchtime we got permission to take a two-hour break. We bundled up in rain gear and life jackets and took a hatchery skiff into Wells Passage. RJ, determined to find orcas, scanned constantly with binoculars. For a half hour, we saw nothing but shrimp pot buoys. On our way back across the passage, the wind picked up. The water got rough. I was daydreaming, kneeling in the bow, bracing myself against each pounding wave, when it caught my eye: a curved fin slicing through waves in the distance. I thought at first it was a wave's shadow, but then RJ saw it too. It was an orca, a female. "Holy shit," RJ said. We angled the boat into her path, and she surfaced very near, passing by the boat and disappearing. We stood clutching the skiff's side, the wind driving pellets of sleet at our faces, waves slamming the aluminum hull. We looked everywhere, but she was gone.

Until that moment, I'd been skeptical of RJ's fixation on "killer" whales. It seemed macho and cruel, like a boyhood obsession with *Jaws*. But after that encounter, I picked up the book I'd bought RJ in Anchorage before we'd come to the island, Eric Hoyt's *Orca: The Whale Called Killer*. Reading it, I learned that orcas are not technically whales but dolphins—the largest members of the family Delphinidae—and are the most widely distributed mammal on earth, inhabiting all the world's oceans. I learned that the Latin name, *Orcinus orca*, translates loosely as "from the underworld." The Haida name for orca, *keet*, means "supernatural being." Some people call them killer, some orca, but in essence both names lead to the same place. Hoyt's book focused on orcas and the people who researched them off British Columbia (B.C.) and in Puget Sound. There, two ecotypes of orca roam the same waters but never interact: residents—fish eaters, and transients—mammal eaters. (Later research would identify a third ecotype, offshores—shark eaters.) Researchers can distinguish the ecotypes on sight. Experts can even tell individual whales apart. Like human profiles, their fin shapes and the scratches on their saddle patches impart to each orca a unique profile and often a descriptive name, like Stubbs, Nikka, or Colossus. Eric Hoyt called orcas "sonic creatures." Their universe is acoustic, while that of humans (unless blind), is primarily visual. Hoyt quoted the controversial researcher of captive dolphins, John Lilly. Lilly pondered the intelligence of whales and dolphins, whose brain morphology resembles that of humans. Lacking hands to construct or write with, whales, Lilly theorized, "may have taken the path of legends and verbal traditions." How could one possibly understand such creatures? I wondered if a musician might.

Before I'd switched to biology, I'd studied music in college, but had been thwarted by stage fright. On Esther Island, evenings, I practiced my oboe in the concrete fish raceway room, so no one could hear me. The idea of an orca "language," or "song," or, at the very least, an "acoustic universe," intrigued me. From Hoyt's book, I learned that resident orcas are "chatty": each pod (a collection of related maternal groups traveling together a majority of the time) identifies itself and stays in contact via a unique dialect of calls. These dialects reflect cultural traditions. Calves learn calls from adults around them. Transients, according to Hoyt, are mostly silent. When vocal, they are terse, their dialect consisting of fewer calls, most of them brief and quiet.

My coworker Tony, a fish culturist and fellow musician, told me to expect orcas to appear in Lake Bay in spring, when herring gathered near shore in preparation for spawning. As March approached, and the days grew longer, I watched for them. Waiting changed everything. It imbued the jade-green water in front of the hatchery with potential energy. My anticipation made tolerable the incessant rain, wind and daily hatchery drudge work, the endless cleaning, repairing, and incubation room tasks interrupted in late winter, blessedly, by the feeding of smolts held in net pens outside. On the net pen boardwalk, I could breathe the iron scent of low tide, feel rain and wind on my face, hear calls of winter ducks, watch for seals, sea lions, river otters, loons, weasels, and orcas, clear my head of the "bushiness," the small-mindedness and claustrophobia induced by a stormy island winter.

As the days lengthened, on weekends, Tony took RJ and me on skiff rides. As soon as we rounded the peninsula buffering the hatchery from southerly winds and waves, our visual scope expanded. The bay with its steep, forested slopes opened wide to Wells Passage. Five miles away, the nearest islands—all uninhabited by humans—hunched on the horizon: Culross, Perry, Lone. Mostly we hugged Esther Island's shoreline, peering down. For the first time I saw sea anemones, sunflower stars, leather stars, nudibranchs. Among the rocks, in the gray winter light, was color: lavender, umber, moss green, burnt orange, rose, pearl. In Quillian Bay, we watched rafts of grooming sea otters, flocks of sea ducks. I learned to identify harlequins, pigeon guillemots, marbled murrelets, and to distinguish Barrow's from common goldeneyes, pelagic from red-faced cormorants. One day, as I scanned Wells Passage hoping for another glimpse of an orca, Tony said, "You know, if you're really serious, you should get in touch with Craig Matkin. He's a commercial fisherman who studies orcas. His wife studies humpbacks. I think I have his address. You should write to him. Maybe you could volunteer on his project. Maybe your future isn't at the hatchery. Wait till you hear him on the VHF. He's got a great voice."

"Okay, I guess," I said, doubtful that this person would consider an assistant as inexperienced as I was.

Finally, one day in March, they appeared. I was inching along the frozen net pen walkway, tossing scoops of fish meal to the smolts, watching the water boil as they rose to feed, when I heard blows, louder than those of sea lions. I looked up to see four fins, ink black against the basalt black of the shoreline rocks, rising and sinking along the far shore. Smoke threads from their exhalations faded against hemlock branches. At high tide, water licked at the forest's skirt. I dropped the bucket of fish food and sat down. Immediately I stood back up, eyes fixed to the spot where they'd dived. A part of me, the part tied to the human world, to RJ, to Tony, to my hatchery coworkers, strained to break free, to run inside and tell everyone. *Come out here! The whales have arrived!* Another part pulled in the opposite direction. It felt like a dream, as if I'd asked, before sleep: *Show me how to be part of this place.* I didn't want to betray something. *I won't tell anyone*, I thought. *Just stay a little longer.* A few hundred yards down the shoreline, they resurfaced. Then nothing. Several minutes later, their blows echoed at the bay's head. Indifferent to the hatchery, to the above-water world, they didn't exuberantly leap out of the water like the resident orcas in *The Whale Called Killer*. Finally, I ran inside. As the whales returned from the bay's head, we stood clustered on the dock. Then the orcas dove under the net pens and disappeared.

After that I started to take RJ's camera, equipped with a zoom lens, with me when I fed smolts. In late March, the orcas returned, a pair. Then in early April, another pair arrived with a calf. In mid-April and again in mid-May, a quartet appeared—two males, a female, and a calf. Once the orcas swam close enough for me to photograph them. I'd read in Hoyt's book about the standards for useful ID pictures: the photographer ought to be positioned parallel to an orca's left side. When the images came back in the mail from the developer—photos not of orcas, but of scenery, a bay with a few small, fuzzy black wedges in it—I sent them, along with the letter I finally wrote—*I'll scrub your decks, cook, clean, whatever, for a chance to volunteer on your boat*—to Craig Matkin.

In the meantime, I read and reread *The Whale Called Killer*. I studied its table of known orca prey, which listed everything from herring to blue whales, from king salmon to harbor seals. Most of all, I agonized over stories of the roundups of the 1960s and '70s, live captures of wild orcas for aquariums, juveniles torn away from mothers. Normally residents stay with their mothers for life. Some of those orcas, having been herded with powerboats and seal bombs, surrounded by seines, culled from their pods, isolated in net pens, and shipped all over the world, still circled tanks, day after day.

In a quest to become more independent of RJ, I ranged the island alone on days off. Often I sat in a cove near the hatchery and watched harbor seals sprawled on granite slabs, or afloat, just their heads, glossy eyes, and black nostrils breaking the surface. They watched me back. I studied the variations of their mottled pelage—bone white, pewter, smoke, tan—imagining I could identify individuals by their coat colors, the markings on their faces. I named the familiars: Baldy, Otto, Waldo, Yorma, Olga. On solitary hikes, with camera, journal, bird book, and thermos of tea in my backpack, I post-holed through disintegrating snow in my gum boots. Dense forest gave way to expansive patches of muskeg, pond-studded, spongy meadows of low-growing plants, easy to hike across. Flocks of chickadees, or crows, or indigo-and-black Steller's jays sometimes followed me. One day I heard an odd buzzing in a stand of spruce, almost electrical—the spring's first varied thrushes—a relative of my childhood robins. I kept lists of birds as spring came on, lists of flowering plants. I counted the consecutive days of rain. Forty-two.

The week before my birthday, in May, I waited for *Itswoot*, the mail barge, already several days late. With no phone at the hatchery, and no floatplanes landing in the bay for months in winter, the barge was our only contact with the world, but it was perpetually delayed by weather, tides, breakdowns, or reasons unknown. In Whittier, in winter, I imagined mornings a skipper might just look out the window, roll over, and fall back asleep. During the dark months, waiting for mail was excruciating. When I see *Itswoot* now (it still plies the Sound), it's odd to remember what longing I attached to a rust-streaked landing craft with a so-called monthly schedule for delivering food, mail, and supplies to the hatcheries. The *Itswoot*'s skipper once presented us, just before Christmas, with a cloth bag full of wet mail. He'd dropped it into the chuck, he matter-of-factly told us. Still, we presented him, more often than not, with home-baked cookies.

The night before my twenty-fourth birthday, the mail arrived unmolested. In it was a letter from Craig. "As it turns out," he wrote, "I do need a volunteer for a few weeks later this summer, after my fishing season. It's good you know how to drive a skiff. Thanks for the photos. Most were too far away, but in one, I could tell that they were our local transients. Interesting that they came into Lake Bay so many times this spring. Probably not after the smolts, most likely sea lions or seals. But who knows? Great if you can get photos when you see them again. Left sides are what we need for IDs. Stay in touch."

After a break in Anchorage later that May, I sat staring out a window as the train I rode made its way, swaying and squealing, through the mountains to Whittier. When it emerged from the last tunnel, rain spattered the windows. Clouds hung down to touch Passage Canal, erasing the mountains. Wind raked the inlet's gray water into furrows from which two black fins rose, paused, and sank. I blinked hard. There they were again. A pair of male orcas swam parallel to the train.

Through a record run of rain that spring, I waited for the rest of my life to begin. On my days off, I hiked the island, practicing biology, not the kind that took place inside the hatchery, with its clanging equipment, its sluicing of millions of gallons of water through thousands of metal incubators, its wet cement floors, its chemical foot baths and malachite green fungicides, but the kind I'd imagined in college, the biology of boots tromping across swamps, of watching, waiting, and writing. At night I studied my field guides. In my journal I kept lists. Every time orcas appeared in the bay, I took notes for Craig.

2

Lucky Star

In late August, after the release of the young hatchery salmon, after egg-take—the collection of another winter's worth of roe and milt from returning salmon—after cooking for a construction crew, after a late-summer stint monitoring a fish weir, I flew to Cordova to meet Craig and his colleagues. I found his seine boat, *Lucky Star*, tied to a float in the harbor. As I walked toward the boat, I watched a lanky, bearded man with a wild head of sandy curls riffling through boxes on the back deck. "Craig?" I called out.

The man looked up with wide, startled, blue eyes. "Oh, you must be Eva." There it was, the voice Tony had described, strong, low, a bit of wind and gravel and salt in it. Crow's feet at the corners of his eyes gave him the look of someone in an ad for pilot bread or clam chowder. Craig straightened, wiped his hands on grease-stained Levis, and strode toward me. He wore a "Spawn Till You Die" T-shirt half tucked into his jeans and the ubiquitous brown gum boots of an Alaska fisherman. His eyes swept past my face to the frame backpack I shrugged off my shoulders and set down on the dock. "Whoops. I should have told you to bring a duffel, like my fishing crew. It's a pain in the ass to stow a pack in the bunks. Oh well. First lesson. Go ahead and store it in the fo'c'sle, bottom right bunk is yours. Mary and Carl are inside, introduce yourself, they're great. You can help Mary put away supplies." Abashed, relieved to be given a task, I ducked into the warm cabin.

An hour later, Carl and Mary untied the lines, pulled up bumper buoys, and pushed *Lucky Star* away from the float. Gulls shrieked from high wooden piers around the harbor. On the flying bridge, Craig stood at the helm, looking behind him as he steered the boat in reverse out of its tight space at the dock. Carl pushed past me to hold a heavy line looped through the power block away from the churning propeller; it was the tow line for the skiff we'd use to work with whales. As *Lucky Star* gained speed, diesel throbbing, smoke trailing from the stack, Carl paid out the line, and soon the skiff swished behind us on the end of its tether. "Got to keep this line out of the way of the prop," Carl said. Not having been aboard any boat larger than a hatchery skiff, I was too shy to jump in and help, but equally embarrassed to stand there doing nothing. *You'll get used to it*, I told myself.

A seiner like *Lucky Star* has what mariners call "beautiful lines." Forty-two feet long, her bow, with its curved bay of windows topped by a flying bridge, sweeps aft to a long, low deck where the purse seine net is piled during the salmon season. Now that net was stored in the hold. Craig had just finished fishing for the summer. I listened as Carl oriented me to the boat's layout. Like Craig, he was both a biologist and commercial fisherman, but he fished out west, in the Bering Sea. Mary, his wife, worked for the National Marine Mammal Lab. Carl pointed out the crow's nest, atop a metal pole, high above the flying bridge. A set of aluminum rungs allowed a person to climb up there to scan for fish or, in Craig's case, whales. As Carl talked, his nautical lingo registered as a kind of birdsong in my ears.

Nine hours later, after transiting Orca Inlet, skirting Middle Ground Shoal, passing Johnstone Point, and crossing Hinchinbrook Entrance, which opened like a maw to the Gulf of Alaska, and after rounding the northern point of fifty-five-mile-long Montague Island, the Sound's backbone, we chugged down Montague Strait. After dinner and cleanup, I sat on the flying bridge, the nautical chart spread out on my lap, binoculars pressed to my eyes, while Craig, Mary, and Carl talked research politics in the cabin below. The remnants of a stiff breeze blew my hair around my face. Scanning the water, I watched flocks of phalaropes flutter from tide rips and settle again like gusted up leaves. Craig had told me that Montague Strait—a five mile-wide corridor between two uninhabited islands, Knight and Montague—was the heart of his study area. Everywhere I looked, seabirds—fork-tailed storm petrels, black-legged kittiwakes, horned and tufted puffins, common murres—winged above the water. Kittiwakes plashed down onto bait balls, and parasitic jaegers chased after the kittiwakes until they disgorged the fish they held in their crops.

Late in the evening, I spotted puffs against Montague Island and hurried below to tell the others. I wanted to be useful, to have "good eyes." But Craig was skeptical. "It's probably sea lions," he said as he grabbed binoculars and followed me up to the bridge. "Or maybe humpbacks. Were they straight and tall blows, or low, puffy ones?"

"Kind of straight, I guess." The puffs surrounded the Needle, a rock slab jutting up from the middle of Montague Strait, like a nunatak from an ice field. The boulders at its base writhed with scarred brown bodies of Steller sea lions. Here and there, a thick-necked, blunt-faced bull gazed solemnly upward, as though holding itself above the fray. Surrounding each bull sprawled sleeping or groaning juveniles, females, and a few pups still cloaked in the black pelage of their first year, all heaped together, fore flippers draped across neighbors' bodies, bellies spooned to backs. The Needle's main rock, a guano-streaked, fifty-foot face, provided nesting sites for kittiwakes. Flocks wheeled off the cliff, circling and then settling back. An ammonia stench wafted toward us on the breeze. A predatory eagle sat atop the Needle, and Craig told me that sometimes a peregrine perched there, nabbing newly fledged chicks from the water.

"I see the blows now," he said. "I'll be damned. They are killer whales." Now the puffs were followed closely by fins. A large group of residents was scattered across Montague Strait, chasing salmon, probably the fat-rich species known as silver, or coho, Craig said. "The whales aren't dumb. They prefer the oiliest fish, the silvers and kings, to pinks. Just like us." He clambered back down the ladder to get his camera.

We worked with the pod until dark. The whales behaved not like the small groups I'd observed in Lake Bay, but like the residents I'd read about in *The Whale Called Killer*, leaping, charging after salmon, and once even playing in the boat's prop wash. Craig told me they were AB pod, thirty-six whales, the hub of resident orca society in the Sound. AB was one of seven resident pods—totaling a little over a hundred individual whales—that Craig monitored on a yearly basis. Of the seven, AB pod was the "friendliest," the most tolerant of boats, the easiest to photograph and follow.

As Craig snapped ID photos of each individual, he called out the names of whales he recognized: Bubbles, a young female who blew bubble clouds beside the boat; Jeannie, the pod's diffident matriarch; and Olsen, Montague, and Latouche, Jeannie's three grown sons. "Mama's boys," Craig called them, reminding me that resident pods were "run" by females. We saw Nellie Juan and Galena, females with gray saddle patches swirled like Persian script over their black skin. Mary checked off in the identification catalog the whales Craig had photographed, and she penciled observations into a yellow-covered Rite in the Rain notebook. Carl drove *Lucky Star*, positioning the boat parallel to the whales' left sides. Craig wanted to get close enough for a whale's fin to fill the camera's viewfinder. That was the ideal ID picture, he said.

While the others worked, nonplussed by all of those orcas, I stood at the rail, clutching my camera, unable to suppress what must have been a look of mad glee on my face. When an orca swam close to *Lucky Star*, I resisted the urge to yip and holler, not wanting to look like a "keener," what Craig and his colleagues called whale groupies.

Before we could photograph each whale in the widely scattered pod, we lost daylight, and Craig turned the boat toward Knight Island, where we'd anchor. After everyone fell asleep, I lay awake, my mind buzzing. Before switching off my reading lamp, I expelled my pent-up excitement in a letter to RJ, who had left Alaska for Oregon. Separated from my ear by an inch of fiberglass, water lapped against the boat's hull. Forward in the boat's belly, the stove's pump periodically blurted. The refrigerator hummed, then clicked off. Every once in awhile, the anchor line rubbed against its metal chock. In the other bottom bunk, opposite me, Craig snored, his feet pushed against mine, wedged together with his in the V of *Lucky Star*'s bow. Boat sounds, water sounds, human sounds finally lulled me to sleep.

As the days passed, I found my sense of purpose, cooking meals, scanning for whales, listening to the biologists' banter, cleaning up, writing everything down in my journal at night. There were, it seemed, countless details to learn, not only about orcas, but about boat life. One of the first evenings, as I was washing dishes, letting the rinse water run, Carl sidled up and reminded me not to be wasteful. "The tank only holds 150 gallons," he said. "Water, water everywhere, and all that."

"Hell, the Australians never rinse their dishes," said Craig. Nothing got past him. He seemed to have the ears of a bat. I was embarrassed he'd overheard Carl's quiet admonishment. During those first days, I learned to turn off the boat's hydraulics after hauling the anchor, and to recognize the burning smell when I forgot. I learned to watch for lines trailing off the boat's side, threatening to get swept into the prop. To latch the refrigerator door during rough weather lest it fly open and spill its contents. To keep an eye out if someone walked to the back deck when we were underway. "If someone falls off, and no one notices, it would be hard to find them out there," Carl said. I learned too to stow my books, journal, boots, and jackets, to make myself small. I was glad for Carl's advice. Craig didn't like telling people what to do.

He did like to talk, though. As we searched for orcas in Montague Strait the next morning, I plied Craig with questions. An escapee from a rural Southern California childhood, from a place wiped away by rampant development, the eldest son of a pragmatist father (a soil scientist) and a red-headed, artistic, Irish mother (a literature and drama major), Craig blended his parents' temperaments. He was garrulous, a rumpled amalgam of surfer, scientist, hippie, farmer, and fisherman, and he talked so openly about so many things that he quickly put me at ease.

Between sips of hot chocolate—Craig was a chocolate addict and anti-coffee zealot (all those alkaloids)—he stressed the importance of photo identification. It was the main tool he and his colleagues in British Columbia used for research. Because of yearly photo ID, researchers had been able to calculate orca life history parameters like longevity and age at first reproduction: an average lifespan of fifty (maximum of eighty to ninety) years for females, and thirty (maximum fifty to sixty) for males. Females bear their first calf at twelve to seventeen. Males, on the other hand, don't reach sexual maturity until their late teens, a transformation marked by the "sprouting" of the fin into its knife-like adult form. Each summer, Craig's group, a nonprofit named North Gulf Oceanic Society (NGOS), photographed every orca in the Sound and sent the films to Graeme Ellis, in British Columbia. Graeme scrutinized every negative strip, frame by frame, under a stereoscopic microscope. The result was a catalog of fins and saddle patches (the gray area behind the fin) and alphanumeric names—AB2, AB17, AT10, AN5—"A" for Alaska, "B" for the pod, and a unique number for each whale. "T" meant transient. The official name of the Chugach transients was "AT1 group." From the yearly photo census, not only could Craig and Graeme count precisely the number of residents using the Sound, they could also tease out relationships among whales, eventually assigning each whale to a matriline, a pod, a population.

A first-year calf surfaces close alongside its mother. As it grows, this one might be replaced by a younger sibling, but it will never stray far from her side. Resident orcas remain in their matrilines for life. For that reason, researchers can track births and deaths from year to year, and calculate population parameters—birth rates, mortality rates, and rates of growth or decline—the baseline normal for resident orcas in the Sound.

In most mammalian societies, including ours, offspring disperse when they mature, in part to avoid inbreeding. Not orcas. Not even humans demonstrate such fidelity to family. After a year, a missing resident is presumed dead. It's different for transients, whose social structure is more fluid. They come and go unpredictably from an area, and a transient might leave its matriline to join another, or disappear for several years, only to reappear. "Well, except the AT1 transients," Craig said. "They're different than true transients." Most summers, he'd photographed all twenty-two in the Sound, sometimes together, most often in small groups.

After two hours of searching, Mary spotted distant splashes: orcas. A group of five—an adult male, three females, and a juvenile—rolled at the surface, socializing. This time, within a quarter mile of the whales, Craig put *Lucky Star* in neutral as Carl pulled the skiff in with the hydraulics. Craig asked me to join him, to get a feel for running the skiff. Carl would drive *Lucky Star* at a distance, while Mary continued to calibrate her sonar equipment, which she hoped to use to examine the prey of feeding humpback whales.

Once the skiff was secured alongside, its engine warming, we rounded up the camera gear. I lowered myself into the skiff. Craig handed me waterproof cases, and then, all long legs, he leapt aboard and staggered past me to the steering station, nearly losing his balance, so eager was he to get to work. I knelt at the skiff's bow, holding onto the rail as we sped across the choppy sea toward the orcas. They were rolling upside-down, exposing their black-and-white bellies, thrusting their flukes high out of the water, then smashing them down. "Lob-tailing," Craig called it. When he tried to maneuver in parallel for photographs, to his surprise the whales charged us. One particularly fearless individual, whom Craig identified as female from her mammary slits—marked by a pair of black daubs on either side of her genital slit—lobbed her fluke a few feet from the bow, so hard it sent up spray. I ducked too late, then gasped, laughing. The frigid water on my face wasn't just any water. It was like holy water thrown at me by an aspergillum. I turned to Craig, overjoyed, but he looked uneasy. He clutched his jacket, holding close the camera zipped inside to protect it from saltwater. "This is weird," he said. "These are transients. Not ATIs. I think they're Gulf of Alaska transients. They don't usually act like this. They're usually shy of boats."

The whales, now lined abreast, surfaced in synchrony, all except the female. She continued to dog the skiff, dousing me again and again. Soon I was soaked. Unconcerned, I raced from port to starboard to watch her. "Damn. She seems determined to get you wet," Craig said. For an hour and a half, she thwarted his efforts to photograph her left side, swimming under the skiff, or so close beside it I could see every scar on her body. Craig told me that most of the tooth rakes were from other orcas, but that some might be from seals or sea lions. Suddenly the whale thrust herself straight up from the water, spy-hopping, so that her eye looked directly into mine. Blue. The iris was blue. Then she breached. I scrunched down. Water spattered my back. I popped up, looking for her. She dropped into our prop wash, lunging. Through her blowhole, she growled, snorted, and whined. Then she surfaced parallel to the skiff, in perfect ID position. Craig reached for the camera he'd tucked into the transom, but before he could snap a photo, she flopped over on her side and slammed the water with her pectoral flipper.

"It's like she knows exactly what I'm trying to do, and she'll be damned if she'll let me," Craig fumed. Finally, frustrated, he decided to speed up and photograph her companions, but the female accelerated too, pacing the skiff, surfacing too close for photos. I leaned over the side, reaching my hand out, lost in delight, oblivious to the imperatives of science. There she was, pumping her fluke, gliding, perfectly visible through the clear water. She turned onto her side, eying me. Finally, the male swam over, and the female departed with him to join the others. Our interaction was over. Craig got his pictures, and when the whales began to shy away from our approach, like "normal" transients, we left them. They headed south, toward their home, the Gulf of Alaska.

That night, puzzling over the catalog photos, Craig finally found a match to a female with several notches in her fin's trailing edge. On the same page was a large male, another possible match. And there was a smaller one, her fin tip rounded, the way our wild female's had been. They were Gulf of Alaska transients, as Craig had suspected, rare visitors to the Sound. Almost nothing was known of them, not range, not feeding habits, not calls, not even how many existed. They didn't mix with the Chugach transients. We named that female Matushka, for a wild, craggy island in the Gulf of Alaska. Many Gulf of Alaska transients in the catalog looked beat-up, the trailing edges of their dorsal fins ragged, saddle patches scarred. The Chugach transients looked less battered, but their fin shapes shared the characteristic broad-at-the-base, pointed-at-the-tip, transient form.

September 4. Two weeks after Matushka locked my gaze with hers, the Chugach transients, as they had in winter, made a brief appearance. If the Gulf of Alaska transients announced themselves with hoopla, the Chugach transients, belonging wholly to that place, appeared out of nowhere, and then just as quietly disappeared. Two adult males. AT13, Aligo, and AT15, Moon. Off the Pleiades, two fins, broad, triangular, tall. Moon was named for the large, scooped-out notch near the base of his fin. Aligo and Moon surfaced, went down. A long time, many minutes, nothing. Then, to the east: one fin emerging, then the other. For a moment, two obsidian shards, side by side, paused at the top of an exhalation. Then sliding back under. Hunting? Resting? Like waves, so much a part of the landscape, barely given notice in the log, in my consciousness, in my journal. Ubiquitous. "The ATIs are always somewhere around," Craig said. "Whenever we're not busy with residents, we find them." We snapped ID photos and left to search for other whales.

Drowned out by the cacophony of resident calls, their silence. Overlooked through days of fifty, sixty, one hundred or more fishing and socializing residents, their stealth.

I didn't recognize it then. Now I know. Those two, like the ones I saw in Lake Bay, like the pair of males—perhaps those same two?—at the head of Passage Canal, seen from the train, were the origin whales. That encounter off the Pleiades was the origin moment.

During those three weeks on *Lucky Star*, first with Carl and Mary, then with a BBC cameraman and producer, finally with Graeme, I receive many variants of advice about my future. The field is too competitive, there aren't enough jobs, said Mary and Carl. The politics burn people out. One day, picking blueberries with Mary near Whale Camp, she qualified her remarks. Despite the competitiveness of cetacean biology, in every field there was room for people with integrity, she said. When he joined us, Graeme observed my dedication to recording calls, and encouraged me to pursue acoustics in graduate school, to talk with his colleague John Ford, who had described the dialects of B.C. resident pods. Perhaps I could do the same in the Sound. Or study the Chugach transients, he said. No one knows anything about them.

Near the end of the trip, in mid-September, Craig asked if I would consider volunteering again the next summer. "I get letters all the time from people wanting to help out with whale research, so it shouldn't be hard to find a field assistant," he said. "You could work out of Whale Camp, run a small boat, take ID photos of killer whales and humpbacks, and think about a project for grad school." I didn't have to think it over. I said yes.

But at night I lay awake in the bunk, wondering what I could study that would be new. Perhaps feeding behavior of the humpback whales we'd followed for hours towing Mary's side-scan sonar. Craig's wife Olga, who studied humpbacks, could advise me. But from listening to the biologists' late-night conversations, I knew that funding for research had to be justified by some political or economic imperative, like AB pod's theft of black cod from fishermen's lines, or Sea World's proposal to capture orcas from the Sound for its aquariums (that plan, thanks to photo-identification data showing just how small the Sound's population was, had been thwarted). No one handed out money for pure science, Craig warned.

Despite my preoccupations, I tried to enjoy those last days aboard *Lucky Star*. On clear nights, the aurora writhed in the northern sky. Sometimes, to get exercise, Craig and I paddled his double kayak around our anchorage cove. Bioluminescence glittered with each paddle stroke, reflecting all I didn't know, about whales, about the Sound, about my future. The quiet of those nights settled my mind. I'd come back to the Sound and let my research subject find me.

3

Whale Camp

I can still see those eyes, glossy and black, too big for its face, staring at me. I can still see the gray body plastered to the rock, how the seal pup craned its neck to see if the orca was gone, how it looked at me one more time, weighing the risks, before it slipped into the sea and disappeared. Sitting here writing more than twenty years later, it feels like a parallel reality, a channel I can tune into, that moment: the sky partly clear, the sea lapping against the rock, the orca fin rising and falling in the distance, heading away. That twenty-five-year-old me on the inflatable, I believe I can slip inside her skin, feel the energy that coursed through her nervous system as she scribbled down what she saw into a notebook, as she picked up binoculars to see what would happen next. That younger me didn't ask where the seal pup's mother was. Did the whales eat her? Was she hiding nearby? The younger me didn't know what questions a biologist was supposed to ask. What she did was back the boat away from the rock and head for the orca, propelled by longing. She jotted down what she saw in code, a field sketch drawn on the fly. The questions came later. *Every time we're with transients, we see something we've never seen before,* she would have said to her field assistant.

Neuroscientists have something to say about origin moments. When we experience things for the first time, our brains, like inner diarists, "write" furiously, recording even the smallest details: a blue sweater, curled orange peels, the tang of salt air on our lips. That's why we remember firsts so vividly, experience them, decades later, "like it was yesterday."

Repeated events over time lay one on top of the other like transparencies, making all the years blend. Time feels slower the first time. Maybe that's why the first summer at Whale Camp, my initiation into fieldwork with the Chugach transients, doesn't feel like the past. It feels like a world side by side with this one, a world I can see if I focus my eyes differently, and then, when it comes into focus, one I enter completely, like a diver. I'm grateful, for in many ways that world I knew is gone.

That's the other reason it's so clear. That summer was the first and, in important ways, the last. The last before the great disaster. Perhaps my vivid memory of that summer has something to do with novelty, and something to do with time and memory, but perhaps it's also cinematic, a pre-shock, a scene lit by a lightning flash a second before the bolt strikes, or the slowed-down seconds leading up to a crash, or exactly what you were wearing when you heard the shattering news: you have cancer. Before. After.

The next summer, I entered the Sound again by Beaver. In May of 1988, I flew from Cordova to the Port San Juan hatchery, not far from Craig's study area in Montague Strait. As we retraced the route we'd taken the previous August on *Lucky Star*, I watched the plane's shadow sweep across Montague Strait, Knight Island's crags on one side and Montague Island's scallops and snow bowls on the other. I watched for orcas amid the whitecaps. Then the plane banked steeply over Chenega Village to skim to a landing in front of the hatchery. As it puttered up to the dock, I turned my mind to the work ahead. I needed to earn money for graduate school prior to the start of my volunteer field season. I'd been accepted as a student at the Institute of Marine Sciences (IMS) at the University of Alaska Fairbanks (UAF), to study with Craig's former mentor, walrus biologist Bud Fay. For the month, I'd been rehired by the same aquaculture outfit that ran Esther Island hatchery, fifty miles to the north, to cook for construction workers and fish technicians arriving for the summer season. This time, I wouldn't be one of the techs, tending salmon eggs in the incubators, scrubbing and repairing equipment, preparing for August egg take.

During my stint as cook, I repressed anxiety about the coming field season. Waking at 5:00 a.m. to start breakfast, prepping for meals, baking cookies, providing an ear for tired workers, cleaning up, I immersed myself in routine, and fell into bed exhausted each night to read a line or two from one of the books I'd packed, mostly biologists' narratives of their field research. Only when it stormed did I pause to stare out past the kitchen window's rain-streaked glass to the forest shaking itself in wind like an animal, rain billowing across the bay, gusts landing punches, and wonder what it would be like for me out there.

On fair days, during my breaks, I hiked, my journal, bird guide, and binoculars stowed in my daypack. Nature on the island felt watchful. Alone I wandered between worlds, the objective world of species, natural history and names, and the subjective world of symbols and signs.

11 MAY 1988

In a meadow of skunk cabbage and moss, I built a medicine wheel with rocks from the beach—whitish stone for the north, clump of moss for the south, yellowish stone for the east, dark stone for the west. The mouse is the symbol of the south, of innocence, and the east is the eagle's place, and I certainly view the world in a mouse-like, as well an eagle-like way right now. Back on the beach, an immature eagle perched on a piling in the bay. I watched an adult eagle fly in, stunned to see it zoom towards the immature and chase it off its perch. They clashed in the air, the adult driving the younger one right into the water. The adult then landed on the piling and cackled proudly. I watched it snatch a fish from the water, the talons reaching, the wings flared, the sweep along the water's surface, the splash as it struck. Then a gang of gulls chased the adult away. Meanwhile the immature sat on a nearby spruce drying its wings.

Inevitably the day arrived, and I met it like an immature eagle about to be thrown into the adult world, to fend for herself. After a sleepless night, my bags packed, my room tidy, I waited in the kitchen, chatting with the replacement cook, until someone ran up to tell me that *Lucky Star* was tying to the dock. I cast my eyes one last time around the familiar space. I was leaving the world of refrigerators, ovens, sinks, running water, flush toilets, and men with a knowledge of mechanics. I'd have no boss to tell me what to do each day, no cookbook with its clear instructions. I'd be clawing my way up a learning curve in front of a stranger. Would my assistant Mary and I get along? I'd chosen her on the basis of a few sentences in her letter: "I've wondered if you think it strange that an artist would want to 'swab decks' or whatever to be near whales. But

I'm sure you know our goals are the same. We (artists and scientists) seek understanding through knowledge and experience. We also feel drawn to share this understanding with others. The dialogue we generate is in two different 'languages,' visual and verbal."

I shouldered my backpack, and walked down the dock to meet Mary, Craig, and RJ, whom I'd convinced Craig to hire as skiff man for his summer fishing crew. On and off, again and again, RJ and I were tentatively on.

In the drizzle they stood on *Lucky Star*'s back deck beside boxes, totes, and gear covered by blue tarps. Craig chatted with the hatchery manager, but was obviously impatient to head out. *Lucky Star*'s engine was rumbling, bluish-gray exhaust drifting from the stack. After hurried hellos and goodbyes, Craig grabbed my backpack and tossed it into the cabin. "Still no duffel bag?" he joked. Mary and RJ cast off the bow and stern lines, and soon I was watching the hatchery recede as we chugged up Latouche Passage.

After stashing my pack, I climbed to the wheelhouse, where Craig sat scanning. I plopped beside him on the bench seat, as I had every day the previous summer, and took up my own pair of binocs. Clouds hugged the islands, obscuring the peaks, entangling in spruce trees, shape-shifting and moving on. Craig pointed out landmarks as he glassed the water for blows, reminding me of places we'd found whales the previous year. Then I'd been a passenger. Now nothing looked familiar. Now my success at finding whales, and my very life, depended on what Craig was saying. I listened and tried to memorize it all. Before long Mary joined us, asking Craig question after question, and I recognized the ten years of life experience she had on me by her easy banter with him. They were the same age. I was, as Graeme had said, just a "pup." Mary's confidence pushed her forward up the passage like *Lucky Star*'s bow. Over her short brown hair, she wore a faded ball cap. She jotted on a pad notes about dangerous rocks, studying the nautical chart spread out on her lap. She'd sailed and kayaked on Lake Michigan. At least Mary had experience running a boat. It hit me then, that navigating, staying off the rocks, reading the charts, understanding the weather patterns, camping, fixing the boat engine, finding whales, and collecting data would be our responsibility. There'd be no one, no Craig, no RJ, to bail us out or back us up.

I fingered my sweater's hem. My mother had knitted it to keep me warm in a wilderness utterly foreign to her. It had arrived in the mail at the hatchery the week before. Somehow, she'd conjured the Sound when she'd chosen the colors—smoky blues and grays in heathery wool. It had seemed, when I'd pulled it from the box, a reflection of the new me, salty and practical. Now it felt talismanic, like the lucky stones I kept in my jacket pocket. I turned toward the stern and watched the snub-nosed *Whale 1* weaving in *Lucky Star's* stern wake, roped to the larger boat like a colt, incapable of independence. It was only sixteen feet long. Craig noticed my gaze but not my misgivings. He glanced back at the boat.

"It was a wedding present from Olga's ex-husband Otto," he said. "I'm not sure if that's a good thing. Plus it's a Boston Whaler. It'll pound your guts out. You'll have to go slow in any kind of chop. But it can't sink. The hull's filled with foam."

"What about the outboards?" Mary asked.

"Good old Johnson 35s, workhorses," Craig said. "Not new—they're rebuilt—but Otto threw in two extras, in case one breaks." Mary laughed. I looked away. Knight Island Passage seemed wider than I'd remembered, the forested islands darker, more impenetrable. I thought back to my camping and wilderness experiences, most of them under RJ's tutelage. He'd been frustrated—even furious at times—with my timidity and impracticality.

But the water was calm, the throb of *Lucky Star's* diesel familiar. In a few weeks, Craig's wife Olga, their six-month-old daughter Elli, and their friend Ralph would arrive to help Mary and me collect humpback data. I glanced over at Mary's aquiline profile, her tanned face shaded by her cap's brim, the fine lines at the corners of her eyes, which spoke of her time on the water, and hinted at a wry sense of humor.

Craig picked up the VHF mike, and told me to put out a whale call. "The fishermen will like your voice better than mine," he said. "Keep track of all the sightings you get on this data sheet." He handed Mary a clipboard.

Hello all vessels, this is the Whale 1, WYM9638. We're doing research on killer and humpback whales in Prince William Sound. If you have any sightings, we'll be standing by on channel 16.

Silence.

"Can we reach the hatchery from Whale Camp on the VHF?" Mary asked.

"Don't count on it," said Craig, "But you can always hail the Coast Guard in an emergency. Just use Olga's rule of thumb: don't leave Whale

Camp if you see whitecaps in the passage, and listen to the Coast Guard weather briefings."

Later in the afternoon, we put out another radio call, and *Arctic Spring* answered, reporting five or six orcas the day before. *Lucky Dove* broke in next, reporting three orcas that day, in the northern passage, two adults and a calf. "Probably transients," Craig said.

Approaching Squire Island and Whale Camp that evening, we passed close to a rock shaped like a whale's finned back. A harbor seal rested just above the lapping water. Cormorants clustered on top, drying their wings. It was Squire Point. Craig warned us to stay outside it: the rock marked the end of a reef. As *Lucky Star* rumbled by, throwing a wake, the seal galumphed into the chuck. The cormorants startled, regrouped, flew in a line toward Italian Bay. Craig explained that Chugach transients liked to hunt through Squire Point. They were so cagey, he said, sometimes he thought they lured you into the shallows to "scrape you off," so you'd leave them alone.

Then he pointed to a cluster of forested humps in the middle of the passage. As our angle changed, the cluster elongated: seven sisters—the Pleiades Islands—marked the passage's bend to the north. The sight of the islands triggered a memory for Craig, one of his origin moments. In 1977, when he'd been my age and newly arrived in Alaska from California, he'd crewed on *Murrelet*, a commercial fishing boat belonging to Pete Islieb, a bird expert and mentor to many would-be biologists and fishermen. One morning, Craig had watched from the flying bridge as *Murrelet* approached the Pleiades from the north, just as a storm was breaking. "The light was streaking out of the dark clouds in shafts, and everywhere I looked, there were backlit killer whale blows, between the Pleiades and Whale Camp. I swear there was a beam of light illuminating the bluff above camp." This was it, he'd thought. He'd finally arrived where he belonged. He'd vowed to return, to set up a field camp under that bluff.

A few minutes later, Whale Camp's pebble beach, fifty yards from end to end, slid into view, rocky headlands forming a small bight. Above the beach, ryegrass partially concealed a few weathered poles, parts of a tent platform. Behind the grass, a scrim of alders flashed new leaves, and above them rose the forest. This would be our home for the next four months. An eagle pair watched our approach from the tallest hemlock.

In the bight, a sea otter floated on its back, rising high out of the water to look at us, ducking under, popping up several hundred yards away.

Because the tide was rising, we anchored *Lucky Star* off the beach in water so clear and shallow I could watch the chain fall to the bottom and disappear among kelp fronds. We loaded the Dynous, Craig's inflatable, and ferried loads of gear onto the shore until a mountain of boxes, backpacks, duffel bags, gas jugs, and tarps formed above the tide line. Inspecting the tent platform, which hadn't been used for a couple of years, Craig kicked a rubber-booted foot through a piece of rotten plywood in one corner. Several side supports had broken, so we went scavenging, Mary and I walking the shoreline toward Squire Point, Craig and RJ taking the skiff to search distant beaches. They were our hardware, marine supply, and general stores. Between the four of us, we scrounged a scrap of plywood, a hank of seine netting, a pink buoy for the mooring, two five-gallon buckets, several two-by-fours, and a four-by-four for the tent's ridgepole. Mary had carpentry experience and went to work nailing boards into place while RJ and I stretched out the canvas tent. It was weathered to a mushroom gray, but smelled fresh. Olga had bleached it and dried it in the sun.

Once the repairs to the platform were complete, we dragged the heavy tent up the ramp, draped it over the side rails, and fitted the ridgepole through two openings. All four of us heaved the ridgepole atop supports at the front and back of the platform, nailing it in place, then pulled a clear plastic tarp over the tent to protect it from rain, bunching the edges around small rocks, tying the ends to logs, stretching the tarp away from the tent's sides. Mary placed buckets at each corner to catch rainwater. When we pinned back the door flaps, light pooled on the plywood floor. In a corner, Craig installed a rusty sheet metal woodstove, the size of a bread box. Then we fanned out to search the beaches for firewood. Craig had his chainsaw. Mary and I used handsaws for smaller pieces, the way we would for the rest of the summer. We stored rounds under the tent platform to dry. Finally, Mary and I stowed our backpacks inside, then stood on the "porch," taking in our view. "Not bad," Mary said. The sun dipped toward Chenega Island, painting salmon-colored swatches on the ice fields of the Kenai Mountains.

Craig proposed a hike before it got dark. We bushwhacked, following a deer trail through an understory of blueberry, copperbush and rusty menziesia. Brushing spider webs off my face, I breathed in the acid musk of sphagnum. Moss blanketed fallen trees, now nurse logs for ferns and saplings. I thought back to spring on Esther Island, when it had rained for forty-two days. In minutes our pants were soaked.

The patch of forest ended abruptly in a muskeg beaded with ponds, their water tea-colored from tannins. Hermit thrushes spun flute-toned whirligigs from the tops of wind-twisted mountain hemlocks that grew to shoulder-height. Some trees looked half dead, their spiked crowns corkscrewing into the air. Craig said that many were hundreds of years old. Natural bonsai, each was shaped, not by a careful gardener, but by prevailing winds. The ground from which they grew sprung back under my feet, all moss and swaths of heart-shaped deer cabbage leaves. The Latin name for deer cabbage, *Fauria crista-galli*, stuck in my head like a fairy's jump-rope song. We were hiking across a sponge, which absorbed two hundred or more inches of rainfall every year and held it in suspension, close to the earth. When I pushed my hands into the sphagnum, my fingertips touched rock. I could peel back moss to reveal wet basalt. What looked so plush was a thin carpet of life. This was our backyard: flowers speckling the muskeg—shooting stars, marsh marigolds, bog violets, blue flag irises, predatory flytraps hidden among lowbush blueberries and tufts of reindeer lichen. Skunk cabbage grew tall as my waist, the leaves big as fan blades. I needed a whole new vocabulary to name the variations of one color: bleached-out green of lichen, shadow green of spruce, tropical green of skunk cabbage, waxy maroon green of *Fauria*, pinkish baby green of rusty menziesia, chalk-dusted silver green of false hellebore.

The muskeg, crisscrossed with animal paths, rose in terraces to the forested face of the Whale Camp bluff. Brooks trickled down, linking pond to pond to pond. We slogged up deer trails into old-growth forest and started climbing the overgrown trail Craig had built years ago with volunteers. In some places it was so steep, we had to pull ourselves up using blueberry branches. Finally, sweating, we broke out of the forest and scrambled over one last rock face, using hemlock roots and limbs to haul ourselves the last fifteen feet to the top. Knight Island Passage lay far below, patterned by darker streaks from wind and currents. To the west, mountains still locked in an ice age cradled a massive sheet glacier. The only signs of humanity, besides *Lucky Star* anchored two hundred feet below, were flashes of the navigational light on the northernmost Pleiades.

Craig pointed to the green mass of Chenega Island across the passage, and to the white floes clogging the entrance to Icy Bay. He told us that, after heavy rains, ice from the glacier sometimes landed on Whale Camp beach, but otherwise, it was a short boat ride to collect chunks for our coolers—"Christ ice," he called them, exaggerating their age. A blue berg could be decades old. In the silence, we heard the glacier rumbling as it calved. I scanned the muskeg below for deer or bears. From that height, the ponds stared back at me, the island's black, inscrutable eyes, refusing to reveal anything, much less whether I'd thrive or fail in that place. Like a cloud-watching child, I tried to tame them by naming their shapes: guitar, hippo, horse head, skiff.

In 1980, during his first summer of whale research, with no boat, Craig and his crew of volunteers had lived at Whale Camp and climbed the bluff each morning with spotting scopes to count marine mammals, the first such census in the Sound. Whales would pass right by Whale Camp, Craig told us. We didn't need to waste gas or time looking for them, and moreover, our boat, small as it was, would be limited by weather. Often we could just stop near the Pleiades, drop the hydrophone, and let the whales find us.

Our study area, stretched out below, suddenly didn't seem so vast, but intimate. I could stretch my arms wide to encompass it. I imagined *Whale 1* trailing a wake as it skimmed the water toward Iktua Passage. Somewhere, along a shoreline, hidden in a bay, right now, were orcas and humpbacks. The Sound would teach me about them, and the whales would teach me about the Sound. And in three months I'd be a different person.

4

First Encounter

The next morning, eager to "go whaling," Craig quickly talked us through *Whale 1*'s operation. Mary, more mechanical than I, took notes on the outboards as the jargon swept past my ears. I'd never owned a car. My father, an old-school Latvian immigrant, hadn't even allowed me to operate his riding lawnmower. The biggest problem we'd face with outboards, Craig said, was water in the gas. We'd be pumping fuel out of fifty-five-gallon drums stored on Whale Camp beach. They'd inevitably collect water. In rough seas, water at the bottom of a fuel tank could get stirred up and stall the engine. He showed us how to check the filter and drain the carburetor.

Finally, we pulled anchor and headed into the passage to search. I watched Whale Camp recede. Now the beach looked inhabited, our fabric house nestled in the ryegrass, the tent flaps held open by clothespins. Less reassuringly, *Whale 1* jigged and jived behind us. *Lucky Star* felt like its mother ship, deck solid underfoot, diesel rumbling steadily, cabin dry and cozy from the stove's constant heat.

We stopped near the Pleiades, where we could listen up and down Knight Island Passage with the hydrophone, a microphone encased in epoxy and soldered to a cable several yards long. Craig called it "the pickle." He plugged it into an amplifier attached to a palm-sized speaker. Hearing nothing but wave slosh, we headed north. Two hours later, Craig spotted blows. Shifting *Lucky Star* into neutral, he turned the helm over to RJ, while I gathered our gear. Then Mary and I climbed into *Whale 1* after Craig, who'd already started the outboards. With each shift in weight, the boat tipped. Loaded with gas jugs, engine batteries, and gear, there was barely room for Craig and Mary in the cockpit, so I sat on the cabin roof. As we pulled away from *Lucky Star*, Craig pushed the throttle, and *Whale 1* bounded across the water, jarring my back as I hung on to the rail. I looked back at RJ, who stood on the *Lucky Star*'s flying bridge laughing. "I hate Boston Whalers!" Craig shouted over the outboards' roar.

As we approached the orcas, Craig throttled down and handed the wheel over to Mary, jotting the time and location in the yellow notebook before pulling the camera out of its ammo can. After checking the settings, he showed me how to take a light reading over my shoulder with a handheld meter. He'd take photos during the first rising. I clambered back into the cockpit as Craig inched his way to the bow, Mary and I instinctively leaning to the other side to counter his weight.

Five orcas—two males, a juvenile, and two females (or subadult males, Craig reminded me; until they sprout into their blade-like adult form, young males' fins are sickle-shaped, identical to those of females)— traveled line abreast, blowing in rapid succession, one fin rising after the other. Sunlight glinted on water pouring off their backs. "They're ATis—Chugach transients," Craig said. He pointed out their saddle patches, which swept far forward of the fins' leading edges. The whales arched and dove. We waited six minutes until they surfaced again, now angling across the passage. After finishing a roll of film, Craig handed me the camera.

I held its heavy body to my eye, focusing the 300 mm lens in and out on trees and waves. "There," Mary shouted, throttling up. The pair of males and the trio now traveled separately. This splitting of groups wasn't uncommon. Once, Craig had observed all twenty-two Chugach transients together, but mostly they hunted in groups of three or four. Waiting for the trio to surface, I stared at the water until a pale spot and darker shadows appeared.

"Here they come," I said. They pumped their flukes, bodies taking shape out of the gloom as they rose. The camera pressed to my eye, I watched a dome of water bulge as an orca's head met the surface. Then the water peeled off like cellophane, boiling and shattering with the blow. Nervous, I held down the camera's shutter, firing off multiple shots.

"Whoa," Craig said. "Easy with that motor drive." I'd learned, looking at the color slides I'd taken the summer before, how difficult it was to fix a camera's focus on a moving whale. Jumpy, that's how I felt—

my hands, my fingers, my brain—while the whales' movements were pure grace.

Craig pulled out the catalog and flipped the pages to the Chugach transients. Glancing from whale to page, he rattled off names. "That male's AT14 and that smaller one is 22 for sure, and I think that one's AT12, but it's kind of nondescript. But that's what we pay Graeme for." As Mary maneuvered the boat between the two groups, I shot through another roll of film. Craig reminded me to take frequent light readings. As the trio swam closer to Chenega Island, light would be swallowed by shadows.

I began to sense a pattern: eight or nine breaths, six or seven minutes below. We guessed they were traveling at 6 knots. I perched on *Whale 1*'s bow, the camera dangling from its neck strap. Below the surface, three bodies glided, motionless but for the pumping flukes. They dwarfed *Whale 1*—the adults were over twenty feet long. Under the reflected slopes of Chenega Island, they appeared to swim through a sunken forest. That forest, which fed itself to the Sound continuously by way of runoff, snowmelt and leaf fall, tinged their white saddle patches green.

Watching the whales through the camera lens, the two hemispheres of my brain vied for dominance, one awash in wonder, the other struggling to memorize Craig's advice. Meanwhile, hermit thrush songs drifted into my ears from the island. Whale blows, birdsong, our voices, the chugging of the outboard, the shutter clicking, all threaded into a strange contrapuntal music. Hemlock scent entwined with the stench of gasoline exhaust and sulfury whale breath. They seemed as much forest as ocean creatures.

The whales followed the shoreline, curving west. If they'd left an ink trail behind them, it would have drawn, along the island's contour, the route a kayak might have followed to Old Chenega, an abandoned Chugachmiut village. Above a salmonberry slope, Craig pointed out the schoolhouse, spared by its elevation from a tsunami that had swept through the village during the 1964 earthquake, killing a third of the inhabitants. Windows gaped, reminding me of the muskeg ponds the night before. The quake survivors had been resettled in Cordova and Tatitlek. Eventually, they'd scattered. After a twenty-year diaspora, some had rebuilt a new village near the hatchery. What would the inhabitants of Old Chenega have thought of orcas passing by?

Our photography complete, we tracked the whales from a distance. Several times we dropped the hydrophone, but they were silent. Over those hours, they passed a harbor seal, two sea otters, three sea lions, and five Dall's porpoises without giving chase. Craig wrote "travel" in the field book. We left the whales as they entered Dangerous Passage. Watching the fins grow smaller, I longed to follow, to see beyond the islets ahead, beyond the island's flank, to explore bays with strange names— Egagutak, Paddy, Iwan—the whales as guides. But Craig said we should look for humpbacks off Icy Bay, to practice taking ID photos for Olga. While we were there, we could grab ice for the coolers. As Mary turned the boat, I watched the transients disappear.

Back at camp, we set a mooring for *Whale 1*, and Mary and I practiced idling up to it in the whaler, grabbing the buoy-topped line with a boat hook and tying up, a challenge in the wind and current. Then we gathered gear and empty gas jugs and paddled to shore in the Dynous. Looking back at *Whale 1*, it struck me that she finally floated free of the mother ship, and the next day, so would we.

That night, RJ and I stayed up late around the campfire after everyone else went to sleep. Sometime, in the nebulous twilight after midnight, RJ spit it out: he wanted to break up, this time for keeps. We needed our freedom to grow. Watching RJ paddle the kayak back out to *Lucky Star*, I felt naked, as though a tide had rushed out inside me, exposing all of the delicate creatures to the stinging air. Then the tide turned, just as fast, and slammed back, cutting me loose. I crawled into my sleeping bag, across from Mary, muffling my crying with my pillow, the waves *lap, lap, lap*-ping me to sleep.

5

Cut Loose

Lucky Star left before dawn. At Whale Camp with Mary, tide licking up the beach, then slipping back down, wind rustling through the alder leaves, the intensity of our solitude and the matters at hand—making the wall tent a home—swamped out my sadness. Every sense felt sharpened, everything lit in stark relief, brighter than normal—my hands sorting rusty silverware, varicolored grays of the beach stones under my feet— and sounds amplified—the flap of the tent's fabric, an eagle's chortling, our voices. Mary and I talked all morning, trading life stories, a kind of crash course in each other. A sculptor, Mary patched together a living from odd jobs, grants, and artist residencies. Single, Mary was childless but motherly, practical and wry. She immediately took my measure as an idealistic, insecure woman hell-bent on proving herself to Craig, Graeme, immigrant parents, and RJ.

As we talked, we sorted and stored the food and supplies Mary and Craig had bought: boxed milk, five-pound blocks of cheese, fishing poles, boxes of a hardtack called pilot bread, matches, jars of peanut butter and jelly, cooking oil, utensils, condiments, pots and pans, sacks of rice, flour, oats, chocolate chips, gorp, granola, and beans, and what seemed enough canned food—from bacon to peas—to stock a convenience store. From the cache behind the tent, we extricated coolers filled with kitchen supplies half-submerged in rainwater.

Washing dishes at the water's edge, I heard crunching. Not far off the moored *Whale 1*, a sea otter floated on its back, eating a starfish. I envied its needs, only its body, maybe a rock to crack shells, while we depended on so much stuff that didn't weather as gracefully as bones, teeth, shells, beach logs, or rock. Our accoutrements turned into junk. Then a seal appeared, lifting itself high to get a better look at us. Later, a hummingbird hovered at the tent opening. The eagle pair flapped by, and we stared until we spotted a nest in a spruce tree at the far end of the beach. Less welcome, red-backed voles scurried across the tent's floor. As we built bunk beds and a desk, they practically ran over our feet. We called them Edgar and Helen, though we knew a legion nested under the tent platform.

Mid-afternoon, satisfied with camp improvements, we pulled the Dynous in from its mooring, loaded it with gear, and began our field season. Each day that followed abided by a seesaw template of empowerment and frustration, eagerness and worry, mirrored by weather, which changed constantly. Much of our angst was precipitated by engine problems, which began a few days after the *Lucky Star*'s departure.

15 JUNE
Delayed by our first boat malfunction. The steering cable jammed.
My initial reaction one of despair and frustration; Mary's one
of action—how to fix it. I have a lot to learn from this woman.
Mainly because of her persistence we found the problem.

By the end of the first week, the outboards themselves began acting up: first, water in the fuel, easily solved. Then, without warning, one of the outboards lost power. We cleaned the spark plugs, and when our repertoire of fixes gave out, we tried switching the troublesome engine with the spares. For a day or so, all was well, but after twenty-four hours, the boat again bogged down. What we didn't know, what we'd find out only that fall, after Craig pulled *Whale 1* from the water, was that the problem wasn't the outboards at all. It was the boat. Its hull pricked with pinhole leaks, its foam core saturated, it was too heavy for the tired outboards to propel.

What we gained from our tinkering was intimacy with outboard anatomy. Likewise, our attention to weather began to reveal patterns. Sunny days, we learned, were just lulls between low pressure systems, some intense enough to kick up gales and lashing rain, keeping us in camp, where we wrote letters, read, fed the woodstove, and experimented with camp cooking. One day, Mary baked "bread"— a hardtack, burnt on the bottom—in the woodstove. We cut off the burned part, slathered it with jam, and chewed happily, leaving the charred rinds for Edgar and Helen. Sometimes we caught fish and cooked them over a beach fire. Gradually, we began to inhabit the island.

One morning, a floatplane landed in front of Whale Camp beach. Mary and I waited at the water's edge as it drifted toward us. From the passenger door, a blonde woman in a red jacket emerged, holding a baby in a front pack. It was Olga, Craig's wife. She smiled and waved. "Hey, you guys! Here, Eva, take this little peanut so I can unload gear." She lifted Elli out of the pack and handed her to me. Eyes wide in her solemn, impish face, Elli looked around her in alarm, then back to her mom. Baby on my hip, I held the plane off the beach with a foot and my free hand. Olga began handing duffels and boxes to Mary. After Olga jumped onto the beach and wrapped us both in bear hugs, a man ducked out from the cockpit, grabbed a backpack, and leaped to shore. In his early forties, an adventurer and sailboat captain whose home base was the Big Island of Hawaii, Ralph was a lean coil of energy, his brown curls cropped close to his head, his nut-brown skin densely freckled from sun. He'd assisted Craig and Olga with humpback research in Hawaii and had volunteered to help Olga at Whale Camp for several days. Then he'd meet his girlfriend in Whittier and kayak with her around the Sound.

By the time Mary and I shoved the plane off the beach and turned back to schlep gear, Olga had rigged a Johnny Jump Up on the tent's ridgepole for Elli to bounce in while we worked. She'd shed her jacket and stripped down to a tank top, revealing tanned swimmer's arms, and an unself-conscious clothing style, her wool Army-Navy surplus sailor's trousers tucked into brown gum boots with the tops folded down—the ubiquitous XTRATUFs, a badge of belonging in a world of boats and muddy roads, the way Birkenstocks had been for my activist friends and me at college.

After arranging Elli in the Johnny Jump Up, Olga strode down the beach to help move gear. She opened a wax-coated box and showed us the first harvest from her garden—lettuce, radishes, and leafy greens— along with potatoes she'd stored in a root cellar since the previous summer. From another box she pulled jars of homemade cranberry-banana jam, cans of smoked salmon, and two dozen eggs from her chickens.

Though jarred out of solitude, after days of futile engine trouble-shooting and frustration, I was relieved to have Olga, Elli, and Ralph at Whale Camp. If I trailed a Latvian cloud of anxiety, Olga's weather was sunny. It emanated from her hair, skin, and blue eyes, which widened when she smiled or laughed or witnessed something that amazed her.

She'd first come to the Sound at eighteen, part of an outdoor leadership expedition. Soon after, she'd married Otto, the son of a legendary Swiss homesteader in Homer. After trade school, the pair had settled in Homer and hung up shingles: Otto's Machine Shop and Olga's Woodworks. A few years later, single again, Olga had enrolled at U.C. Santa Cruz to study biology. When she'd returned to the Sound for her undergraduate thesis research, a photo-identification survey of humpback whales, she'd contacted Craig for advice and logistical support, and in the summer of 1980, she and her friend Beth had set up a primitive camp in Whale Bay, working from an inflatable boat. She'd studied the Sound's humpbacks ever since. As a first-time mom, Olga intended simply to continue her work and adventures. Elli would crawl naked in garden dirt, bounce in a backpack up mountains, fly in a floatplane to a remote camp, sleep in a tent with whale blows as lullabies.

After setting up their tents and storing gear and food, Ralph paddled out to *Whale 1* with Mary and me to take a look at the engines. On the hatchery mechanic's recommendation, they'd brought new parts. With Ralph watching over her shoulder, and me handing her tools, Mary replaced the power pack and coil. To our relief, when we untied from the mooring and throttled up, *Whale 1* ran like a top.

6

Into the Labyrinth

Morning. Late June. Daytime breeze already ruffling the passage. While doing calisthenics on the beach, Olga spotted three blows threading upward in rapid succession against Gage Island, across the passage. Humpbacks. Some days, a particular quality of light, wind, and humidity made spouts stand out. Ralph, Mary, and I loaded up *Whale 1*. Since Elli was still sleeping, Olga stayed behind at camp. A few moments after departing, I spotted smaller, fuller blows off Squire Point. "Stop!" I yelled. The three of us stared through binoculars until the whales surfaced again—three orcas slinking close to shore, heading toward camp. Recalling Craig's warnings about Squire Point, Ralph crawled onto the cabin roof and knelt on the bow, watching for rocks while Mary paralleled a male, female, and juvenile. I stood behind her, camera at my eye. "Once we're past the point," she said, studying the nautical chart, "it looks clear."

The trio swam past Whale Camp. Olga, hearing our engine and the whales' blows, stuck her head out of the tent and waved. In deeper water, the orcas finally dove. We drove ahead, stopped and waited. Would they continue into the labyrinth of rocks and islands ahead of us? Or angle out into the passage? Mary spotted them near a grassy island. Idling in close, we saw that the female was gone. The juvenile nosed up to a tide-exposed rock, its fin wobbling as it pushed its body into the shallows, the male milling a few dozen yards away. A seal pup crouched on the rock, scrambling higher as the orca tried to shove itself up and over a lip to get nearer. We stared, stunned, through our binoculars. Here it was. Seal predation. "I wonder if the juvenile orca has the advantage in shallow water," Ralph said.

"Maybe it's learning how to hunt?" I said. "I don't know if I'm going to be able to watch this."

The seal's eyes widened. It craned its head back toward the orca, then lurched a few inches higher. The male circled the rock. From behind, his dorsal appeared rippled. Mary checked the tide book. Fortunately for the seal, the tide was ebbing. I thought of Barry Lopez's writings on the predatory behavior of wolves: "Predator and prey grow stronger together by means of a series of tests, through all the years of their lives, tests that pit them against each other at both psychological and physiological levels, tests that weed both culturally and genetically." We were witnessing such a test.

For ten minutes the young orca tried to charge the seal from various angles. Finally, without fanfare, it gave up. The male had already departed. The juvenile turned, inhaled, and dove. We inched *Whale 1* forward with a paddle to see if the seal had been injured. Unharmed but shaken, it transferred its worried stare to us briefly before slipping back into the sea.

"Wow, lucky seal," Ralph exclaimed. "Lucky us."

"Hurry and start up, Mary," I said. "Or we'll lose them." When we caught up, the orcas had reunited and the three were hunting, searching every nook along Mummy Island's shoreline. They ignored a sea otter and a small group of Steller sea lions, which bunched tighter, rose high out of the water, and huffed as the orcas passed. Hauled on numerous rocks and islets were their likely prey: harbor seals, the main food of West Coast transients in British Columbia.

As the whales penetrated further into Knight Island's protected waters, Mary kept her eyes on the chart, and Ralph kept watch for bottom from the bow. It took our three sets of eyes to avoid hitting a reef or losing the whales. They were unpredictable, traveling north for a while, then abruptly reversing direction. Each time we dropped the hydrophone, it was silent. Mary flipped through the catalog. "I think Ripple Fin is AT11," she said, pointing to a photo. "And that female looks like AT9, with the tiny nick." According to the catalog, the juvenile was her offspring, AT10. Finally, in water too reef-choked to follow, we lost the whales.

As we headed back toward camp, I studied the chart. Countless unnamed rocks and islets dotted the entrances of bays that cut deep into Knight Island's body: Drier Bay, Copper Bay, Johnson Bay, Lower Herring Bay. The archipelago continued for several miles, to Channel Rock, creating a navigational challenge but a refuge for seals, sea otters, and birds. On the chart, large swatches of water appeared impassible, shaded in blue, riddled with asterisks and crosses for rocks. I imagined that world from the orcas' perspective, an intimate geography they obviously knew as home. Sometimes their bodies probably scraped against rock, or brushed past eelgrass or kelp ribbons. We called that stretch of water the Labyrinth.

That night, we sat inside the tent drinking cocoa laced with peppermint schnapps, recounting our encounter to Olga. "Hey, speaking of seals, an older guy from Chenega Village stopped by while you guys were out," Olga said. "His name was Mike, said he grew up in Old Chenega. He said he'd heard you on the radio a lot, wondering where the whales are." Olga laughed. "He'd been hunting in Icy Bay. He said there were a lot of seals in there. He sees orcas hunting in the ice a lot. There was dead harbor seal in his skiff."

Later, after Olga took Elli to bed, Mary and I labeled film rolls and filled data sheets. In the catalog, I checked off the Chugach transients we'd seen so far: AT12, 14 and 22 with Craig. AT9, 10, 11, and 18 with Ralph. "I'll never remember those numbers," Mary said. "We should name them." We already had Ripple Fin. Sitting by the fire, we studied the photos, and tossed around ideas. We settled on Chenega, for AT9, the nicked female, and Mike for AT10, the young seal hunter. The second adult we named Iktua, after the seal haul out in Iktua Bay. Something had begun, a door cracking open.

Two days later, it opened further. As we readied *Whale 1* for travel one morning, two orcas, a male and a juvenile, surfaced off our stern, heading toward Squire Point. We decided to split up, Mary and Ralph taking the again-sluggish *Whale 1* to find humpbacks, and Olga, Elli, and I taking the Dynous to follow the transients.

We threw equipment into Olga's army-issue ammo cans—green, watertight, metal containers like giant lunch boxes. Olga bundled Elli into a life jacket. Once Olga was settled in the inflatable, I shoved it away from shore, and she yanked the pull cord until the engine sputtered to life. "Hang on!" Olga cried, squatting on her heels in front of the outboard, Elli peering out of the bib of her rain pants. Kneeling in the bow, I watched for rocks, the camera zipped inside my jacket. At Squire Point, the whales—Ripple Fin and Mike—paused, circling the outermost rock. As before, a harbor seal crouched there, out of their reach. Did adult males train juveniles to hunt, I wondered? How did they know the seal was up there? Both whales nosed in, but within minutes they abandoned the seal and dove. We debated what to do. They might continue across the passage or they might return to the rock. The tide was rising. It wouldn't be long before the seal was swimming. Five minutes passed. "Let's listen for blows," Olga said, killing the outboard. I stood up, wide-legged for balance, and scanned.

At first I thought it was Elli, muffled against Olga's chest. Something stirred the air, a moan. But it wasn't Elli. It was coming from below, crescendoing into a trumpeting wail that twined around our ankles. I looked back at Olga. "Oh, my God, they're calling," she said. "They're swimming right under us. Quick, get the recorder going." I scrambled for the ammo can while Olga, clutching Elli, threw over the hydrophone. Fumbling with the plugs, I cursed until I found the right arrangement and the static stopped and calls poured from the speaker. They echoed off the passage's underwater canyon walls.

This was not the chatter of residents, the catlike whines and yips and whistles. This was something other: long, descending cries, and high-intensity blasts ending in upsweeps, like questions. This was a voice at once strident and mournful, a strange hybrid instrument, part trumpet, part oboe, part elephant, part foghorn. And loud. In the calls' echoes, I imagined the passage mirroring back to the whales: *You are, you are.* Soon, in silences between vocalizations, we heard distant, answering calls. Mike and Ripple Fin burst through the passage's surface, charging west. We yanked up the hydrophone and raced to catch up. As we passed, I snapped ID photos, kneeling in the bow. Approaching Iktua Passage, Olga spotted more blows. Ahead of the pair, we dropped the hydrophone again: wild ululations, mingled with cacophony, the passage resonating like an amphitheatre. Without the hydrophone, we wouldn't know this. It would be like wearing earplugs and watching, from behind a half-drawn curtain, an orchestra flailing away on their instruments.

At last, in tandem with the male and juvenile, we reached the mouth of Iktua Passage. The pair entered a fray, eight more orcas slapping flukes, charging after one another, lunging in tight arcs. We dropped the hydrophone, turned on the recorder and listened to a sound poem, like something composed by Philip Glass: upswept squawks punctuated by silence, and bangs and cracks, like axe blows against planks, some we could attribute to fluke slaps, and some not. Now and then a syncopated blast of echolocation, like automatic gunfire. No more mournful wails; these calls were higher-pitched, abrupt, gashes of sound, some degenerating into raspberries or harsh, thudding pulse trains, no two calls the same. A looping improvisation of molten glass, spinning, shattering, all of it stunningly audible in the still water. It reached a climax and suddenly stopped. The whales gathered into a line, nine abreast, one adult male behind. They circled slowly for an hour in formation, silent. *Rest*, I wrote in the notebook, along with the time. At seven in the evening, Elli fussing, all of us hungry and chilled, we left the whales and headed across the Passage toward camp, talking all the way, retelling it, piecing it into a story.

A few nights later, behind on journal writing, I hiked the trail behind camp to a big hemlock tree on a moss-covered knoll. King Tree, Olga called it. Below, I could hear waves slapping the beach, voices murmuring. Grateful for solitude, I stretched out my legs, leaned against the tree's trunk, and opened my journal. Pausing, pen pressed to the page, I looked back on the last couple days, during which a graduate project had sprouted in my mind like one of those surprising bonsai hemlocks in the muskeg. It seemed, in retrospect, so obvious, transients repeatedly passing camp, as if saying, *Wake up, hello, we're here.* Olga studied humpbacks, Craig studied resident orcas, but no one studied the Chugach transients. Turning to the page in my lap, I considered the nature of guidance, perhaps reliably present to an attentive mind. The Sound cultivated awareness. When I let go of my dramas, nature revealed perpetually opened doors. Over the course of weeks, the transients had swum repeatedly by, and now I'd follow.

And then the Chugach transients vanished. Eleven days passed without them. In the meantime, Olga and Ralph left, taking with them their seasoned approach to every day as an adventure, limping outboards or not, whales or not. Olga had chided me to relax: "Remember, you're volunteers." After they left, camp echoed with their voices, Elli's peals of laughter in the Johnny Jump Up, pots and pans clattering, tent zippers unzipping, campfires crackling, a happy chaos greeting each morning as we prepared to set out on the boats.

Gradually, Mary and I adjusted to working one-on-one again, seeking our own adventures: swimming in ponds, showering under waterfalls, beach-combing. Olga had left her kayak. Evenings, we took turns, one of us paddling, one of us cooking supper. The engines, a continuous vexation, provided a subplot to our whale research story. When all else failed, we banged on the outboards with hammers, alternatively swore at and pleaded with them. Once we even smudged them with a smoking bundle of sage. Mary called us "whale girls." As we lived deeper into July, the fair weather gave way to longer rainy spells, punctuated by a day or two of sun, just enough time to dry ourselves out. We waited for the Chugach transients to return.

7

Memorize These Things

With our small boat, we kept to the shelter of Knight Island Passage, but after ten days without seeing orcas, we decided to venture farther. In its southwestern part, around Whale Camp, Prince William Sound constricts into a network of passages, the remnants of Pleistocene ice rivers, snaking between islands and linking the Sound to the Gulf of Alaska. As you travel north up Knight Island Passage, the geography opens to a deep, oval basin rimmed by mountains clad in glaciers, ice sheets, and perpetual snow—remnants of the forces that shaped the Sound. In the north, a few large islands—Culross, Perry, Lone, Naked, Seal and Smith—interrupt the long fetch from Hinchinbrook Entrance, but in storms, the water is treacherous for small boats. Out in the open, without landmarks, orca blows are hard to spot.

Nevertheless, on a calm, drizzly July day, we packed for travel: sleeping bags, extra food, rain gear, water, a thermos of hot tea. In the notebook, I wrote, portentously, *0900, set out for the North.*

Motoring slowly so as not to miss blows, we hugged the Labyrinth's periphery, Mary driving, me sitting on the cabin roof, scanning. Pod after pod of Dall's porpoises interrupted their feeding to ride our bow before darting away. Lying on my belly, I leaned out, my hand stretched, watching the stout black-and-white bodies crisscrossing below. Occasionally, when a porpoise tilted to its side, I glimpsed an ancient-looking eye.

Off Herring Bay, I spotted splashes, then black fins knifing and sinking back down. Orcas. They appeared to be chasing something. As we neared, a Dall's porpoise charged by our bow and vanished. The orcas ignored it. They'd isolated and stunned its offspring, a gray-skinned, first-year calf. The calf circled, a juvenile orca swimming close behind it, an adult male milling a few yards away. We studied the catalog. The male wasn't Ripple Fin. The broad, triangular dorsal and rake marks on the saddle matched those of AT14, the male from our first encounter. We'd named him Eccles.

The porpoise gasped and dove. The young orca twisted sideways, then upside-down, and, like a gymnast executing a backbend, it lunged chin first and belly up out of the water, arcing back into the porpoise's wake. The water rippled closed behind them. A few minutes later, the young orca resurfaced and swam under our bow with its mouth agape, showing us its teeth. I didn't know at the time to look at the other side of its mouth, from which, most likely, flesh protruded. Out of nowhere, three more orcas appeared, and the five dove repeatedly in the same spot. On the hydrophone, calls began, wavering whistles, and bangs, accompanied on the surface by fluke slaps and breaches. The juvenile broke the surface in a headstand, its whole torso above water, fluke waving. The calls intensified, then quieted, then intensified again. The whales converged, then spread apart. From the north, four more approached, and then all was fortissimo: cymbal taps, whistles, shrieks, and nine whales launching themselves skyward. In the notebook, I frantically tried to tally everything, matching behaviors to a segment of cassette:

1445   Tape 2 Side A
    0–95, rolls, tail slaps, juveniles active
    95 headstand
    114 juvenile breaches
    148 quieter
    160–70 circling more, less active
    190 tail slaps
    206 bang

Two hours into the fracas, some of the orcas approached *Whale 1*, twirling beneath us, chunks of flesh in their mouths. Too much meat to be from one small calf, I thought. Probably the distant whales had killed another porpoise, and brought it to share. For the next hour, they fed. Gulls appeared, swooping and diving, picking scraps from the water, squabbling. Like a gyre of energy in an otherwise calm sea, the whales and birds drifted northeast. When we finally left, after seven hours, we'd filled an entire 180-minute cassette plus half of another with calls. We'd shot two rolls of film.

Still wired, Mary and I studied the chart. Eager to anchor someplace new, we decided on Disc Island Cove, its entrance a barely navigable channel. The boat in neutral, I sat on the bow watching for rocks. I could almost reach out and touch the basalt pillows along shore, gnomish lobes of rock formed by rapidly cooled magma oozing, as our geology guidebook put it, "like toothpaste," on the sea floor millions of years ago.

We dropped anchor in the lagoon, paid out scope, as Mary instructed, seven feet of line to every foot of depth. Then we gathered up and stashed the equipment. While Mary inflated *Puff,* our tiny raft, I filled out data sheets. With our cooking supplies, we paddled to shore and made supper on the beach, listening to Disc Island come awake with hermit thrush song as dusk fell. Finally, mosquitoes drove us back to *Whale 1,* where we fell asleep hard to the turning of the boat in the tide.

Remember these things, I want to whisper to that younger me, asleep on *Whale 1. Remember the entrance to Disc Island that first time, the darkness of the basalt, which will be so much darker next year. Remember the smell of spruce needles, the salt tang of kelp beds at the back of your throat, the quiet in the cove, not even a lap of water against the hull. Remember the transients, jubilant after a kill, jubilant to be together. Remember the juveniles. Remember the water, incredibly clear. Remember your feet in your sleeping bag touching Mary's feet in her sleeping bag, both pairs jammed together in the V of the bow. Remember water roiling in the pot over the campfire, the smell of noodles and smoke, the warmth down your throat and in your belly, the cold stones underneath, the thrush songs from deep in the island. The pigeon guillemot pair drifting by. The sizzling of low tide. Don't be distracted,* I want to whisper, *by questions about RJ, your parents, or the future. Stay right where you are. This is your childhood in the Sound. Memorize everything as it is now. Stare hard at the water, which will darken, and die.*

8

The Survival Value
of Exuberance

Dear Dad, I wrote. *It's stormy today, rainy, windy, foggy, so Mary and I are holed up in our "home." You can't imagine the luxuries one can have living on a remote island, with no electricity, running water or even solid walls.* I described our showers, gasping under waterfalls in Mummy Bay, where we'd tie *Whale 1* to a steep ledge and stand naked under the frigid cascade. I was sure my father and mother, Latvian immigrants, a college librarian and a phlebotomist, couldn't imagine, much less understand, the life I'd chosen, but I never stopped trying to convey it.

By afternoon, the buckets at the corners of the wall tent overflowing, we heated a kettle of rainwater on the woodstove for bathing. But first I asked Mary to cut off my waist-length hair. All we had was a Swiss army knife. "Are you sure about this?" Mary asked.

"I'm sure. It's a pain in the ass to have long hair out here," I said, but it went deeper. I wanted visible change.

When the water was hot, we filled a solar shower bag and hung it from a branch in the alders behind camp. Then we took turns showering in the rain. After washing my hair, I sat beside the woodstove, finger-combing it dry, amazed at its sudden lightness.

Toward evening, the wind died. Mary rowed out to *Whale 1* to put out a radio call for sightings. To her surprise, Ralph answered from his handheld radio. He and his girlfriend were camped in Iktua Passage, having paddled from Whittier in the past week. They'd lost a paddle and were low on food. Ralph asked if we'd bring over a spare and some supplies from the stash he'd left at camp. And, Ralph said, they'd spotted orcas heading our way. They'd meet us in their kayaks for the drop-off, so we wouldn't lose time.

When we left the mooring, it was 8:30 p.m. With the cloud cover, light for photography was fading. Sitting on the bow, my skin twanged, cleansed like everything around us. The Sound scrubbed by the storm, the passage gleamed. Fog clung to the forests in strips. I swear I could feel the barometer rising. All day, the low pressure had pressed against my skull, inducing lethargy. Now everything felt spacious. It amazes me even today, how a storm engulfs the Sound, heaps up waves, and just as rapidly the water lies down, like an angry ruff smoothed flat by a few hand strokes. After a day in a twelve-foot-square tent, we relished wind on our necks, wrists, and hands as we crossed the passage.

Near Iktua Point, two red kayaks drifted amid seven cavorting orcas. With barely any light left for photography, we headed for the whales. If residents were acrobats, socializing Chugach transients were contortionists. They leapt higher, executing bending, twisting maneuvers, the most dramatic being a backward "handspring," belly arching toward the sky as a whale plummeted snout-first back into the sea. According to animal behavior theories, to expend energy on play means it contributes to survival—for instance, through training and conditioning juveniles to be hunters, or through reinforcement of social bonds. Was there survival value to exuberance, to the celebration of feeding, to pure joy? Any explanation I assigned to their behavior, whether scientific or emotional, was a product of my mind, subject to its limited understanding of causes and effects. All I saw were effects. There were causes foreign to my way of knowing. To fully understand, I'd need to enter an orca's mind. As I scanned the water churned by their bodies, I spotted a pair of males on the periphery. Eccles and another male surfaced quietly near the shore of Fleming Island.

In near darkness, we left them. Early the next morning, we raced back to the same spot and dropped the hydrophone, but, as quickly and completely as the storm had dissipated, they were gone.

9

Boys in Blueberry Season

Late July and August is blueberry season on the coast. Blueberry muffins, jam, cobbler, crisp. Blueberry pie. Blueberry-stained hands. Eating our blue-studded pancakes early one morning, we heard blows. An orca male surfaced off Whale Camp beach. Like ptarmigans spooked from the snow, we erupted from camp chairs, gathered breakfast dishes, pulled pants and sweaters over long johns, loaded the Dynous with gear. By the time we caught up to the male, he was entering Squire Cove. I recognized the squat, broad fin, almost equilateral. When he arched high before a deep dive, I saw the dark splotch in the center of his saddle patch. It was AT1, the first Chugach transient Craig had ever photographed. At twenty, he was physically and sexually mature. Mary and I named him Eyak.

He milled briefly at the cove's entrance, then dove, next surfacing in the Labyrinth, so close to an island that he appeared to be scraping its side with his dorsal. For an hour, he hunted his way north. When we dropped the hydrophone, he was silent, and we soon lost him in the Labyrinth. At the time we thought it odd, an orca traveling alone; there must be others. But his appearance and disappearance didn't usher in a bout of transient encounters. It ushered in another, less silent, season.

The season of blueberries is also the season of salmon. That year, the commercial seine fleet, including *Lucky Star*, arrived in the study area along with the resident orcas: whale chatter, whistles, and echolocation clicks competing with a thrum of boat engines and hydraulics. Using sonar, the residents plucked silver salmon from massive schools of hatchery-raised pinks. On the hydrophone, we listened to what sounded like a typing pool. Sometimes fifty or more residents socialized and foraged in the passage. Charged with photographing all of the whales, not just transients, Mary and I had our hands full.

One morning, not finding residents, we headed north. Along the Labyrinth, a primeval stillness prevailed, a world apart from the floating industrial zone that had taken up residence in the lower passage. Near Channel Rock, a harbor seal haul-out, we found five Chugach transients. They angled away offshore, into a growing wind chop, disappearing for several minutes at a time, following no discernable compass heading. I managed to photograph two, the males Aligo and Holgate, before we lost them. One moment we were working, taking notes, the dorsal fins in our sight, and the next moment we bobbed alone in the waves.

Two days later, Aligo and Holgate reappeared with a third male, Moon, and in a different mood. I remembered Olga's description of a trio of odd transient males she'd seen over the years. "The Boy's Club," she'd called them. Belly up, Aligo rocked lackadaisically, slapping his paddle-shaped fore flippers against the water's surface. Moon and Holgate lifted their flukes high, lowered them slowly, swishing the water as though stirring paint. Their bodies brushed together. From the hydrophone speaker drifted crass, distorted calls, guttural groans and squeals. For several breaths, they'd grow quiet and travel, but then the calls would resume and they'd stop again to roll upside-down and laze. We slowed too. For once, we could truly see them, the glistening of their skin, the patches of black pigment on their white bellies, the contrast stark, like calligrapher's ink on snow-white paper.

"Lazy whales," Mary sang as the trio meandered up the passage, steadily north, all the way to Channel Rock. A fish-buying tender chugged south past them. The whales seemed unperturbed. The only sign of disturbance was one male rising headfirst to eye the bright, above-water world. What did that world look like to him? I knew his vision was acute. Was the tender, and our boat for that matter, an annoyance, an intrusion, or a presence long ago accepted as part of the environment? The only world he'd known included engine noise. A whale of silence, he'd been born into the twentieth-century underwater din. Yet, that day, I didn't feel foreign or apart from him.

As the trio dove, they raised their flukes into the air like humpbacks do. All three had the down-curved fluke tips of mature males. We shadowed them, stopping often, dropping the hydrophone. As the recorder inscribed calls onto a strip of tape, I sat on the bow, taking notes. Mary, leaning on the dash, holding a stopwatch, called out dive times. We'd stripped down to tank tops, rolled up the cuffs of our jeans. I dangled my bare toes in the water. Mary and I passed a water bottle back and forth. There was something tender in the males' interaction, no indication of competition or dominance. Their play was reciprocal, relaxed. I hadn't imagined transients as relaxed animals. I'd imagined them as dogged, secretive predators, aloof, continually on the hunt. I'd imagined so little of what they were. Far more than eating machines, they were, like us, creatures of moods and personalities. Like wolves and lions, like humans, they could be as gentle and playful as they could be fierce.

As the cassette recorded part of their call repertoire, my pencil recorded part of their behavioral repertoire. But the word "repertoire," with its implication of a limited set of repeated states, seems inadequate. Perhaps the word reflects more the limits of the imagination. The life story of Chugach transients was beginning to seem more a labyrinth. They were part of a complex society. Unlike many species, females live decades after reproductive senescence. The old females become matriarchs, the locus around which daily life revolves. Clearly, the adult males had a family role to play as well, standing by as juveniles practiced hunting. But they also cultivated male–male bonds, perhaps lifelong. Their ties to one another were another kind of food, as essential, it seemed, as seal fat.

We tracked the trio for two hours as they gradually quieted, their tandem surfacing followed by longer and longer dives. Drawing inward, they reverted to their transient personae, inscrutable and silent.

10

No Passage Out

By August, my thoughts turned to endings, to wondering what it would be like to return to civilization. In our final Chugach transient encounter, on August 29, we followed Chenega's group from Point of Rocks to Squire Island, just a few miles. Once, they passed close to our boat. It was the only goodbye we'd get. Without witnesses, they continued their hunts, their social gatherings, their travels. We were the transient ones. Orcas—even so-called transients—don't migrate. The names "transient" and "resident" reflect temporary states: the summer residence of fish eaters in salmon-rich waters, the unpredictable comings and goings of mammal eaters. Because of our transience, because of darkness and storms, winter was a great unknown, like the Gulf of Alaska. It was wildness, a realm I edged up to and left that fall with reluctance.

7 SEPTEMBER 1988
*On Lucky Star with Craig, RJ and Ralph, anchored near Cape
Elrington, getting ready to leave the Sound, but a storm delays our
departure. I can't fathom that I've left Whale Camp. It goes on,
without us. We built a banya on the beach last night out of logs
and tarps. We heated stones in a fire and threw them inside, then
poured on water to generate steam. After crouching inside the
humid dome, I ran into the ocean to cool off, then stood naked on
a log watching the passage through steam rising off my skin.*

I don't want to leave my twenty-five-year-old self, standing naked on that log. I don't want to write the next chapter. I've drawn it out, that first summer, grown a forest around it, sketched in waves and current lines, added dabs of color. I dig in my heels. I never want to leave the Sound, but especially not now. Because, unlike the younger me, I know what happens next. I won't be able to stop it. No matter what, the oil will pour from the ship's breached holds. The oil will spread. It will coat rocks and barnacles and kelp and otters and harbor seals and birds. It will kill orcas. It will change everything I know, everything I love.

That younger me didn't foresee that she'd never truly leave the Sound again. It was imbedded within her, as geography, as biology, as spirit, as names. Aguliak Island, New Year Island, Mummy Bay, Clam Island. Chenega, Iktua, Eyak. She'd carry dorsal fin shapes, and the shapes of unnamed islands. She'd carry routes penetrating Knight Island, where the passage out wasn't always apparent. Following transients in the Labyrinth, she'd followed a vein to the heart of the place.

Leaving the Sound, I didn't recognize the connections. I didn't recognize myself in my study animals. The solitude and silence of the Chugach transients—and the Sound—mirrored something inside me I didn't yet own. That knowledge would come much later.

II

Vegans and Carnivores

That fall, in preparation for grad school, I flew to Oregon to visit RJ and earn money cooking at a vegetarian restaurant. In my off time, I read orca literature, papers Craig sent me, others I tracked down at the Oregon State University library. Almost all of what was known of orcas, besides stomach content data, came from British Columbia and Washington State, from the research of Mike Bigg, Graeme Ellis, John Ford, and Ken Balcomb. Now they were mentors to what Craig called a "crop" of students like me. Three of those mentees, Robin Baird and Pam Stacey in southern B.C., and Alexandra Morton in northern B.C., studied transients. Robin and Pam had already published some of their observations in magazines like *Whalewatcher* and *Cetus.* They described kills of harbor seals near haul-outs, the whales cooperating to hunt and share food. Occasionally, they watched transients bash a seabird around. Much of what they saw matched my observations. Nearshore foraging, they wrote, occurred when transients "closely follow the contours of the shoreline," venturing "through narrow passages between reefs and islands," just as I'd observed in the Labyrinth. Offshore foraging involved "frequent direction changes" in open water. Robin and Pam had seen a porpoise killed as a result. West Coast transients also killed Steller and California sea lions. The transients Robin and Pam had observed—and the groups observed by Alexandra Morton—were silent and stealthy while hunting, noisy only after kills.

I studied the table of known transient food in *Orca: The Whale Called*

Killer, baffled at the diversity: Bearded seal. Crabeater seal. Blue whale. Leopard seal. Northern elephant seal. Bowhead whale. Northern fur seal. Ringed seal. Steller sea lion. Walrus. Weddell seal. Leatherback turtle. Emperor penguin. And more. Basically, every available species. I searched out obscure references from Russia and Japan, which suggested that some orca populations specialized seasonally on locally abundant prey—for instance, fur seals off Kamchatka in summer.

I turned next to the literature of acoustics. In John Ford's papers about resident orca vocalizations in B.C., I encountered a whole new language: *Stereotyped pulsed calls. Whistles. Echolocation. Variable calls. Aberrant calls. Discrete calls. Pulse repetition rates. Frequency modulations. Call components. Hertz. Decibels. Side-band intervals.* Ford described orcas' three basic call types: pulsed calls, whistles, and echolocation clicks. Pulsed calls are wails, shrieks, screams, squeals, catlike whines, sounds I could imitate with my own voice by plugging my nose and humming. They appear on a sonogram—a graph of frequency versus time—as a series of evenly spaced horizontal bands representing the "pulses" or harmonics making up the call. Our own voices, talking or singing, would appear on a sonogram in that same way. Some pulsed calls are discrete, or stereotyped, repeated over and over by all members of a pod. They make up the pod's dialect. Other pulsed calls are called "aberrant," as when the whales turn their stereotyped calls into playthings, warping familiar calls into barely recognizable variants. Variable calls are pulsed, and, as far as we can tell, invented on the spot—random, one-time-only utterances— which is to say, we don't know much about them. Like variable calls, whistles, which are single-frequency tones, without harmonics, appear random, improvisational. Echolocation clicks are entirely different. On a sonogram, they're represented by vertical—not horizontal—bands, each a single pulse of high-frequency, broad-band sound projected through the oil-filled melon in the whale's forehead, traveling out into the sea ahead of the whale, bouncing off a target, returning its echo to the whale's mind via fat channels in its lower jaw. That echo tells the whale what's farther than its eye can see: king salmon or pink; harbor seal or rock; boat hull or island.

I wrote my notes on index cards. In a composition book, I wrote my questions. Every day, I biked to work, and spent my hours chopping vegetables, grinding sesame seeds, clarifying butter, marinating tofu, dicing garlic, squeezing oranges. Now a vegan, with my fellow prep cooks, wait-ers, bussers, and chefs, I smoked pot and drank carrot juice behind the restaurant during breaks. At night, I melted soy cheese on my tortillas, cooked up pots of beans for protein. I volunteered at the food co-op. But in the OSU library, I prepared my mind to study carnivores.

Kaj's group swims beside the grounded and leaking *Exxon Valdez* on the day after the disaster, on Bligh Reef. (Rosemary Kaul / Los Angeles Times)

PART 2

Season of Dead Water

12

Refugia

In November, I moved to Fairbanks to start graduate school. "You're gonna eat meat up there, you watch," Craig predicted. "I used to be a granola cruncher too, in Santa Cruz, but after my first winter of forty below, I started eating moose. Peanut butter doesn't cut it in the far north. Just ask the Athabascans."

I dismissed him. But one thing was true, in Interior Alaska, I entered another kind of wilderness, populated by people who ate a lot of wild game. Like most biology graduate students at the University of Alaska Fairbanks, I lived in a one-room log cabin without plumbing and skied or biked two miles to the university. As was my habit, I wrote in a journal to pin experience to paper, so I could scrutinize it later, to make sense of my new life. There I described each five-hour-long January day, how the mercury on my porch thermometer crept downward until it bottomed out at record lows: forty, fifty, then sixty below zero. How my stove stopped working on the coldest days; the propane gelled in the copper pipe. How a friend came over one night with a torch to thaw out my frozen sink drain. Some nights, I thought the star-choked sky would split me in two. Other nights a sickly greenish aurora heaved above me as I biked home by headlamp beam. Then in late February the sun flooded back and the temperature climbed to zero, ten, twenty above. I marked the changes by evolving ski wax color: special green, green, extra green, blue.

But on Good Friday, March 24, 1989, the day everything changed in the Sound, in my work, in my life, I didn't write one word in my journal.

On March 26, I mentioned the oil spill only briefly. *Today I'll attend a meeting about what IMS, the University of Alaska's Institute of Marine Science, will do to help out in the Sound.* My writing evaporated into silence. It would take twenty years to unearth that buried narrative.

In Fairbanks, four hundred miles from the Sound, the spill remained abstract in those first days. A high pressure system held time and the snow-blanketed Alaskan Interior in suspension, the clear sky stretched taut as a seal skin tacked up to cure. For two days after the supertanker *Exxon Valdez* ran aground and spewed millions of gallons of crude oil into the Sound, the archipelago throbbed under that same dazzling late-winter sun. On those windless days, the oil spread in a slow-moving acre from the point of rupture, as though uncertain. Time was an open window, waiting. Something would be done, I thought, the oil boomed off, sucked up, burned. But little was done, and the window slammed shut.

Sixteen hours before the tanker had struck Bligh Reef, Cordova fisherwoman and activist Riki Ott had testified to the Mayor's Oil Action Committee in Valdez, where the laden *Exxon Valdez* prepared to leave the pipeline terminal. "Fishermen feel that we are playing a game of Russian roulette," she'd said, arguing for greater industry oversight and disaster preparation. "When, not if 'The Big One' does occur—" Her words, like the spill's timing—exactly twenty-five years after the Good Friday earthquake that had devastated the Sound—were prophetic. As the powers that be—the pipeline service company Alyeska, Exxon, the state, the feds, the Coast Guard—argued about what to do—as they scrambled to find enough boats, skimmers, and booms from around the planet to suck up and store the oil; as they argued over using chemical dispersants to break apart and sink the crude, or fire to burn it; as they ignored warnings of fishermen, who spread maps out to show them how the oil would travel when the wind started blowing, as it soon would; as they dug booms from under ten-foot-high snow drifts in Valdez—a storm bore down on the Sound.

Meanwhile, Interior Alaska remained clear and still, adding to my sense of disconnection. On the evening of March 27, as I sat down in a crowded auditorium on the university campus, fellow grad student Matt Hare beside me for support, sixty-knot winds were churning millions of gallons of crude into a toxic lather called mousse, spreading it beyond any hope of containment. Wind and currents drove it south and west, just as fishermen had predicted, eventually, over the course of months, besmirching thirty-two hundred miles of shoreline, from the northern Sound to the Alaska Peninsula.

Before IMS scientists took to the stage, the lights dimmed, and images of the Sound were projected onto a screen, photographs taken by reporters and biologists of oiled beaches, oiled corpses of murres, pigeon guillemots, sea otters, and eagles flicking by in a numbing progression. I strove to recognize places in the photos, hoping I wouldn't. But then I did. Blue sky, pale blue water snaked with shadows, the Pleiades, their tide-exposed sides tarred, gleaming black in the sunshine. And then. The massive black hulk of the tanker's bow, its name painted white in block letters on the side. Nothing could be darker than that hull, I thought. But then I saw that something was darker. Black against black, four dorsal fins, four orcas, two males and two smaller ones, swam a few hundred yards off the bow. An *L.A. Times* photographer had captured the image the day after the tanker had run aground. The photograph jarred me from numbness. Were they transients?

My throat tight, I listened as the IMS scientists took to the mike, waiting to hear what they'd do to "help out in the Sound." I'd approached some of them the previous fall, hoping to inspire more research with my reports of abundant marine life and few scientists. Logging and development threatened what was in essence a wilderness, I'd argued. No funding, they'd said. Now millions of dollars were poised over the scientists' heads: federal money for damage assessment, in preparation for litigation against Exxon; Exxon money for counter-assessment, to fight the litigation. Most studies would commence without baseline data. Most damage would be reported as body counts. I remember nothing of the proposals advanced that night. I remember only one speaker, one of my professors, calling the oil spill a "great opportunity, a great experiment." Whatever bedrock of logic underlay his words was lost on me. A few years before her death, the last full-blooded Eyak, Marie Smith Jones, of Cordova, spoke to a *New Yorker* reporter about the impending extinction of her language. When the reporter asked how she felt about being the last speaker of Eyak, Chief Marie replied, "How would you feel if your baby died? If someone asked you, 'What was it like to see it lying in the cradle?'" *Great opportunity. Great experiment.* Like Marie, I tried to wrap my mind around an alien viewpoint. When I told Craig about the orcas in the slide presentation, he said the photo had been published on the front page of the *Anchorage Daily News*. He'd asked the photographer for a copy of the negative, so Graeme could examine it under his scope. Even in the blown-up newspaper version Craig could tell they were transients, from their fin-shapes. On the trailing edge of one fin, he could make out a large notch. It was probably AT7, the Chugach transient we called Kaj. Craig had more disturbing news. When word of the spill had reached him, he'd been preparing *Lucky Star* for the spring herring fishery. After the storm broke, knowing the herring season was doomed, he, Olga, and Elli headed into the Sound. Olga was pregnant.

First, they'd joined a group of volunteer fishermen desperately trying to boom off the Port San Juan hatchery and Chenega Village before oil reached the southwestern Sound. Hearing reports of orcas off Point Helen, on March 31, eight days after the tanker grounding, they'd motored to Knight Island Passage. They'd found AB, AI, and AJ pods—over forty whales—resting north of Point Helen, five miles south of the advancing oil. As they'd photographed and checked off whales in the catalog, they'd realized that several AB pod members were missing. Two juveniles traveled without their mothers. On the data sheet Craig had summed up the encounter:

31 MARCH 1989
Whales reported in this area for previous couple days perhaps enjoying this oil-free environment. 0810 animals move slowly most of the day, resting. Some echolocation and vocalizations in morning but then quiet. Begin heading up Knight Island Passage 1500, traveling. 1530 head through heavy sheen of oil 1 mi. N. of Gage Island. Rick Rosenthal observes whales swimming through oil from airplane.

As Craig and Olga had followed the whales north into the oil, past the Pleiades, past Whale Camp, *Lucky Star*'s hull had blackened along the waterline. Choking on fumes and worried about Elli and the baby Olga was carrying, they'd turned back toward the hatchery. Soon after, with a wildlife filmmaker, Craig had traveled to Herring Bay, at the Labyrinth's northern end. Entering the bay, he'd gagged on hydrocarbon fumes. In a cove at the bay's head, dead animals had floated in thick windrows, so coated they'd been unrecognizable. A few days later, his friend Rick Steiner and sea otter biologist Chuck Monet, from a small plane, had photographed orcas swimming through heavy slicks. They'd sent Craig an aerial photograph of fluke prints marking the whales' paths on the sea surface. Each dark splotch in the sheen represented a whale's inhalation of volatilized hydrocarbons.

Craig urged me to hurry to Homer to prepare for the field season. We'd be doing damage assessment, and I could continue to collect data on Chugach transients. Three field camps would be set up around the Sound. Two young biologists from San Juan Island would work from a camp on Point Nowell, at the north end of Knight Island Passage. A couple from British Columbia, former lighthouse keepers, would monitor Hinchinbrook Entrance, in the eastern Sound. As before, I'd work out of Whale Camp, first with my friend Matt, then with Mary.

"Plan to be at Whale Camp for four months," Craig said. "Prepare yourself. It's awful out there. It's going to be a different kind of summer."

On May 23, Matt and I trailered *Whale 1* behind Craig's battered Ford pickup 150 miles north to the depot in Portage, where we drove it onto the train. In a half hour, when we emerged from the second tunnel, we'd be in the Sound.

It was a moment I loved. Between the tunnels, the train emerged in a wind-swept valley of willow, alder, and cottonwood. Avalanches left fan-shaped trails down the mountainsides, ending in twenty-foot-high snow cliffs messy with trees swept up during the descent. Often moose grazed near the tracks. Nothing of the maritime was apparent. Then the windows went black. Twenty minutes later, they brightened, and the head of Passage Canal flashed into view through rain-lashed windows. I told Matt about seeing the two males from the train in 1987. Now I speculated as to who they might have been, perhaps Holgate and Aligo, or Eyak and Eccles.

Whittier harbor, normally quiet in May, bustled, as if the military that had built the outpost had been resurrected. Like cancer and sports, Exxon's spill response was spun in military language: war, battle, assault, battalion. Packed with boats and people, everything happening in Whittier was connected in some way to the spill. Near the narrow harbor entrance, the harbormaster had set up a cleaning station to mop oil from hulls of boats returning from the spill zone, twenty miles south. With *Whale 1* launched, tanks filled with gas, we hightailed it out of there.

On the fifty-mile journey to Whale Camp, I jotted sightings of marine mammals: one sea otter feeding in Perry Passage; one resting in Culross Passage; one harbor seal off Foul Bay. *Saw booms in Culross Passage,* I wrote in the log. Momentarily, there on a rocky shoreline, I mistook black lichen for oil.

Then we entered the spill zone. No more sea otters or harbor seals, just two small groups of Dall's porpoises in Knight Island Passage. I was terrified of two things: the presence of oil and the absence of life. Of the creatures I'd encountered the previous summer—seals, otters, sea lions, porpoises, whales, eagles, seabirds, shorebirds, ducks—how many were dead or sick? What about the Chugach transients? So enigmatic, appearing and vanishing like ghosts. Could the oil wipe them out? Drive them away from places they'd hunted for generations? Could oil alter their behavior? In late September, what story would my data tell? What story waited to be lived out?

We arrived at Whale Camp in the afternoon. The mooring buoy still bobbed off the beach. Matt and I grabbed the oil-smeared ball with the boat hook and stripped the rope of a winter's growth of kelp, then yanked on it, testing to see if it would hold. We wiped oil off the buoy and our hands with a sorbent pad, a square, white, polypropylene rag used to mop up spills. Satisfied with the mooring, we idled *Whale 1* to shore to unload. The boat lay low in the water, packed with the wall tent, a month's worth of food, personal gear, plastic gas cans. Anxiously, I scanned the beach as Matt nudged the bow ashore. Cackling erupted at the far headland, oystercatchers scolding us. When I jumped down with the bow line, I breathed a scorched, noxious scent of petroleum. The stones oil-spattered, tar balls and clumps of oily eelgrass and kelp washed against the pebbles. It could be so much worse: on some beaches, the oil was ankle-deep. Three wandering tattlers scurried along the water's edge. A part of me welcomed them, and another wanted to scare them away.

I'd regaled Matt with stories of Whale Camp, of wildlife we'd watched from the tent porch while we ate pancakes, the birds and mammals that had, in our isolation, come to seem like neighbors. Matt, a rationalist, had humored me, sure I was exaggerating. He'd rolled his eyes at the names I'd given the voles. Would the seals, sea lions, river and sea otters still feel safe in the bight off camp? I recalled an op-ed cut out of a newspaper taped to Craig and Olga's refrigerator, written by Chief Walter Meganack, of Port Graham, an Alutiiq village in the spill zone. "The excitement of the season had just begun," Meganack wrote of the weeks preceding, "and then, we heard the news, oil in the water, lots of oil killing lots of water. It is too shocking to understand. Never in the millennium of our tradition have we thought it possible for the water to die, but it is true." His words spoke equally to the plight of the tattlers and oystercatchers on Whale Camp beach. Nothing in their evolutionary history prepared them for the oil stuck to their feathers and feet, for the poison they breathed and ate.

"Look, Matt," I said, pointing out two white spots against the spruce and hemlock forest above the headland. It was the eagle pair. They'd survived. Though I knew they weren't safe from the oil on the beach or in the water, I let relief wash through me. I turned back to the boat, positioning it sideways to the beach, and Matt began handing out gear and boxes.

The tent platform stood stark among flattened mounds of dead rye-grass from which new green shoots poked. Barely leafing out, the alders smelled resinous, the buds sticky, leaving their beeswax scent on my fingers. The terrestrial world, just a dozen yards from the oiled shoreline, appeared pristine, though I knew it wasn't. Eagles and river otters eating contaminated fish, defecating in the woods, could bring poison inland. I walked to the cache, where we'd stored supplies and a few full gas jugs the previous fall. Someone had rummaged through it. The gas was gone.

At six the next morning, I nudged Matt. "Listen," I whispered. A sea otter pup squealed from the bight. "It's our sea otter's new baby," I said, smiling, glancing over to gauge his reaction. He groaned and turned over on his side. I closed my eyes. A breeze rattled the alder branches and flapped the tent fabric. Waves sloshed against the beach. The otter pup cried. I could almost believe it hadn't happened, that the Sound was safe, intact, as it had always been. I crawled out of my sleeping bag, stretched, and peered through the flaps. Overhead, broken clouds crept past, opening and closing patches of sky. *Whale 1* bobbed in a westerly chop. Nearby, the otter pup lay on its mother's stomach, quieted. Behind me, Matt lit the Coleman stove to start water for coffee.

After breakfast on the porch, sitting on stumps in our long johns, we spent the morning finishing camp chores, then set out in *Whale 1* to look for whales, but first to find a fuel tender. Off Fleming Island we spotted a barge I didn't recognize, *California Star*. The crew said they worked for VECO, the primary clean-up contractor to Exxon. They'd come down the passage from the north earlier that morning. I'd expected villainous Exxon employees, but these were ordinary young Cordova men, hired to service the clean-up operations with fuel. The response was still gearing up; they were bored. They chatted with us and filled our tanks, refusing payment. When we asked about whale sightings, they said they'd spotted an orca pod early that morning, off Chenega Island, heading north. We thanked them and sped off, finding, a few miles up the passage, not Chugach transients, but AK pod, residents.

The pod traveled slowly south in two subgroups. Matt took the wheel and I sat on the bow, explaining how to approach the whales' left sides. The first group, surfacing slowly, bodies touching, shied away as we neared, arched and dove deep. We dropped the hydrophone. Their silence told us they were resting, so we waited. After two and a half hours, the whales awoke. Picking up speed, the groups dispersed, the silence on the hydrophone replaced by calls and clicks. A matriline approached us, and we took it as permission to begin our work. This time the whales allowed us near. As I shot pictures, then scrutinized the catalog, confirming IDs though binoculars, Matt drew a check beside each photo and jotted notes. To my relief, all the AKs were there: no new calves, but no deaths.

Four hours and over ten miles later, we turned back toward camp, entering the Labyrinth off Drier Bay, hoping we'd find the Chugach transients in their familiar haunt. But I also wanted to take Matt to a place I'd described the winter before. Praying it would be oil-free, I navigated *Whale 1* through a tight entrance slot into Cascade Cove, a drowned glacial cirque. A raft of sea otter mothers and pups rested in water reflecting mountains that appeared to arise from below. A few seals dozed on a rock. Waterfalls snaked down cliffs from snowfields high above. We drifted, listening to snowmelt streaming off peaks, the otters' plashing. I pointed to the spot where Mary and I had taken waterfall showers. The air smelled ionized, clean. The place felt ancient. During the Pleistocene glaciation, some animals and plants had survived ice advances in refugia, "islands" of earth or water surrounded by blue-white wilderness. That evening, Cascade Cove was a refugium, for the animals, for us.

Back at camp, near midnight, I looked up from transcribing notes and rested my eyes on the scene outside the tent. I never tired of that view: Point of Rocks casting shadows on the water, the Pleiades light blinking. Like a visual mantra, I could lose myself in it. The wind had died, leaving the water silvery. Just off the moored *Whale 1*, a head appeared. "Matt," I said, pointing to the water. He looked up from the book he was reading. "It's my buddy, the harbor seal."

He followed the point of my finger, then smiled. "Okay, I'm beginning to believe you about his place," he said.

The next day, we headed south. "That's Point Helen," I said, pointing to the island's southern tip knuckling into Montague Strait. "That's the place I told you about, where I'd love to have a whale camp, where—" I stopped. Point Helen's geography was entirely familiar, yet something was out of whack. Then it came clear. On its exposed, eastern beach, the boulders and drift logs gleamed black in the sun. A puff of wind carried a stench of crude oil, which stung my throat. Matt throttled back and let *Whale 1* drift, then scanned the shoreline with binoculars. The shock turned my sight inward, to memory. I wanted Matt to understand. As he studied the damage, I talked. I told him stories. I recounted the excitement I'd felt the first time I'd beach-combed Point Helen with Mary. Its exposure to Montague Strait allowed wrack to make landfall, and storms and tides washed everything high, where it formed a berm Mary and I had mined for wood, buckets, buoys, and rope for camp. Hidden by a screen of forest was a lake where we'd swum. I told Matt about bears and deer we'd spotted on the beach, the eagle nest atop a grandmother hemlock just above the day marker at the island's tip, the sea cave below it, how sea lions patrolled the point and Chugach transients skimmed through the kelp beds, searching for seals. Now I imagined bears, after foraging the tide line, frantically trying to clean their oiled paws and fur.

My stories spent, Matt and I sat quietly.

"You doing okay?" he asked.

"Not really. Let's go."

Matt started the engine. "Where to?"

"Let's try the Needle, check the sea lions." I braced myself, grasping the rails, as *Whale 1* accelerated, closing my eyes, and letting the wind cleanse me of memory and dread. When I opened them again, I reached for my binoculars and scanned for blows.

The acrid smell of guano hit us long before we arrived at the Needle. When we cut the engine, its ruckus was replaced by groans and shrieks. A skein of kittiwakes rose off the Needle's face. Glassing, Matt spotted a peregrine perched on top of the nesting cliff. Jaegers chased gulls, and two horned puffins floated near us. No obvious oil, we counted over three hundred sea lions lolling on boulders at the Needle's base.

As we drifted, I let myself forget the toxic fringe of Point Helen, the oil-spattered cobbles of Whale Camp beach. "Look," Matt said, pointing at the water. Streaming past were thousands of ctenophores—comb jellies—planktonic carnivores translucent as wet tissue, some phosphorescent with rainbow-colored lights. These were part of the spring plankton bloom without which the Sound would be a biological desert, without which, ultimately, there would be no transients. They were a sign of the Sound's resilience, a balm to my fear; they nourished my hope that the water itself hadn't died.

Dragging our attention away from the ctenophores, we scanned separate parts of the strait for blows. Matt spotted humpbacks to the north, toward Grass Island. As we approached, we noticed a skiff bobbing nearby. A couple in orange Mustang suits watched the humpbacks. Guessing by their garb that they must be agency biologists, we motored closer, recognizing Lloyd Lowry and Kathy Frost, long-time Alaska Department of Fish and Game researchers from Fairbanks. They were carrying out damage assessment of harbor seals. Iconic Alaskans, they lived in a log cabin, raced sled dogs, and spent months in the Arctic and Bering Sea studying ice seals, collaborating with indigenous hunters. When I'd met them in Fairbanks, I'd felt too young, too green, too soft. But here we shared fear at the fate of our study animals. They told us they hadn't seen any orcas, and their news of harbor seals was grim. On many haulouts, including those at the northern end of Knight Island, every seal was oil-coated.

"Eva, they're 100 percent oiled in some places," Kathy said. She described oil-intoxicated seals swimming lethargically, oblivious to boats. Necropsies would reveal neurological lesions caused by breathing aromatic hydrocarbons. "They're sitting ducks for your orcas," she said.

Would Chugach transients eat oil-coated seals, I wondered? And what would that do to their digestive tracts, immune systems, and livers?

"We'd better get going, Kath," said Lloyd, starting their engine. "We've still got to survey Danger Island."

For the rest of the afternoon, we searched west of oil-devastated Grass Island and across to Knight Island's north end, but spotted no whales of any kind. Curious about the cleanup presence at Grass Island, we motored closer, until we could see workers blasting the blackened beaches with hot water hoses in an attempt to dislodge oil. Orange booms snaked along the shorelines to catch sheens. The air stank of petroleum. It throbbed with engine noise from skiffs and landing craft. How could any creature survive such an onslaught, I thought, first the oil, then boiling, pressurized water? Grass Island, with its shallows and rock-strewn channels, normally sheltered hundreds of seals and sea otters. Oystercatchers lay speckled eggs in shallow depressions on beach gravel. Eagles nested in the forests covering the low island from tip to tip. In coves at low tide one could dig clams to the accompaniment of loons' quavering and the peeps and trills of migrating shorebirds. It was spring. How many gull, tern, and oystercatcher nests would be trampled by human feet? Where would the seals, wary as they were of boats and people, go?

Later, sitting off Applegate Reef, another harbor seal hot spot, suggested by Lloyd and Kathy as a place to look for transients, Matt and I released our angst in words. Together we composed an editorial in the field notebook, expressing our concern about the cleanup causing further injury to the Sound.

That evening, motoring into Disc Island Cove to anchor for the night, Matt drove through the narrow entrance channel and I sat on the bow watching for bottom, but my eyes, watering from petroleum reek, were drawn to shore. Blackened rockweed and eelgrass hung from oiled logs half submerged in shallows filmed with oil. After anchoring, we rowed to the beach. I forced myself to look directly at what I least wanted to see: memory fouled by oil. Our gum boots slipping on black rocks, I kicked through thick mats of oiled wrack at the high tide line. Poking into them with a stick, I uncovered dead crabs.

When we couldn't abide it anymore, we scraped muck off our boots on rocks and ducked into the forest. Hiking into the heart of Disc Island, I focused on hermit thrush song, stream song, colors of wildflowers, ghost breath of cold air around snow patches in shady spots. When we finally climbed back on the boat, after dark, we scrubbed oil off our boots and hands with dish soap. My jottings that night in the daily log expressed the duality we'd experienced: signs of spring, evidence of damage, something unprecedented and foreign entering the life of the island, the Sound. *Total insanity on Grass Island, army on beach and tons of boats. Anchored at Disc Is. Badly oiled with much oil on rocks and oily film on water's surface. Took hike. Blueberries forming, skunk cabbage flowering, blue and yellow violets, crowberries, shooting stars.*

In the morning, as I hauled anchor, I watched a pigeon guillemot dipping its bill into the center of the cove, over and over.

13

When It Happens

If something is boring after two minutes, try it for four.
If still boring, then eight. Then sixteen. Then thirty-two.
Eventually one discovers that it is not boring at all.
—JOHN CAGE

Searching for transients, not finding them day after day, a numbness settles in your mind, not a lack of expectation but an expectation of nothing. Nothing but shorelines gliding past the eye. Nothing but water churning past the bow. Rain forest sky—clouds obscuring tops of islands—adds to the hypnotic effect. As skin and clothes soak in moisture, your mind soaks in the Sound's mood: melancholy, pensive, meditative, inward. The eyes absorb every imaginable shade of gray, and sometimes, all the more startling for its contrast, the sudden blackness of a bear wandering the shoreline or the phosphorescent blue of a berg bobbing in the wake. The only object in life seems to be searching and waiting. Patience morphs into frustration, then into monotony, then not even that. You are cold on your fiberglass perch, shivering under your rain gear, fantasizing about the tent's woodstove, and then cold and damp is all you've ever been or will be. Coziness is a story you heard once; sun is a rumor. You are nothing but a set of eyes combing the line where water meets land or sky, as indifferent as a lighthouse beam sweeping the sea's surface. You clutch binoculars until the skin of your fingers swells, whitens, wrinkles. You stare through binoculars until the imprint of the eyepieces remains on your face when you put them down.

The boat stopped, Matt and I scanned in opposite directions, conversing in phrases so intermittent and random that they became just another part of the concert of birdcall and waves slapping the hull. The familiar mind-set and routine of searching known routes stitched a common thread between past years and that season of oil. For moments, I forgot to worry that we couldn't find transients because they had been killed or traumatized by oil or the cleanup response. We couldn't find them simply because they were whales and we were humans. As long as the bulk of the cleanup remained in other parts of the Sound, I could let myself be lulled by the timelessness of geography, by the undisturbed forested slopes disappearing into cloud. Many places, at least from a distance, appeared as they might have to a Chugachmiut hunter scanning the same shoreline five hundred years ago from his kayak.

So, when it happened, when my eye slid momentarily across a puff of gray dissolving against the forest, I waited to say *I think I just saw a blow* until I saw it again. That's how it happened on the second to last day of May, after a week of rain and wind and nothing but humpbacks. Drifting off Whale Bay, I shifted my binoculars back a few inches toward the spot where I thought I'd seen that blow. Perhaps it had just been a shred of mist. Several minutes passed. There.

"Matt," I said. "Look toward the middle of the bay. I'm pretty sure there are orcas in there. I'm pretty sure they're not humpbacks. There they are, toward the left arm, at ten o'clock. There's a dorsal fin, a male. There's another male. They've got to be transients."

"Got them," Matt said, putting down his binoculars and starting the engine, his eyes locked on a spot along shore. I scuttled off my perch and rooted around in the cabin for the camera and recording gear. My numb hands, in fingerless wool gloves, fumbled with the camera case latches.

By the time I crawled back onto the cabin top with the camera dangling from my neck, Matt was easing up on the throttle as we approached the whales. "Looks like four," he said, pulling his slicker hood over his ball cap as another squall overtook us. "Two males and two smaller ones." I buttoned my jacket over the camera. The whales were spread out, milling, slapping flukes on the bay's rain-pitted surface. Suspecting they'd killed something, we motored slowly through their fluke prints, scanning for bits of flesh.

"I don't see anything," Matt said.

"Let's drop the hydrophone. If they've killed something, they'll probably be calling." Matt positioned the boat in the middle of diving orcas and shut down. I dropped the hydrophone and hooked it up to the recorder tucked in the cabin, out of the weather. Slumped on the bench seat, I adjusted the volume.

"They're calling a little, some quiet calls and whistles. Definitely Chugach transients," I said. I glanced out the windows, but the whales were down. Immediately, I felt conflicted. We needed ID photographs—the four whales were survivors of the spill's initial assault. But I wanted recordings, and their erratic behavior would make them hard to approach, so we stayed put.

"Don't lose sight of them, Matt."

"They're still in the same spot, just milling around," he said.

"I know, but these transients can't be counted on to keep doing the same thing for long. They can disappear just like that."

"Don't worry," Matt said.

After twenty minutes, the whales grouped together and began traveling. Rather than quieting, they grew more active, groaning, whistling, slapping flukes, and breaching. They must have killed something, I thought, frustrated that we hadn't picked up evidence. But at least now we could get photos. Matt maneuvered as close as he could to the orcas while I shot a roll of film. I recognized Eyak and Eccles, but the females were nondescript, with unmarked saddle patches and dorsal fins, one more sickle-shaped than the other. Compared to the bulky males, they seemed small. Finally, we matched them to photos of Gage and Lankard.

As the orcas traveled out of Whale Bay, Eyak separated from the others, swimming back toward shore. The trio, silent now, continued toward the Pleiades. Matt and I fell into a rhythm, running ahead to drop the hydrophone, letting them pass, over and over. I tallied the time accruing, each minute precious. During a long dive, we heard calls, and when they surfaced, Eyak was back. They crossed Knight Island Passage to the Labyrinth, foraging among rock piles. Again they stopped to mill, calling and slapping their flukes. Probably another kill: they'd dispatched the animal so quickly, we'd missed it. The papers I'd read from British Columbia described short "handling times" during harbor seal predation. Larger, more aggressive prey, like sea lions, sometimes required hours to subdue. I thought about long-term studies of lions and wolves. Those predators didn't spend most of their lives underwater, out of an observer's sight. If a wolf killed a caribou while a biologist watched, he or she would know for certain who'd done the killing, who'd been killed, who had gotten to eat first, who'd had to wait. Sometimes it seemed that what we observed most could be summed up as swimming and breathing. "This study is going to take a long time," I said. "Years."

"I don't think Bud's going to be happy about that," Matt said. "I'm pretty sure he doesn't want you around for ten years, like some grad students."

By 7:30 p.m., we'd traveled twelve miles, from wilderness to its opposite. Outside Herring Bay, we entered an industrial zone of ships, skiffs, and—deep in the bay, above boomed-off, oil-drenched shorelines—beach crews hosing rocks. Lloyd and Kathy had described seal haul-outs in Herring Bay as completely fouled, every seal oiled. Where were those seals now? Would the transients enter the bay to forage, as they had in the past? When we dropped the hydrophone, engine noise blared from the speaker. How could the orcas stand it? How could they hear their prey or one another? The whales milled, slapped their flukes. Then they turned west, away from the chaos. We decided to let them go, into a silence devoid of even one small boat's mechanical din. We turned south to find quiet for ourselves.

A few days later, I dropped Matt off in Whittier and picked up Mary. In his backpack, stowed with his camera and books, was our editorial letter, written longhand on pages torn from my journal, which itself remained largely a chronicle of silence:

Anybody who has walked a rocky shore at low tide knows that it literally speaks to you with the crackling of countless invertebrates making it their home. When we walk the beaches, we can hear that community speaking, trying to breathe under a black blanket of poison. Equally disturbing is the human occupation, the domination and scouring of this poisoned wilderness. Helicopters and planes regularly crisscross the sky at low altitude; fishing boats, tenders and support boats working for Exxon/VECO abound. The hydrophone with which we listen for whale calls picks up the noise of propellers. The relentless activity has the feeling of war, dramatized by the presence of military personnel carriers and landing craft. The latter are parked on the shore of an island where armies, literally hundreds of workers, are concentrated on beaches using pressurized hot water to combat oil.

What is best for Prince William Sound? From our observations, we believe that Exxon's concentrated beach assaults are doing more harm than good. Already one grizzly bear has been shot in the sadly ironic defense of Exxon's beach crews as they try to remove oil before wildlife gets slimed. Please, let's take the armies away and pay the locals who know and respect the Sound to make a reasonable cleanup effort.

14

Where the Whales Are

A few days after Mary's arrival, *Whale 1*'s engine died in the Labyrinth. Died not in the usual way, sputtering, then conking out from water in the carburetor. It died grinding and popping. Fortunately, anchored nearby was a seine boat, oil-stained and battered. We limped over to ask for help. The boat belonged to a commercial fisherman named Tom Copeland, from Cordova. After fiddling with our engine to no avail, he invited us in for a warm-up of coffee. Tom and his crew were part of "the bucket brigade," a group of local volunteers who, frustrated with a lack of rapid spill response, had taken matters into their own hands, and were picking up injured and dead animals, and collecting thousands of gallons of crude in five-gallon buckets. Like us, they thought hot-water blasting of beaches was doing more harm than good. As evening wore on, our talk quieted. I was distracted by our engine predicament. Aware of the irony, Tom suggested we head north, to Herring Bay, where Exxon's cleanup command post had taken up residence. He knew of a mechanic barge stationed there.

If a boat could be said to crawl, that's what *Whale 1* did those few miles. We found the barge anchored on the outskirts of a concentration of larger ships and black, boomed-off beaches. The armada, Mary called it. The mechanics said they'd look at the engine in the morning, told us we could tie to the barge for the night. Relieved to be safe, close to help, we agreed, but soon realized that the men were mind-numbingly bored. "We just sit here day after day, on hold, getting paid a lot of money to do nothing," the skipper said. He seemed trapped in an ethical bind, happy to collect a paycheck, but frustrated at the lack of meaning-ful work. Many cleanup workers truly wanted to help the Sound.

The next morning, after a fitful sleep, the boat thudding all night against the barge's bumper buoys, the breeze carrying whiffs of hydrocar-bon, we woke to a voice blasting across Herring Bay from a loudspeaker mounted on the bridge of a Navy warship. I looked at my watch: 5 a.m. I couldn't make out the words, some kind of cry to action, but recog-nized the song trumpeted next, "The Star-Spangled Banner." Through binoculars I made out an insignia painted on the ship's stack: Exxon's tiger logo, the cartoon cat bursting forth with its paws fisted in defiance, as though it could conquer anything, even an oil spill of unprecedented magnitude.

All morning the mechanics tinkered with our engine, finally conclud-ing that it was a lost cause. Reluctantly, I called Craig via the marine operator with the news. He told me to hang tight. He'd pick us up with *Lucky Star* in a couple days.

At noon, the skipper, to relieve his boredom, climbed the barge's rig-ging in swim trunks and cannon-balled into the bay. More men arrived from surrounding boats, all at loose ends, offering advice. A mechanic emerged from the wheelhouse and said Exxon had radioed, ordering him not to help the whale researchers, "But I convinced him it was good PR," he said. Mary, sensing my fraying nerves, urged me to go ashore. She'd stay with the boat. Relieved, I packed my journal into my backpack, blew up *Puff*, climbed in, and paddled away.

7 JUNE 1989

Lying in an alpine meadow on top of Ingot Island, sun beating down, warming the ground, my body. The landscape looks pri-mordial, boulder-strewn, craggy trees, tumbling meadows, tundra giving way to forest. Like it's always been. I curl up in a hollow and pretend nothing's changed. Nestled, I feel safe, part of the earth. Per-haps Matt's right and it's possible to become animal-like with time, completely at home in the wild. When I first arrived here, I thought I'd left the other, bizarre world behind. But a helicopter landed over the ridge from where I was eating lunch by a pond half-filled with melting snow, half-filled with trash, shiny and new. What was a helicopter doing there? When it took off and flew over me, I pan-icked. Hyperventilating, I wedged myself under a hemlock.

After several days in Whittier installing a new outboard in pouring rain, Mary and I returned to Whale Camp. That evening, a helicopter hovered over us, flew off, and then circled back for several more passes. I ran into the tent, peering out from between the door flaps. From its shelter, I cursed the human invasion of the Sound. Mary sat me down. "I'm worried about you," she said. "You had a crazy look in your eyes when that helicopter flew over. Maybe you need to take a break." But how could I take a break when every whale encounter felt crucial, every non-encounter ominous? Thoreau wrote that "silence is the universal refuge." Where was silence? With the Chugach transients. Between encounters, I'd just have to find it within.

On June 13, a rare sunny morning, low on drinking water and eager for a shower, Mary and I loaded empty buckets, bottles and jugs, towels and soap onto *Whale 1* and headed for Mummy Bay, to the waterfall that plunged down the mountainside onto a flat-topped boulder. Sitting on the bow, scanning for transients as we went, I imagined the exquisite sensation of clean skin, clean hair. I imagined how at the waterfall, we'd tie *Whale 1* to the boulder, clamber up, and position buckets beneath the cascade. How we'd stretch our arms to fill bottles, pausing to drink draughts until our teeth ached. How I'd crane my neck to see what I was drinking: snowmelt and rain filtered through moss, forest duff, muskeg, fern, and dark soil, ionized by its plunge down the mountainside. How, after filling our vessels, we'd strip, hold our breath, wrap our arms around our chests, duck our heads and step under the downpour, swearing at the shock. How we'd leap back into the sun to soap our chicken-skinned selves and duck under once more, this time able to stay long enough to uncross our arms and rinse off, skin tightening and tingling. How afterward we'd sprawl on the sun-warmed boulder to dry. How I'd bring my forearm to my nose and smell the island, not one thing—sphagnum, humus, hemlock, violet, or rock—but a sweet distillation of all.

But when we rounded the headland and the bay opened before us, we saw that it was dotted with boats—a gleaming white tour ship, bow-pickers, and barges—the water around them fuel-sheened and necklaced with orange booms. We took showers anyway, collected water as usual—our spot hidden from view—but we left depressed.

A week later, the consequences of the cleanup presence on Chugach transients, and on our ability to study them, became apparent. During an encounter with three orcas near Mummy Bay, boats repeatedly crossed the whales' paths at high speed. The orcas turned west and dove for ten minutes, surfacing more than two miles away. After another boat charged them from behind, the orcas disappeared. When we spotted them again, they'd traveled several miles across the passage. The trio never allowed us close enough for photographs. *Persistent boat traffic all day*, I wrote in the log, *boats moving at high speeds, fishing vessels, barges, ships*. Discouraged, we headed north, searching Icy Bay and Dangerous Passage. In the evening, we returned, hoping to find the trio again, but instead we found four others. From their deeply notched fins, I wondered if they were Gulf of Alaska transients. They traveled side by side, tolerant as we eased in parallel. Through the camera's viewfinder, I recognized Kaj, one of the whales who'd been photographed in front of the *Exxon Valdez* right after it hit Bligh Reef. The catalog confirmed the identities of the others: Shadow, Totemof, Egagutak. They were alive.

The whales surfaced in synchrony several times, stayed down five minutes, then resurfaced a quarter mile to the southeast, following the same course, as though guided by a compass. Within half an hour, I'd shot an entire roll of film, thirty-six frames. It was a relief to work with cooperative whales, "well-behaved," as Craig would say, with plenty of time to adjust the focus, to fill the frame from saddle to fin tip, to know I'd documented each one. I wanted to read something into their tolerance: that we were accepted. We motored ahead, shut down, dropped the hydrophone and listened, but the whales were silent. They skimmed the rocky coast of Knight Island, the two adult males falling behind Kaj and the juvenile, Egagutak. Intent on travel, they rounded Point Helen and swam along the oil-coated outer beach, through toxic rainbow sheens washed off by the tide.

Something about them struck me as unusual. Perhaps I was swayed by appearances. Those scars hinted at hunting stories we'd never know. Why did they, alone, among Chugach transients, have those notches? Or perhaps it was their indifference, their single-minded travel, their utter silence. Out in the strait, we lost them. Had they decided they'd had enough of us? We wouldn't get to know, in that encounter, what they hunted, where they were headed, if they'd find other Chugach transients. We'd never get to know. We didn't realize that it was the last time we'd see Kaj and her group, that they'd be seen only once more by anyone, on August 16, 1989, in Hinchinbrook Entrance. Innocent of that knowledge, we gave up searching and headed for camp.

JUNE 22, 1989

Dear Mom and Dad,

Morning. I just woke up in a meadow near camp. Song sparrow and golden-crowned warbler songs replace the hermit thrush songs that put me to sleep last night. From my spot on the ground, I can see the sun cresting the bluff, and through the trees, wind rippling the water. The hemlocks, gray-barked and bearded with lichen, remind me of ancient men in Tai Chi poses. Gnarled, wind-scoured, half alive, they seem to hold each cry, each gasp of the Sound under oil, under boats, under trash, under storms, like memory given form. When I lean my body against one, I'm dizzy from their knowledge.

Afternoon. We have the engine turned off and are drifting. No whales yet today. A week ago, a large clean-up operation moved into Mummy Bay, just south of Whale Camp. Coincidental, perhaps, but the whales have been more difficult to find since this "armada" arrived. It came while we were up north, where there are few whales and plentiful boats. We returned to "our" part of the Sound only to find what feels like an invasion, power boats barreling across the passage, and one evening, a barge towing what someone told us was the world's largest crane. All day skiffs charge across the paths of whales, otters, seals and porpoises.

The talk is that the spill will be "cleaned up," that the devastation is media hype. Easy to believe from this vantage, a half mile from shore. Even walking on what appeared to be a clean beach yesterday, I was oblivious until Mary pointed it out—push the boot into gravel, boot toe comes back oil-coated. The insidious, idiotic, unthinking, stinking poison has seeped down below the surface. The animals struggle to survive and there is some spark of hope because isn't the beauty and immensity just too powerful to destroy?

Evening. Anchored among granite boulders in a palette of earth tones: tan, blonde, auburn, buff, charcoal, gray. Animal-like, as though we've discovered the hidden refuge of Steller's sea cows, slumbering here all these centuries. This place, so sheltered and quiet. We used to take this kind of purity for granted.

That's it, the end of a typical day searching for whales. Write soon.

Love, Eva

15

Part of the Darkness

Five days later, after a run to the hatchery to pick up mail and make phone calls, we pulled up to the old wooden seiner *Point Steele* to buy gas. A Cordova boat, it had been contracted by Exxon as a fuel station, but with much down time, *Point Steele's* crew of Chugachmiut men fished for hours, anchoring often in front of Old Chenega for the night. Pete, the skipper, passed on a sighting of five orcas reported by another boat, but when we asked for location details, he was vague. "Not sure, somewhere down here," he said. He was preoccupied with other news. It was so disconcerting, so unbelievable, I placed a question mark next to my notation about it in the log: *Pt. Steele rept. 37,000 (?) gal. spill off USS Cleveland last week.* More than anything, Pete worried about looting of Chugachmiut archaeological sites at Old Chenega.

We never found the five orcas, but the next evening, clean from waterfall showers, sitting in front of the tent eating dinner, blows interrupted our conversation. Four orcas surfaced off the beach. We scrambled, throwing our saltwater-rinsed plates into a washtub and grabbing cameras and notebooks. From behind, Mary recognized the male in the group, Ripple Fin. With Chenega, Iktua, and Mike, he was combing Squire Cove's shoreline. In the catalog, check-marking their photos, I added them to the roster of survivors: twelve so far.

When we dropped the hydrophone, the silence was broken sporadically by the quietest of vocalizations: short bleats and hiccups. "Quiet calls," I told Mary. Analyzing my recordings the previous fall, I'd teased those calls out of background noise, wave laps and hydrophone flutter.

I'd thought at first that it was the hydrophone cable rubbing against the boat hull. But on the sonograph analyzer, I'd seen that they were stereotyped calls: quick, quiet, and low-pitched, two distinct types, one upswept, one down.

The whales traveled on into the Labyrinth, milling at bay entrances, now silent, listening for the sounds of prey. At Mummy Island, they searched water so shallow, they turned on their sides to clear reefs. Sea otter mothers with pups floated nearby, unconcerned. Finally, the whales swam toward a haul-out rock where fourteen seals sprawled, grunting, basking in the late sun. The orcas surfaced a few yards away. A seal, perhaps an inexperienced juvenile, startled and splashed into the water. The whales dove, then resurfaced, milling. Immediately, gulls swept in, plunging. We motored over, vying with the gulls for a sample. For a half hour, they fed. We floated nearby, listening, but Ripple Fin and his family called just a few times, and quietly. Except for one spy-hop, there was no after-kill socializing. Apparently, they didn't want to blow their cover. How long could a single seal satisfy four whales' hunger? They resumed hunting.

In the lowering light, among the Labyrinth's innumerable rock piles and islands, there were so many ways to lose them. Only by constant scanning, our focus aided by chocolate-covered espresso beans, were we able to track them. At 9:45 p.m., they entered Drier Bay, a fjord cutting deep into the heart of Knight Island. At its head, in the 1930s, had been a herring saltery. Nearly all traces of a once-vibrant, noisy operation had vanished into the rain forest's silence. Into that silence the whales traveled, swimming sideways through shallows along islets. We followed, so close to shore we could smell hemlock and spruce resin and hear the night song of thrushes. The orcas skimmed the margin of sea and land, their fin tips practically brushing overhanging branches, their blows echoing through the forest to reach the ears of bears and deer. At 10:30 p.m., they stopped and milled. Gulls swept in, first a few, then hundreds. The orcas had killed another seal. Again they called quietly as they fed, then moved on. By midnight, they were back in the Labyrinth.

Just past summer solstice, the light of the long dusk barely allowed us to distinguish the whales' fins against the silhouettes of islands. I couldn't discern a single star in the sky. Ripple Fin's group hunted on, sliding along the flank of Clam Island. At 1:00 a.m., eyes aching, we finally turned back toward Whale Camp.

16

Into the Ice, into the Oil

Whales of intertidal zones and forest and night, and one day, whales of ice. In between, days of waiting. Immediate reality often eclipses what we know, deep down, of nature. A few days without orcas, and we imagined the worst—they'd left the Sound. Alternately, we agonized over all the ways we could be missing them. Searching Pleiades Bay, we knew they might be five miles away, off Point Helen. Waiting off Point Helen with the hydrophone down, we knew they might be foraging in Drier Bay or passing Whale Camp. But all we felt was absence in our narrow field of vision. The presence of oil, and of the cleanup operation, fed this. I wondered how long the Chugach transients would continue to hunt in an area polluted and overrun with boats. But some urges are stronger than catastrophe, at least in the short run. Humans continue to live in places ravaged by hurricane, flood, monsoon, war, volcanic eruption. Orcas continue to hunt in oiled water.

I'd read John Ford's paper about orca vocal traditions—an aspect of their culture—calls taught to calves, maintained through adulthood, and passed down the generations. Hunting habits and routes are another aspect of culture, another tradition. Calves learn to navigate the Labyrinth by following adults. They learn seal haul-out rocks, points where Dall's porpoises feed. They learn silence. Place binds the heart beyond sense sometimes. Wedded to place, the Chugach transients hunted in their old haunts for better and for worse.

Every time we passed the schoolhouse on the hill above Old Chenega, I was reminded of the opposite impulse, to flee a ravaged place, to come to think of one's home as haunted or cursed. When a place is abandoned, culture changes. New Chenega, near the hatchery, had called some of the quake survivors back to the Sound, and also newcomers, Native and non-Native. Some Natives even arrived from other villages and cultural groups. New Chenega drew the dedicated, the place-bound and also the placeless, to a raw patch of earth, to brand-new, vinyl-clad HUD houses sprung from the gravel like Lego flowers. In New Chenega, subsistence culture intertwined with consumer culture: seal ribs, octopus, clams, and smoked salmon set out at the table alongside soda, white bread, packaged chicken, and even pizza flown in on the mail plane from Cordova. Something old and new and hybrid was growing up in New Chenega. Now disaster had struck again. This one threatened the most basic tradition: food. When all else changed—kayaks replaced by motorboats, seal oil lamps by lightbulbs, shamanism by Russian Orthodoxy—food endured, just as it did for my immigrant parents, who cooked Latvian dishes thousands of miles from their home. Food is place; food is culture. For us, for whales. The way an animal hunts, the way a human hunts, is culture.

We sensed anger when we stopped at the village to use the phone or take a walk. Exxon had shipped in containers of groceries to "replace" subsistence foods like octopus, clams, mussels, limpets, and salmon contaminated by oil. "We will make you whole," they claimed. Exxon had set up an office at the community center, installing banks of phones. Reporters swarmed the village, seeking stories. Strangers wandered the two dirt roads through the cluster of houses, where every face and figure had once been familiar. While some villagers welcomed the influx, hoping for jobs, others recoiled, felt invaded and used. No one asked the important questions, sought their knowledge and experience.

These thoughts preoccupied me as we searched for transients. I knew that many seals along Knight Island were oiled. I knew the water along the shoreline was tainted. But the transients hunted as they had for millennia. How did they perceive what had happened to the Sound?

One place they hunted was safe from oil and boats. Icy Bay. One evening Mary spotted blows off the Pleiades. By the time we caught up, it was half past eight in the evening. Scrutinizing the catalog, we finally identified the three orcas: AT19, 20, and 21, an adult male, a female, and an immature. We named them Berg, Hermit, and Icy. We followed them into Icy Bay. To our surprise, they entered thick floes. We knew from Lloyd and Kathy that harbor seals hauled out on ice near tidewater glaciers to molt and give birth. Perhaps during those vulnerable periods, they found shelter from predators close to the faces of calving glaciers, where the ice was thickest, impenetrable to boats, and possibly to predators. Here and there, we spotted seals perched on ice, their back flippers tipped up into the air. Darker blots on the ice turned out to be grooming sea otters.

Black fins rose and fell among blue-white chunks and milky blue water. All around us, ice hissed and churned in currents. A seal resting on a floe craned its neck toward an orca blow. Hermit surfaced a few hundred yards away. Then the seal turned to look at us. Between whale and boat, it hunkered on its ice refuge. A mile into Icy Bay, we maneuvered ahead of the orca trio as they navigated ever-thicker floes. When I lowered the hydrophone, I noticed how it disappeared almost immediately into the turbid water. When we turned on the speaker, we heard only static. At first, thinking it an electrical problem, I fiddled with a wire. Then I realized it was centuries-old ice melting, releasing its load of silt scraped from the land, particles falling to the sea floor, laying down a story of millennia, making a bed for crabs and shrimp.

How could the whales hear or see a seal? Yet they swam purposefully, as though covering familiar ground. We would come to find out that they used quiet, sporadic echolocation clicks to navigate and hunt. Entering thicker floes, they slowed. We slowed even more, Mary driving at idle speed while I sat on the bow pushing ice out of the way with an oar. Suddenly a seal popped up alongside us. Mary threw the gear shifter into neutral. The orcas surfaced, the seal hidden by our hull. I told Mary about harbor seals taking shelter beneath skiffs in British Columbia. Sometimes they'd even climbed on boat transoms to escape pursuing transients. *Whale 1*'s high sides protected us from such a dilemma: shelter a seal or push it back off. No one I knew of had chosen the latter. After a few minutes, the young seal dove, and we motored on.

As light in the fjord faded, the whales pushed deeper, entering a cove dotted with ice. For a half hour they milled, probably feeding. It was too dark to tell. We checked our watches: 11:00 p.m. We checked the chart, which showed shallow water but no rocks. We checked the tide book. Still flooding. It would ebb at 3:00 a.m. Not a big tide, so we dropped anchor. After its clatter, we heard the whales' departing blows. Then we crawled into our sleeping bags. Half awake, I listened to thunder, Tiger-tail Glacier shedding another ice wall. I imagined the pressure wave rolling out from its face, hauled-out seals rising and falling with the swell. I shivered. The air was cold, much colder than at Whale Camp. Those three Chugach transients were ice whales. The Chugach transients were whales of every way the Sound expressed itself.

17

Groundings

The next morning, sun poured through the cabin windows. Silence. Warmth. Stillness, absence of wave laps against the boat's hull. Something was wrong. The boat tilted at an odd angle. I sat up in my bunk and stared out in disbelief. All around, gray silt stretched to the cobbled beach. Along with several dozen ice chunks, we'd grounded on the low tide. We'd have to wait until the flood floated us again. In the meantime, we put on gum boots and hiked on the sea floor, each footfall triggering thin, arcing streams of water from buried clams. If only we had a shovel, I thought. After the tide flowed in and freed us, we searched the fjords, scanning below the faces of Tigertail and Chenega Glaciers, counting hundreds of hauled-out seals, but Icy, Hermit, and Berg were gone.

Late in the afternoon, bouncing back toward Whale Camp, we saw from a distance something blue on our beach, a cabin skiff high and dry, two figures crouched near the bow. When they heard our engine, they stood, waving and calling hello, and I recognized Lance and Kathy, the B.C. lighthouse keepers.

"We tried calling you on the radio off and on all morning, but didn't get an answer, so we went ahead and beached *Boomer*. Had a bit of a mishap, I'm afraid," Lance yelled.

As we tied *Whale 1* to the mooring and loaded the inflatable with gas cans and gear, I realized that in an instant we'd turned a page in the field season's log. Now we'd be part of a team of researchers operating out of widely separated camps. And we'd be switching boats. We'd be turning *Whale 1*, the more seaworthy vessel, over to Lance and Kathy, who'd take it to their camp on Hinchinbrook Island. *Boomer*, Olga's boat, would be ours.

"I'm pretty attached to *Whale 1*," Mary said. "It's been great, with this new engine, not having to worry about mechanical problems." I tried to reassure her. Olga had installed a new outboard on *Boomer*, identical to *Whale 1*'s. According to Craig, people used to fish cabin skiffs on the Copper River Flats, back in the days before bowpickers.

Lance and Kathy met us at the water's edge, reaching out to take our gear. "You must be Mary," Kathy said, as they hugged. "And Eva, so great to see you, out here, in your element." Earlier that spring, Kathy and I had spent hours sitting cross-legged on Craig and Olga's shop floor, sorting food, gear, and equipment, getting to know one another. A veteran of bush living, she'd been systematic, her lists precise. While I stood overwhelmed in grocery stores, trying to eyeball how many cans of beans or boxes of soy milk we'd need, she'd used math, even calculating the number of teabags they'd go through in a season.

Town-clean in new jackets, gum boots, and jeans, they didn't seem daunted by the jagged hole punched in *Boomer*'s plywood hull. They bantered with the ease of long partnership. Kathy, with her sea-green eyes and long brown braid, was nearly as tall as Lance. He was compact and fit, with a wild head of dark brown hair and a thick beard, and spoke with an accent that was part Australian, part Canadian. In their early thirties, they'd already accrued years of nautical experience. As lighthouse keepers, they'd come to know the B.C. orca researchers. Encouraged by Graeme, Mike, and John, Lance was applying to graduate school. Craig and Graeme considered Lance and Kathy master field biologists, and that's why Craig was sending them to Hinchinbrook Entrance.

"So, what happened?" I asked.

"Well, it's a little embarrassing," Lance said.

"Yes, Lance got a little cocky with the throttle."

"Ahem," Lance began, looking down, scratching his beard, striking a contrite pose. "*Boomer*'s a bit overpowered for her weight. We came down Dangerous Passage, and halfway to the Pleiades, I hit a piece of ice. It was actually pretty hard to see with the sun glare. And *Boomer*'s hull's a bit thin, I'm afraid. I was surprised. The berg wasn't that big, and it punched right through."

"How did you get to camp without sinking?" I asked.

"Well, it does have a bilge pump, and we've got a five-gallon bucket and bailer. Kathy kept driving slowly toward camp, and I stopped the hole up with a flannel shirt and Crisco."

"Crisco?" I asked.

"Yup. I always keep a can on a boat. It works amazingly well in emergencies. But I sure learned my lesson about ice. We don't have that problem in B.C. It's floating logs we have to watch out for."

"Come on, love, we'd better fix the hole before the tide comes up," Kathy said.

"Mary and I will get dinner going."

Lance wrapped an arm around my shoulders and gave me a squeeze. "No worries. We have a repair kit. And we found some plywood behind camp. We'll patch the bow and she'll be as good as new. But I have to say she feels a bit light in choppy water. Definitely overpowered with that huge outboard. And I'm not sure how seaworthy she is. You'll just have to be careful."

Boomer felt like an origami bird, flitting, almost airborne, across the water on our first day out. Mary shrieked with delight as we skimmed toward the Pleiades across smooth water. We reached the islands in no time. Returning to camp in the wind chop, however, we slowed to a crawl, feeling the plywood hull flex under our feet when she pounded. We took the waves slowly, relieved to see, at day's end, that the cabin had stayed dry, even with waves breaking over the bow.

The day before Lance and Kathy departed for Hinchinbrook, we finished the final transfer of gear between boats and headed out in separate directions to search. *Boomer* officially became *Whale 1,* Lance and Kathy's boat *Whale 2.* Mary and I were photographing humpbacks when we heard Kathy's voice on the VHF. "We've got your friends here, transients in Shelter Bay," she said.

When we intercepted them, Eyak's group was traveling rapidly toward Icy Bay. Like Icy and Berg, the four whales swam straight into the ice floes. Stopping to mill, to dive repeatedly in the same spot, we assumed they'd killed a seal, but ice blocked us from getting closer. At 10:30 pm, inside Jackpot Bay, they had killed another seal. Again they arched high to propel themselves straight down toward the carcass, an oil slick spreading from that locus, gulls swooping in to scavenge. Then calls began, mostly Call 3, its tight snarl opening to a quick moan, up and down a little hill of pitch. Even those few recorded vocalizations felt precious, one segment of cassette tied to a specific behavior. For once, I could say without equivocation what the whales were doing. In the dusk, their blows, loud and quick, infiltrated the forest, echoed off cliff faces. I imagined them working against gravity, consuming the seal before it sank to the bottom. One whale or the other took turns resting at the periphery. After a half hour, they quieted, grouped up, and left the bay. The gulls flew off to their nighttime roosts, and we to ours, Whale Camp, our nightly grounding point. What, I wondered, grounded whales continuously on the move? Perhaps it was movement itself, the constant retracing of geography, the one thing holding steady amid so much change.

18

Beast and Beauty

And the blue earth resumes its measureless dialogue
Between catastrophe and plenty.
—CYRUS CASSELLS, "DOWN FROM THE HOUSES OF MAGIC"

No matter how deeply we penetrated bays and passages, how closely we followed transients, we couldn't escape the spill, which revealed itself in odd and unexpected ways. One morning, anchored in Hogan Bay near an unfamiliar boat called *Lion of Judah*, a gunshot startled us. Someone had fired at the beach, and the bullet ricocheted. We scanned with binoculars but couldn't see a target. The gunshot was one of several random occurrences, meaningless unto themselves, yet taken together with other anomalies—cigarette butts floating in Mummy Bay, a dead seal washed up on Whale Camp beach, an oil-stained plastic pom-pom (a clean-up tool) wrapped in our prop, oil pooled ankle deep beneath a boulder—constituting a story I tried to keep separate from the whales' story. And of course it was connected. The exposed film we sent to Graeme told a different story than the one we told ourselves to survive that summer. Raw data is unequivocal, devoid of wishful thinking or denial.

Take for instance our illogical hope that the "armada" in Mummy Bay would be temporary. One day at the hatchery, I phoned Olga, and after describing the scene there, she said she'd make inquiries. After all, Mummy Bay was significant orca and humpback feeding habitat. When we next called, Olga told us that she'd been assured that "the task force" would move out of Mummy Bay. But Eric, the hatchery manager, scoffed. He'd heard that the task force would stay through the summer, with equipment stored in the bay over winter for the next season's cleanup. When I told him about Olga's phone call, he shook his head. "The beast is too big," he said. Eventually, the spill wore down my defenses. Every zooming skiff, every blackened beach, every harassment of whales triggered ire, until it seemed the oil was inside me. While I channeled my anger into work, Mary yearned for refuge. She'd left a new romance behind in Michigan. She pressed me to go to the hatchery more often to check mail and make phone calls. Uncharacteristically, she complained of tiredness, cold, and frustration at long days and nights anchored out, cramped together in *Whale 1*'s cabin. For the first time, we snapped at each other, then brooded in silence. At camp, soothed by a meal, the woodstove's warmth, the earth underfoot, and space, the tensions eased. Still, one day Mary asked if I might find someone to replace her so she could go home early.

Our lives no longer played out as an adventure story of two women alone in the wilderness, but as a work assignment in a war zone. We weren't volunteers. The National Marine Fisheries Service (NMFS) paid us to collect data that would hold Exxon accountable for damage to whales. At the same time, Exxon was mounting its own research to counter our data. Yet I felt accountable to Mary also. She'd taught me new ways to see—the sculptural in nature, its shapes, lines, and colors—but more: together, we'd endured catastrophe. Alone I would have cracked.

9 JULY 1989
Yesterday, Mary and I hiked on Crafton Island, not realizing it had been heavily oiled. We found an oil-coated river otter skull. Even the grass above tide line was black. I told Mary about the first time I'd come there. One spring day in 1987, a fisherman friend had invited me for a skiff ride. It was an old, wooden skiff, and he'd perched atop the outboard's cowling so the engine wouldn't fall off. Here, I told Mary, was where we'd searched for glass balls among bleached driftwood. Here's where we'd found wild irises. Here's where we'd sat on the wreck of an old boat and talked all afternoon. I'd never met anyone so earthy, so entirely of a place, embodying an all-out, organic love for the Sound. I'd only begun to recognize that in myself. "Why aren't you married to him?" Mary asked. I told her I was married to the place.

Now, I'm sitting in a meadow on Squire Island, surrounded by old trees. A few moments ago, I opened a bag of almonds, rustling the plastic. When I looked up, my eyes met those of a deer, twenty feet away. Her body tensed, ready to spring. Her ears tipped sideways away from her face. She sniffed, trying to catch my scent. My heart stilled, the world stilled as we stared at each other. She turned and slowly walked away.

Every day is like this: life and death, beauty and disaster.

19

Quiet Sounds

When the war came, I decided to use only quiet sounds.
There seemed to be no truth, no good, in anything big
in society. But quiet sounds were like loneliness, or love,
or friendship.

—JOHN CAGE

A cluster of transient encounters, four in five days, ended with Eyak. The day after our evening with his hunting group in Jackpot, he turned up alone off Mummy Bay, traveling silently along the shoreline, swimming past the moored armada. Soon after, we lost him. A clue to his whereabouts came the following day, when a woman radioed to report four orcas, two males and two smaller whales, combing the east side of Perry Island, twenty miles north. "They met up with a group of sea lions," she said. "There was a brief scuffle, and then the whales kept on going." We headed that way, but never found them.

Looking back, I see myself that summer as a mouse finding her way through a meadow, winding her way among stems, climbing one stem until it bends to touch another, unaware of the meadow's shape or relation to a larger geography. That's how it is with data points, data gathering. Two decades later, I mine chronology, the research logs' day-by-day unfolding. But that's no story. A story has trajectory, meaning. Now I lift events off the logs like fingerprints, studying them, considering them in the context of all that unfolded, all that came after. When I open my old journal with its now-missing cover, I find little written there. My private voice lodged under my breastbone, overwhelmed by life in the spill zone, co-opted by the voice of science I believed I had to master.

Often that summer I read from a book Mary gave me, Judith Duerk's *Circle of Stones*, a kind of instruction for rethinking what it means to be a woman. In Fairbanks, in my classes, I'd sought instruction in the paradigm of science, its language, its laws, its methods, its structure. In the circles of stones I arranged in the woods when alone, and in that book, I sought instruction of a different sort: how to navigate my voicelessness and anger.

One morning, I opened the book to the following question: "What is asked of us?" In the shadow of the spill, it was my question, but until then, I hadn't verbalized it. What was being asked, specifically, of me? The book answered: "To find a voice . . . a voice to cry out . . . to make us all attend to our woundedness, our pain, our anguish . . . in nature, itself . . . that vast woundedness which has been so ignored, so denied . . . and, at last, to honour it. . . . in hope and faith that it may heal."

In the calls of orcas, on the oiled beaches, I heard that voice. "I'm still here," it said. During hours with transients, or in the silence of 2:00 a.m. dusk when I'd wake and momentarily believe the Sound was whole— no, never wounded—I heard that voice, when even the cleanup "show" playing incessantly all over the Sound slept and dreamed of something deeper. In the end, the true story of the oil spill is perhaps best expressed in the words of composer John Cage: "Language can only deal meaningfully with a special, restricted segment of reality. The rest, and it is presumably the much larger part, is silence."

But the heart of that summer throbbed with traffic. We put out more frequent VHF calls, and hailed passing vessels, explaining our research and asking for sightings. Increasingly, our searches turned up spill-related trash and oil itself, in various forms: slicks, sheens, tar balls, puddles. We collected what garbage we could, calling Exxon or the Coast Guard or the DEC—the Alaska Department of Environmental Conservation—on the radio to find out where to deliver it. Rarely did we receive any response, so we stored it at camp. One day, in the northern Sound, we discovered a drifting coil of oiled boom, and, tied to one end, garbage bags filled to bursting. Mary pulled apart an opening, and her fingers touched oily fur. The bags were crammed with dead animals. We dragged the mass five miles to the nearest armada, at northern Knight Island. Shuttled from one official-looking boat to another, finally a man confided that he'd been instructed not to talk with us. Furious, we tied the boom to the *Corinthian*, a gleaming white ship housing Exxon officials. Deckhands called down that we couldn't leave garbage there, but we motored away, resuming our search for whales. At the time, it felt like civil disobedience, but when I turned the incident over in my mind, I wondered if it meant anything. Should we have searched harder for reporters or a DEC boat? Or had the beast grown so big that such an incident lost meaning or significance? Who would add those individual deaths to what poet Bei Dao calls "the roster of the missing?"

Another evening, we delivered an oiled boom to the armada in Mummy Bay. The hull of a ship housing cleanup workers towered above us as we eased to its side. We craned our necks to talk with people leaning over the rail, jigging for bottom fish, relaxing after a day of labor. The air was thick with diesel fumes, like a harbor, not Mummy Bay, place of williwaw winds, sacred place where, pre-contact, the Chugachmiut had interred their mummified dead in sea caves, place where Mary and I, the summer before, had watched a humpback calf breach again and again. Would Mummy Bay's original essence return after a winter of storms?

Just around the corner, in Thumb Bay, sprawled the ruins of another herring saltery. Only one marginally habitable cabin remained, a ramshackle abode for a series of misfit caretakers, growing pot and raising chickens among twisted metal, creosote-soaked pilings, and half-collapsed rendering tanks—a Superfund site. Encroaching on the ruins, a mass of salmonberry crept forward year by year. Nature's own restorer, salmonberry flourished in waste places, regardless of history, not asking why. The same plant engulfed the ruins of Old Chenega. It colonized avalanche slopes. It gave me a weird kind of hope.

20

Scientific Magic

During Mary's last transient encounter, with a lone male we hadn't seen yet that summer, Holgate, we followed him as he traveled rapidly toward Bishop Rock. We soon lost him, but not before Mary captured his image on film, one broad fin amid angry gray seas.

For Chugach transient encounters, it was a slow time. And mid-July was a distinct in-between time for residents and humpbacks, too early for both the silver salmon run and the August plankton bloom. Nonetheless, we kept in radio contact with skippers, including Lloyd and Kathy, who reported their first orca sighting of the summer off Applegate Rocks, a lone male. We befriended a young biologist named Pete on the DEC boat *Silver Spider*. Now he collected the oily trash and dead animals we found. Some whale-less days, I jotted petroleum sightings into our log:

15 July 89: Strong diesel smell on water near Bishop Rock.

16 July 89: Skimmers trying to clean up a thick oil slick between Point Helen and Grace at 1200. They said it "got loose off a beach somewhere." We called Coast Guard and Silver Spider. Skimmers still working at 1800; slick appeared to have moved 2–3 miles north.

17 July 89: 1/8 mile off Point Helen, found smelly skin of oil with brown bubbles. Called Coast Guard.

Weeks of fair weather broke the day I dropped Mary off in Whittier, a storm shoving the Sound past its in-between season into one of simultaneous abundance and decline. As always, muskegs burnished, flowers went to seed, blueberries ripened, pink and silver salmon flooded the passages, choked the streams. But in many streams, salmon deposited eggs in oiled gravel.

When I hugged Mary goodbye at the train, I knew she was torn, both relieved and sad. I stood there crying, words stuck in my throat. Together, we'd grown intimate with the Sound, the transients and one another. No lover had known me better.

Matt's familiar presence blunted my sadness. It helped too that our long dry spell without transients ended. Crossing Perry Passage on our way from Whittier to camp, Matt spotted four orcas, a male and three smaller ones, perhaps Ripple Fin's group, but it was too rough, *Whale 1* surfing down four-foot seas, to alter our course and get close enough for IDs.

The next day, after a morning weathered out at camp, Matt and I found four more transients. Eyak and Eccles milled near Italian Bay, rolling over each other, socializing, Lankard and Gage surfacing erratically along the shoreline. Matt spotted more blows to the south, a pair. They shied away from our approach, diving for several minutes. When they surfaced, I studied their fins through my binoculars. It was Icy and Berg. After two hours, the five whales approached each other with a frenzy of fluke lobbing, but they never joined, just fell back to milling. Were they feeding? Up, down, milling, surfacing, diving, tail slaps. Their behavior revealed itself only through context, and often that context was the presence of other life forms: a seal, a porpoise (or its parts), diving gulls, the arrival of others. Lacking context, Matt and I speculated. Perhaps they'd been taking turns on a carcass as it slowly sank, one group resting, the other feeding. Perhaps Eyak's group had killed a porpoise or seal, attracting Icy and Berg.

Indifferent to our questions, the whales, now silent, traveled south, Eyak not with his companions, but side by side with Icy and Berg.

A few days later, a familiar voice responded to our radio call of "Hello, all vessels."

"Empress of Latvia," David Grimes hailed back. "This is *Orca 2*."

"Empress of what? Who the heck is that?" Matt asked.

I'd met David in 1987, when he'd joined us briefly on *Lucky Star.* A Renaissance version of a jack of all trades—musician, naturalist, story-teller, activist, commercial fisherman, river guide—David was a bit of a wandering minstrel, a bard. In his mid-thirties, he owned neither house nor car. Each March, like a migratory bird, David arrived in Cordova from his Santa Cruz, California, wintering grounds, carrying a battered guitar case, wearing a black beret on his head, trailing a long, dark braid down his back. "The coastal temperate rain forest," he'd say, "starts around Santa Cruz and ends in the Sound. That's my home range." Over the years, he'd helped Craig with orca research, yin to Craig's yang.

The spill had hit David hard. With his friend Rick Steiner, he'd thrown himself into the political fray in Valdez after the tanker grounded. Looking for purpose like all of us, he'd recently bought an exquisite wooden boat he'd found in Juneau, a salmon troller built in 1947 and christened *Orca 2.* David brought her to the Sound as a vessel of "fair witness," taking environmentalists, reporters, politicians, bureaucrats, writers, musicians, and artists to ground zero, for the disaster but also for the Sound's heart—his heart. His heart's absolute ground zero was Sanctuary Bay, shadowed by Knight Island's highest mountain.

That evening, David anchored *Orca 2* in Squire Cove and rowed his entourage—a group of environmentalists and reporters from Washington, D.C.—to Whale Camp. Matt and I brewed cocoa for the crowd while David built a campfire. A modern-day Pan—wildflower tucked into breast pocket, crow feather woven into his braid—he wore flip-flops, a forest green wool jacket, wool trousers, and his ubiquitous beret. We sat late into the night listening to David's stories of spill politics, the battle he and Rick were waging with Exxon over the cleanup, over industry oversight, and, more than anything else, over the story of the spill. Exxon's story involved a freak accident and a heroic industry response: a billion dollars and thousands of people unleashed on the Sound to battle the oil. The damage wasn't as bad as people feared, their biologists claimed. It was a war story, ultimately a triumphant one, in which technology and human will prevailed. Its villain was Captain Joe Hazelwood, the tanker's drunken skipper.

David and his friends told an alternative story. Theirs involved triumph over adversity also, but with the heroes a collective of fishermen and citizen activists taking on Exxon and forcing changes in tanker safety, energy policy, and public perception of the true cost of oil consumption.

"All over the US, people are destroying their Exxon credit cards," David said. David, Rick, and fellow activist Riki Ott had met with the president of Exxon Shipping and the head of the DEC, with reporters for CNN, CBS, and NPR. Their advocacy would contribute, eventually, to change: close citizen oversight of the oil transportation industry, the buyback of timber rights and land for habitat protection, state-of-the-art monitoring of oil-laden tankers exiting the Sound, new spill contingency plans, and yearly training of locals in spill response. I thought of the dead animals in the bags we'd found, invisible to the public eye. How did they fit into that story?

Isolated as I'd been from media, I absorbed David's news of the big world. The reality we lived with daily affected people I didn't know. Could the spill be a catalyst for a shift in consciousness, as David dreamed?

"What I'm really interested in," David said, his tone softening, "is the spiritual cleanup." Then he told a story. On his first trip to the Sound after the spill, brought to his knees by the devastation and by the recent death of his friend Lars, he'd steered *Orca 2* toward the one place on earth he knew to go for solace, Sanctuary Bay:

> Just past the turtle rocks at the entrance, four orcas suddenly surfaced beside the boat, one a big male. For a moment, we all hovered together, and then they disappeared, leaving behind their mysterious swirls on the water's surface. It was as if I were being welcomed at the end of my pilgrimage. Focused on the last bit of tricky navigation into the bay, I thought how curious it was to be inside the ribs of an old wooden boat named after orcas a generation earlier, with my friend Lars's name welded on the anchor, Lars who'd been my spiritual anchor, and most amazingly, here we were about to enter the sacred heart of the Sound. And at that moment, just as I steered into the narrow keyhole entrance to the inner bay, the big male orca reappeared and dove right under *Orca 2*'s keel. Kind of like "X marks the spot." I had the strongest feeling that the universe was keeping an appointment. And I had somehow made it right on time.

"Just one male?" I asked.

"That's right."

"It was probably Ripple Fin, and Chenega, Iktua, and Mike."

"Really?" he said. "I never thought I'd know who those friends were. That's what I call scientific magic."

Then David told us about his friend David LaChapelle, who'd had a dream after the spill. "He was rising through a mist above Knight Island, and the mist was the spirits of all the animals that had died in the spill. They said to him, 'Yes it's true, we're still here, we haven't left yet, because we have a message to deliver, and the message is love.' That's how I see it," David said, "the way it most makes sense to me. The spill on Good Friday, the day of sacrifice, was a sentient act of the earth to wake us up to what we love, to make sacred what we hold most dear."

When someone asked about our orca research, out flowed my untold stories of oily trash, of Chugach transients weaving their way through cleanup boats. Chugach transients were the ones, I said, photographed swimming by the grounded tanker. David's companions wanted to know if we'd seen AB pod. Craig's encounter back in March had made national news. Had we seen the missing ABs?

"No," I said. "We haven't seen them yet, not many resident pods at all down here. It's still early."

The Chugach transient story receded. I felt obscure too, a novice biologist, not a key actor in a public drama. I had nothing newsworthy to offer. As the talk wound down, I retreated inside myself. I'd wanted David's environmentalist friends to tell me that my work mattered, that I was also heroic. My own oil spill ego trip.

As though reading my thoughts, David caught my eye. "In the end, we all just want to repay with our lives some measure of the love we feel. Don't you think?"

It would take years for me to understand the Chugach transient story within that context. Repaying with my life—and love itself—was at its core a silent endeavor. The transients thrived on obscurity. They were nowhere, and everywhere. In a sense, they were common. But at the same time uncommon, mysterious, surprising. I had no choice but to follow them, not away from obscurity, but into it. Finally, David picked up his guitar, and my angst vanished, drowned out by the music. It drifted down the beach with the smoke from our fire, perhaps telling the truest story of all.

21

The Whale Called Eyak

After David left, we resumed our routine. Matt claimed that the hydrophone was a waste of time. We'd found both residents and transients by scanning with our binoculars. Nonetheless, out of habit, I still dropped the pickle every time we stopped.

One morning, when I threw it over and turned on the speaker, a long, mournful call cut through the static. "Chugach transients," I said, grinning at Matt in self-satisfaction. He scanned until he spotted the spout, then a male dorsal fin a mile and a half distant.

"Keep your eyes on him," I said, shutting off the speaker and yanking up the hydrophone. Matt leaned back against the windshield, binoculars pressed to his eyes. I started the engine, pushed the throttle, and turned the wheel until the boat lined up with Matt's outstretched arm, indicating his last sighting.

"Which way is he going?" I shouted above the outboard's roar.

"Toward the strait." With one hand, Matt clutched a cabin rail; with the other, he held his ball cap to his head so it wouldn't fly off. It was early afternoon, the sky clear, but already a breeze was making whitecaps on the water in the strait. We had little time to photograph and record before we'd enter unworkable seas.

"Do you see any others?"

"No, just a male, and he's pretty active."

"Weird. There must be others. Why else would he be calling? Maybe they've killed something."

Upside-down, the male's white chin and belly rocked back and forth as he slapped one pectoral flipper and then the other against the surface. Rolling upright, he canted his fluke into the air, water droplets spraying off the down-curved tips. Slamming it down, he blew explosively, arched high, and dove. No other orcas. No blubber bits floating at the surface. No diving gulls. What was he doing? I eased up on the throttle, shut down the engine, and threw the hydrophone over. As we glided toward him, I ducked into the cabin to retrieve the recorder.

"It looks like he's coming to check us out," Matt said. We clambered to the bow and stood, looking down. Out of the green-black gloom, a black-and-white form resolved into an orca. He glided beneath us, on his side, pumping his fluke, his pectoral flipper pressed against his body. A glistening ellipsis of bubbles trailed from his blowhole. Just below the trailing edge of his oblong white face patch, an eye gleamed, a liquid bead. My eyes locked with that eye. Faint calls rose through the hull. The only other sound was the *plunk-plunk* of jumping pink salmon. As he drifted past, I recognized the dark patch at the base of his saddle, the fat triangle of his fin. A few stronger fluke pumps took him under, out of sight. I turned to Matt, who was holding his binoculars in one hand and smiling like a twelve-year-old. "It's Eyak," I whispered. "Do you hear that? He's calling." And then time started up and I snapped back into science mode. "Oh, my God, he's calling." I worked my way along the boat's side and groped for the start button on the recorder. Calls blasted and crackled through the speaker, so near, so loud, I had to turn the recording level down to almost zero.

"I can't believe this. There must be other whales. Why would he be calling like this, all alone?"

Matt kept scanning. "Don't see anything." Meanwhile, we timed Eyak's dives with a stopwatch. I jotted shorthand to describe his behaviors and calls and wrote down the recorder number, tying his behavior to a segment of tape. But what was his behavior? Play? By himself? The dial turned, the seconds accrued, the recorder capturing his voice on the ribbon spooling round and round. The notebook page was a crude transcription:

1331—three surfacings (milling), then down, silent
1337—up (milling), (tape 1, 352), a few calls
1339—down, calling
1342—up, silent, moved S (milling)

There was something magic and illicit about listening to Eyak, as though I were eavesdropping on the underworld. I tiptoed around the boat like a spy. Matt and I whispered. Crouching near the machine, I tweaked the recording level; he was getting farther away.

"We'd better start up," I said, though it was hard to stop recording for even a second, to miss even one vocalization. Because the longer I listened, the more I discerned a pattern in Eyak's calling, something I'd never heard before. I began to anticipate the next call the way I would the next lyric in a familiar song. He didn't vocalize until after he dove, and each time, he began with Call 1, a long, insistent, descending yawl. I started drawing symbols into the notebook, squiggles that reflected the calls' shapes to my ear.

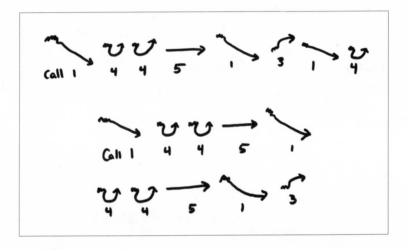

Three calls: the long wail followed by a few higher-pitched, tight blasts with questioning upsweeps, then a long blast on a steady pitch, like a cab's impatient horn. Call 1, Call 4, Call 4, Call 4, Call 5. He repeated the sequence, at full volume, over and over. As though he were proclaiming, "It's EEEEEEEEEyak. You there? You there?"

Of course I had no idea what he was saying. Graduate school trained me not to anthropomorphize. Besides, if orcas had language, it would follow different rules than ours. But whatever message his calls and actions carried, I couldn't help but sense it was urgent. "I wonder if he's looking for his group?" I said.

"He's at least a quarter mile away now," Matt said. I shut everything off and hauled up the hydrophone. Matt settled back on the cabin top, pointing toward the spot where Eyak had last dived. We stopped again in choppy seas south of Point Helen. From there we could see, to the north, miraged, the blue-white Chugach Range, forty miles distant, and to the south, the Gulf of Alaska, open ocean, a realm as forbidden to *Whale 1* as the moon. On sunny days, the wind blew from that direction. With such a long fetch, waves built quickly. Much farther, and we'd be out of Knight Island's shelter and in seas big enough to swamp *Whale 1*. So we stayed put, bobbing, recording Eyak as he swam into the strait.

Despite the noise—the *whop-whop-whop* of the prop of a tug pulling a barge down Montague Strait, the slosh of chop slapping the boat's sides, the churn of waves against Point Helen—Eyak's calls came through on the hydrophone for a long time. We stood there, jostled by the seas, until we lost sight of him, until his calls faded to nothing. It had been a scrap, a fragment of his life. But as we headed back into the passage, I clutched it to myself like an artifact unearthed from an archaeological dig. I thought about the day I'd met Mike Bigg in British Columbia. He'd been the first biologist to use photo identification to study orcas, the first to suggest that there were two types, fish eaters and mammal eaters. He'd devoted his life to their study. My first moment alone with him, he'd asked: "So, do you plan to study transients for the rest of your life?"

Taken aback, I'd stammered, "I hope so." How many lifetimes of gathering tidbits of data like that—a few minutes of recording, a photograph, a page of scribbled observations—would need to accrue before I could understand Eyak? That day, I'd encountered the unexpected, something new. A lone male calling—it could almost be called singing. A door had opened, and questions blew in like a flock of unruly birds.

That evening, in the wall tent, I transcribed the field notes to a data sheet by the light and hiss of the Coleman lantern hanging from the ridgepole. Matt, sprawled by the woodstove, read a book, a mug of tea by his side. The breeze had died, and wavelets washed wearily against the beach. The data sheet asked me to condense our observations, to assign behavioral categories, to note times and tape counter numbers. I read and reread my jottings, trying to fit what we'd witnessed into one of four basic categories: Social, Rest, Forage, Travel. Most researchers broke up a creature's life into those elemental imperatives. But categorizing what we'd seen seemed not only impossible, but simplistic.

What if Eyak, unbeknown to us, had been studying our behavior? I put the question to Matt. We tossed suggestions back and forth. What would he think about all the hours we spent traveling, searching the passages, stopping and starting? What about our feeding behavior, the incessant snacking in lieu of lunch? And our hike to the bluff behind Whale Camp to watch the sunset? Play? What about me bent over data sheets? Would he call it resting? What about Matt drinking tea and reading? Every act had intention. But he wouldn't know our intentions. We existed in different worlds, separated by a physical barrier and mutually incomprehensible languages. So how could I know Eyak's intentions? What had he really been doing that day? Traveling. Yes, he'd been swimming toward Green Island. But he'd stopped, flopped around, slapped his fins and flukes, agitated, like a caribou harassed by mosquitoes. Was that social? Could a whale play by itself? Or had he been annoyed at our presence? Or frustrated because he couldn't find his companions? Or disturbed by the presence of oil off Point Helen? I ruled out foraging. His loud calls alerted every seal and porpoise within miles: "Traaaansient whale, hungry, hungry." And he clearly hadn't been resting. Had he been amped up because he'd wanted to mate? He was about twenty, sexually mature. He didn't have many females to choose from, out of a population of twenty-two. Would he mate with orcas besides Chugach transients? Maybe he'd been lost, somehow separated from his group. Could a whale screw up, get lost? What if something had happened to Eccles, Lankard, and Gage? The questions whirled.

I flipped back through the field notebook. A lone male had passed camp three days before. On the page for July 7, I skimmed notes about our last encounter with Eyak. About his behavior, I'd written only "traveling, silent." And seven days after that, Mary's last encounter, with Holgate: "traveling rapidly toward Bishop Rock—silent." Finally, a lone male seen by Lloyd and Kathy. How odd that I hadn't seen it—lone whales, always males, passing through the study area. Like a nearsighted mouse, my eyes fixed on data points, I hadn't discerned a pattern. I felt something incipient, like the first puff of wind before a gale. Stashing the data folder, I pulled on my boots, and walked outside to watch the afterglow of midnight behind the Pleiades, to listen for whatever might be breathing out there.

22

On Being Hushed and Silent

Storms define the Sound, not its rare sunny days. Salmon streams, plankton blooms, muskegs—all depend on rain, lots of it, two hundred or more inches a year. Storms sweep the Sound clean, drive back fair-weather boaters, discourage tourists, drench kayakers. They hide the Sound from jets descending toward Anchorage. The ceiling lowers to envelop mountain passes, until even floatplanes can't get through. In a gale, the world shrinks to the size of an island. Even an oil spill dissolves for a day into the periphery.

When a late-summer storm arrived, Matt and I welcomed it. We stoked the stove and arranged our canvas chairs near its warmth, each claiming a few square feet of floor space. The weather gave me a chance to catch up on data transcription and letter writing. If I could motivate myself to suit up in rain gear, I might even take a hike to the bluff top, to watch the wind-ripped passage from above. By early afternoon, my notebooks, film canisters, teacup, and books were spread around me on the plywood, and Matt scolded me for encroaching on his space. Every half hour or so one of us added more wood to the firebox until the sheet metal glowed. Wind snapped the tarp and billowed the tent fabric, but we felt cozy and secure. We had anchored *Whale 1* deep in Squire Cove the night before. For breaks, I stretched, then padded around sock-footed, grabbing handfuls of gorp or an apple, separating the tent doors to check on the storm's progress, the scene outside a study in grays. Overhead, clouds of varying shades, from smoke to ash to dishrag, sped by. From that, I guessed the wind was blowing a steady thirty knots. As squalls marched in, clouds descended to touch the water, hiding the Pleiades entirely in fog. Iron gray waves streaked white with spindrift churned down the passage. A wild music accompanied the storm: jostle of waves against shore, spatter of rain against plastic, shrieks of veering gulls, trickle of water, snap of canvas, crackle of wood, hiss of kettle. Behind the tent, the wind soughed through the hemlocks. Rain fell in sideways sheets, running down the tent's tarp, overflowing our drinking water buckets.

In the evening, the wind dropped to twenty knots, but the rain fell steadily. A voice from the water broke our heat-drugged lethargy. John, the DEC biologist, paddled a kayak over from the cove, where *Silver Spider* had anchored to wait out the storm. His blonde hair, darkened by rain, clung to his forehead. Rain dripped off his slicker sleeves onto the wooden ramp in front of the tent. We invited him in for tea and spent a couple hours talking. For him, the summer, his first on a boat, his first in the Sound, was an adventure. The Sound was beautiful, his work purposeful. And he believed the cleanup was helping. As I listened, my insides twisted. The Sound choked with boat traffic, the Sound smeared in oil, was his reference point. It bothered me beyond reason, and I stumbled over my words, trying to express why. Finally, I managed to sputter a few sentences: "Do you know what it's like to want to leave here? When other years, I cried when I left the Sound? This spring, I cried when I got here. I can't stand to see it like this." It was something I hadn't admitted until then, and I had a month and a half of fieldwork to go. Obviously, the cleanup armada was in Mummy Bay to stay, as the hatchery manager had predicted. Now beach crews blasted at Point Helen with their hoses. Even a storm couldn't change that.

Despite the "I can't go on" depth I'd plunged into, when the storm relented the next afternoon, Matt and I loaded up the boat and headed out, as always. That's how a person gets through, I thought as I lugged a gas jug down the beach, one everyday act after another, pushing through grief as though it were head-high grass in a meadow you can't see the end of, going on faith that there has to be an end.

Off the Pleiades, we spotted a male dorsal fin. Pure dumb luck. With the rain and fog, the visibility for blows was terrible.

"I only see two," Matt said, "and they're down now, but it looks like they're traveling." We ran ahead and stopped, throwing over the hydrophone. No surprise, they were silent. I glanced at my watch. Five minutes. Six.

"Damn, I bet we lost them already. If it wasn't for the male, we'd never have spotted them in the first place," I said. Seven minutes. Eight.

"There," Matt said, "ahead, toward Verdant Island."

"Let's hurry and get photos," I said, ducking into the cabin for the camera.

As soon as I focused on their fins and saddle patches, I recognized Icy and Berg. Again, no Hermit. We followed the pair, timing their dives as they rounded the headland into Icy Bay. As always, the ice stopped us, but not them. I couldn't deny a tinge of relief, watching them disappear. Maybe it was fatigue. Maybe the sense of exposure induced by the cleanup, as though the lights of a surgical theater illuminated once hidden aspects of the Sound, driving its mysteries into what shadows remained. I wanted nature—weather, ice, the Chugach transients—to thwart human effort, even with our motors, binoculars, hydrophone, and autofocus cameras. Some essence, I believed, dwelled in what was most obscure, the way a blurred photo, an abstract painting, or a poem reveals a truth no science or logic can account for. It felt right, that some parts of their lives remain unseen.

We left Icy Bay. Motoring toward the Pleiades, I heard Craig's familiar voice on the VHF. "*Whale 1 . . . Whale 1. Lucky Star . . .* WYM 9639."

I scrambled for the radio. "*Lucky Star,* this is *Whale 1.*"

"Channel 72, Eva?"

"72."

Craig was at Whale Camp unloading a gas barrel. We hadn't seen him in weeks, and I imagined a drop-off of garden vegetables and hopefully chocolate. We'd been relying on beach greens, cabbage and carrots for days. Also on board, he had our boss, from NMFS in Seattle, and Noah Adams, a reporter with NPR. Craig invited us for dinner, so we headed straight into Squire Cove, where he'd anchored *Lucky Star.* I hadn't met our boss Marilyn and was eager to put a face to Noah Adams's familiar *All Things Considered* voice, but I was nervous. Would we seem bushy? Unprofessional? When was the last time I'd looked into a mirror?

"Don't worry," Matt said as we shed our rain gear on *Lucky Star*'s back deck. "They're just people. Be yourself."

When we ducked into the cabin, I blinked at the brightness. The air felt dense with heat. I wouldn't have been surprised to see steam rising off my cuffs. Noah and Marilyn, sitting at the settee, turned to greet us. Standing at the diesel stove, I warmed my hands, my fingertips shriveled, white raisins. Salmon fillets sizzled on the cast iron pan. "Dinner's almost ready," Craig said. I picked up a spatula to turn the fillets, calming myself with a familiar gesture. After our meal, Cajun-spiced salmon, garden potatoes, and greens, followed by the wonder of ice cream, we sat squeezed into the settee with teacups. Marilyn asked about our field season. I launched into anecdotes about whale encounters, and about the cleanup and its impact on the animals.

"Well, I need to talk to you two about that," Marilyn interrupted, her demeanor changing. "Your editorial in the *Anchorage Daily News* was totally out of line. The word from above is to put a sock in it, Eva. The data you're collecting is for litigation against Exxon, and everyone on this project has to be unbiased. There's a good chance you'll be called as an expert witness, and Exxon's lawyers will try to take you apart. You can't be spouting off to the media about anything related to the spill. No more letters. You're putting the government case at risk."

I froze. Noah sat quietly beside me, looking into his cup. Before I could respond, Craig, who'd been leaning against the window beside the helm, sat up and put his cup on the table. "That's just bullshit and you know it, Marilyn. What does their opinion about the cleanup have to do with their credibility as biologists? They're two separate issues. You're talking about censorship. A gag order. That's Exxon's game, not ours."

"We're potentially talking millions of dollars in damages. This is no joke to Exxon. It plays right into their hands to paint you as an environmentalist with an agenda. They'll say your data can't be trusted. There's too much at stake."

"Photographs don't lie, Marilyn. No one can create seven missing AB whales out of thin air."

It went on like that, Matt, Noah, and I fading to the periphery as they argued. I was gratified to hear Craig defend me, but felt embarrassed at my silence. My heart pounded, words formed in my mind, but before I could utter them, they sputtered and died. "We should be hushed and silent, and we should have the opportunity to learn what other people think," said John Cage. When not writing, being hushed and silent came easily. It served me well, studying transients. In the end, I told myself, that's what mattered. But another voice nagged: "What is asked of us?"

Before we left for the night, Marilyn hugged me. "You're doing a good job out here. Just no more letters."

23

Tallying Icebergs

Now our encounters threaded back to Eyak, to the day we'd heard him sing alone. One day, Ripple Fin's group of four, along with the male Moon, appeared off Chenega Point, resting for an hour. When they began to travel, Moon left them, and we followed him until he disappeared into Icy Bay. A week later, listening on the hydrophone, we heard loud calls, then spotted a lone male off Chenega Point. He quickly disappeared. Hoping another boat might see him, we put out a radio call. A half hour later, someone reported a male orca at the mouth of Icy Bay. By the time we arrived, he was deep in the ice. The next day, we found Eyak's group foraging for seals in the Labyrinth. After three hours, Eyak disappeared. When he returned late in the afternoon, the entire group vocalized and milled together. That evening, he disappeared again. This time, the whales vocalized as they parted ways. The next day, we found Eyak traveling alone off Chenega Island, silent, intent on his own mysterious purpose. We lost him in the fog. A pattern was emerging. Males coming and going from their hunting groups. Did they act as scouts? Or was there some other reason?

In the catalog, I kept up my tally of Chugach transients we'd seen so far—seventeen of twenty-two. At least that—presence, absence—was unequivocal.

One night, I wrote a progress report to my major professor. I wanted to reassure him that I'd soon head north for the fall semester. In his last letter, he'd sounded worried that I might disappear into the Sound for good. "I've collected 60 hours of observations so far," I wrote on the back of an unused data sheet. "I feel like I'm chipping away at an iceberg, gathering the tiniest fragments of understanding. Every other ice chip is a question."

I tried not to think about the number of hours in an orca's life. I tried not to think about how I'd been watching the icebergs that were the Chugach transients through a slit in a dark fabric—the unknown. I told myself that sixty hours was more than nothing and that next year I'd tear the slit a little wider. I tried not to think about the oil, how it was changing what I barely knew. I told myself that next summer the spill would be over, and some of my questions would be answered.

The following day, not far from Herring Bay, we found not orcas, but a diesel slick a half-mile long and five hundred feet wide. I remembered the 37,000-gallon diesel spill that Pete on the *Point Steele* had described. We hailed the Coast Guard, and to our surprise, a pollution control vessel responded. For once, someone seemed eager for our report. The dispatcher told us a helicopter had reported the slick earlier. They asked us to collect a sample. Heading south with a jar of greasy water on the dash, we spotted blows off Whale Camp. At least thirty orcas rested in three lines. It was AB pod. I pointed out Galena to Matt, her saddle patch shaped like a horseshoe, and Montague, his fin canted forward, and the matriarch, Jeannie. As I shot roll after roll of film, Matt flipped through the catalog, checking off whales. When we finished, there were unchecked photos: the missing seven. We dropped the hydrophone to the sound of intense echolocation. Preceding the whales down the passage, the clicks returned as news: silver salmon, food. A boat hull. A buoy. Pink salmon: not food, but maybe silvers among them. A strange object dangling from a line: our hydrophone. Would they detect the diesel slick miles ahead? To our relief, they kept to the opposite side of the passage. As the whales passed Herring Bay, boat noise grew louder until it drowned out their calls. Their direction of travel had kept them away from a slick but led them straight into the cleanup chaos. A boat pursued them, chasing a first-year calf. We hailed it on the radio, but no one answered, and when we approached, they motored away.

The AB encounter ushered in the season of residents, the ensuing weeks dominated by pods converging on the southwestern Sound, hundreds of whales chasing salmon amid hundreds of cleanup boats, whales swimming repeatedly through oil sheens. From a distance, no one could detect seven missing AB whales. Invisible to a distant eye, a rupture that would eventually split the pod in two. That eye would have to wait, focus in and focus out, to see what was actually happening.

I didn't recognize them as transients at first. Like the ABs a week earlier, they rested in a line, their bodies touching. They surfaced in unison, fins and sweeping saddle patches filling my camera's viewfinder. From time to time a juvenile slapped its flukes. They circled a patch of water, diving for ten minutes at a time, in deep rest. After photographing them, we shut down the engine, dropped the hydrophone, and sat listening to their breathing, and then, when they dove, their silence. When they surfaced, I studied their fins through binoculars. There was Chenega's tiny notch. There was Mike's shadowy, square saddle. There was Eccles's isosceles triangle beside Lankard and Gage. There was Ripple Fin. Our familiars. Like the residents, they were bound to the passage, despite oil, despite boat noise. Only Eyak was missing. I didn't worry. He was off on one of his walkabouts. Perhaps the others were waiting for him. Perhaps they were listening for his calls.

24

Wild Horses, Green Skies

It was September 4. Asleep on the gravel alone in front of Whale Camp at dawn, dreaming a herd of wild horses had thundered down the beach to surround me, their breath on my face, their hooves stomping the ground, I startled to a human cry.

"Hey, you on the beach! Hey, wake up!"

Eyes sleep-glued shut, my mind knitted data, cool air on my face, wave laps, kelp scent, idling engine. Yes, that was it, I'd slept on the beach. Could it be possible, I thought, my ire rising, that a cleanup worker was waking me to ask for directions, to ask for a fishing pole or a can of gas, on my last morning at Whale Camp? I sat up in my mummy bag and turned toward the water.

"What?" I screamed, projecting all my rage at the stranger.

A man leaned over the side of a skiff. Behind him, a lurid yellowish sunrise tainted the sky behind Chenega Island.

"I saw you sleeping on the beach and figured you didn't know. There's been a big earthquake. They've put out a tsunami warning. Head for high ground or deep water!"

"You're kidding," I said, still dream-befuddled. Was that what I'd felt, the thundering hooves, the ground shaking under me? "Thanks for telling me. Thanks a lot."

But the man didn't hear—he was already pushing off the beach with an oar. I grabbed my shoes, kicked myself out of the bag. Clad only in long johns, I gathered the sleeping bag and ran up the beach. Everything was packed, waiting for *Lucky Star* to pick up gear, to help dismantle the tent. I'd asked to spend a night at camp alone. I'd slept under the stars, which now, in September, showed themselves in the returned darkness, along with vague green auroras, on the rare clear nights between autumn gales. I'd wanted, in sleep, to breathe salt air and low tide musk, to absorb night sounds, gull cries, oystercatcher chatter, wave laps, the tide licking up the beach and back, the crackle of barnacles, so all those sensations would be implanted, so they'd carry me through the frigid winter in Fairbanks.

I stood inside the tent, staring at packed boxes, my half-empty backpack. Should I hike up the bluff? No. I had to protect the boat. I remembered stories of the wave that had destroyed Old Chenega. Moored in such shallow water, a tsunami would sweep *Whale 1* into the forest. And what about *Lucky Star*? What if they'd turned off their radio? What if they hadn't heard the warning? Grabbing my daypack, already loaded with bags of exposed film, tapes, and data, I crammed in the camera and tape recorder. I unzipped my duffel and rummaged through it, seized whatever my mind latched upon—my mostly unused journal, a packet of letters from friends and family, favorite books, a bag of shells, an eagle feather. No time for more. I layered on clothes, the sweater my mother had knitted me over Capilene and cotton. Then I grabbed *Puff* from behind the berm and ran with it to the water. I waded out, climbed in, and paddled hard, *Puff* zigzagging its way, too slow, too slow. The tide was high, the boat far from shore. My breath came in gasps. After several minutes, I realized my knees were getting wet. Two inches of water sloshed inside *Puff*, the nylon crinkling beneath me. By the time I grabbed *Whale 1*'s side, *Puff* was folding in half. In my haste, I must have brushed it against barnacles, puncturing the nylon hide. I hauled myself over the gunwale, pulled *Puff* in after me, started the engine, and ducked into the cabin to turn on the radio. I glanced at my watch. Six-thirty. Preparing to cast off, I caught fragments of warning: "Pan-pan, Pan-pan, Pan-pan. Hello all stations. A large earthquake . . . a tsunami warning . . . Possible significant coastal damage . . . United States Coast Guard Kodiak Alaska Out."

"*Lucky Star, Whale 1.*"

"*Whale 1, Lucky Star.* Channel 11, Eva."

"11."

"You're up. Good. Olga wanted to go find you. So, I guess you heard the tsunami warning. When I went to pull anchor, I found a huge oil boom caught on the line, wrapping around the hull. It took forever to free the boat. Pretty ironic if we got trapped here because of Exxon. You might as well hang out off the Pleiades, it's deep. We'll head that way after it's over. Don't worry, it's probably nothing."

"Did you see the sky?"

"Yeah, it's wild. But I don't think it's a portent of doom. There's a storm coming. You know, red sky in the morning, sailors take warning."

I watched that sky as I untied *Whale 1* from the mooring and motored into the passage. It wasn't red; it was the color of antifreeze. The passage was filled with vessels, the cleanup boats heeding the Coast Guard warning, drifting in deep water. I took my place among them. For that hour, we were one fleet, compatriots, all of our individual, conflicting purposes erased, even the largest vessels toy-like considering the force we imagined lumbering toward us. Between Coast Guard updates, I listened to radio conversations, skippers checking on other skippers, making sure friends and coworkers were in a safe place.

Finally came the station reports as the disaster that wasn't to be passed town after town, island after island, boat after boat, voices of strangers announcing, to everyone's collective relief: no wave, no wave, no wave.

But I felt something else. It was grief. In a poem, Li-Young Lee asks: "Is it praise or lament, hidden in the next moment?" I thought back to the clear, calm night when the *Exxon Valdez* had left port. Asleep in our beds, we'd had no warning of the enormous black wave lumbering toward us then, the wave that would change everything, forever. Something in me, as it does after every life-altering disaster, obsessively rewinds the tape, scrutinizes each increment, trying to find the one word or gesture that would have turned the tanker away from the reef—a few degrees north, a few moments sooner— allowing us all to awaken to ordinary rhythms of water on a blessedly ordinary day: no wave, no wave, no wave.

That fall, when Graeme sent the spreadsheet of the summer's photo identification results, I scanned the table for the Chugach transients. To my relief, between four boats, we'd documented all twenty-two whales. But the news for AB pod was disturbing. Seven of thirty-six pod members were unequivocally dead, many of them reproductive females. I prayed that winter would be gentle on the survivors.

While I analyzed my data in a university lab, Mary expressed her "results" and her grief in another form. She built a sculpture, an igloo-like hut constructed of wooden blocks. Painted black, from the outside the hut resembled a humpback whale's arched back. From the inside it was an overturned hull or rib cage into which viewers crawled and huddled in the darkness. She called it *Memory House*. She photographed it for me, finishing off a roll of film still in her camera from the summer, not realizing that the film wasn't advancing. Images of *Memory House* were superimposed upon images of the wall tent's interior, the Pleiades, a lone male orca.

25

Mercifully Untranslatable

During spring break, I traveled to Vancouver to work in John Ford's lab. One night, alone in his office, I leaned across his cluttered desk and pressed a picture book to the window of the orca tank. Hyak, the aquarium's adult male, eyed the pictures from the other side of the glass. I watched him scan photographs of wild orcas breaching, and I wondered what he was thinking, what he was feeling. John Ford had shown me this obsession of Hyak's when I'd first arrived. "Hyak's only interested in pictures of other killer whales," John had said wryly. "If you work here at night, he'll bug you until you show him photos." I'd been wowed at the time. Eye to eye with an orca, a transient no less—an orca wanting something from a human, wanting to connect.

Hyak had lived at the Vancouver Aquarium since his capture from Canadian waters in 1968. As a teenager, he and his companions had been herded with boats and explosives and held in a pen. He'd been sold to the aquarium, separated from his family, and brought to Vancouver to join a female named Skana. After she died, he'd lived with a pair of Icelandic orcas. His eyes hadn't seen a wild Pacific orca for twenty-three years.

An orca's irises are blue. It's something you'd never know if you didn't see one like I did that night, from five feet away. In the wild an orca's eyes are nearly invisible, appear black, subtly placed just beneath the showy white eye patch on either side of its face. In the wild, an orca rarely comes near enough for you to notice its eye. To see an orca's eye in the wild, it has to swim close to your boat and look at you by spy-hopping— thrusting itself headfirst from the water—so its eye is level with yours.

Or it has to swim beneath your boat, on its side, looking up, the way Eyak had the summer before, the way Matushka did, my first summer. I could count on one hand the number of times a wild orca had looked me in the eye. What does it see? What does it think and feel? I know what I feel. I feel my heart pinned in its gaze. I feel seen and known in ways I could never see and know myself—the iceberg of my own being. I can't see my reflection in a wild orca's eye, and I can't ask for an interpretation. But there's no question who's in control, who's chosen to see and be seen. I'm never more alive than in that moment, exposed, a part of my soul stolen and given back, reshaped.

Hyak's blue eye didn't meet mine. Hyak's blue eye roved as he scanned the photograph, the way a person's eye flits searchingly when skimming a newspaper article. Watching him, I felt the way I had the previous summer, seeing orcas swim through crude oil sheens—culpable, part of the mechanized world, reducible to the sum of my destructive, human parts. Did Hyak file those images of wild orcas away for later, for the hours he spent circling the tank? Did they act as an antidote to the images that daily clogged his mind, the faces of humans pressed to the glass? Or was he scanning the photos for something familiar?

After a minute, Hyak backed away and stared at me. Bubbles streamed from his blowhole as he called impatiently. I flipped to another page, another orca photo, pressed it to the window, and Hyak sank a little and readjusted his position, his eye parallel to the book. Hyak could do that indefinitely, but I couldn't. I felt guilty and depressed when I leaned the book, open to a new page, against the glass, and turned my back to him. I walked across the dimness of John's office and sat down at the sonograph analyzer, where I'd been stationed all day, listening to recordings of wild transients, measuring each call, filling blanks in columns on data sheets.

It was 11:00 p.m. I kept the lights low in John's office to better see the monitor, and the glow of Hyak's tank cast the space in a greenish murk, as though I too, were under water. Though it was eerie, it was preferable to working during the aquarium's business hours. I had just a week to analyze the summer's recordings, and during the day John talked on the phone constantly, fielding requests for papers and interviews, advising students in Norway and Russia and Austria, answering questions from volunteers and graduate students and trainers streaming in and out the office door. A compact, energetic, sandy-haired man in his thirties, John was the world's expert on orca vocal behavior. Though I was thrilled that he'd agreed to serve on my graduate committee, getting a moment to ask his advice was nearly impossible, though I sat in his office for hours every day. But the wall beside me was lined with shelves of books and file boxes of scientific papers and reports, surely the most complete library of orca-related literature in the world. When I wanted a break from analyzing calls, when John was busy, I pulled out a paper, read, and took notes. When John focused his gaze on the screen in front of me, I hung on his words. "These don't look anything like West Coast transient calls," he said. And: "I don't think that's a distinct call there, but a subtype of that other one you showed me." And: "Their dialect is really big for transients. Are you sure they're really transients?"

That night, halfway through the summer's tapes, I'd identified twelve discrete calls in the Chugach transient repertoire, but to describe their dialect, to distinguish it from dialects of other orcas, I had to measure hundreds, even thousands, of individual calls. For each segment of tape, each span of minutes, I'd assigned a behavioral category. More than describing dialect, I wanted to understand the calls' purposes, a bigger challenge.

Finally, from my box of tapes, I pulled out one labeled 27 July 89. I started the analyzer, put on the headphones, and waited through the static and churn of water noise. And then I heard him. Eyak:

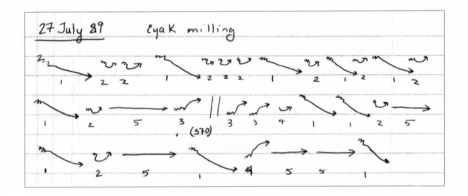

On one data sheet, I transcribed every vocalization I heard, using symbols, each representing a call's tonal pattern. Stopping, rewinding, repeating segments of recording, I drew until the data sheet resembled a musical score, the soundtrack to an extraterrestrial sonata. As I transferred Eyak's calls to paper, I began to see what I'd heard out in the field with Matt—a repeating pattern. They were the same vocalizations I'd heard in social encounters, seemingly emitted at random. I remembered the encounter with Olga in 1988, when we'd heard loud calls through the inflatable's floorboards. I'd listened to that tape so many times, measuring calls, staring at the sonograms scrolling by on the monitor, that I'd memorized it. That day, there'd been two whales, an adult male and a juvenile. Hadn't there been there a pattern to their calling? And what if only one of the two had been vocalizing? What if it had been the male? Just to be sure, I dug through the box until I found that encounter, 30 June 88, and listened to it again. The pattern matched Eyak's. The pair had charged across Knight Island Passage to join other whales. The calls had been so loud, they'd overwhelmed the recording system. Perhaps whales used those calls to find each other. I thought about the lone males I'd seen, how often I'd lost them. If I stayed with them, listened to them long enough, would I discover that they eventually vocalized? And if lone males used loud calls for long-distance communication, why in sequences? Each call in an orca's dialect didn't represent a word, according to John. So a pattern of calls didn't make a sentence. What information did they send, on pressure waves through the ocean, to distant whales? I carefully measured each of Eyak's calls. Perhaps they conveyed not only the whale's intent—finding a mate or companion—but also identity. Here was one whale's voice, isolated from the others. No "signature" call, as had been found in dolphins, said "I am Eyak." But perhaps the quality of Eyak's voice was distinct. Could I learn to distinguish his voice, the way I could pick a loved one's voice from the roar of a crowd? Humans communicate in words, yes, but so much more comes through tone, accent, inflection, through the emotional force behind our words, not to mention our silences.

Like a stone dropped into the center of a cove, my question radiated outward, getting broader, the further it traveled from its point of origin. The possibilities of meaning carried by a single call expanded to the exponentially more complex possibilities of meaning packed into a sequence of calls. Eyak sang in language beneath the language I knew. Underwater, where sound travels seven times faster than in air, where vision past a few feet is largely useless, where orcas see with sound and hear through their lower jaws, what could I hope to understand? Eyak's calls reverberated off underwater canyon walls, mapping terrains and histories shared between him and his relatives, passed down the generations. I loved the possibility of discovery, that I might some day crack the language of the Chugach transients, and I loved equally the mystery, the possibility that no one could crack it, that it was beyond us. "There is another world and it is in this one," the poet Paul Eluard wrote. Eyak lived in that other world.

Hours later, I took off the headphones, ejected the tape, and gathered my data sheets. It was past midnight, time to walk back through Stanley Park to the bus stop. Only the occasional cry from Hyak broke the aquarium's silence. Before walking out the door, I stopped at the window above John's desk, lifted the picture book, and flipped through the pages, searching for an image to carry Hyak through the night, until trainers arrived to run him through his paces and hand-feed him herring. Hyak whistled as he glided over—not to connect with me, not to steal my soul. Not to see into me. No. Only to ask for a look at photographs of his wild relatives. He didn't live in the "other" world anymore, a world of depth, a world of layers. He'd been yanked out, imprisoned in this world. As though his life had been flattened into one dimension. But what did I know of the mind of a whale?

Having recognized the role of males like Eyak as roamers, long-distance travelers, I couldn't delight at my proximity to Hyak, couldn't see him as an ambassador, the way the thousands of visitors to the aquarium did, couldn't imagine his calls as an attempt to communicate with me. Like Eyak, Hyak was an adult male, but unlike Eyak, there was no hope that his calling would reunite him with kin. His calls reverberated off the tank walls and returned to him, through his jawbone, into his brain, a language of echoes, mercifully untranslatable.

Chenega attacks an adult Dall's porpoise in lower Knight Island Passage, summer 1990. (Eva Saulitis)

PART 3

Survivors

26

A Human Silence

On April 17, 1990, Cordova bush pilot Steve Ranney, flying over Beartrap Bay in northeastern Prince William Sound, saw from his plane the body of an orca floating upside-down. Beartrap Bay was largely ice-covered, with just a bit of open water at its shallow head. There the carcass drifted and eventually beached. Craig and a colleague flew to Beartrap to perform a necropsy. By then the carcass was rotting. They found nothing in the stomach, but looking back on that day, Craig can't be sure they'd examined every cranny. As we'd discover over the coming years, an orca's stomach is a mass of pouches. Claws, whiskers, flippers, and skin collect deep inside, and are easy to miss. One thing was clear: the whale hadn't eaten anything recently. It was a female, twenty-two feet long. From the double nick on her dorsal fin, Craig recognized her as Berg, twenty-one years old, in her prime. He saw no bullet wounds, no obvious cause of death. Aromatic hydrocarbons, crude oil's most lethal components, don't accumulate in blubber, like PCBs and DDTs; they damage tissues like lungs, stomach, and liver. No funding had been allocated for the expensive necropsies and toxicology to quantify those effects.

The math of Berg's loss equaled more than one. The loss represented an unknown quantity: the number of potential calves over her lifetime. And for each female calf she might have borne, the loss of all her potential offspring. Craig wondered if Berg might have been trapped by ice and shallow water. I wondered why she'd been alone. I remembered my encounters with Icy and Berg the previous summer, the ease with which they'd navigated ice floes to hunt seals. What did it mean for her to die that way? Cause of death: undetermined.

12 MAY 1990

The border between water and air dissolves as we enter a fogbank. Heading south toward Whale Camp on Lucky Star, towing Whale 1, here and there an island peak suddenly appears, reminder that 5000 feet above us, the sky is perfectly clear. Only one otter and one sea lion so far. Sounds intensify—gull shrieks, porpoise blows. When I spotted cormorants, I thought "survivors." Every living thing I see is a survivor, having come through the spill and then the stress of winter after. But there's much I can't see: all the oil that remains, buried under gravel, sunk to the sea floor; all the weakened animals; all the animals that didn't make it. I think of David's friend's dream, of the spirit animals hovering above Knight Island. What other orcas besides Berg are in that number, we don't know. Nor who the survivors will be. Sun pierces a thin spot in the fog, glints on water. The water shades from dove gray to gray-blue-white and back to dove. The fog closes the thin spot, the air cools. The dampness penetrates my jacket, fingers under my hat brim, slips under my collar, wraps a tendril around my neck. The fog takes us, still trilling with town energy, into silence. Earlier this morning, in a fog like this south of Perry Island, we heard whales blowing but couldn't find them. That's how limited we are all the time. The fog just reminds us.

In the Whittier Harbor, in early May, *Lucky Star*'s back deck was loaded with boxes, fuel barrels, totes, and crates, all wrapped and tied in a blue tarp. It would be a four-month-long field season. During its second half, Whale Camp would house two research teams, my assistant and me searching for orcas, and another pair of women photo-identifying humpbacks for Olga. The North Gulf Oceanic Society had again been awarded contracts with NMFS to conduct oil spill damage assessment and monitoring, and I'd received funding for my Chugach transient study. Lance had begun a graduate study too, on orca echolocation. He and Kathy would return midsummer to run the "new" *Whale 2*, a liveaboard boat. Over the winter, Craig had found a bowpicker abandoned in a field outside Cordova. Her diesel engine rusty but serviceable, her bathroom-sized cabin leaky and mildewed, Lance had been tasked with weathering the drenching Cordova spring to revive her. Meanwhile, at Craig and Olga's place in Homer, Kathy and I had sorted gear, prepared data sheets, and organized field supplies.

Craig, Kathy, and I met Sandra, my new field assistant, at the train in Whittier. When Sandra opened her truck's tailgate, out hobbled Silver, her wolf-husky—gray-muzzled, with huge paws and long wolf legs. Sandra lifted him off the tailgate onto the gravel before pulling coffin-shaped wooden boxes out of the bed. "This isn't all going," Craig said, eyes widening.

"Of course it is," Sandra replied. "It's my camping gear and supplies, six weeks' worth." Craig looked from the dog to the wooden boxes to me. He shrugged, then turned to slide the first box out of the bed. My mind spun back to my talks with Sandra about working as my field assistant. Had I been vague in describing Whale Camp, how our basic shelter would be provided? I didn't know Sandra well. She'd been recommended by the man I'd been dating, her friend John. A lifelong Alaskan, she'd run sled dogs and built her own cabin. Now she was a biology student at UAF, hoping to work in the medical field. On the long boat ride to Whale Camp, we found out that Sandra had met Olga years before, in a remote Inupiaq village on the Arctic Ocean. Twelve years older than I, Sandra reminded me of a log cabin: sturdy, practical, private, self-effacing. In my exuberance, I plied her with questions, anticipating an intimate friendship as I had shared with Mary. But Sandra was not Mary. Reserved, she responded tersely. The cabin door cracked open, then quickly shut.

I puzzled over Sandra's coldness in my journal that first night, and many nights to follow. But as we motored closer to Whale Camp, as Squirrel, New Year, Clam, and Mummy Islands emerged and were swallowed by fog, I relaxed. By the time we dropped anchor in front of Whale Camp, the invisible sun was pearling the sea to the color of oyster flesh, burning the fog away.

Now 11 pm, exhausted after a day pushing fuel barrels up the beach and setting up camp, so tired I can barely think. I learned what was in Sandra's wooden boxes. She brought her own camp, wall tent, wood stove, cook gear, cans of food, everything. She set it up far down the beach, behind the alders. So I have this tent to myself.

Sightings off camp: two sea lions, three bald eagles. A hummingbird buzzed the tent. Oystercatchers jabbering. I'm home. Now time to sleep.

For the first thirteen days of the field season, Sandra and I found no orcas. Each morning and evening, I drove *Whale 1* to Whale Camp beach so Sandra could load Silver into and out of the boat. A retired sled dog, he was arthritic and nearsighted, and spent hours sleeping on the bunk, but he perked up when we stopped to photo-identify humpbacks. Then he paced the cockpit, ears and tail erect, in response to the whales' blows. Most days, we anchored off a beach for lunch, so Sandra could bring him to shore for a walk. Mornings I looked forward to seeing him outside my tent, nosing for a treat.

Thirteen days. We searched the Labyrinth, Dangerous Passage, Icy Bay, Knight Island Passage, Montague Strait. We photographed humpbacks, collected water, fished ice out of the drink to fill the coolers, cut firewood with handsaws and dragged it back to camp, recorded sightings of seals, sea lions, porpoises, minke whales, and we did it all almost entirely in silence. Sandra bristled at my questions, or at any mention of John. Some nights, we ate silent dinners sitting on stumps in front of my tent. Other nights we ate apart.

Even more than Sandra's cold shoulder, I was troubled by the lack of orcas, by fear that they'd died over the winter, or that the cleanup, which was back for a second summer (this time employing a new, worrisome tactic, bioremediation—the "fertilization" of beaches with chemicals to encourage oil-consuming bacteria), had finally driven the transients away.

And then, like the burning off of fog, like the Sound opening a door previously barred and suddenly letting us see inside, we found them, four Chugach transients at the mouth of Jackpot Bay. We'd been searching Pleaides Bay late in the evening, and it was dark in the mountains' shadow. A male and three females traveled line abreast, their fins jet black against spruce green water, their blows barely visible, disappearing as quickly as breath on glass. "They must be hunting," I said. When I checked the light meter, it was already too dark for photographs, so we followed at a distance as the whales traveled deeper into the bay. They were in no hurry. At the bay's head, the group broke up. It was like watching modern dance, interpretation based on scattered, telling gestures. The male and a female rapidly combed the shoreline. The other two surfaced at unpredictable intervals and locations. In contrast to their synchronized surfacing as they'd traveled into the bay, this looked chaotic. The hydrophone told another story, in the language of groans, cracks, squeals, and bangs. On the back deck, Silver paced, alert, his nails clicking audibly through the speaker.

> *2019–2039. Apparent attack. Loud bangs recorded but no orcas at surface. Terns flying, big splashes, irregular, aggressive swimming. Oily substance spreads around whales. Calls begin.*

Sandra dropped her reserve. She could predict where a whale would surface by watching where Silver fixed his stare, she said. It was clear the whales had killed something, probably a harbor seal. A faint fishy smell arose around us. They surfaced slowly now, milling in the bay's center, *Whale 1* drifting nearby. One of the females swam toward us, dove ten yards away. From the speaker, we heard the flush of her surfacing, the wheeze of her inhalation, the drips of water off her fin, then a violent churn as she bashed into the hydrophone. In the cove's stillness, every sound was amplified due to ambient silence. No wave noise. No boat engines. Separate echolocation clicks quickened into machine-gun bursts, ran into each other, blurred into rasps. Then the bangs, squeals and clicks ceased, and the bay was silent, but for the buzzing of terns as they dipped into the water, grabbing bits of fat. Then sounds resumed—groans, staccato clicks, horn blasts, quiet calls here and there amid the improvisation, with silence at irregular intervals. If it was music, it was a postmodern kind, mostly percussion, with a few oboes.

As below, so above. For moments, the bay appeared empty. Then an orca burst through, lobbing its fluke before turning over to swim belly-up, slapping its pectoral flippers, rocking on the keel of its dorsal. Sandra idled the boat into the fracas, and I stood on the bow with the swimming pool net. A greasy sheen flecked with hairs and fat tendrils spread over the surface. Satisfied with our samples, we shut down again, recording calls and jotting notes as the orcas fed and socialized and rested. No effort. I sat, notebook on lap, binoculars pressed to my eyes with one hand, pencil pressed to paper with the other, like the researchers I'd envied. It was as close as I could come to observing animal behavior the way Jane

Goodall or George Schaller might. The encounter lasted less than two hours. And though it revealed more than most long-term encounters with Chugach transients, their calls provided only suggestions of meaning. What had been the purpose of the loud underwater bangs, which hadn't coincided with breaches or tail slaps? I pictured a seal hiding in a crevice, an orca driving it out with a barrage of sound. Or had the bangs been caused by a sudden direction change, a fluke powered through the water like a whip crack? Those blasts were nothing like the typewriter-click trains of residents hunting salmon. They sounded like weapons. I pictured a seal quietly feeding in the cove, its world suddenly crashed into by that sonic onslaught, by the hunger of predators. How would it be to live like that? With that ever-present menace?

At nine, the whales, still calling and thrashing, the gulls and terns pursuing, disappeared behind rocks at the entrance channel. We stored the notebooks and took off after them, but they were nowhere to be found. When we dropped the hydrophone, we heard nothing. Within Jackpot Bay, they could make as much noise as they wanted, the bay a sonic antechamber. Once they reentered expansive Pleiades Bay, where sound could travel for many miles, they quieted. Motoring away, I felt a curtain close to the world they inhabited apart from us, hunting on through the night. We dropped in and out of that world only briefly, and, it seemed, at their bidding. By the time we tied onto the mooring in front of Whale Camp, Sandra and I had returned to our separate, human silence.

27

In Named and Unnamed Coves

MIDNIGHT, NORTHWEST BAY

Almost June. Kathy and Lance showed up at camp yesterday morning—they'd anchored in the cove at 2 am after following a group of transients into Drier Bay. The whales killed a seal. We've only seen them once. Have I been too preoccupied, not pushing hard enough? On the way past Herring Bay, I heard John, the DEC biologist from last summer, on the radio. We had a good chat. It was insanity up there at the north end of the island, just like last year, helicopters and boats and radio traffic.

The next day, we spotted blows off Brandt Island, in the Labyrinth, the same configuration of orcas Lance and Kathy had seen the night before, two females and a male. It was Ripple Fin, Chenega, and Iktua, but without Mike. They were offshore foraging, difficult to track, with six-, seven-, eight-minute dives. When they suddenly surfaced off Whale Camp beach, I thought of the fat seal that often watched us from the bight. That seal was obviously elsewhere, or well hidden. The orcas moved on, combing the shoreline toward Squire Point. Then they angled offshore again. After a seven-minute dive, Ripple Fin surfaced alone in the passage. A few minutes later, three more whales surfaced around him, including Mike. Gulls circled. They milled briefly, silent. I scanned the passage. Not a porpoise in sight.

That night, transcribing my notes, I thought about their meandering behavior. Craig called it "laying low," transients making themselves inconspicuous to potential prey. Lance and Kathy often remarked that on days when porpoises were scarce, they saw transients. As though porpoises were the ones "laying low," sensing the presence of predators. The transients' culture was a hunting culture, their senses constantly attuned, even when at rest or on the move, to the errant splash or squeak of prey. I closed my notebook and piled everything onto my plywood desk. It was past midnight, a full-moon tide. Standing on the porch brushing my teeth, I listened to waves churning against the berm just below the tent's walkway. I imagined the tide carrying the platform off into the night as I slept. A blast of air startled me. A humpback surfaced beyond the mooring. In the moonlight, I could just make out the broad fluke slipping beneath the surface, water zipping up around it, like a secret.

After three long days, we spotted Chugach transients, again off Brandt Island, again offshore foraging. But this time, we counted ten. In the midst of intermittent quiet calls, I heard something new, a low tone, like the voice of a humpback or a distant foghorn, slowly rising in pitch for several seconds, quavering. They repeated the call twice, then fell silent. Sandra and I worked our way through the group, taking ID photos, checking them off in the catalog. Ripple Fin, Chenega, Iktua, Mike. Marie, Ewan, Paddy. The young male Egagutak, who normally traveled with Kaj. No sign of Kaj, Shadow, or Totemof, though—the whales, along with Egagutak, that had been photographed beside the tanker.

There was Eyak, also without his group. He surfaced near Holgate, another adult male. Ten Chugach transients, ten survivors spread across the passage, heading into the strait, where it was too rough for us to follow. We'd wait ten days to see them again.

> *End of a weather day. Sitting on a rock south of camp watching for whales. Just got scolded by a pair of crows. They must have a nest. Found a mass of barnacle cyprids clinging to kelp, rocks, other creatures' shells—they "read" a site for survival potential before choosing to settle. How do they perceive oil?*
>
> *A big squall passes through; it sprinkles. Now the clouds shift to reveal Chenega Island. The water's calmed into a tight chop upon which a marbled murrelet bobs. A bubbling of silvery fish flips at the surface; suddenly a second murrelet pops up in the boil's center, a fish in its beak. In the woods behind me, songs of evening birds. I*

spot a kinglet in the alders using its tail as a rudder, hanging upside
down. Psip, it says. There's so much I don't know that's rudimentary.
Like why the kelp on one part of the beach is orange, not golden
brown. And what is that plant with whorled leaves and translu-
cent orange flowers? A phrase runs through my head like a mantra:
"Live the questions now." What choice do I have? Slow whoosh of
air above my head, a crow escorts an immature eagle away. Now
a mink bounds down the beach, disappears in the kelp. The next
squall creeps forward, descends. The mink galumphs toward me,
stops, sniffs, then hides under a rock. And now a seal. Floating near
a submerged boulder. Sitting still like this, I fall prey to mosquitoes,
but so much is happening, I don't want to move. A sleeping sea
lion lifts its nose to take a quavering breath. A louder blow. Two
blows. Silence. A humpback. Then another sea lion, darker than
the first. A merganser croaks as it flies past. Behind me a drone of
insects. Here's a sea otter lying on its back looking around, a starfish
clutched in its paws. If I sat here all day, what would fill these
pages? Out of nowhere, a helicopter. Clouds sink and rise, wind
rises and stills, the air becomes moister and cooler. It's impossible
to predict what will happen next.

A few days later, our solitary lives at Whale Camp ended. On a stormy morning, *Lucky Star* arrived, Craig and his teenaged deckhand Davin delivering a third wall tent, lumber, chain saw, fruit, cheese, eggs and veggies. A few days later, Olga would bring Molly Lou and Beth, the humpback team, in *Boomer*. In front of Whale Camp beach, *Lucky Star*'s engine throbbed. Pink and orange buoys, some tarred from pilings, swung against the flying bridge rails. The deck was crowded with gas barrels. The tide midway up and rising, Craig nosed *Lucky Star* in close, smiling at us from under his orange rain jacket hood, and told us to suit up for barrel-rolling. Towheaded Davin stood beside Craig, looking expectant, awaiting instructions. While we donned rain gear, Craig backed *Lucky Star* even closer to the beach. "Let her go!" he shouted to Davin. We heard a splash as a barrel hit the water, momentarily sank, then burst up and bobbed. After Davin hoisted over two more, Craig gunned the engine, sending a whirlpooling prop wash to push the barrels toward shore, where Sandra and I waited, our sleeves rolled up. We waded in to the tops of our gum boots and each grabbed a barrel by its lip, yanked it into the shallows, then rolled it above the tide's reach. An hour later, soaked from rain and sweat, we heaved the final barrel over a log and into place beside the others.

"Now let's eat lunch and look for whales," Craig said. "We can set up the wall tent when the rain backs off. Bring overnight bags in case we end up far from camp. I want to go north. Olga's due tomorrow from Whittier, and the weather forecast isn't good. We may end up meeting her halfway." I packed up my journal, toothbrush, book, a change of clothes, and we hopped, Silver and all, on *Lucky Star* and headed north along the Labyrinth, Craig and I sitting as we always did, back to back on the bench seat, he watching for residents in the middle of the Passage, me scanning the coastline for transients. If my gaze strayed too far west, he elbowed me. "Hey, get out of my quadrant," he said.

I settled into a welcome break from our routine on *Whale 1*. Under the "sissy lid" on *Lucky Star*'s flying bridge, Craig and I stayed dry while we scanned and chatted. Below, a kettle perpetually steamed on the diesel stove, and when I got cold, I climbed down, slipped into the cabin, and warmed my hands as a tea bag steeped in my mug.

After several unsuccessful hours, we anchored in an unnamed cove. The next morning was stormy, so we made pancakes, and waited for the wind and rain to subside. Lulled into lethargy by the low atmospheric pressure, the heat of the stove against my back, I gazed out the window. Breezes puffed through, ruffling papers on the dash. I ran my hand down the fogged-over window glass beside me, clearing it so I could see the shore. The forest dripped over rain-glazed rocks. Something black caught my eye. I rubbed the glass, blinked.

"Holy crap, it's an orca," I said.

"No shit. Where?" Craig dropped his spatula and stumbled out of the galley onto the back deck.

"I see it," he said. "Right against the shoreline. I'll be damned. It's got to be a transient. Who else would come into a place like this? No rest for the wicked."

"There's another one," I said, "a male. Looks like a male and a female."

While Craig checked the engine, and Sandra and Davin pulled the anchor, I ducked into the fo'c'sle to pull jeans and a sweater over my long johns. From the line over the stove, I grabbed socks and eased my toes into their warmth. Then I worked on my still-damp boots. Binoculars in hand, I hurried up to the bridge, grabbing my rain gear and my tea mug.

Lucky Star's engine rumbled, the silence of morning broken. Everything—water, sky, islands, the whales' blows, even the paint on *Lucky Star*'s deck—was murky gray or green. Except for those black fins combing the shoreline. Impatiently, I listened to the *clink-clink* of the anchor chain, the clang as the anchor rounded the chock and settled into place, the shift in throttle as Craig maneuvered *Lucky Star* around to follow the whales. He thrust his head out the cabin window. "For now, we'll follow from the big boat, since it's so wet," he called up to me. "I'll stay down here for now, where I can watch the depth sounder." I wondered if the whales could sense the intensity focused suddenly upon them. Did they startle at the engine, or had they been well aware of our presence the moment they'd entered the cove? It was barely big enough to hold *Lucky Star*. But here a seal might hide out. Here transients might hunt and kill a seal, and most of the time no one would know.

The orcas—it was Eccles and Lankard—foraged through the Labyrinth's tangle, combing the shoreline of Johnson Bay, marked blue on the chart, riddled with asterisks and crosses for rocks. A mariner's nightmare, for transients it was an ideal hunting ground, full of hidey-holes for seals. At Drier Bay's mouth, the pair paused to mill, perhaps listening before deciding on a course. They headed into the bay, but then abruptly backtracked, continuing south down Long Channel, where harbor seals clustered on rocks and sea otters floated in kelp beds in coves too small for any vessel bigger than a kayak or rowboat. Watching them for hours in that cold, I got hungry. Craig got bored, and taunted me, as he often did, claiming that residents were more interesting than transients. Even Davin's fascination ebbed. He retreated into the warm cabin and chatted with Sandra.

"Just wait," I told Craig, "something amazing is bound to happen. They've got to make a kill." But nothing happened: no calls, no kills. I didn't mind. "If residents are around, we'll hear them on the hydrophone," I reminded him, as he climbed down from the bridge to take a nap.

"Whatever. Transients make me incredibly tired."

I stayed on the bridge, drinking cup after cup of tea, tossing handfuls of gorp into my mouth, driving, stopping, dropping the hydrophone, taking notes, watching the hours of observation time accrue. Back out in the passage, the pair milled, breaching, tail slapping, as though they'd bored even themselves. Then they swam a beeline toward Icy Bay. The glacier still miles distant, bergs appeared nevertheless, glowing bubble-gum blue in the gray water, as though phosphorescent. Finally, Craig emerged from his nap to say it was high time to photograph a few hump-backs for Olga before turning in for the night. I watched them disappear into the ice at the mouth of Icy Bay, where perhaps Eyak was waiting.

That evening, I studied the catalog. We'd accounted for all of Eyak's group except Gage. Twelve certain survivors. One certain death. Nine still unaccounted for. As I transcribed notes, I felt anxious that I so rarely saw kills. What was barring my vision? Part of it, I knew, was my focus on acoustics. Most of the time, I sat watching, listening, recording one aspect of their lives, missing another.

Sometimes those years at Whale Camp, standing on top of the bluff, looking down at Knight Island Passage, I felt a kind of pressure against my skin and bones, concentrated in my chest. I wanted to open my eyes as wide as possible, to enlarge my sight to take it all in. I wanted to know everything about the Chugach transients. I wanted the edges that separated me from the Sound to disappear. Until I discovered another way, science was my tool. And science depended on that very separation I wished to erase.

28

The Smallest Island

The next day, the storm peaking, we headed north up the passage, Craig calling every few minutes: "*Whale 3, Whale 3, Lucky Star*, WYM 9638. You there, Olga?"

Finally, she answered. While they talked, I set to work making soup and cake. It was Father's Day. When *Boomer* pulled up to *Lucky Star*, three drenched, rain-gear-suited figures scurried to drop buoys and hand over lines. As always, Olga's blue eyes beamed out like sunny weather from beneath her orange hood. Elli, chin to thighs in a baby-blue life jacket over toddler-sized rain gear, stood clutching the gunwale. "Daddy!" she shrieked when she saw Craig. *Boomer*'s deck was a mess of gas cans, bunched up survival suits, fishing poles, and plastic buckets. Clearly aftermath. I tried to read Beth and Molly's faces, slick with rainwater and salt spray, tendrils of brown hair stuck to their foreheads.

Soon we were crowded in the cabin, bodies taking up every open space, windows fogged from moisture evaporating from hair and clothes and skin. As the storm wind whistled down the stovepipe, we ate soup, drank tea, and listened to Olga's account of their crossing of notorious Port Nellie Juan. They'd surfed down six-foot following seas, so scared that Olga had called the Main Bay hatchery to let someone know their location, just in case they had to put out a Mayday call. Halfway across, they'd pulled survival suits over their clothes, Olga zipping Elli into her own. Olga laughed as she described the chaos, fuel cans sliding back and forth, gear tumbling around in the cabin, but Beth and Molly looked shell-shocked. Later, Beth would tell me of her terror, and her skepticism at the seaworthiness of *Boomer.* She hadn't wanted to make the crossing.

Beth, a dark-eyed, petite woman in her early twenties, a NMFS employee, was not used to Craig and Olga's rough-and-tumble style. She'd just finished her master's project photo-identifying Dall's porpoises in Puget Sound. Molly Lou, nineteen, petite and delicate-featured, had just finished her first year at college, studying environmental science. She'd grown up on a homestead near Craig and Olga's, in a hand-built log house without plumbing. Summers, she and her sisters crewed on their father's commercial fishing boat. Molly Lou wanted time in the field, to ensure biology was the right career path.

Later, Molly Lou would mirror back her first impression of me in my bulky sweater and oil-stained Carhartts, holding the Father's Day cake I'd baked and decorated with wildflowers. "You seemed so open, a magical person, with your Latvian cheekbones," she would say. While I felt the opposite of magical, in the face of my tense relationship with Sandra, I certainly was open that afternoon, hungry for connection.

Dusk fell early. After clearing the supper dishes, Craig pulled anchor and we headed for Whale Camp, dozing as the boat lurched down the passage.

The next day, the sky clear, the clouds erased in the night as though swept by a hand, I woke early to the rumble of *Lucky Star*'s engine as the boat dropped anchor in front of camp, preparing to unload gear, lumber, and the new wall tent. We spent the morning building a second platform. Now we'd have a sleep tent and a cook tent. I realized how worn our old wall tent was, how much light it let in through its threadbare fabric. The sleep tent, with its heavy waterproofed canvas, was dim, and smelled of freshly cut spruce.

That evening, we sat on drift logs around the campfire, eating halibut and beach greens on tin plates, toasting marshmallows for dessert, sipping mugs of smoky tea. Olga perched the teapot on a tripod of logs. Elli ambled around the beach, collecting twigs and pebbles and tossing them toward the water. It felt like a different place. The stories bandied among eight people replaced the quiet, unresolved story Sandra and I had lived out on Squire Island. I felt a door close against what seemed already an irredeemable past.

A week after Molly Lou and Beth's arrival, we decided to switch crews for a day. Sandra and Beth took *Boomer* to look for humpbacks. Molly

Lou and I headed north along the Labyrinth, stopping inside each bay to drop the hydrophone, to listen for blows, to scan the shorelines for fins. Molly Lou studied every inch of the chart, memorizing names. Seeing and hearing no orcas in the Labyrinth, we crossed to Dangerous Passage, heading south, photographing humpbacks on our way, then stopping to strip down and jump into the water, what would become a ritual for us in the years to come. By the time we exited Dangerous Passage, it was 9:00 p.m., but we didn't want our day to end. There was a kind of magic between us. "Let's find an island to explore," Molly Lou suggested. We snacked on trail mix and apples to stave off hunger. Then we chose an island along Chenega's shore, so small that our wall tent wouldn't have fit on top of it. I followed Molly Lou as she crawled on her hands and knees into the blueberry understory along a river otter trail. Soft new growth on spruce branches brushed my face. My hands sunk wrist-deep into moss. We traced a cinnamon smell to its source, crushed rusty menziesia leaves. Emerging on the island's other side, we laughed to tears at seeing each other: our wool sweaters stuck all over with lichen and twigs. We pressed more forest detritus into each other's sweaters and hair, to see if Sandra and Beth would notice. Later that night, in what would become another repeated gesture, Molly Lou handed me a book open to a poem. It was called "Their Heads Bent Toward Each Other Like Flowers."

29

It Barely Makes a Sound

Iktua Bay, a wide scoop out of the side of an island, is marked at its entrance by a prominent, bare outcrop, Iktua Rock. Every time Sandra and I passed it, we slowed to count harbor seals hauled out around its base, and wondered why we never found Chugach transients there. It was one of the haul-outs Lloyd and Kathy regularly surveyed.

It had been another ten-day stretch without transients, and when we spotted them that afternoon, I wasn't really looking. We'd come into Iktua Passage to take shelter from the wind. I certainly didn't expect to see, through my binoculars, the entire body of a female orca airborne, frozen for a second against the backdrop of the shoreline. If not for that breach, I would never have spotted those three orcas. I was focused on staying dry as we transited steep seas. To our relief, they surfaced in the lee of tiny islands. I sat on the bow watching for rocks as Sandra idled closer. She glanced back and forth from the chart squashed under the dashboard to the orcas.

Eyak, Eccles, and Lankard breached and milled off a cobble beach. Again, no Gage. The engine had been running rough, so when we got close, we shut down, threw over the hydrophone, and I took notes while Sandra cleared water out of the filters and carburetor. All day we'd dealt with water in the fuel, stirred up from the bottom of the tanks by *Whale 1*'s pounding.

Judging by their excited behavior, it was likely the whales had just killed something. After twenty minutes, they began to travel rapidly into the passage, not stopping to forage along seal-crowded Iktua Rock. They seemed determined to get someplace. Paralleling them, *Whale 1* again bucked into a chop. But then the whales veered inshore, entering a maze of islands, rocks, and channels, some coves so tiny that we could barely maneuver. For two hours, they charged through the complicated geography, not like stealthy hunters, but like party crashers. Agitated, Eccles split off from the others, lobbing his fluke against the water. When we dropped the hydrophone, we realized he was vocalizing, repeating the same unfamiliar call. In the shallow, rocky channels, the shrill tone reverberated, reminding me of the whistle a kid makes, holding a grass blade between both thumbs, putting mouth to the gap between, and blowing hard. If there were a frustration call, this would be it. I wondered if some social altercation had taken place, a whale spat. With the racket caused by that shriek and the crack of Eccles's persistent tail lobs, every seal in his path would be on alert. *Travel,* I wrote in the notebook, not knowing what else to call it. Finally, four hours later, still within the island maze, Eyak and Lankard slowed, milling and vocalizing. Eccles caught up. The trio joined, their bodies close, as though reestablishing bonds. After that, everything changed. They turned and swam back the way they'd come, foraging now in earnest like real transients, silent, slinking along rocks and islets. If there'd been a spat, it was done. It took them two hours to cover four miles. Not until much later, in the shadow of Evans Island, did they kill a seal.

It had been one of the best days with Sandra. I could no more divine her mood shift than I could an orca's, but I was grateful for the gift of that twelve hours, the two of us working in tandem, equally tuned into the whales, engine mechanics, and weather. Three days later, Sandra, Silver, and the camp at the far end of the beach would be gone. The rest of that summer, and all the years after, when I'd hike the path to the blueberry thicket, I'd pause to contemplate the platform she'd nailed together of scavenged lumber, the life she'd lived inside her canvas tent. I'd remember the awkwardness with which we'd coexisted. For six weeks, we'd lived within a few hundred yards of one another, for much of that time the sole inhabitants of an island you could hike across in one day. We'd spent hundreds of hours together on a boat smaller than a king-sized bed. Yet I didn't know her at all. The poet Rilke wrote: "As it happens, the wall between us is very thin. Why couldn't a cry from one of us break it down? It would crumble easily, it would barely make a sound." Neither one of us had uttered the right cry. We didn't speak the same language. Though

I'd sometimes pass Sandra in the halls of the biology department that fall, she'd look away from my hello with an enigmatic half smile. I'd learn that when she spoke of her summer, she made it sound like she'd been alone. Essentially, it was true. To her friend John, who eventually became my husband, she'd say little about what went wrong between us. She'd never speak to me again.

30

Breathing in Never-Night

Midsummer. One night, transcribing data in the tent, I looked up to let my eyes rest on the glimmering water in the bight. A pod of sea lions breathed somewhere out of my line of sight. An eagle uttered three questioning cries, then stopped, as though it couldn't muster the effort to finish its query. I listened for blows. I imagined transients slinking through the Labyrinth. We'd been counting seals on our searches, finding fewer hauled out on the rocks than I remembered. According to Lloyd and Kathy, the oil spill might have steepened their decline. They worried about the impact of Native hunting, lingering oil, contaminants, depleted feed fish, predation. I worried about the impact the decline could have on the Chugach transients.

A few days later, those worries were temporarily allayed. As they had in 1989, Eyak's group and Ripple Fin's group returned to the study area and stayed. With Matt, who'd arrived to replace Sandra, I followed them for the better part of four days. Of all the transients, those two groups seemed most tied to Knight Island Passage. They were called transients, but during July, they took up residence near Whale Camp. I fell asleep each night to waves churning against the beach, reminding me that I lived on the edge of their world, almost a cohabitant.

We first spotted Chenega's group while the four of us sat in front of the tent eating breakfast: four blows evaporating against the Pleiades, and then, through binoculars, dorsal fins. Matt and I rushed to gather gear, while Molly Lou and Beth hauled gas jugs to the water's edge. By the time we were underway, the orcas were milling off Squire Point, diving repeatedly in the same place. "Let's listen," I said. "It looks like feeding."

Matt tossed the hydrophone over the side and turned on the speaker. We heard calls and the cracks of their flukes thwacking the water's surface. For forty minutes, we sat recording and writing notes. As always, conflicting desires yanked at me, the desire to get closer, to look for scraps of flesh, the desire to get photographs, the desire to record calls. For my oil spill work, the photos took precedence; for my graduate study, the recordings came first.

Finally, the whales moved on. They disappeared into Sanctuary Bay's narrow entrance channel, past David's "turtle rocks." Most likely they were the same four who'd surfaced off *Orca 2*'s bow the year before. Already attached to Knight Island's geography in my mind were stories I'd heard, encounters I'd had with Chugach transients, and stories I'd lived with Mary, Matt, Sandra, Olga, and Craig.

We shut down at the bay's entrance. Waiting for the whales to resurface, I thought of all the seals I'd watched when we'd anchored in Sanctuary Bay, the hippo-like way they floated, nostrils barely clearing the surface, following me as I paddled *Puff* to shore, diving with a splash if I spun around and caught their eyes. Just as I was about to tell Matt to pull up the hydrophone and head into the bay, the whales emerged. On down the coast they hunted, ducking into Mummy Bay, where they milled, calling, echolocating, whip cracking, the same sounds they'd made during the seal kill in Jackpot. From my hours at the sonograph analyzer, I now simultaneously heard and saw their sounds. I filled a field book page with symbols reflecting modulations in pitch, X's for bangs, W's for whistles. Like a score, I could later read the page and hum it back to myself. "Talking about music is like dancing about architecture," it has been said. Well, talking about orca language is a lot like talking about music. I couldn't help but think I might be hearing it all wrong, missing nuances and underlayers, perceiving only at the most unsophisticated level. The real meaning—intention, emotion, mood—was imbedded in what was beyond my perception.

Sometimes I grew bored and frustrated with the dullness of my notations: *Silent, traveling along shore to Little Bay. Infrequent surfacing. Foraging along beach. Spread out. Moving slowly and getting closer together. Moving out of Little Bay. 30 m from shore, all together. Slow surfacing. Move to 100 m offshore, then back to 30. Travel toward Point Helen.* Naturalist Henry Beston wrote of animals that "in a world more complete than ours they move gifted with extensions of the senses we have lost or never attained, living by voices we shall never hear." Science asked me to observe, take notes, collect data, test hypotheses, and then say something meaningful and new. But the more I watched, the greater my sense that saying something meaningful and new, and most importantly, saying something true about the Chugach transients, required a language I hadn't yet acquired.

The next morning, under a high, broken overcast, Matt and I skimmed across a mirror of milky blue and lead gray. At the Pleiades, we sat a long time listening and scanning, trying out a strategy of patience and fuel conservation. On a day that calm, the hydrophone had a ten-mile range. So we scanned, chatted, sipped tea from the thermos, and waited.

Matt spotted the blow against one of the Pleiades, then a familiar squat fin: Eyak, traveling south at a good clip, following a steady compass course, 330 degrees. Matt kept the boat on that heading, and I sat on the bow snapping ID photos. "I've got the pictures, now let's run ahead and listen," I said, bracing myself on the cabin top. "He's alone, and maybe he's calling, like last year. Remember our encounter with him? I'd love to get more recordings."

"Of course I remember. The singing male." Matt pushed up the throttle, and we roared ahead and then stopped. Calls blared out of the speaker, sure enough, the same as the summer before. I scribbled my hieroglyphics. There it was, Eyak's song. The long descending wail, the series of abrupt hiccups, the horn blast. He dove. Silence. He surfaced, tilted on his side, dorsal almost parallel to the water. Changing direction, he traveled back to the Pleiades, and then abruptly stopped, turning 360 degrees, projecting calls in all directions. He then swam between two of the Pleiades, surfacing erratically, as though drunk. There he veered, belting out his song again, now heading east across the passage with purpose, now slowing, his dorsal wobbling from side to side, then canting over. What was wrong with him? He was staggering, if a whale could stagger. And that's the way he continued north, up the passage, traveling, staggering, singing.

Suddenly Beth's voice drifted from the VHF speaker.

"*Whale 1, Whale 1*, this is *Whale 3*."

"*Whale 3, Whale 1*. Channel 14?"

"Switching to 14."

"Hi, Beth, what's up?"

"Hey, just wanted you to know we're off Crafton Island with six transients, and they're going crazy. We're sitting here with the engine off, and they're all around us. We could hear them vocalizing through the hull. One swam over and rubbed against the boat. There was this echolocation burst right before."

"Can you stay with them? We've got Eyak here, and he's heading that way, but he's acting weird, meandering around, calling really loud. Maybe he's trying to find your whales."

"No problem."

I looked at Matt. "Pretty cool," he said, grinning. "I'd better get ahead of him again, he's traveled quite a ways north."

When we stopped again, a few hundred yards in front of Eyak, he'd reached the Labyrinth. More agitated, he lunged from the water in a half breach, and I was stunned at his size and girth. He resumed calling. When he finished, he lobbed his fluke against the water. Was this whale frustration?

For two hours he repeated the pattern: traveling, stopping to call and mill and lunge or tail-lob, skimming the Labyrinth's edge. Then we lost him. Matt spotted an evaporating blow beside New Year Island, then a fin sweeping along the rocks, as though Eyak were hoping to scrape off a seal. "Foraging," I wrote in the notebook. Had he given up trying to find the others? At the next island, Squirrel, Eyak again hugged shore, nosing into the rocks. He combed the island's entire length, then resumed traveling and vocalizing at full volume. How far away, I wondered, could his calls be heard? Past Squirrel Island, he lashed his fluke, then dove.

"Listen, Matt," I said. "I think I hear distant calls." Faint though they were, I could tell they were Chugach transients. "It must be the others. How far away is that, I wonder?"

"Let me check the chart," Matt said, ducking down into the cabin.

That's when Eyak began screaming. His body exploding from the water, his whole head exposed for a few seconds, thousands of droplets flying past his face with the force of his momentum. He crashed under, then burst back up a few seconds later. Emitting the same wild banshee cry, he porpoised north toward Crafton Island. On the speaker we could hear water rushing past his body with each surfacing. Only when his cries began to fade did we pull up the hydrophone and race toward him—the black-and-white and crystalline rocketing of him into and out of the sea.

"He must be going fifteen knots. It feels like it's taking forever to catch up," Matt said. "I've got the throttle all the way down."

I sat on the bow leaning forward as if I could eek a few more knots out of *Whale 1* with my body's yearning. When we stopped again, Eyak was still screaming, and in the background of those screams, more distinct now, we could hear the excited vocalizations of the others.

Whale 3, Whale 3, Whale 1."

"*Whale 1, Whale 3.*"

"Eyak heard the others finally, and he's charging your way. Are you still in the same place? Are they still doing the same thing?"

"Yup, they're still just socializing here, crazy high leaps and upside-down swimming."

"You should see us before long," I said.

No dives. I wrote in the notebook. *Porpoising—rapid travel—mid-channel toward Crafton Island.* It was hard to fathom the musculature that propelled eight tons of orca for a full hour against the resistance of water. He never slowed. *1719, now silent and porpoising violently,* I wrote, just before he closed in on Eccles, who milled apart from the others, as if waiting. To our surprise, Eyak charged by him, Eccles turning and following. The other whales slammed their flukes at Eyak's approach, the blue *Boomer* bobbing amid tilting fins. Eyak disappeared into the fracas. We stopped within shouting distance of Beth and Molly Lou. *1743. All together socializing. Whistles, calls. Eyak upside-down, fluke slapping.*

Molly Lou and Beth stood barefoot on *Boomer*'s bow in sunglasses, their jeans cuffs rolled high. The water between us was so still it seemed gelatinous, tide-shivered and beribboned with color and shadow: ice blue, platinum, indigo, smoke. But around the whales, it churned. Eyak, Eccles, Lankard, Ripple Fin, Chenega, Iktua, and Mike twisted and rolled, slashing at the water's skin with their flukes, swishing it sideways, shattering it, throwing it up into the sky. Taken inside, air became another plaything, modulated like putty in the intricate hollows and pockets of their nasal passages, forced through structures called monkey lips to create whatever sound they wanted—clicks, whistles, pulsed calls. Though in play they blew rude-sounding bubble clouds from their blowholes, they didn't have to release air to vocalize like we do. No larynx, no vibrating vocal cords, no tongue or mouth sang or spoke. They used their mouths solely to kill or eat or carry a wand of kelp or bite one another. They used their blowholes to capture air, then move it around, recycle it, sculpt it into sound. They sang through their foreheads. That pulse of sonic energy could travel, as we'd seen, fifteen miles to call a roaming male home. Tape after tape captured the vocal rumpus, sounds at turns so wild, eerie, or raucous they could easily fit into the improvisational segment of a Grateful Dead concert called "Space."

When the pink penis of a male flopped at the surface, we motored closer. Eyak swam behind Iktua and Chenega. I saw a flash of silver as Iktua threw a pink salmon into the air, leaving it stunned on the water. Swimming on his side, Eyak trailed the females, his penis still extended. He tipped up partway and blew a raspberry from his blowhole, then dove beneath Iktua and Chenega, who porpoised away. Then Iktua slowed, allowing Eyak to catch up, and the sexual cat-and-mouse game continued. By then, it was almost 9:00 p.m. Molly Lou and Beth left to head back to Whale Camp.

"Do you mind if we stay with them a little longer?" I asked Matt.

"Of course not. I don't mind if we stay with them all night. But I've got to eat something or I'll get grumpy."

In the few minutes of distraction, of saying goodbye and digging out cheese and crackers, trail mix, chocolate, and apples, the orcas vanished. We glassed the water frantically with binoculars.

"They can't have disappeared," I cried. Fifteen minutes passed. "I swear you can't take your eyes off them for a second."

"There they are," Matt said, pointing toward the north end of Knight Island.

But the animals we approached at the entrance to Lower Passage were like another kind of orca entirely: silent, skulking along the shoreline in three separate groups. For a few moments I wondered if they were different whales. But then we took stock: three males, Eyak, Eccles, and Ripple Fin. Four smaller ones. While our backs had been turned, they'd transformed back into hunters, zipped on different skins. They combed the shoreline of the narrow passage before entering Montague Strait.

Something strange happens to the Sound at night in midsummer. Notions of illumination turn upside down. The sky grows dusky, but the sea gleams, as though it absorbs sunlight all day and then releases it slowly, imperceptibly, like a fugitive exhaling a long-held breath. Darkness doesn't fall. At dusk, it leaks out of the forests like an infusion of ink. People talk about a "midnight sun," but this far south, the sun does set. It's just that night doesn't arrive. My poet friend coined a term for it, "never-night." It's the most accurate name I know for the time of day when people up here finally drop off to sleep. But Matt and I would not sleep. This was it, we knew, our chance to follow Chugach transients for twenty-four hours.

At midnight, Chenega's group broke away from Eyak's and turned into Bay of Isles, a convolution of coves and islets. In the twilight of that place, we'd be blind. We had no electronic instruments, and Bay of Isles was full of rocks. Eyak's group continued down the strait, so we stayed with them. During the darkest hours, we followed Eyak and his resting companions by listening for their blows. We learned to distinguish the terminal breath, the last in a series, by its greater volume. The whales would be holding that breath for several minutes. Once we knew they were down, we started the engine and motored forward, trying to place ourselves ahead of them, but within earshot. Then we shut down and listened. *Whoosh. Whoosh, whoosh.* Like owls, we strained our ears to gauge direction and distance, refining our hearing as the hours passed. Fortunately, the strait was calm and the whales resting. Matt and I took turns dozing in the cabin. Gradually, in a reversal of the evening's process, light bled back into the air drop by drop. This time, the sea retained night's shadow as the sky overhead brightened. Just as we'd strained our ears, we now strained our eyes to see the whales when they surfaced. At 6:30 a.m., they woke up, traveled inshore, and rounded Point Helen, just a few miles from where we'd first spotted Eyak the day before.

"Hello, all vessels," Kathy's voice piped out of the VHF speaker. "This is the research vessel *Whale 2*." It was the first radio call we'd heard in hours. *Whale 2* sounded close. Punchy with exhaustion, I called Lance and Kathy to ask if they'd take over for us. I didn't want to let Eyak's family go, but Matt and I needed sleep. And Lance needed data on transients for his echolocation study.

We left the whales at 9:30 a.m., three hours shy of twenty-four. Back at camp, after a breakfast of granola and boxed milk, I hiked out to the muskeg where I'd set up a tent, and let myself collapse into sleep. During those hours, Lance and Kathy followed Eyak's group to Icy Bay.

In one day, Eyak circumnavigated Knight Island, as though drawing a map of the center of his family's range. The line I drew on the data sheet that night, depicting his path, described as well the center of my life, the locus from which I grew, both as a biologist and as a person. I now understood why David thought of Knight Island as the heart of the Sound. James Galvin, in his novel *The Meadow*, writes of a man named Lyle living on the edge of a field in the Medicine Bow country of the Rockies: "He lived so close to the real world it almost let him in." Lyle had his Neversummer Mountains. I had Prince William Sound's never-night. In the twilight, alone on *Whale 1*'s deck while Matt slept, listening for blows, I'd come as close to that "real world" as I'd ever been. The whales breathed. I moved.

The next day, rested, Matt and I loaded the boat with food and fuel and headed out as always, into gray squalls. Bobbing off the Pleiades, we glassed the passage but saw nothing. In that regard, it began as most days did, full of expectation and waiting. The twenty-four-hour encounter over, the slate of our fieldwork was wiped clean. No residual luck kept us tuned into the Chugach transients. We had to start over from the beginning each day. The norm: hours of searching interrupted by hump-back encounters or minor engine repairs. That's what we were doing—fiddling with the carburetor, clearing it of water—when Molly Lou called on the radio. She and Beth had found transients in Dangerous Passage. We scrambled to put the fuel system back together, then started up and high-tailed it north. We were ten miles away.

We found the whales swimming out of Ewan Bay, one of four long fingers cutting deep into the mainland side of Dangerous Passage. Eyak, Eccles, and Lankard foraged along the shoreline, then rounded the corner into the next bay, with Paddy stopping to mill behind a cluster of islands. A seal watched the whales from its haul-out rock. Below it, in the water, another snugged tight to shore. Two sea otters craned their necks. The whales, dead silent, swam toward the rock. The seal in the water held itself motionless. Unable to reach it, the orcas turned and left.

Back in Dangerous Passage, the whales grouped together to rest. Line-abreast, their bodies touching, they surfaced in synchrony, inscribing a big slow circle. For two and a half hours, this circle drifted from one side of the passage to the other. It was the behavior Craig called "deep rest," and I'd seen it only with residents before. We shut down the engine. We took out our thermos and drank tea. We talked, and gradually, it turned into deep talk, down below surface layers, past science, past careers. I'd given Matt a copy of *The Little Prince*. We watched the whales and mused about the book's meanings: the rose, the fox, the tiny planet, the volcano. *You are responsible, forever, for what you have tamed*, the fox tells the little prince. What did that mean, to be tamed? Was it a good thing? A bad thing? What did it mean about friendship? About love for a place, for animals? We ate supper. We fell silent. Once in a while, we moved the boat a few hundred yards so as not to miss a quiet call, but the whales were silent too. Hidden there, Eyak and his family slept. How often had they done this precisely here, I wondered? How often did they need to deeply rest? Why hadn't we seen it before? Did they have secret hideouts all over the Sound for just this purpose? And how often did our presence inhibit them? Or shorten the duration of their sleep?

Soon even my questions turned to rest, to silence. All that mattered in that moment was this: the whales were at ease, safe, Eyak, Eccles, Paddy, and Lankard asleep, and a small boat at the periphery of the circles they inscribed on the water, almost, not quite, in their midst.

31

Transients Outside the Box

In the following days, wind, rain and low visibility hindered our search efforts. From radio reports of small groups of orcas, we pieced together possible Chugach transient scenarios. But from what we'd learned following them, the reports were, in their specifics, about as reliable as ghost sightings. The best they could offer us was an imagining, a tale spun of scattered facts. On July 7, a single orca was spotted off Jackpot Island, not far from where we'd left Eyak and his family. Later that day, two males were sighted inside Granite Bay, at the northern end of Dangerous Passage. And then the next day, a fisherman radioed a sighting of a single male off Herring Bay. I mentally drew lines on a map, connecting those three sightings to our encounter with Eyak's group. They were trees falling in the forest of my study. Only hermit thrushes, seals, sea lions, bald eagles, and perhaps the bays and islands themselves felt the water displace as a male orca surfaced. Only they heard his blows and perceived his absence after he left.

In the meantime, a storm kept us in camp, each inhabiting a small territory of the tent to read, write letters, or catch up on data work. Sock-footed, clad in long johns and T-shirts, we skirted bodies sprawled on the plywood floor to boil water for tea or to make lunch. Whoever sat nearest the woodstove fed it almost continuously. When we got too claustrophobic, we donned rain gear and hiked, searching for early blueberries, combing the beaches for interesting drift.

On the storm's dying day—squalls still marching down the passages, the seas still choppy—resident orcas, AB, AD and AN pods, appeared off camp, as though blown in on the gale's tailwind. Matt and I followed them all day as they hunted for salmon in Pleiades Bay, filling the so-often silent underwater amphitheatre with their clicks and squeals. We anchored that night in Ewan Bay, chilled from eight damp hours with the whales, but hopeful at the evening's clearing sky. The last dry day seemed a surreal memory. That night, hunched in my sleeping bag in *Whale 1*'s cabin, I labeled three rolls of film, knowing that inside those canisters was evidence. Six more ABs were missing.

At 7:00 a.m. the next day, after heating water for our thermos on the camp stove, we motored across the bay's glassy surface, trailing a thin cirrus of exhaust, and I wished, as I often did, that we too could travel in silence.

We decided to search north up Dangerous Passage, eating granola bars for breakfast. When we emerged into Knight Island Passage, we found the water calm, a languid expanse silking north to the base of the mirage-warped Chugach Range. I dried the dew off the cabin top with a towel and sat searching with binoculars, barefoot, bare-headed, wearing jeans and a sweater, feeling reborn out of the stiff rain gear I'd worn for days, and five pounds lighter. Matt and I bantered. The lifted cloud ceiling had, it seemed, removed any heaviness from our heads. Leaning back against the windshield I turned my face up to the sun's warmth and stretched my arms over my head.

"Don't get too relaxed," Matt said.

I bolted up, turned to look where he was looking.

"I see spouts, all the way across the Passage. I'm pretty sure they're orcas," Matt said. "The blows seem right."

Twenty minutes later, we were watching Eyak and Ripple Fin's groups diving repeatedly in the same spot, staying down for a long time with each breath, changing direction, as though working against currents to hold their position. Soon we began to hear clicks and calls. Perhaps those clicks helped them keep tabs on a sinking carcass. After an hour, the whales began to socialize, echolocation fading away, calls intensifying, including a vocalization I didn't recognize, a strange, ethereal chord. I drew a symbol for it in my notebook: four stacked parallel lines. It sounded like a bow drawn across the strings of a stand-up bass.

Calling and thrashing, the whales swam into Lower Herring Bay, directly into the path of cleanup boats. A skiff roared in from the north, stopping within shouting distance. It was a crew of Fish and

Game, Exxon, and Coast Guard personnel, surveying the cove for pre-bioremediation. To our surprise, they knew we were researching the whales, even asked if they should hold off their work until the orcas were gone.

"That would be great," I said. "They're pretty social right now, but usually these whales tend to avoid boats." The skiff hung back, its crew standing at the gunwales, watching. Off the bow of a Mississippi mud boat, the whales milled briefly, then swam out of the cove into the passage. They moved like a bait ball of fish, a concentrated fist of energy. Then it all subsided, the way bait balls dissipate and feeding gulls land in a scattered flock on suddenly quiet water. They floated, just their melons, blowholes, and fins above the surface, in classic orca "sleep," the only time an orca holds completely still. They gradually sank, fluke-first, and when water lapped at their blowholes, they abruptly awoke to inhale, then floated again. Catnap over, the calls, echolocation, and play resumed. They flipped upside-down, white bellies flashing, then enacted every acrobatic move in the orca repertoire: breaches, fluke and flipper slaps, lunges, surface skims like hunting sharks, sideways slides, spy-hops. Clicks built to a crescendo, and an orca burst from the water. Pink salmon jumped everywhere around them. Off our bow, Chenega rose headfirst from the water, once, twice, a third time. Under again, she blew a bubble cloud, then breached, a salmon flying off her snout.

"Did you see that?"

"I saw it," Matt said. "Maybe they do eat salmon."

The group began to move, so we pulled up the hydrophone and started the engine, motoring slowly toward a female swimming erratically near the shoreline. Her fin wobbled, as though she were braking. Then she drifted just under the surface, angling toward us. We leaned over the side and watched a salmon dart under the bow, just ahead of her snout.

The whales headed into Herring Bay, following its convoluted coastline. The year before, Herring Bay had been completely fouled by oil, loud and crowded with cleanup boats. Now it was quiet, from a distance, returned to its pre–oil spill tranquility. The whales swam in, as David Grimes would say, quoting Brer Rabbit, "just like there ain't been no hard times." Now silent, they angled toward shore. In a cove, the whales milled. *Strange roaring noises*, I wrote in my notebook. *Vocalizations and clicks.* An orca swam toward us, echolocating, then veered, sweeping its body along a sheer rock face. Ripple Fin and Eyak rolled over each other's bodies. Upside-down, their penises waved in the air. The group expanded and contracted, their choreography impossible to interpret. After circumnavigating Herring Bay, they again grew quiet. When we left, fourteen hours after we'd spotted them, they'd returned to the Labyrinth, silent, hunting transients again. We'd filled three cassettes—nearly four hours' worth—with their calls.

But what did it mean? I was baffled by their behavior. Were they indeed chasing fish to eat them? Or were the schools so thick along the shoreline that the orcas were using them, in their excited state, as playthings? The notebook was full of penciled observations. In one encounter, I'd doubled my recordings. But what could I say? It was as if an inverse relationship existed between data and knowing, as if the small pictures needed to accrue, the window into their lives first get more clouded, before the glass cleared and a big picture clarified. The mind of field biology, like the mind of art, requires equipoise of innocence and experience: open, unencumbered, what some call "beginner's mind," coupled with serious practice in observation, plus knowing how to ask good questions. From what I'd read about transients, from what I'd been told to expect by other orca biologists, I'd constructed assumptions and expectations. It's amazing how quickly the mind falls into its storytelling groove, fitting what the eye sees to a familiar narrative.

In British Columbia and southeastern Alaska, researchers have watched transients killing and abandoning seabirds, using them to train juveniles. We've watched Gulf of Alaska transient juveniles bashing sea otters and seabirds senseless, and then leaving them behind after the practice session ends. Residents in Puget Sound have played porpoises to death. Were the fish that day prey, tool, or toy? I wish I could go back with twenty years of experience, and grant myself permission to get in closer. I might have spotted flesh or a fish in an orca's moth, or a seal tucked under an orca's flipper. All I can say in hindsight is that the Chugach transients' behavioral repertoire was complex, spilling out of the boxes into which I'd crammed it.

18 JULY
Sitting on shore in a cove of Herring Bay. The water laps just as gently and the fog drifts by just as softly as it does in all the coves of Knight Island this morning. Yet this beach smells like a freshly

tarred road. Even now, after more than a year, tar balls entwine with eelgrass, kelp and twigs in the wrack-line. In rock crevices, oil is wet. I sit on a log, my feet tangled in beach peas. When I toe under the peas, I find a matt of oil imbedded with spruce needles. New plants grow out of this matrix, grass blades poking up through tar. Driftwood is plastered with the same amalgam.

One gull cries out.

Slowly approaching the shore where I sit, a shiny, red bioreme-diation balloon drifts, suspended over the gray water, turning in the wind. It's knotted with string to a stick, which floated free with last night's tide. We retrieved another balloon last night, tied to a small rock covered with barnacle spat. To think of the cleanup lodged here all last summer, yet oil so visibly remains, and now the assault of bioremediation: chemical fertilizers sprayed on beaches to spur the growth of oil-eating bacteria. Chemical fertilizers made of oil. The balloon floats closer. What does this place need to heal? There's only wind, alder leaves brushing against one another, thrum of insects, drip of water, quiet swirl of tide as it slips up and enfolds the rocks. Maybe this is the beginning of healing, the repeated lick of the tide, like an animal worrying a wound clean and raw.

As the balloon drifts closer, my throat tightens. It's emblazoned with a "face" intended to scare wildlife: black eye slashes and a jagged, angry pumpkin mouth. I grab it from the water and stab it with my pocket knife to let out the air. Its message deflates: biore-mediation area, keep out. The message is lost on the animals and it's lost on me. Out of nowhere, a sea lion breathes off the beach, lifting its head and pushing air out of its nostrils, which flare and close, flare and close.

32

Uncommon Language

A few days later, after a storm rolled through, two resident pods, AE and AK, passed Whale Camp. Across Pleiades Bay, clicking and calling to one another, they foraged for salmon. Throwing up rooster tails around their heads, "bow-riding," Dall's porpoises dogged the orcas. One whale, after several minutes, slammed its fluke on the water in annoyance. When the orcas dove, the porpoises, like us, slowed and waited. Bored, they entertained themselves with our boat. No one had come up with an explanation for this behavior other than play, other than mischief. Acoustically, no doubt, Dall's porpoises can tell residents from transients.

Waiting, Matt scanned the periphery with binoculars to make sure we weren't missing far-flung groups.

"I see a few a ways to the south, coming toward us," he said.

"Maybe they're new whales joining in. One more and it's a superpod."

Instead, we found Eyak, Eccles, and Lankard traveling straight toward the residents. First fish bouncing off transient heads. Now this. The conventional wisdom was that transients avoided contact with residents. Now was our chance to test the ground truth of this theory for Chugach transients. We dropped the hydrophone. The familiar AK resting call, a groan, issued from the speaker. Then a few transient quiet calls. Then the strange, upswept whistles of the AEs, like the signals of extraterrestrials. Then a few more transient quiet calls. *Now within a mile of each other*, I wrote in the notebook. The transients hugged the shoreline, not slowing. *200 yards apart.* Passing the resting AEs and AKs, whose calls had died to nothing, the transients, still emitting the occasional quiet call, didn't try to disguise their presence or avoid the residents, which they must have heard from miles away. But neither did either group cross the invisible boundary between them. I thought again about the Dall's porpoises, now vanished. Had they used the residents as an acoustic shield? Did traveling for a time with residents grant them a reprieve from their constant vigilance?

Eyak, Eccles, and Lankard were intent on one place, Icy Bay. Once inside its wide mouth, they separated, working their way deeper through the ice. As always, we struggled to penetrate floes the orcas navigated effortlessly. Matt sat on the bow with the paddle, pushing away chunks when the ice got so thick we couldn't find a lead. Finally, in the evening, one whale slapped its fluke, then lunged across the surface. We watched the trio tightly circling and diving across the boundary separating us, a field of ice. *Feeding*, I wrote in the field book.

At 8:30 p.m., the whales circumnavigated Verdant Island, a small, forested hump at Icy Bay's entrance. Lankard swam close to its rocky, kelp-clad side. Movement caught my eye. A sleek brown form scurried straight up from the water's edge. Immediately, Lankard thrust himself after it. It was a river otter. From his high perch, the otter stared down at Lankard with intense black eyes. Lankard slid down until the water closed around his head. He swam on. Within seconds, the otter leaped into the sea and disappeared. Did it consider itself orca food? I thought of the odd items on the prey list in *Orca: The Whale Called Killer.* River otters were on that list, along with sea otters. Orcas have even attacked swimming moose in South East Alaska. But those were anomalies.

In Denali Park one autumn, friends and I waited an hour for a mother grizzly and her two cubs to descend a draw and cross the park road. When they finally put their paws on the pavement, one friend, who'd been standing near his car, spooked, bolting for the car door. Instantly, one of the cubs charged him, then just as quickly stopped and continued ambling across the road. It had stunned me, the instinct with which the cub had reacted: a running figure inciting immediate chase. Perhaps the river otter, startled, leaping onto the rocks, triggered a similar response from Lankard, who was hunting, not for river otters, but for seals. Or perhaps Lankard was just curious.

As August approached, the world closed around us and turned gray. The weather, not windy enough to keep us at camp, was wet enough to drench us despite rain gear. All night, we stoked the fire to dry our clothes. Sometimes in desperation I placed my felt boot liners on top of the woodstove, where they steamed, then scorched. Even our sleeping bags grew clammy. Our musty-smelling rubber boots never dried out. On the boat, we kept hand towels in our pockets to wipe the camera lenses, and rigged a plastic bag over the camera's body, with the lens poking out of a hole cut in the bottom. Still, by the end of long encounters, the autofocus acted up, the electronics rebelling against the moisture.

By the time the sun returned, life at Whale Camp had reconfigured itself again. I'd reluctantly said goodbye to Matt. Beth's fiancé, a whale researcher from Southeast Alaska, arrived to assist her, freeing Molly Lou to help me. On one of our long days of searching, I asked Molly Lou if she'd come back the next summer as my assistant. To my relief, she said yes. I now understood that life as a field biologist was as much about *the field* as it was about biology: it encompassed searching but not finding, weathering out, and breaking down, all the while inhabiting small spaces with another human. The choice of that other person mattered as much as the choice of a boat. It shaped a field season.

With Molly Lou, each day felt shaped, whales or no. We searched, we tinkered with the engine, we spent hours following orcas and humpbacks, but we also took breaks to hike barefoot across muskegs or swim in ponds. We gathered wild plants, baked bread, read, wrote letters, and philosophized—"speculated," as she put it. In matters of research, she followed my lead, but in most other ways I followed hers. She was uncertain about science as a career. Educated in the East Coast, she still loved Alaska, the wilderness, boats, water, the language of weather and seamanship and botany. She loved language most of all, especially poetry. Nightly she wrote in a journal. Inspired by her, I wrote more. The poems she shared spoke to me in a new, visceral language. Often Molly Lou read poems and stories out loud while we worked on tasks at Whale Camp. They were contrapuntal lines to the lines of scientific inquiry and self-inquiry I'd been following. There was a way, I saw, to turn all of it—spirit, thought, reflection, description, science, desire—into one thing, not just into art, but into a life. In those weeks with Molly Lou, I got an inkling of something one of the poets she introduced me to called "the dream of a common language."

One day that summer, John, the man I'd been dating back in Fairbanks, arrived at Whale Camp in his kayak. For a few stormy August days, he accompanied Molly Lou and me on *Whale 1*. When we took him into Sanctuary Bay, it was as if we'd invited him into our private world. A gifted photographer, he snapped a picture of Molly Lou and me standing in a field of fireweed taller than our heads. It sits on my desk to this day. It captures the way we lived a second childhood in the Sound, like sisters separated since the age of five, reunited to reclaim lost time, to school one another. It was a strange bilingual education: poetry and predation.

33

The Poetry of Predation

After Molly Lou left to return to college, Olga, two-year-old Elli, and baby Lars flew in to take her place. To accommodate life with a baby and toddler, we left camp later, and stayed out later, and took daily beach breaks to give Elli a chance to play on shore. Lars, sturdy and mellow, was content to spend hours dozing, bundled inside a sleeping bag, in *Whale 1*'s bunk. I cooked hearty meals for Olga, who lost many of her calories to Lars, as voracious an eater as the orca calves we photographed.

Though we searched relentlessly for transients, motoring slowly along the Labyrinth's edge, then down Dangerous Passage to Icy Bay, we didn't find them until late August.

Preparing to write about that encounter, that origin moment, I gather the day's records: the log, with its weather report, its extreme shorthand synopsis: *Headed N & found AT1's—foraging for porpoises. Watched them chase and kill 2 & followed for 10 hrs.* The encounter form with its tape numbers, whale identities, locations, times, behavioral categories. The composition book with its painstaking narrative of field notes. The call transcription sheets, like a score to the field notes' libretto. Added to that, memory with its gaps and illuminated scenes: the whales swimming past the seine fleet working the waters off Shelter Bay, the rumble and shriek of diesels and gas-powered skiffs and hydraulic motors drowning out the whales' quiet calls. Evening sun casting the fleet in a more romantic light than our hydrophone did. The dash of *Whale 1* crowded with binoculars, notebook, sunblock, water bottle, apples, granola bars, Elli's baby doll. Olga in a red jacket and wool hat, sitting on the swivel seat in front of the steering wheel, holding Elli on her lap. How we kept the kids occupied, content and fed for ten hours on a twenty-foot boat while tracking seven orcas is something I can't reconstruct, only state as a fact.

And then there's my tattered personal journal, with its unscientific preoccupations. Finally, falling out of a folder of data sheets, four pages of yellow legal paper covered with my careful cursive script, retelling the encounter in yet another language, this one deader and in some ways less credible than the others. *There were scores of jumping salmon and schools near the whales, and intense seining activity ~ 4 miles to the south, but no behavior of the whales indicated pursuit of or feeding on salmon. (They might have been doing it; we didn't observe it.)* I vaguely remember Craig asking me to write up the encounter as a narrative, so he could use it for the book he was writing. I begin to read, thinking it will make the job of reconstructing what I thought and felt and saw that day easier. But it doesn't. It clarifies, more than the whales' behavior, my own struggle to understand what it meant to be a scientist, to think like one. A scientist, I must have imagined, is impassive, deadpan, objective, linear. A scientist's vision isn't manifold but singular. A scientist equivocates. A scientist rejects certainties. A scientist wouldn't wilt under cross-examination by Exxon lawyers. Reading that account now, I recognize voices I'd internalized, criticizing me for speaking out, or out of turn—from my father to my professors. Trying to demonstrate that I was an impartial observer, not an overexuberant "keener" or "orcateer," not one to leap to conclusions but a worthy initiate into an exclusive society of scientists. To be, in my father's words, prudent, cautious, patient, quiet.

It takes decades for the final alchemy to occur: observation into insight, data into understanding, knowledge into wisdom. Eyes of innocence, turning questions over to the mind, mind working the questions until the grit rubs off and some truth emerges.

It was a perfect day, sunny and calm. Olga and I wore T-shirts and ball caps, slathered sunscreen on our faces and arms, on Elli's skinny limbs, on Lars's fat cheeks. It was the perfect day to *not* see whales. That's what we told ourselves, because so many times, on perfect days, we turned up nothing in our searches but tired eyes. This time, right away we spotted transients: Marie, Ewan, Paddy, Lankard, and Aligo. Foraging offshore, the group pulsed, separating and then coming together, like communal breathing. Diving eight minutes, they'd resurface in some unexpected quadrant. Then, out of thirty-five minutes of silence, arose their "ghost call." Abruptly they joined together and charged south.

"Six knots," Olga said, watching our gauge. I sat on the bow, snapping photos. For fifteen minutes they pushed their faces up, one after the other, through a quicksilver sea, which flexed before peeling off their bodies. Around them, the passage spread flat and empty as an ice sheet. And then, pandemonium: Dall's porpoises darting away, orcas pursuing; two orcas closing in on a porpoise; blood fountaining; the pair stopping to feed, the other three still chasing another porpoise.

That porpoise flitted across the surface. For twelve minutes, feinting right, then left, it deftly eluded the whales, which in comparison seemed ponderous. But they were relentless, never losing ground, lunging free of the water's resistance to gain speed. And then it was over. One orca breached on top of the porpoise, and we never saw it again. The orcas stopped and milled. The other two joined—with or without the remains of their own kill, we couldn't tell—and they fed together. Olga motored through the fluke prints, and I stood on the bow, scooping bits of flesh with the swimming pool net. From nowhere, Eyak and Eccles arrived, and the seven whales joined, reversed direction, heading north, hunting again. At 11:00 p.m., we left them. Elli and Lars asleep in the bunk, we motored slowly across the passage toward Whale Camp, our wake cutting apart ribbons of shadow and light entwining in that water of death and survival.

That night, transcribing my notes while Olga sang Elli and Lars to sleep, I thought about wolves. As always I longed for the visual field a wolf biologist could cast across the tundra, watching predators worry a caribou herd. My visual field felt miniscule. How exactly did the orcas single out one porpoise from the exploding, fleeing pod? How did they share their kill? What had Eyak and Eccles been doing on the periphery of the scene? Had the ghost call signaled that one orca had detected prey? In an article called "Wolf Kill: Predator and Prey Engage in a Conversation of Death," Barry Lopez speculates: "When a wolf 'asks for an animal's life' he is opening a formal conversation that can take any number of turns, including 'no' and 'yes,' and can proceed either ritually or personally from there." This, Lopez says, is a "conversation of death."

The death of a porpoise is brutal to watch. Nature in that moment appears merciless, the killer aspect of the orca unequivocal. I identify not with the orca, but with the porpoise, as the object of relentless pursuit, nothing more than prey to another creature. Yet Dall's porpoises are exuberant, far from haunted or wary. You'd think that they'd steer clear of all orcas, but they don't—they're attracted to residents. One year, a Dall's porpoise joined AB pod for an entire summer, after a time even altering its breathing patterns to match its adopted pod's. If there's a conversation of death, there's also an equally inscrutable conversation of life. There is death and there is play, and both are mysterious.

Yet the idea of co-evolution—predator and prey influencing each other over millennia—spins what seems merciless, the absence of moral order, into something elegant, a dance of survival. Perhaps within the chase itself, animals enact what is already encoded deep in their cellular structure. Because death is fate. And animals—us included—are born knowing how to die.

The traditional indigenous hunters of the Alaskan coast seem to understand the moral universe of nature. "To us, the killer whale or orca is *aqlu*," writes Inupiaq anthropologist Herbert O. Anungazuk. "The name does not signify that the animal is a wanton killer, but the *aqlu* is a supreme predator. The *aqlu* is a hunter and he has gained an extremely high status in the lore of the northern hunter, yet is not a mythical being, although to some who do not understand our ways, the *aqlu* may have the nature of a myth. In the ancient stories of the Inupiat the *aqlu* is at its own level in the hierarchy of predator and prey, and the majestic mammal resides at the top of its own universe. His position is absolute."

From watching the Chugach transients hunt and kill, I learned that the world was more complex, less understandable, and at the same time more absolute than I'd known. Nature operates by laws, and at the core of things they are our laws too. We've simply forgotten. We've separated ourselves. We'd rather not hear the conversation of death in which we all participate.

The next evening, Olga and I picked up Craig from *Lucky Star*. Fisheries managers had shut down seining for a few days, and Craig left his crew in charge of the boat so he could spend time with his family at Whale Camp. So, when the blows of Ripple Fin and Mike woke me early the next morning, I pulled on my long johns and called out to the tent down the beach: "Don't get up. I'll follow them myself." It was, as Craig put it, "severe clear" and "flat as a plate." Glancing up every few minutes to see where the whales were, I stuffed gear and snacks into my back pack, and lugged a couple of gas jugs to the water's edge, loaded them into *Puff*, and paddled hard for the mooring, excited to have the boat and the whales to myself.

I caught up with the pair off Squire Rock. Soon after, they separated from one another, angling offshore. I kept my eyes on Ripple Fin, his adult male dorsal more visible above the calm sea than Mike's stubby, subadult fin. When Ripple Fin dove, I shut down the engine and listened for his blows. With the seine fishery shut down, with no wind, I could hear him breathe long before I spotted him. *Silent*, I wrote, again and again in the notebook.

I felt like a predator myself, every sense keyed to tracking. From the speaker came the ghost call's low-pitched *whoooo*, like someone blowing across the mouth of a bottle, half breath, half tone, tremulously ascending in pitch, one second, two, three, four. Farther away, I heard another ghost call, this one shorter, with an upswept tail. Shortly after, Chenega and Iktua appeared far across the passage. The calls ceased. For an hour, silently they meandered. And then, just as before, they arrowed south, like they'd been shot from four separate bows toward the same target.

I raced the boat ahead, dropped the hydrophone, and scanned. At the point of their eventual convergence, Dall's porpoises threw up rooster tails, chasing small fish. In moments the transients were upon them, high-leaping, all four whales working together, some chasing, some tail- and pec-slapping. By the time I arrived, all the porpoises had scattered and disappeared except a single adult, and the locus of the four orcas' collective intensity honed in on that one hapless animal.

I abandoned any notion of listening, intent this time to not miss anything. Now the three adults took turns, one pursuing, the others hanging back. Mike, the juvenile, as though berserk with anticipation, breached and slapped his fluke through the entire attack. Whatever whale was chasing launched itself high out of the water after the porpoise, which zigzagged just out of reach.

Then the oddest thing happened. Everything slowed, as in a child's game of tag, when someone shouts "freeze!" and everyone stands there holding their sides and panting. The porpoise rolled as if resting, and the three adult orcas surfaced lazily behind it, only Mike still thrashing his fluke. Then they dove. After a two-minute beat, *resume*, they all surfaced in a frenzy, the porpoise darting this way, that, trying to confound the orca pursuing inches from its madly pumping fluke.

And then the porpoise was flying in the air. Ten feet above the surface, the whole black-and-white body of the porpoise, frozen against the sky to this day in my memory, and behind it, Chenega, her whole black-and-white body airborne, in a perfect arch of muscle and power, water streaming off her fluke. Predator and prey flying together, crashing down. The whales formed a line behind the porpoise, each orca in turn breaching beneath it, catapulting it into the air, until it could barely swim.

I leaned across the dash, snapping photographs, my heart pounding, a sob stuck in my throat. *Finish it off*, I thought. *Get it*, I thought. "Oh, my God, oh, my God, oh, my God," I said aloud to no one. A hand had reached into my rib cage, seized my heart, and was squeezing and releasing it. Here was nature, red in tooth. Here was suffering. Here was death. Here was the black-and-white, muscled, ruthless will to survive. It was one thing to write "milling" in my notebook, to drift through the smooth ovals of water left by a diving whale and net up bits of seal fat. To write "harbor seal kill" in the log. It was another to see the kill itself, to witness the true nature of my study animal. What could it teach me? "When death comes," writes Mary Oliver in a poem of the same name, "like an iceberg between the shoulder blades, . . . I want to step through the door full of curiosity." How did a porpoise step through that door? What to make of the moment when both orcas and porpoise called "time out"? Was it the dance of death? I'd even heard it called a contract. Had I seen it? I wanted to believe I had. I wanted that belief to salve the ache in my chest as I watched the porpoise, rammed and battered, still struggling to swim.

The whales swam a tight circle around it. All dove, water zipping closed around them. Everything stilled, except for the plunking of salmon, the screech of gulls. And then the world went on: orcas resurfaced, diving repeatedly in that spot, feeding on the porpoise, for nearly an hour. *Whale 1* drifted, the hydrophone down, but the whales were silent. No frenzy of socializing and calling marked their kill.

When I looked up from my note taking and spotted three more orcas approaching, I wasn't surprised. I'd seen groups of five Chugach transients suddenly become seven or twelve. But when I trained my binoculars on the trio, I didn't recognize a single whale. Was that why the feeders had remained silent? To not advertise their kill to unfamiliar transients? I started the engine and motored closer to take pictures, then paged through the catalog until I matched them to Gulf of Alaska transients, part of the wild bunch that had three years before charged around Craig's skiff, spooking him, thrilling me. At the strangers' approach, the Chugach transients grouped tightly and began traveling. The others trailed them. There was no perceptible friendliness, no territoriality or aggression or tension, simply a subdued and silent procession. Near the Needle, they parted ways. The Gulf of Alaska transients, sea lion hunters, foraged briefly around the Needle, then turned south and disappeared. The Chugach transients turned north, heading deeper into the Sound.

I headed back to camp quieted, feeling that I'd been privy to something inscrutable, the ritual of a foreign culture observed without aid of interpreter or translator.

34

Nine Silences

At the end of the seining season, Graeme flew up from Nanaimo to join Craig on *Lucky Star*. Curly-headed, with a boyish face and a gap-toothed grin, Graeme reminded me of a river otter, sharp-witted and intense. The arbiter and judge of our identification photographs, I feared his yearly critiques and was in awe of his observational prowess. A field biologist with an eye for orca identities and human foibles, he didn't have academic degrees, just time, experience, and devotion under his belt. His life was water-centric, the view from his living room window a passage that orcas frequently traversed. I knew of his tender side through stories, how he'd raised an orphaned river otter pup, and a harbor seal named Lucy, who still returned to his dock each spring, hauling herself up to be hand-fed a few herring.

Through his eyes I imagined myself just another here-today, gone–tomorrow dilettante, "studying" orcas for the adventure before moving on to the rest of my life. I wanted to prove him wrong, but often ended up only looking more inept in my striving. It didn't help when the first day I drove up to *Lucky Star* to say hello to Graeme, and in an effort to skillfully maneuver in choppy seas, managed to ram bow-first into its side, with Graeme standing above me, grinning, trying to fend *Whale 1* off with a buoy, shouting, "What are you trying to do? T-bone us?"

A few days later, I joined Lance and Kathy on *Whale 2* for a change of pace. We'd been searching Montague Strait for residents when Craig radioed to say that he and Graeme had found transients in the passage, harassing humpback whales. This was unusual behavior, something all three of us were eager to observe. We raced over to find Eyak and Lankard surfacing a few yards behind a humpback, *Lucky Star* drifting nearby. Each time the humpback took a breath to dive, it raised its flukes high in the air. Stopping within shouting distance of *Lucky Star,* we dropped the hydrophone, then grilled Craig and Graeme. What exactly had they seen? They evaded our questions, our conversation going something like this:

"What have they been doing?"

"Surfacing around this humpback."

"Attacking, or just playing around?"

"I don't know."

"I mean, did you see any sign of aggression?"

"I'm telling you what I saw."

We were pushing Graeme's buttons, as he was skeptical of behavioral studies, with their speculations and interpretations based on endless tallies of dive times and blow sequences and numbers of tail slaps and breaches. He believed in what the eye could see. An orca wasn't feeding on fish unless we saw a fish in its mouth, unless we collected scales drifting at the kill site. An orca hadn't killed a seal unless we had a blubber sample to prove it, or a photo of a seal in its jaws. He dealt in the unequivocal, primarily photographic negatives, proving presence and absence and association. Conclusions about behavior, Graeme thought, were suspect, when most of the story happened under the water, out of sight.

In the moment, it was maddening. Half joking, egging each other on, Craig and Graeme refused to relent. I sat with my pencil poised above my notebook, the point breaking against the page. Disgusted, we gave up and turned our attention to the whales.

After decades of studying orcas, contending with people's intractable belief that they're voracious, opportunistic predators—sea otters flying into the air around them "like popcorn," herds of sea lions killed in "blood baths"—I understand better Graeme's skepticism and caution. We hear wild interpretations of whale behavior all the time, read scientific papers based on scant data. But in the moment, on that August day, during my last orca encounter of the field season, after hundreds of hours observing transients, I took his derision personally. What did I need to do to prove myself? Of course the answer was to simply go about my work, collecting data carefully, patiently, writing, growing into my own species of biologist, hoping there was a place for me in their world.

Late that fall, Graeme sent me a copy of the spreadsheet of photographic data. Six more AB pod whales were dead, for a total of thirteen. All of them were juveniles or reproductive-aged animals, 33 percent of the pod. Eighteen times the normal mortality rate for orcas. I studied the large gaps in the columns for Chugach transients. Even with our intensive field effort, four boats searching the Sound over four months, nine whales—41 percent of the population—were missing. Whales I'd barely come to know. What those percentages, those numbers, didn't convey was the individuality of loss, each whale's unique traits, personality, habits, skills, predilections. None of the missing whales were old. They included two teenagers, Gage and Hermit, and two twenty-somethings, Icy and Berg. Moon and Trident were thirty-three-year-old males. And three were from Kaj's group: twenty-one-year-old Kaj, and two males, Shadow and Totemof. We knew unequivocally that two of the missing were dead. Berg had beached in Beartrap Bay. A second carcass found on Culross Island that summer, an adult male, was genetically identified as a Chugach transient. His stomach contained bones, whiskers, and hair from harbor seals and the fin of a Dall's porpoise. Two orca carcasses are a lot to find in one year. Their bodies generally sink after death.

We had only studies of West Coast transients to use as a template for deciding when to pronounce a transient dead, and science was cautious, for good reason. Because transients disappeared for years at a time from B.C. waters, because they sometimes dispersed from maternal groups, we couldn't conclude, as we could for residents, that the seven unaccounted for were dead. But knowing what I knew of the Chugach transients, those blanks on the spreadsheet alarmed me. The Chugach transients didn't range thousands of miles, like West Coast transients. They lived in the Sound. In seasons of focused effort, they'd all been accounted for. And it had been nothing if not a season of focused effort.

If they were dead, what had happened? All twenty-two had survived the oil spill summer. The nine whales had disappeared over the ensuing winter. I wondered how compromised they'd been, going into those cold, dark months, all summer having eaten oiled seals, having breathed volatilized hydrocarbons. I wondered about their livers, their immune systems.

In Fairbanks, I took more classes and summarized my data, preparing to give a talk at an orca symposium in Vancouver. But first I traveled back to John Ford's lab to analyze the summer's recordings. I added two calls to the Chugach transient dialect, the ghost call and the choral call. I grouped the calls into categories: quiet hunting calls, loud calls, and social calls. I hypothesized that, unlike John Ford's residents, some Chugach transient calls were behavior-specific. The orcas used quiet calls when hunting, loud calls when trying to locate each other, and social calls, which included whistles, variable and aberrant calls, when playing. I analyzed more recordings of Eyak, Mike, and Eccles alone. To my ear, their "voices" sounded distinct, but I'd have to collect many more recordings of lone whales, then measure components of hundreds of calls to quantify my impression. With all of my data, I'd need to convert notes to numbers in columns, feed spreadsheets into computer programs. In the end, I'd interpret the lives of Chugach transients from probabilities. There was something disconcerting yet beautiful about the process. Eyak's fin breaking the surface, his exhalation breaking the stillness of a calm afternoon, the glint of sun on his skin, a scrap of meat in his jaws, the disappearing fluke print he leaves behind him on the water, his haunting cries ricocheting off island walls, his blue eyes: the irrefutable, flesh-and-blood truth of him. Translated into numbers: what we give ourselves permission to say, to claim as knowledge. Our caution. In that sense, the numbers are a reflection of our respect for what can't be known or concluded. It was, perhaps, Graeme's subtext that day, perhaps what his recalcitrance, his unwillingness to engage in speculation, had been trying to teach me.

As part of my conference presentation, I added to my growing "activity budget" of the Chugach transients. A strange co-opting of an accounting term, the currency of an activity budget is energy expressed as time. How animals spend time, and thus energy, reflects something of their ecology. In the metaphor of an animal's life as a pie, each slice represents the portion of time spent socializing, resting, foraging, and traveling, the broadest categories. Energy and time given over to play or rest is energy not available for hunting. Many scientists besides Graeme find these budgets speculative, foremost because interpretation of surface behavior is subjective—each researcher sees through a unique lens. How do I know that what I call foraging someone else wouldn't call traveling or resting? In essence, we draw conclusions from breathing patterns, squiggles on water. To breathe—that's why whales surface. But, lucky for us, also to play, to rest. To kill, to drive prey toward and against the surface. Even so, over 90 percent of what they do occurs under that surface. Squiggles on water, that's what we see. Broad categories applied to a group are unreliable, too. Do we ever do only one thing? Craig jigs for halibut and scans for whales simultaneously. We eat and travel. Are transients ever just traveling or resting? Or are they always foraging, keeping an ear constantly attuned to the squeaks, bleats, swishes or plops of prey?

I studied the activity budgets of other researchers and tried to follow their standards. Even if there was fuzziness at times in my classification of behaviors, it was clear that Chugach transients portioned their energy differently than West Coast transients. They spent much more time socializing. Why? Did a small population occupying a small range act more like a pod? Was the maintenance of social bonds more critical to their survival than it was for West Coast transients, part of a much larger population with a huge range?

Another unequivocal difference was that their dialect consisted of far more calls than that of the West Coast transients, as many discrete calls as some resident pods. Why did they need all of those calls when other transients made do with just a handful? All the fragments I held in my hands—dialect, range, diet, behavior, social interactions—floated before my eyes. I could almost see the shape of a larger view, a view that necessarily encompassed the Sound itself. The Chugach transients were a manifestation of place, more resident to the Sound than most of the whales we called residents. If language is a reflection of place, as linguists claim, then the language of the Chugach transients, both acoustic and behavioral—no, *everything* about them, including their dying—was a reflection of place. Nine subtractions. Nine silences.

Eyak, as a young male, travels in Montague Strait, early spring 1988. (Craig Matkin)

PART 4

Into Great Silence

35

Hunger

It's all one thing, it's the humming through the trees, through the chairs, through our bodies, the water we drink, it's all humming. If we're quiet enough we can hear it.

—LI-YOUNG LEE

All night Chenega, Iktua, and Mike skimmed the island's perimeter, resting but alert, in case a seal pup bleated or splashed. Now, after nearly ten minutes down, she rises toward the ocean's meniscus, the impulse to breathe overwhelming all else. On either side of her eddies and currents ribboning off the bodies of her sister and her son thrum along her skin. As she nears it, the gelatin-silver barrier between worlds materializes. The never-night of June in the other world, the world above, patches the ocean's ceiling like a fresco with polygons of shadow. She meets the sea's skin with her face, already breathing out, her blow fountaining, and then her face is free, and she gasps, refilling her lungs with air, the smell of land, pungent tang of seaweed, resin of hemlock. The water rushes past her dorsal fin and slips off her eye; above the sea, momentarily, she feels the fin's weight. Even after fifty years, air is quenching. She hears her sister and son take their breaths and they're under again, home, dim, enclosing, edgeless. She pumps her flukes, rises to breathe again, again, again, and then, lungs bursting, oxygen circulating, she sounds, returning to darkness, where she'll glide, buoyant, listening, until the need to breathe drives her up, or until she hears a faint animal cry that stirs her hunger, or until a familiar song calls her to come. There's no question of what to remember, of what might come

*to pass. Only the hunt, the breath, her kin. Only the hum she
feels along her skin, through her body, in her bones. The way it's
always been.*

*Every moment, they are present to the hum of being alive in that
home. Every bleat, wave lap, squeak, outboard drone, light dap-
ple, echolocation click, water current, cloud shadow, hydrocarbon
molecule, basalt face of whatever cove or passage they're in right
now. That's what I imagine.*

That spring, I bought a journal exactly like Molly Lou's, a lap-sized artist's notebook with a black cover, sewn binding, and unlined pages. I
bought a fountain pen too. I liked the way it blotched the journal's pages
if I pressed too hard, or paused too long, thinking, tip to page. I liked
the way, when the words flowed, the ink glided in rivulets across white
expanses. I liked the way the ink stained my hands. I saw those stains as
a mark of my labor, like garden dirt or boat engine grime. I pasted poems Molly Lou sent to me onto the journal's blank pages. I studied their
strange constructions of language and their silences. "Taom," Molly Lou
told me, of one poem she sent, by Moya Cannon, was Irish for "a great
wave." I wanted to discover in myself the "territories of the voice" the
poem described, "that first articulation . . . when someone, in anguish, /
made a green and mortal sound." I'd failed to give voice to that green and
mortal sound during the oil spill summer, and that cry was still in me.
I thought of the surviving thirteen transients' voices giving "testimony
to waves succumbed to and survived." They'd outlived the great, black,
uncontained, unexpected wave of oil. How was I to translate their voices
into language, much less unearth my own? In my attempts, I filled pages
with words.

I packed that journal into my backpack, along with my new book
collection: poetry, writers' journals, essay anthologies. With my science
books, they reflected my new cross-discipline curriculum in understanding the world.

MAY 20

*Evening. Anchored in Eleanor Cove, out here with Craig setting up
the field camp. Two days ago, after putting up the tents and rolling
fuel barrels up the beach, I walked behind camp to the King Tree,*

*and lay down over one of its roots, my face inches from a partially
eaten starfish. Nearby, I found the remains of a crow, its feathers
wet, flattened, spread out across the moss. No skull, just a beak,
some bones, a pair of leathery feet. In the woods, sphagnum so thick,
it felt like I'd sink to the knees if I stood still too long. The deer had
eaten all of the skunk cabbage down to nubs, their hungry noses
pushing hollows into the earth. Back on the beach, another kind of
hollow—two recently excavated holes, the top layer of rocks shoveled away, several inches of gravel dug into, probably by biologists
looking for oil. Oil clogged the spaces between pebbles. Those who
say the Sound is back to normal are liars. Now here at the galley
table, Craig sleeping, kettle steaming, it's warm. Dusk, and across
the water, a large boat—probably a tanker—blinks its lights. There
are still cleanup crews around the Sound. I want the spill to be over,
but it's not. Will it ever be? Today we passed an anchored Mississippi
mud boat, and on a nearby beach, red-suited people swarmed. We
asked them what they were doing. Checking beaches, a man said.
When Craig asked how the beaches seemed, he said, "Pretty good."
I look away from memory to now. Out the window, the moon half
full, bright in tonight's denim sky.*

It seemed an omen of a good field season when the next day, the sky clear,
the water still, we found Chugach transients not far from our anchorage
cove. We counted seven, with no adult males: Chenega, Iktua, Mike,
Egagutak, Marie, Ewan, and Paddy. In two groups, they meandered
slowly northeast, into the middle Sound, the adults resting, the juveniles
rolling, breaching, fluke-slapping. That area, fifteen miles north of Whale
Camp, was out of our everyday search range, but I knew from sighting
reports that it was, like the Labyrinth, habitat, a hunting grounds. Still,
it felt like traveling with them off the map of the known world.

When we dropped the hydrophone, calls exploded from the speaker:
whistles, clicks, aberrant and variable calls, what I'd come to know as
after-kill chatter. We searched for a bit of blubber, an oil slick, but saw
nothing. If they'd killed something, it was already consumed. For nearly
two hours, the whales socialized. I sat with my stopwatch and binoculars,
new yellow notebook, and mechanical pencil, at home again with my old
routine. Like the whales, I chattered, giving Craig my explication of what
we saw and heard as though it were a poem I'd spent years deconstruct-

ing. And I had. Nonetheless, I scribbled notes furiously, knowing that every encounter would shore up my ideas. Bud had been telling me it was high time I analyzed the data. I already had started writing my thesis.

But I wasn't measuring bones or working with captive animals. My study animal was long-lived, slow to reveal its secrets. And I didn't want the study to end, ever. I felt like a cartographer who'd just drawn the basic contours of an island, named it, and described it as forested or not. Now I wanted to crawl all over it, go deeper, into the island's heart.

"Where did that male come from?" Craig asked, interrupting my thoughts.

I lifted my binoculars. A tall dorsal rose and sank behind the others. On its next surfacing, the male tilted over, his fin nearly parallel to the water's surface.

"It's probably Ripple Fin," I said. "He's always with Chenega."

We motored over for a photograph, but it was Aligo, not Ripple Fin. Soon after his arrival, the whales fell silent and began to travel, stopping occasionally to mill. I timed their dives at six minutes.

"Definitely offshore foraging now. If we stick with them long enough, they'll kill something," I said, glancing over at Craig, knowing he was antsy to find residents. "This is exactly what they were doing last year, right before those porpoise kills." For hours, the silent whales hunted. How patient they were. And it took equal patience for us to wait out the long dives and the silence, to perpetually scan so as not to miss a surfacing. After lunch, Craig went below for a nap, leaving me to my note taking. Despite my prediction, for seven hours the whales foraged without incident or sound. I didn't see a single porpoise. Even I grew restless by mid-afternoon, my eyes aching from staring into the sun's glare. Finally, Craig declared the encounter over, and we headed back toward the passage.

The next day, a boat reported four orcas off Herring Point, heading south, and again we found Chenega's group, still without Ripple Fin. The whales hunted down the Labyrinth, circling seal haul-outs. We left them inside Drier Bay and then found the others from the previous day's encounter off Whale Camp: Ewan, Paddy, Egagutak, Eccles, and Aligo.

I could see why Graeme described transient social organization as "fluid." It was the perfect adjective: individuals flowing in and out of a still point, home—the maternal unit—to hunt or socialize, adult males leaving on their solitary walkabouts, temporarily joining other groups. I wondered how the oil spill deaths affected their association patterns. Had their bonds loosened or tightened? That kind of question opened a maw of silence behind me, all the things I couldn't know, would never know: what they were before the spill. I barely had an inkling.

Two days later, Craig and I headed for Homer, where Molly Lou waited to help me prepare *Whale 1* for another field season. We had plans: installing a woodstove to keep the boat cabin warm and dry on rainy days, and a vent for the fuel tank to prevent air locks; rigging curtains to make sleeping aboard easier in midsummer, when it never got dark; nailing up a bookshelf for our library; gluing carpet to the inside walls to reduce condensation; replacing the wiring; building raised floorboards. We looked forward to life at Whale Camp but also wanted Lance and Kathy's live-aboard-the-boat freedom. Like the Chugach transients, we wanted to be fluid. We wanted a still point, a home, and we wanted to roam.

2 JUNE 1991

Dreamed I was sitting on the beach in front of Whale Camp. Two harbor seals floated in the water, and I wondered what would happen if orcas came by. Just then a fin broke the surface, then another. Two transients dove under the seals. One tried to grab a seal, and the other turned and swam toward me. I knew it wanted to touch me, was going to put its snout on the little ledge I was sitting on. I decided to trust that it wouldn't bite my hand off or hurt me, so I reached out, and it closed its mouth on my fingers, then let go and sank back into the water, leaving the indentations of its teeth on my skin.

In the season's first weeks, my hand throbbed with the impressions left by those dream whales. On June 28, I wrote in my journal:

I'm extremely frustrated and anxious at our inability to find transients. It's been 24 days. But I remind myself that it took Sandra and me almost as long to find them last spring. Maybe they're still up north. Each day, I begin with a seed of anticipation. Perhaps today. I peer out of the tent each morning at the passage stretching to the Pleiades and beyond. Transients might arrive from the north, from the Labyrinth. They might arrive from the south. They might

be just out of sight, off Squire Rock, or in Long Channel. Every-
thing is possibility. But by late afternoon, Molly Lou and I are
so tired from searching, so discouraged (I hate to admit this,
bored even), I begin to hope we don't find them. I want only to
hike on the island, sleep, get to that moment of possibility again,
like the line by Robert Duncan, "that is a place of first permission,
/ everlasting omen of what is." Morning is that place for me, all
permission, omen, possibility. I miss the transients like I miss friends
or family, I miss following the careful paths they weave along the
shoreline, quietly. I miss their almost inaudible hunting calls, their
black fins against the basalt, the mystery of where they'll go, what
they'll do, the constant wondering what their intentions are.

Those twenty-four days in June, we roamed the southwestern Sound photographing humpbacks. Occasionally a pod of resident orcas passed through. Often we cruised slowly north through the Labyrinth, me sitting on the bow scanning with binoculars, Molly Lou driving, stopping at each bay entrance to listen and scan. One day, we searched Drier Bay all the way to its head. At lunchtime, we anchored and paddled *Puff* to what we knew, from our chart, was the site of a herring saltery, but we saw no evidence of it, no broken pilings, no rusting hulk of machine or rendering tank. In the muskeg, we stumbled upon cabin remains, scatterings of fireplace bricks. The forest had reclaimed everything else. Back on the beach, we found bags of oily trash left by cleanup workers. How long would it take the Sound to reclaim evidence of the spill? When would it become irrelevant?

Watching, waiting: June passed thus. July brought rain and wind but still no transients. We returned to camp nightly damp and chilled, despite the woodstove on the boat. As always, camp life was grounding: baking bread, tidying, hiking, trading books, writing, talking. Sometimes I felt no imperative but to inhabit the Sound. To dwell, to dry seaweed and can kelp pickles, to collect goose tongue, salt bush, beach greens and lovage for supper, to catch a fish. To be taken in. Even in rain and wind, we stripped off our clothes and dunked ourselves in muskeg ponds. It was the only thing that revived us from boat lethargy and weather numbness, the only thing that loosened our limbs, that startled awake our foggy brains, as though we carried weather in our heads, an occluded front, and only cold-water immersion could clear it. Restored, skin tingling, hair damp, we resumed searching.

7 JULY

I'm filled now with gnawing worry for the Chugach transients.
Even if our search methods were faulty, we'd surely have run into
them by now, or heard reports. We need to renew the intensity of our
efforts, even if it means miles of travel and frustration. We need to
see if they're using other areas. I kayaked around the island yesterday
and counted seven harbor seals in Long Channel, surely enough
for at least a quick visit. And our porpoise sightings have increased
lately. I'm anxious to talk to Lloyd and Kathy about their seal sur-
veys. The decline here seems dramatic. At some point it must impact
the animals that prey on them: but when and how?

The nature of studying transients, and the isolated nature of our field
camp, caused our inner lives, our physical bodies, everything around and
within us, to magnify, as though we viewed ourselves and our surround-
ings through a macro lens. A tide rip. A spindle or puff of breath against
a shoreline. An off-key remark. A shift in wind. The first drops of rain.
The approach of a squall. Menstrual cramps. Cold. Oystercatcher calls.
A perceived slight. Sea lion blows. Wanting to find transients so badly
it hurt. My naked body, arms wrapped around my breasts, dunked in
a muskeg pond. Silence stretching minutes, hours, between Molly Lou
and me. The sudden resumption of conversation. A black bear swimming across a passage. A familiar unnamed island.

And finally this: Chenega drifting toward *Whale 1*'s bow, a harbor
seal clenched crosswise in her jaws. All of those other moments leading
to and away from that one. Whatever was going on in my mind in the
moments before we watched her gliding toward us, whatever kind of
weather, it was erased. My eyes fixed at the water. A moment of giving
and taking, of being given sight, like the ringing of a meditation bell
calling me back from the world of thought into the world of immediacy.
Nothing but her fluke print, blood pouring out of the seal's body in a
slow pulse, reflecting the beat of its dying heart. Standing on the bow,
looking down, then and now. I am still there. It's still happening, the
eternal perfect progressive tense of Chenega drifting beneath the bow
with the seal in her mouth. Turning to Molly Lou. "Did you see that?"
Her nodding.

We'd spotted a blow off New Year Island, at the edge of the Labyrinth. As we'd approached, we'd seen her wiggling her body in an odd
way. Arching high with each breath but not diving. She must have been

shaking that seal to kill it. Alone, she had no companion to help subdue it. Alone, she looked small, like a juvenile, and in her jaws the seal looked small, like a juvenile. But my perspective was off. When she drifted under the boat, I saw how large she was. Twenty minutes later, she was traveling across Knight Island Passage. We pulled up the hydrophone and sped to catch up. Now she porpoised across the water. For a half hour, she charged toward the Pleiades before slowing, silent. Off the Pleiades, she milled. We spotted another orca to the west, and then Lance and Kathy called on the radio. Three transients off camp, they said, a male and two females. Lance and Kathy had followed them through Squire Rocks. They were following still, but the male had disappeared before they could get a photograph.

Off Gage Island, our whales and theirs joined. No excited reunion after a long separation. Together they hunted along Fleming Island. It seemed, despite the miles between them earlier in the day, that they'd been one sensory organ scouring the passage for prey. Later, the whole group fed together on a seal in a rocky bight. Then they hunted on down Iktua Passage. An hour and a half later, they killed again. The behavioral cue was subtle, but after three summers, unmistakable: milling, splashing, silent at first, then vocalizing, then bangs and cracks on the hydrophone. We drifted into a spreading sheen of blood and oil. The whales blew explosively, arching high with every breath, diving straight down to the carcass. Gulls whirled, picking up bloody bits. We collected scraps in our net. As though scripted: the agitated whip cracks and splashes of the attack, the chorus of quiet calls signaling the sharing of food, then five minutes of play—aberrant and variable calls, whistles, surface splashing. Temporarily sated. Resting.

Then traveling away. Falling silent and stealthy, crossing Iktua Passage into a maze of islands. Hunting again. Disappearing into that silence of a barely relenting hunger. Now I sensed it in everything: trees, salmon, seals, gulls, myself. Hunger for knowing. Hunger for another day in that place.

36

More Than We Understand

13 JULY
I dropped Molly Lou off in Whittier today, for her fishing trip with her father. We're a pod. Like the transients: group size of two, hunting companions. At the moment of parting on the train, the words finally came, and though they sounded lame, they were true: "I'll miss you." Our closeness feels fragile. Our skins are thin. Too many words might break something.

As I roved alone, clues to the Chugach transients' movements trickled in through radio reports, many of them from the northern Sound. One male in Port Nellie Juan, heading toward the glacier. Three orcas feeding on harbor seals off the Dutch Group. Lance and Kathy watching transients harass humpbacks in Montague Strait. It started to feel like a trend, the whales no longer centering their foraging in the study area.

One August day, after Molly Lou's return, Craig and his crew anchored in Squire Cove during a fishing closure. One of Craig's crewmen, heading for Whittier in his own boat, volunteered to search for transients as he traveled north. He would take the passage's western shore; we would take its eastern, along the Labyrinth. Other friends guiding a sailing charter radioed to say that they would search around Perry and Lone Islands. Craig would skiff out into Montague Strait. Lance and Kathy would cover Grass Island.

We all left from camp that morning, our wakes fanning out in a starburst. Molly Lou and I set off feeling buoyed, knowing that many sets of eyes hunted for transients, covering much more ground than we could on our own, mimicking the whales' strategy, the way they broke up into smaller groups to hunt seals, then regrouped to socialize, then scattered again. Join and fan out, join and fan out, a communal rhythm.

So we fanned out, sighting conditions perfect. Craig found residents in Montague Strait. We searched all day. Almost ready to give up and find an anchorage, at 8:15 p.m. I spotted a fin, then another, then a third. Widely separated, Chenega's group—again minus Ripple Fin—surfaced slowly, hunting, their blows nearly invisible. On the hydrophone: nothing. We'd seen five porpoises earlier in the day, that was all, and those had seemed quiet, slow-rolling, lying low. The porpoises were telling us something. Not playful, not bow-riding our boat or chasing fish, rooster tails spraying up behind them. They were acting like prey. "The transients are somewhere out here," I'd said, knowing it was hubris, but unable to resist. "The porpoises know it." The day—flat water, recent sightings of transients in the area, all those other boats searching too—inevitability throbbing against my eardrums—and then there they were, foraging in the northern Sound's wide open spaces. After an hour hunting, they found their target, a pair of Dall's porpoises. Two orcas, bodies sprung high above the water, chased fleeing forms. When we drew near, we saw a porpoise calf surfacing slowly in front of them. The whales surfaced slowly too, taking the porpoise into their mouths, letting it go, then breaching beneath it, throwing it into the air. It never got easier to watch. Finally, to our relief, they took the porpoise under. Quiet calls followed. They dove over and over, feeding for fifteen minutes before moving inshore to hunt seals. A continuous cycle. By then, it was dusk. We left them at 11 p.m. to anchor.

It was almost what you could call dark. Making our way into Eleanor Cove, we saw our first star in months. Night had returned to the north. In my sleeping bag long after midnight, I felt myself sliding down an inclined plane toward the field season's end, toward Fairbanks, toward winter.

The next day, we searched miles of the northern Sound, and then motored slowly south back to camp along the Labyrinth. One of Craig's crewmen told us he'd seen a male orca swimming past Whale Camp that morning. Exhausted, I threw down my gear and headed alone into the woods. No reports, nothing on the hydrophone, no encounters with transients for weeks in early summer, and suddenly they seemed to be everyplace and no place at once, sightings a scattershot of dots across the map.

Over the next several days, Molly Lou and I kept heading north, finding another arrangement of Chugach transients south of Naked

Island. Finally Lankard. Finally Eyak. Eyak's group together again. All the Chugach transients alive in 1990 accounted for, except Ripple Fin. Ripple Fin was dead. He had to be. Dead at twenty-seven. Traveling with Eyak's group was the young male Egagutak, the roamer, the only survivor of Kaj's group, the "tanker four." Like a young male wolf recently dispersed from his mother, he seemed to be searching for where he belonged. The whales circled, widely dispersed, miles offshore of the island. *Milling in open water,* I wrote. *Silent. Very slow surfacings, blows quiet and invisible. All diving at different times.* Perhaps some quirk of the day's atmosphere damped the sound of their breathing, but it struck me as surreptitious. And no calls, just the steadily intensifying drone of a boat engine. During the boat's passing, Eyak rolled over onto his back, lifted his fluke, rolled upright again, and spy-hopped. For forty-five minutes, until the boat was well beyond them, the whales socialized and called. When its engine throb receded, they fell silent again and resumed hunting.

Did they abort hunting because of that engine? Or was it one of the inexplicable aspects of their gestalt: the fact of being both predator and social animal? In *Of Wolves and Men,* Barry Lopez presented the following summary of wolf predation on moose in Michigan observed from the air by biologist David Mech. Out of 160 moose "judged to be within range of hunting wolves: 29 were ignored, 11 discovered the wolves first and eluded detection, 24 refused to run when confronted and were left alone. Of the 96 that ran: 43 got away immediately, 24 were surrounded but not harmed, 12 made successful defensive stands, 7 were attacked, 6 were killed, 1 was wounded and abandoned." Lopez concluded, "It would appear that the wolf is either inefficient or not very serious about killing moose. Or that more is going on than we understand." I knew what he meant. The Chugach transients were neither inefficient nor lacking in intent. More was going on than we understood. In a study filled with uncertainty, I could be certain of that.

Two days later, near Whale Camp, Chenega's group appeared, socializing and calling. When we began hearing AB pod calls on the hydrophone, the transients, as if to avoid contact, fell silent and traveled north, around the bend in Knight Island Passage, out of earshot, and then milled again, calling loudly. *More is going on than we understand.* Did they react differently to AB than they did to AE pod? Was their relationship to each resident pod unique? Now they rolled upside-down and slapped their flukes. A little later, they swam into the Labyrinth, hunting their way north, then south again past Whale Camp, through Squire Rocks. At 10:00 p.m., in the twilight, we left them.

Ten days later, we had our final encounter of the summer, this time with a lone whale, Mike, the youngster from Chenega's group, learning how to be an adult, a roamer. Along the Grass Island shoreline, in Montague Strait, he vocalized loudly. Like Eyak, a bout of calls was followed by a bout of silence—perhaps listening for an answer. *Appears to be sending calls in different directions,* I wrote. Down the strait he zigzagged. The next day, we heard the same loud calls again but never found their source. At two that afternoon, a boat reported a single male orca traveling north up Iktua Passage. Transients drawing the contours of the Sound. Coming together, coming apart. There is more going on than we'll ever understand.

37

What the Numbers Say

That fall, it was time not just for call analysis in John's office, but for number crunching, as Bud called it. "Time to get down to brass tacks," he said. I took more statistics classes, consulted with professors and fellow grad students. Intimidated, in a notebook I kept a log of each day's progress. The descriptions I wrote in the yellow Rite in the Rain notebook morphed into numbers in columns on spreadsheets that fed into statistical programs that extruded results. The results were qualified: with such and such a margin of error, with such and such degree of certainty, I could say something.

This is how you do science: Develop precise questions, what are called "null hypotheses." Devise a method to answer those questions, to test the hypotheses. Observe. Collect data. Analyze. Report the results. Discuss. As the notebook pages filled, I realized over the months of winter that I was going to do it—I was going to finish that thesis.

In November, I flew south to an oil spill research meeting at NMFS, in Seattle. Kathy, Lance, Craig, and I presented various facets of the data we'd amassed since the spill. Soon, a three-year progress report would make public, for the first time, the results of our study. Actual court litigation against Exxon was now unlikely. There would be a settlement. Nervous to be standing before federal scientists, I clicked through slides of photos and charts, glanced at my notes, which I'd written on index cards. My talk focused on the Chugach transients. Up to that point, public and scientific attention had been on AB pod, the thirteen deaths.

A subgroup of AB pod had broken away and joined AJ pod, an unprecedented event.

The Chugach transients' unique dialect suggested that they were distinct from both residents and Gulf of Alaska transients, a separate population, I said. Graeme had confirmed that we'd photographed only twelve animals in 1991. Nearly half the population had disappeared since the spill. I wanted to say: *Look at these unique, secretive whales, hardly seen by anyone. They're of the Sound. They're disappearing. Because they're transients, we can only call them missing. But they aren't missing. They're dead. They're quiet, silent a lot, but listen. Something's happened. Something's happening still.* But I couldn't say those things. Instead, I presented data, hard facts. I described their behaviors, how they seemed to differ from West Coast transients. I presented a slide of activity budgets, one for West Coast transients, and two for the Chugach transients: before and after the spill. I suggested that the Chugach transients were spending more time hunting porpoises, less time hunting seals.

When I finished, I walked to the back of the room to listen to Craig's presentation. My hands shook. Kathy waited for me there. She took my arm, led me off a ways, and told me I'd made a mistake. My data on behavior were too preliminary. Such a thing could jeopardize the integrity of the project. Dazed, I skipped lunch and walked with my journal to a nearby lake. I sat at the water's edge watching a raft of ducks preening and dabbling. Three Canada geese drifted near, eyeing me, as if to ask, "What do you presume to know about another animal anyway?" *I tried to defend myself,* I wrote in my journal, *but I couldn't, and I'm slammed with the thought that I'm not thinking like a scientist, that I don't know how. I speak another language, come from another culture. I think this lesson tells me to be quieter. It's a gradual process, learning not to say too much, too soon.* Kathy, Lance, and Graeme embodied the caution of scientists. They scoffed at researchers who published speculative papers based on a season or two of data. I remembered Marilyn's earlier injunction to "put a sock in it."

But at the same time, I wondered, who was I responsible to? The enterprise of science? Or the whales, the Sound? Or was I responsible to my own observations and intuition? After the meeting, I took the ferry north to Vancouver, to analyze my tapes in John Ford's lab, to try again to enter the mind-set of the scientist. Back in Fairbanks, in a kind of displacement behavior, I dove into environmental issues, protesting against aerial wolf control, collecting hundreds of signatures to protect the Arctic National Wildlife Refuge from oil development, organizing a letter-writing campaign to ban fish farms from Alaskan waters. If I had to be cautious about the Chugach transients, I could be reckless in other arenas. In doing that, I told myself, I fought for the whales. In Eyak's eyes everything was reflected—the Sound, its ecology, hunger, knowing, and what was true, wild, and essential. And in the spring, I'd be back out there again with my notebook, stopwatch, pencil, binoculars. With my own eyes.

38

What the Silence Says

The silence is primal.
    —LI-YOUNG LEE

This is what the silence says: We are listening. We are searching.
We are hungry. This is what the silence says: I am this place. I am
a prayer of this place. Surface still: the moment before rain. Surface
chopped apart by waves: it's windy. Surface punched in by kitti-
wakes, plunging onto a school of fish. Surface dashed by the lunge
of a porpoise. Depth a great silence brush-stroked here and there by
disturbance, the feathering of a salmon's fin, bleat of seal pup, high-
pitched clicks of a hunting porpoise, halibut gliding over a rock,
crab walking on the bottom, crackle of shrimp, sizzle of iceberg,
crunch of bone. Surface split by dorsal fin.

In 1992 I returned with Molly Lou to the Sound in early June. While we
were setting up camp, four Chugach transients appeared off the beach.
We dropped everything and followed them into the Labyrinth, where
they skimmed the seal haul-outs. Bodies pressed to the rocks, bawling in
agitation, the seals watched them pass. It was a promising beginning, but
proved ephemeral. We didn't see them again for six weeks. Once again
we set off from camp every morning full of yearning, our vessel tracks
radiating out from Squire Island.

That year, Molly Lou and I inhabited the Sound with renewed intention. It would be her last summer. In the fall, she'd head to Iowa for
graduate school, to study poetry. And it would be my last summer as
a graduate student. By then, our friendship was so intimate, it was its
own solitude, one of the unclassifiable, unquantifiable things we learned
from the Chugach transients: solitude and silence while in one anoth-

er's presence. One day, discussing my guilt about getting edgy when we had to share Whale Camp with others, Molly Lou said, "Well, perhaps you're a solitary person by nature." Was I? It had been a long time since RJ had insisted on my hyper-dependence. My relationship to John, a self-contained, reflective person who could happily spend hours alone skiing, running, or walking through the woods with his camera, was its own solitude, "two solitudes," in Rilke's words, cohabiting a two-room log cabin.

As the days passed, I watched myself and realized that perhaps Molly Lou was right. I sought time alone. We both craved it. The Sound gave it to us. Even the whales gave it to us, vanishing for weeks at a time. Solitude and silence were like the flow of time or tide through our days.

Alone outside in the rain and wind with nothing but waves in my ears, crows cawing their scratchy arguments, leaves jostling against each other, wind brushing along my skin, it feels as though I'm taking some profound rest. My eyes clear and around me the smallest things become vivid: frilled edges of lichens, twitching tail feathers of an eagle adjusting its movements to turbulence. I find myself awake when it's still dark, silently crawling out of the sleeping bag, tiptoeing over to the cook tent for solitude. Time with Molly Lou is often quiet, a walk in the forest becoming a prayer. One night, we hiked up Disc Island. No set intention, we just kept climbing. On a grassy ledge, we found a single iris, and from then on, spoke only in whispers, like foraging transients. There was expectancy in our quietness, possibility that we might see an animal. In the forest, it was already getting dark. Slants of light illuminated hemlock trunks. No birdsong. Setting our feet down on the moss as lightly as possible, following deer paths up and up, adding our tracks to their fresh prints pressed into the mud, we climbed. I imagined us curling up under one of the trees and going to sleep, like wild animals. "Do you think we should keep going?" Molly Lou asked me. It was steep in the forest. "Yes," I said. Finally we broke out of the trees, sweaty and panting, onto the crusty alpine. Hemlocks hip-high and flattened by wind. In twilight, below, Montague Strait drenched in blue. The wind drew us higher, to escape clouds of black flies. Just below the summit, I saw it. Silhouetted against the sky, a deer lay on top of a knoll. We sat where we were. The deer shook her head and tail, every once in a while glancing in our direction. She faced Montague Strait too, into the wind. When we descended from the ridge, she followed us. Molly Lou led, moving instinctively. Our steps sure, we crept over logs and moss. A feeling that everything else, every bird, every insect, was sleeping.

Of six encounters we had with Chugach transients that summer, one stands out in memory, that of July 26. In a grainy black-and-white photo from that day, Chenga, Iktua, Mike, Marie, Paddy, and Ewan sleep in Knight Island Passage, bodies so close that they could be one six-finned organism. What passed between them, skin to skin? What communication? What assurance or reassurance? The sea too I imagined as reassurance, a familiar skin, voice, rhythm. The orcas had survived the spill, the cleanup. Looking at that photo is an encounter with a long echo, repeating and diminishing forward and back, having something to say about evolution, and something to say about survival. Those six whales are still alive in the Sound today.

39

Spaces Between Facts

As I consider the graduate thesis I wrote that winter, which would eventually become two scientific papers, the words of William Blake come to mind: "To see the world in a grain of sand, / and heaven in a wild flower, / hold infinity in the palm of your hand, / and eternity in an hour." It was over 220 pages, my scientific story of the Chugach transients. It was drawn from nearly 230 hours of observation during five field seasons, over six thousand calls. Fourteen discrete call types in their dialect identified. My conclusions: They hunted most of the time, and thus were mostly silent, especially when offshore foraging. But there were exceptions. Their calling patterns changed with behavior. Lone males like Eyak emitted loud calls in predictable sequences—more like refrains than songs. As with transients elsewhere, they were noisiest when socializing, with whistles being predominant. When hunting, they used quiet calls—cryptic, short, low-frequency, nearly imperceptible bleats—to communicate. Lance discovered that they used quiet, intermittent sonar as well—he called them "cryptic clicks"—to orient themselves. Most significant, and most worrying, the Chugach transients shared no calls with other populations, suggesting genetic isolation.

I held the pages in my hands, feeling their heft, before turning them in to my committee. I felt the weight of hours, the stress, the lack of sleep, the nights in the computer lab, the struggle with statistics, the library searches, the learning of the foreign language of science. But what had I mastered, really? Only eleven Chugach transients remained alive. Over the winter of 1991, Lankard had vanished. In important ways, my thesis weighed as much as one of his breaths. One encounter with the Chugach transients revealed a snippet of their lives. My thesis was a collection of snippets. It was as if I'd taken a pair of scissors and clipped threads of six, ten, twenty-four hours. If they'd colonized the Sound after the retreat of the ice, as the Chugachmiut had done, then the Chugach transients had occupied that place for nearly ten thousand years. How many hours are there in ten thousand years? Nearly eighty-eight million. What does it mean, then? Can I see eighty-eight million hours cupped there, in the palm of my hand?

It's impossible to view the Chugach transients—all that they are—in a handful of sand grains. But if sand grains are all you have, you treat them as precious, each a crystal of knowing, inside which other, unexpected, truths might arise.

After turning in my thesis, relieved of the strictures of science, its attention only to observable facts, in my journal I considered what couldn't be seen. I considered the spaces between facts:

> *What is it to remember Eyak when I'm so far away, in a cabin,*
> *surrounded by forest, five hundred miles from the ocean. Study-*
> *ing whales is like watching someone swim. Once, a field assistant*
> *of Craig's stripped down and dove into the ocean near a pod of*
> *sea lions. She plunged under, popped back up, and treaded water,*
> *just her blonde head bobbing above the surface. Craig said, "Right*
> *now, those sea lions are zipping around her at about 90 miles an*
> *hour checking her out, and she has no idea." Watching Eyak is like*
> *watching that bobbing head, not seeing what's holding it aloft, the*
> *arms and legs kicking and swirling. The observing mind transcribes*
> *words into a data book, while something inside carries on another*
> *conversation. That's why listening to whales is so compelling. When*
> *you lower the hydrophone and slip the headphones on, you realize*
> *the water's surface is all illusion. I think of the transients' sounds,*
> *mournful, echoing, while above, it's just a whale breathing. I imag-*
> *ine slipping into the sea and swimming along a rocky shoreline,*
> *hunting for seals. I might find one sleeping near the bottom of a*
> *cove, or wedged into a crack in a rock, hiding. Eventually, like me,*
> *it will have to breathe, so I wait. I imagine hunting in dim light.*
> *An image of the world returns through my jawbone as an echo from*

a single click I emit from the top of my head, telling me where I am,
what the dark holds. I imagine the beginning of a call, something
from nothing. An eerie ghost-moan amplifying as if lifted off the sea
floor, a rope of sound rising, ending in an upsweep like a question. I
imagine slipping into the smallest bays, the narrowest constrictions,
listening. Or like a hunter in a forest at night, shining the lights of
my listening ahead of me. I imagine that kind of listening.

In Fairbanks, even while immersed in my life with John, I felt split in two, displaced from the Sound. So I ate moose heart. I skied alone by headlamp light. I wrote about water and whales. I practiced meditation. I bestowed myself to silence, in the words of poet Adrienne Rich, "a severer listening." As I practiced letting the transients go into their own silence, their own listening.

40

Silence as Survival

If things and creatures who live on earth don't
possess mystery, then there isn't any.
—GALWAY KINNELL

There's a great silence that opens, a great silence the remaining Chugach
transients retreated gradually into. Silence is an aspect of their survival; it
always has been. Like humans, they live by survival's imperatives: finding
food and mates, avoiding danger, searching the perimeter of their home
range, connecting to each other. They've always done this, through enormous anthropogenic changes to the ocean—the erasure of silence by the
arrival of steamships, outboards, and diesels; the arising and vanishing
of human enterprises; a state bounty on harbor seal "noses" chipping
away at their prey base; the collapse of herring, at the foundation of so
many food chains; the altering of shorelines during the 1964 earthquake;
an oil spill.

The truth is that my impression of the transients retreating into silence is partly personal, a consequence of my own retreat. I let them
go. After my graduate study ended, I had no justification—and no
funding—to trail them for hours at a time. I grew reluctant to inter-
fere with their lives, aside from documenting their presence with photographs. Moreover, in those years after my graduate study, my focus,
once tight on the Chugach transients, expanded to the long-term monitoring of all the Sound's orcas. But my impression of their retreat into
silence is partly ecological, a result of further changes to the Sound.
After the spill, the harbor seal decline, already underway, accelerated

in oiled areas. Seals vanished from many haul-outs in the study area. Where once they formed a living, grunting surface, I saw bare rocks. Bays without eyes.

Other things changed. Funding tightened. Craig pared our effort down to one boat, *Whale 2*. No longer would my track lines radiate from Squire Island. No longer would I roam the Sound with Molly Lou, or commiserate with Lance and Kathy around a beach fire at camp. I'd have to drum up new field assistants. To my relief, John agreed to help for part of the summer. Like me, John loved the Sound. He was a photographer. His grain of sand was the image framed in his camera viewfinder. For him, it was about framing, about putting things in the right light. From the silence of his images, stories arose. But also like me, John was no diesel mechanic, and *Whale 2*'s diesel was old and cantankerous. Lance and Kathy's mechanical expertise had kept it running. For us, it was a monster, an iron hulk lurking in a cramped space under the bunk, and I sat beside it, again at the bottom of a learning curve, a pile of engine manuals on my lap, a maintenance schedule pinned to the wall.

On a May trip to set up our fuel cache with Craig, one morning I sat alone on *Lucky Star*'s flying bridge, scanning. Above a silvery after-storm sea, I spotted three black wedges rising and disappearing. I fought my impulse to yell down to Craig, forced myself to sit tight until I saw them again. Only then did I lean over the side and shout toward the open cabin window, "Killer whales!"

Craig climbed up to the bridge with his own binoculars dangling from his neck, said, "The gods are with us. Must be AE pod." Superstitious, I wanted to pluck his words out of the air. Bad luck, I thought, to name them already, besides, my guess—my hope—was Chugach transients. We sat there scanning to no avail. I started to believe I'd conjured them out of clouds.

We dropped the hydrophone. Faint calls of a single Chugach transient emanated from the speaker, first distant, then louder. Finally, Craig spotted a dorsal fin back the way we'd come. As we drifted, listening, waiting for it to arrive, a squall engulfed us. I frantically scanned. Finally, after the squall passed, Craig spotted the male. He'd passed us. Was he looking for the three I'd seen earlier? We pulled the hydrophone, fired up *Lucky Star*, motored toward him. Easing in alongside, I saw that it was Eyak.

He swam slowly, milling and calling. He circled around us. He glided under the bow, then surfaced close, on one side of the boat, then the other. And then he disappeared into the next squall, and that was all. That was enough.

Finding the journal entry describing that encounter, two decades later, it retains its surreal quality. On *Lucky Star* with us that day was Craig's friend Mike, whose wife had been diagnosed with breast cancer. She's been dead for many years now, and I have just come through my own breast cancer experience. In my journal I read the impressions of my twentysomething self, touching the edges of someone else's grief: *Mike is reading an issue of* Ms. *magazine about breast cancer. He looks earnest. I can't imagine living every day with the fear that your partner may die.* Since the spill, I've lived with the fear that the Chugach transients will disappear. Every spring, I've returned to the Sound with trepidation. Now I wonder, will I survive them? Or they me? The past and present loop and stitch, stitch and loop, a strange and continuous dream.

Whale 2 being far more seaworthy than *Whale 1* kept us in Montague Strait much of the time. That's where, one mid-July day in 1993, John and I found Chenega's group. Through binoculars, I spotted blows and splashes from humpback tail lobs vivid against Knight Island's dark shoreline. When we approached, we could see the cause of the humpbacks' agitation. They smashed their flukes on the surface and exhaled wheezy, trumpeting breaths. Chenega, Ikua, and Mike chuffed among them. "They're killing something," I said to John.

"Do they attack humpbacks?" he asked, peering over the rail, his camera in one hand.

"I've never seen an attack, just harassment. We've heard about it, though."

The humpbacks swam toward, not away from, the transients. I joined John at the boat's side. Chenega surfaced, swam by with a chunk of flesh in her mouth. Gradually, the orcas drifted away from the humpbacks. John and I raced around, photographing flukes, easing in as close as we could to look for injuries, but we saw no blood, no wounds, no scratches. "No sign of humpback attack," I wrote in the field book. After feeding together, Chenega, Iktua, and Mike traveled away toward Grass Island, silent.

Now I can place that long-ago encounter alongside many strange accounts of humpbacks attracted to scenes of orca predation on marine mammals. In Southeast Alaska, humpbacks once joined an attack of West Coast transients on a Steller sea lion, at times striking the sea lion with their flukes. A Sitka-based researcher once watched a humpback accompany transients who'd gravely injured a sea lion, the three species swimming in tandem for miles. Recently, researchers in Antarctica observed humpbacks interfering with orca attacks on seals. In one instance, a humpback lifted a seal onto its belly to save the seal's life. Biologist Bob Pittman, an eyewitness, described the incident in *Natural History* magazine: "When a human protects an individual of another species, we call it compassion," he wrote at the article's conclusion. "If a humpback whale does so, we call it instinct. But sometimes the distinction isn't all that clear."

That summer, when we encountered Chugach transients hunting porpoises in Montague Strait, as we did often in the mid-1990s, they seemed shier. When we tried to photograph them, they changed directions. I drew jagged lines depicting their travel path on my encounter maps. I thought of my thesis result, offshore foraging being the most silent behavior, and wondered if boat noise was a bigger issue then, masking subtle sounds of porpoises. So we took our ID photographs and let them be, let them hunt unmolested.

But science can't leave things alone. Science with its never-ending questions persists, pursues. Sometimes the answers it pursues are about survival.

41

The Story Inside the Flesh

In the fall of 1994, Lance and Graeme flew to Alaska to begin a new line of questioning. They joined us on *Lucky Star*, along with tow-headed Lars, now four years old. Lance was in the midst of a PhD project investigating orca genetics in British Columbia and Alaska. He and Graeme had painstakingly developed a minimally invasive method to collect biopsy samples. Lance shot a dart at a whale's flank from an air gun. The dart, attached to a light aluminum body, hit the whale, extracted a two-inch-long cylinder of skin and blubber, and fell out. Tipped with an orange cap, the dart floated upright at the surface. They retrieved it with a swimming pool net. Through video documentation of each darting and follow-up approach, they'd been able to show that the whales reacted very little to the pencil-thin darts. The skin samples would allow Lance to describe population genetics of orcas in the North Pacific. The fat samples would reveal the contaminant load borne by the whales.

Anchored in Squire Cove. Stars glittering between racing clouds, the sky cold and foreign. Perhaps it feels that way because we're here to do something foreign. We're in the center of change. I've felt edgy, though never so much accepted as an equal. I keep busy, Lucky Star and my role familiar. Lance seems more serious, thoughtful, preoccupied. I imagine this enterprise of collecting biopsies wears on him. If anyone has the integrity to do it, it's Lance, so careful. Today, our first attempt at darting a humpback. A cylinder of flesh in a metal tube, surreal. The whales' reaction, instantaneous, a fluke slap.

Lance says the humpbacks are much more sensitive to darting than orcas, and I hope he's right.

The next morning, we found AB pod off Chenega Point, feeding on salmon. As I drove the skiff toward them, Lance braced himself in the bow with the gun, Lars beside him, laughing as the bow rose and fell. Craig and Graeme bantered, the catalog open in front of them. They picked a whale to biopsy, an adult male, Olsen, and I drove slowly parallel. Serious now, Graeme stood near Lance, camera to his eye, talking quietly. Lars scrunched into a tight ball, a finger in each ear, eyes closed. I felt everything inside me scrunch, my heart trying to bang its way out. Time compressed, then stopped. The tip of Olsen's dorsal broke the surface, then his head. He blew. Water slid off the fin, the saddle patch. I heard a pop, watched a dart fly, hit Olsen's side. "Good hit, no reaction," Graeme said, bending to jot notes in the field book. "Keep your eyes on that dart."

Lars popped up and turned toward the water, clutching the rail. "There it is," he shouted.

"Good eyes, Lars," Craig said.

The orange-tipped dart tilted back and forth in the whale's fluke print. I motored in close, and Craig leaned his long body over the side and plucked it from the water. "Good sample," he said, his voice ebullient. Relief swept through the boat like a gust, touched every one of us, softened the expression on Lance's face. By the end of the day, we had seven samples.

In the evening, we returned to Whale Camp to take down the wall tent for Olga, leaving only the platforms, skeletal and ramshackle. Graeme asked, "So, how much land does the Forest Service lease give you here? How big is your kingdom?" And I laughed at how unlikely it was that any part of the Sound could be claimed. From our encounter that day, we had one roll of film and some tiny samples of blubber and skin. They reflected the size of our claim to any of it. The camp put away for winter, Lars and I climbed up to King Tree to say goodbye. "Let's hug King Tree," I said and he did, willingly, a small smile on his face, reaching his arms out, his fingers curled on the bark.

In April, I returned to the Sound with Craig and Lance to help collect more biopsies. I'd never been there so early in the spring. Though it appeared wintry—snow thigh-deep on the islands—the yearly arrival of herring inshore to spawn signaled spring's beginning. Craig had spent many Aprils in Rocky Bay, on Montague Island, taking part in a herring roe-on-kelp fishery. The spawning herring drew not only fishermen, but other predators: harbor seals and sea lions, king salmon, gulls, humpback whales, and transients, who patrolled the shorelines.

In Montague Strait, we heard distant Chugach transient calls, but didn't find them. In Hinchinbrook Entrance, a few hours later, we watched a large aggregation of harbor porpoises, normally inconspicuous, shy cousins to the boisterous Dall's, spread out across an acre of water, their gray bodies scuffing the lumbering sea surface. Whitecaps would have concealed them entirely. I'd seen them only inside coves before, a pair here or there, never in such numbers. I knew that in B.C., harbor porpoises were part of the West Coast transient diet, but I'd never seen an attack or even harassment by the Chugach transients. I wondered if their gray coloration—like that of Dall's porpoise and beluga calves—helped camouflage them from predators.

The next morning, we rose early to broken clouds above Eleanor Cove, the water so unearthly still that I'd startled upon waking, imagined for a moment we'd gone aground. Snow covered Eleanor Island, all the way to the waterline, white cliffs rising several feet above the beach. When I stepped out on deck to brush my teeth, the air smelled sharp, like wet aluminum. It stung my face. "Bracing," as Molly Lou would have said. Frost melted under my bare feet. Varied thrushes buzzed in the trees, defying the snow. Pairs of marbled murrelets drifted along the shore, their whistly peeps keeping them in constant contact. Like the Chugach transients, murrelets, once ubiquitous, had suffered great losses during the spill, and hadn't yet recovered. Still in black-and-white winter plumage, they flipped up their tails to dive for fish. The tableau was ancient. A hunter in a skin boat, wearing an orca hunting hat, could have in that moment paddled in, and we would have been the anachronism.

After coffee and granola, we headed north, sharing the seat on the bridge, scanning with binoculars, cups of steaming tea held between our legs. Craig and Lance talked about research politics, and I half listened. I kept my journal open on my lap, pen in my hand, field book on the dash. As we searched our way north, stopping every few miles to drop the hydrophone, I jotted marine mammal sightings. Every ten minutes or so, we spotted another group of Dall's porpoises. "Must be a lot of feed fish around," Craig mused.

"Should be transients around," I said. "Somewhere." Four hours later, dorsal fins rose and fell at the horizon. Four orcas, tightly grouped, slowly traveled north. From a long way off, we knew they were transients, by the way they moved, by their silhouettes. I took the wheel and angled in parallel. Craig and Lance snapped ID photos: Chenega, Mike, Iktua. But who was the adult male? I momentarily thought it was Ripple Fin, but he'd disappeared in 1991. This male was Eccles. "Eyak must be around somewhere," I said, jotting notes in the field book, then lifting my binoculars to scan.

"Well," said Lance, with a sigh. "I suppose we should try to biopsy these guys."

"They're pretty tolerant right now," Craig said, "but you know it won't last. We should do it while they're friendly. We've got just a few close approaches before they say 'Enough.' Eva, stay backed off while we get the gear and skiff ready." I eased the throttle, angled away from them. Below me, Craig and Lance hustled, loading the camera case, gun case, and cooler of darts and disinfectants into the skiff. I heard the hydraulic winch squeal, the lines creak as the skiff lifted off the deck.

"Okay, Craig, it's clear of the side. You can let her down," Lance yelled.

"Keep the radio on channel 14," Craig called to me as the skiff zoomed away.

I dreaded what was about to happen, glad to remain behind on *Lucky Star*. I maneuvered ahead of the whales, shut down, dropped the hydrophone, and picked up my binoculars.

Craig was right. The whales' tolerance was already spent. Offshore foraging, every time the skiff pulled near they dove. In my head, I cajoled the whales, knowing how self-serving it was, how full of justification and wishful thinking. But I couldn't help myself. Perhaps it was a way to clarify intention—my intention. After all, though I hadn't conceived of the project, I wasn't just a bystander. I'd chosen to participate. I was culpable. *We'd like to take biopsy samples from you just this once. We're doing this so we can work to protect you. Please allow us to do this.* The voice in my head unceasing, I stared through the binoculars, jotted notes: *3 br/6 min* [three breaths, six-minute dive]*; 4 br/4 min; 3 br/5 min; 3 br/6 min.* With so little surface time, it was impossible for Lance and Craig to get a sample.

"You've got to gain their trust," I half-joked on the radio. "Be patient, Craig."

"We're trying," Craig said.

Gradually, over an hour's time, the whales' behavior changed. They stayed longer at the surface, as though they'd relaxed or given in to our presence. After a short dive, they surfaced beside the skiff. I watched Lance lift the gun to his shoulder, cock his head slightly to sight on Chenega's saddle patch. One beat. I saw the gun lower, the whales dive, one after another, as before. Craig pointed at the water and turned the skiff sharply. Lance leaned far over the side. He lifted the dart out of the water, turned to Craig, saying something. I watched Craig lean down to take the VHF microphone.

"Good sample!" Craig said over the radio. "She didn't react at all."

I took a head-clearing breath. On the next surfacing, Lance darted Mike. I could see the reaction from *Lucky Star,* a shake of his whole body, then a quick dive, the others following.

Craig's voice crackled from the radio. "I think we'll back off for a while now. We hit him at a slight angle; he didn't like that."

Over the next hour, their dives grew longer again: seven minutes, eight. Off Smith Island, they spread out. Eccles disappeared. Through binoculars, I saw, scattered over a square mile, dozens of harbor porpoises, some surfacing singly, but most in small groups of up to seven. The transients, now dispersed, swam among them. Were they resting? They must have been aware of the harbor porpoises. Were the porpoises aware of them? Was it some kind of strategy, to lull the porpoises, the way the skiff's persistent following at a distance seemed to lull the whales? Or were the orcas simply not that hungry? For an hour more, orcas and porpoises surfaced together. Nearby, two sea lions dozed on top of a can buoy marking a reef.

And then a harbor porpoise was flying, with Chenega flying after. She threw the porpoise into the air twice, then took it down. Mike and Iktua arrived. The whales milled. After twenty minutes, they lined up and began traveling. *Not a porpoise in sight,* I wrote in my notebook.

Again the whales dove every time the skiff approached. Finally, Lance fired off another dart, this time at Iktua. When the dart hit, all three whales startled, as though sharing one skin, and quickly dove. Eight minutes later, they surfaced far away. Craig retrieved the dart, and they roared back to *Lucky Star.*

"Thank God that's over," Craig said. I was relieved to hear him admit some discomfort.

That evening, my hands in rubber gloves, I screwed the extractor onto the end of the dart tip and watched blubber, then a quarter inch of gray skin, tumble into a Petri dish. I pulled the barb out of the sample with a pair of pliers. It dangled from a tweezers, a piece of Chenega. I'd never touched her or any Chugach transient. They'd always kept just out of reach of my outstretched hand. This time, we'd crossed that gap. We'd touched them, not with our hands, but with stainless steel. Had they allowed it? Or had we simply taken what we wanted, against their will? How would they react next time, as the skiff, or *Whale 2,* motored toward them? Had we betrayed them? Would it be worth it?

As if reading my thoughts, Craig said, "Don't worry. These are transients. They're tough. Look what they did to that porpoise. They're used to being roughed up. It was like a mosquito bite."

But I thought of the young Yupiq woman I'd tutored in Fairbanks. When I'd told her about the biopsy project, she'd warned me: "The elders say you're not supposed to touch killer whales, or bother them. Bad things can happen."

With a scalpel, I cut the blubber from the skin, one clean slice. Then I sliced the skin in half lengthwise. I dropped Chenega's skin into two separate vials of fixative, one half for Lance's genetic analysis, the other to be archived. I dropped the blubber into a glass vial. I labeled each one, not with the names I called the whales, but with their scientific monikers, which kept us separate enough, detached enough, to do what had to be done: AT9, AT10, AT18.

In June, back in the Sound with Craig and his crewman Ted, a few weeks before my own field season on *Whale 2* was to begin, we found Chenega's group hunting in the place where they'd killed the harbor porpoise. To my relief, they were no more, no less diffident than they'd always been. They combed the coast of Little Smith Island, a place that had been heavily oiled in 1989. Here and there, seals clung to rocks or held motionless in shallows. The transients made no kill, swam back offshore. A swell was running, and we lost them among rolling hills of water.

The next day, anchored in Hogan Bay, riding out a storm, still in our pajamas, syrup dripping from the tines of our forks, Ted suddenly said, "Holy crap. There's a killer whale just off the bow—right here!" Two males, two black knives, sliced open the bay's rain-pocked surface. Eyak and Eccles. We jumped up, Craig starting the engine, Ted pulling the anchor. I pulled rain gear over my long johns, sweater over my T-shirt, slicker over that. While Craig readied the skiff for launching, I gathered up the camera and biopsy equipment.

The whales traveled side by side along the shoreline toward Point Helen, passing groups of chuffing sea lions, who craned their heads from the froth, as if in indignation. In the seas and rain, we banged along in the skiff, Ted trailing us in *Lucky Star*. I drove, a lump in my throat, my heart racing. Craig snapped photos, and then reached for the biopsy gun. I eased in parallel, and when Eccles surfaced, Craig fired. I watched Eccles startle, the dart sticking in front of his saddle patch. He tilted to the side. Both whales dove. We searched through their fluke prints but never found the dart. Craig, wild with frustration, explained that he'd dialed down the gun's power, thinking we were too close. That's why the dart had stuck in the whale. Hitting the water when the whale dove, it probably broke apart and sank.

By the time we saw Eyak and Eccles again, they were halfway across Knight Island Passage, lunging through three-foot waves, side by side. "It looks like they're fleeing," I said under my breath. I didn't know whether to be angry at Craig, at science, or at myself for participating. *Please whales*, the voice raced in my head, *let us get these samples and then we'll leave you alone.* The last time I'd pursued transients aggressively, Eyak had lashed his fluke at *Whale 1*'s bow. But we were committed now, I sensed it, so I angled the skiff in close. Craig braced himself. Eccles surfaced, slashing his fluke. Craig shot. The dart hit the center of his saddle patch. Eccles seemed not to react at all. "I think I hit him from a slight angle last time, that's why he reacted," Craig shouted, pointing at the water where the dart bobbed. He leaned far over and grabbed it. "Good sample!" he shouted. "Hurry and catch them again. Let's go for Eyak this time."

I tried to calm my heartbeat with deep breaths, scanning the water for the whales. When I spotted them, still traveling as before, I pushed the throttle, focusing my attention, emptying my mind of thought or doubt or pleading. We pulled up alongside. Still porpoising, the whales' bodies broke free of the water with every breath. Water opened around them like a collar, green and translucent as bottle glass. They arched high. I saw the gray, scarred patch of Eyak's saddle. I watched a dart hit, fly out, fall into the waves. "There," I said.

Craig followed my finger. "I see it!" he shouted. As we pulled near, I saw white blubber protruding from the tip. Eyak's flesh. It was done. Darts in the cooler, we let the whales go.

At the time, I had to rely on faith in the integrity of my colleagues and mentors to believe that the theft of those bits of skin and blubber from orcas was justifiable. Only now, two decades later, do I see the story held within each millimeter of flesh. In his office, Craig recently pinned up a poster titled "Killer Whale Ecotypes and Forms." It illustrates ten distinct orca types now known to exist in the world, six of them in the Antarctic. Each ecotype occupies the ocean in a unique way, from the "carousel feeding" herring eaters of the North Atlantic, to seal hunters of the Antarctic, who work as a group to create pressure waves to wash their prey off ice floes. There are penguin eaters, shark eaters, and minke whale eaters. One mammal-eating type, named "Bigg's killer whale," includes the Chugach transients. Like nested Russian dolls, ever more intricate stories reside within those ecotypes, the stories told by those skin samples. Within an ecotype are separate populations, each with its own narrative. Within Bigg's killer whale are West Coast transients, Gulf of Alaska transients, Eastern Aleutian transients, and Chugach transients. All stocky, tall-finned, black-and-white, nonetheless each population lives an entirely different lifestyle—and has for thousands of years.

The blubber samples would tell another story. In terms of PCBs, PBDEs (flame retardants), and DDTs—all immune suppressors and endocrine disruptors—transient orcas, at the top of the marine food chain, are some of the most contaminated creatures on earth. Mothers pass contaminants to their calves through their milk. The poisons originate from leaking barrels dumped decades ago into the Gulf of Alaska by the military. Or they arrive within air masses from Southeast Asia, warm air hitting the cold air over the Gulf of Alaska, raining the toxins down. Within each cylinder of blubber is our human story.

Within each skin sample is an old story overturned. There is no one thing called *Orcinus orca*. What we thought one thing is many. What we thought abundant is not. What we thought invulnerable is fragile, existing in that form nowhere else on earth.

Two weeks after darting Eyak and Eccles, Craig and I heard the loud calls of a male transient near Whale Camp, and, using the directional dish, we found him. Like Eyak when he was alone, Eccles slowly traveled, blasting his song in various directions. Through binoculars, I saw no scar, no evidence that we'd taken a piece of his flesh. Off Point Helen, the place we thought of as a crossroads, the apex of three passages, Eccles's calls grew shrill, their tail ends sweeping up. On the hydrophone, we heard distant, answering calls. Scanning the water of Montague Strait, I spotted white sprays to the north. It was another whale, porpoising toward Eccles. Eccles bashed the water with his fluke. Still a few hundred yards away, the second whale dove, then surfaced beside him. Of course it was Eyak. Side by side, the pair traveled out into the Strait.

That night, at midnight, I sat up writing in my journal, the bleating of geese drifting in through the open window. Just past solstice, it was light enough to scan the beaches for those geese, or for brown bears or deer. A movement along the shoreline caught my eye, but it wasn't a bear. One black fin, then another, broke the surface, slid back under. Then again. Two male orcas surfaced and dove, their blows hanging in the air, dissolving. Something no genetic sample could quantify or describe: what it was like to see them appear in a cove at dusk; their brotherhood; their singular lives in the Sound.

42

Snippets and Transparencies

The next day, leaving the cove, I spotted splashes. Eyak and Eccles social-ized with Chenega's group: the five darted whales. With nothing to do but photograph and watch them, I felt calm. "Now we can regain their trust," I joked to Craig. Quieting, the whales foraged along Montague Island, a shoreline rock-riddled, like the Labyrinth. They passed sea otter nurseries, mothers resting placidly, pups on their bellies, unconcerned with the orcas or our boat. In a kelp bed, the whales milled briefly. I wondered if they'd found a seal, but they veered offshore, charging back toward us. When a pair of seals surfaced off our bow, Craig yanked the throttle back. One seal lifted its head high out of the water, and for some reason I picked up the ID camera and trained the viewfinder on its sil-very face, its enormous black eyes. The seal rose even higher, eyes fixed on mine. "Holy shit," I heard Craig say. A shape passed beneath, a flash of white. Then Chenega's open mouth clamped around the seal's body. Through the viewfinder, I watched her take the seal down. The other seal disappeared in the melee that followed, Iktua and Mike arriving, then Eyak and Eccles. The orcas swam a short way, the seals crosswise in their jaws. Then they thrashed at the surface, dove, and moments later chunks of blubber, bits of organ, and clouds of blood—all that remained of the living animal I'd stared at—floated around them. "I guess the whales knew those seals were there, even with our engine running. How the hell do they do that?" Craig asked.

Everything had happened so quickly. Perhaps we'd missed some clue.

Perhaps the orcas had startled the seals in the kelp bed. Perhaps the seals had fled. Perhaps the orcas had tricked them, doubled back.

After feeding, the whales moved on, nearshore-foraging. "Look," Craig said, pointing toward the beach. The whales were down. A brown bear stalked the water's edge. When the whales surfaced, it startled, stood on hind legs like a person, and watched them swim past.

A few days later, rolling a barrel up the beach on Grass Island, I turned to look at the water, and I could almost see, like a transparency laid out across my view of the narrow passage, three fins, three Chugach transients that had swum past that beach years before. I'd been there with Kathy, and she'd just said, "I wonder why we never see transients in here?"

It was that way in the Sound, as though time itself were layered, multidimensional, holding the present alongside a moment of "first permission," the first time I'd seen Chugach transients in a particular place. The beach on Montague was forever altered by that brown bear standing to watch its oceanic counterparts swim by. How many memories were layered under the place names on my nautical chart, ancient, forgotten names of forgotten incidents. I thought of the names I'd given the Chugach transients, each carrying a specific association, geography, history, narrative, meaning, saying as much about me as it did about them. *Call me by my true name*, I imagined Eyak saying. A lifetime didn't feel long enough to discover that name.

Every once in awhile, something entirely unfamiliar laid a new memory down. Even after nearly a decade, the Chugach transients still surprised us. Like the day in 1994 when I followed AE pod north toward the Pleiades with John, now my husband. I'd spotted blows on the periphery of the foraging residents, and said, "Maybe we should check them out, in case there's an incoming pod." But it wasn't a new pod, and it wasn't AEs either. Three transients surfaced tightly together, traveling rapidly north. A young male followed just a few feet behind them. When John pulled the boat alongside, I caught my breath. The male wasn't Eyak or Eccles. It was Eshamy, an AE teenager just sprouting his adult dorsal fin, swimming behind Chenega, Iktua, and Mike, who charged toward the Labyrinth. "What the heck," I said, baffled. Gradually, Eshamy dropped further behind the trio. Finally he turned back toward AE pod, now a mile away. Could he have been chasing the transients? Or was he simply curious? Perhaps he didn't know the rules of resident-transient avoidance yet. A flicker of hope arose. If Chenega or Iktua mated with an unrelated male, they might have a calf. They might have a chance.

Chenega's group disappeared into the Labyrinth. We backtracked and found Eshamy foraging with his mother. I remembered Graeme's odd story of residents in B.C. driving transients into a cove and "thrashing them." The residents had had a new calf. Did residents perceive transients as a threat to their calves? My story and Graeme's were like two excerpts clipped from an enormous, hidden text, laid side-by-side, curiosities. All we could do was continue to collect more fragments, building a mosaic that might one day illuminate that larger story.

Another encounter, another fragment. Near the Needle, Chenega's group, which had been offshore foraging, milled. Near them, something floated, pale like a bleached balloon: a pair of still-inflated porpoise lungs, the heart between them. Chenega surfaced with a slab of flesh balanced on her snout, a cow and calf humpback swimming close behind her. A few hours later, writing notes in the field book, I startled at John's shout. "Porpoises, racing away!" I looked up to see a porpoise flying, an orca airborne behind it. Then everything slowed. The three orcas converged. The porpoise, a calf, swam weakly away. The whales turned. Chenega lunged, grabbing it. I stood on the bow as I had so many times, watching her swim over to us, holding the porpoise crosswise in her jaws. The whales began diving, calling quietly, oil spreading across the water's surface. We drifted close enough to see flesh in their mouths. Storm petrels arrived. Iktua swam under the bow, the porpoise's flukes in her mouth. It felt like we'd been allowed in. It felt like permission. Did they know me? After nearly a decade?

Another snippet. Sleepy Bay. Egagutak and Mike, older male with younger, vocalizing, rolling over and under one another, penises extended. It was like the play between those three long-ago transient males, like the sexual play we saw often between resident orca males. Was Egagutak, the most solitary of the Chugach transients, training the younger male, Mike, to be an adult? Or was it some form of competitive male sparring, establishing dominance for mating? Was it simply play? Or was it a sign that, even with their social structure shattered, the Chugach transients still dwelled in possibility, living as if?

43

The Other World

In September of 1994, with *Whale 2* tucked in the Cordova harbor, Craig, Lars, and I returned to the Sound on *Lucky Star*. The fall storms were upon us, and signs of the bird migration were everywhere: flocks of phalaropes in the strait, knots of shorebirds on beaches, the V-shaped tendrils of geese, and one day, over the north end of Montague Island, a spiraling prayer wheel of sandhill cranes, thousands of them, riding updrafts, gaining altitude. We stood on deck with our heads thrown back, listening to their creaking voices. From time to time, a line of birds, like a torn-off scrap, blew east across the strait, toward the Copper River Delta, where they'd stage before migrating farther south. Replacing them, continuously, incoming birds from the west joined the spiral. A sound like raindrops hitting drew our eyes away from the birds, toward the water. "Look," Lars said, pointing. Around the boat, thousands of sand lances finned at the surface, flashing silver, like a gesture of response to the cranes.

In fall, while most things die back or depart the Sound, other things flourish: humpbacks lunge-feeding through schools of sand lances or herring, resident orcas feeding on late runs of silver salmon, the last pinks spawning in streams. There Lars ran barefoot, chasing dying fish, catching them in his hands, shouting, "Look, I got one, Dad!" As we walked along, sometimes we'd find a strip of bones, sometimes a shred of skin folded over itself, sometimes skin shrunk over skeleton, mouth agape, eyes plucked out by gulls.

In the darkness, water glittered with phosphorescence, and on clear nights, the sky with stars, and often an aurora throbbed in the north. The air felt sharp after storms, the clouds like alabaster, and the wind never stopped, even in clear weather. After supper, Craig often played his guitar, singing Lars to sleep. One of his favorite songs was called "The Urge for Going," describing "winter closing in." But I had no urge for going. I liked knowing that up in Fairbanks, graduate students were ensconced in a new semester, and the first cold nights were freezing the puddles on the dirt road where John and I lived. In the interior, it was winter. But I was in the Sound. Despite the dusting of white on the high peaks after storms, it was still autumn, and I wasn't going back to Fairbanks until December. *Whale 2* waited for me in Cordova. After our trip, I'd live aboard her and work on our data at the Prince William Sound Science Center.

One evening, at dusk, Craig, Lars and I rowed to shore and walked to the outer beach of Grass Island. Wading through waves of dead ryegrass, ducking under alder branches stripped of leaves, I held Lars's hand, trying to keep up with Craig's strides, which led us far down the beach. We reached a headland and stood leaning against it. The strait gleamed, though the sun was long down, so it seemed as though light, not water, sloshed against the shore below us. Everything was dying back, but the water was alive. I felt the cold air in my hair, the grittiness of rock beneath my hands. I felt like we might just disappear forever into that place. My time with the transients felt as if it were being reclaimed, gathered in. It was not mine, had never been. It felt, in a strange way, like death, a dissolving, the way a salmon or orca carcass dissolves into beach stones and leaves behind a necklace, a shadow of its life. Now Lars held Craig's hand. I put my hand on Lars's head, to fix that moment, that connection, that knowing, into permanence. And yet I knew that moment was less mine than anything, passing as quickly as the clouds overhead. Soon we'd climb back onto the boat and turn on the lights and clang pots and pans and cook supper, and then we'd fall asleep into our separate dreams.

A few days later, on the way back to Whittier, we watched Eyak, Eccles, and Egagutak reclaimed too. In the dusk, slapping their flukes, turning upside-down, laying pectoral flippers across one another's bodies, they reminded me again of that long-ago trio of males. Night pooled around them, as though spilling out of the forest. We followed until we could barely see their shapes against that greater darkness.

Later that fall, I lived aboard *Whale 2* in the Cordova harbor. For hours each day, I pored over data sheets going back to 1984, to Craig's first years in the Sound, entering everything, including track lines, into a geographic database called GIS. A complex analysis would allow us to look at how individual pods and populations used the Sound, to document critical habitats. One field log, one encounter, one track line at a time, I relived every hour I'd spent on the water, entire days reforming in my memory, triggered by a few sentences: *Stormy in morning, calming. Headed down KIP searching, filled water buckets in Mummy Bay from falls, found Icy and Berg in Icy Bay, then 5 humpbacks in Port Bainbridge. Craig brings gas in evening.* I worked late into the night, walking to the boat past rowdy bars and dark canneries. I lay awake listening to the wind rattling the stovepipe, howling through the rigging of sailboats in slips near mine. One weekend, John flew in for a visit. On a drizzly morning, we took *Whale 2* out. Sitting on deck drinking tea at the mouth of Nelson Bay, I heard blows. Along the shoreline, two male orcas traveled. I grabbed the camera, and John took his familiar place at the wheel, driving us toward them. It took several moments to recognize Aligo and Holgate. I hadn't seen them in two years. After photographing, we drifted with the engine off. I felt no compulsion to follow them farther. John and I sat quietly watching Aligo and Holgate swim out of the bay.

I imagine Nelson Bay holding the echo of Aligo's and Holgate's breathing even now. I imagine it holding John and me together in that moment, fixing it forever, though in the other world we'd all go separate ways.

44

Where the Seals Are

In January of 1996, with Craig, I attended meetings of the Exxon Valdez Oil Spill Trustee Council, funders of our post-oil spill research for years. The buzz phrase was "traditional ecological knowledge." My Chugach-miut friend Mike Eleshansky, an elder and master subsistence seal hunter from Chenega village, was there as a liaison between villagers and the scientists studying ongoing impacts of the spill. I listened to him try to relate his impressions of the harbor seal decline, something of utmost import to his people. They'd relied on seals for food since "time immemorial." In his halting, storytelling way, he described how, from the 1920s to the early 1970s, the Chugachmiut, along with other locals, hunted seals not only for food but for a bounty of three dollars per harbor seal "nose," collected by the territorial, and then state, government. During those years, 360,000 "hair seals" (mostly harbor seals) were shot in Alaska as a result of the predator control program. In the 1950s, about 50,000 were killed on the Copper River Delta alone. A decade later, a hot commercial fur market led to the killing of tens of thousands more seals annually for a few years. Craig had told me of the dynamiting of harbor seal haul-outs on the Copper River Flats in the 1960s to decrease competition for salmon. Not until the Marine Mammal Protection Act of 1972 did seals and sea lions gain some safeguarding, though they still could be shot if they interfered with commercial fishing operations. In 1973, 125,000 harbor seals were estimated to inhabit Prince William Sound.

The seals "always seemed to bounce back," Mike told the panel. Now, he said, there was much less hunting, but the seals no longer bounced back. Since 1973, their population had declined by 80 percent in the Gulf of Alaska. The moderator kept trying to interrupt Mike, who spoke slowly, pausing often to choose his words. Kathy Frost, who was also on the panel, who'd worked with Mike and other villagers to collect data from seals harvested for subsistence at Chenega, tried to paraphrase what he was saying. I kept listening for the story under Mike's words, what wasn't being said. Part of that story was the responsibility he was willing to take. In his view, it was simple. "We just shot too many," he said. His "we" was broad: government biologists, bounty hunters, subsistence and commercial hunters, fishermen. Another part of the story under his story spoke of imbalance: some resilience, some equilibrium in the Sound had been upset. The seals had bounced back and bounced back up to a point. For years, state biologists would study the decline, just as federal biologists would later study the Gulf of Alaska sea lion decline, but they'd come to no firm conclusion of cause. "Possibly a change in feed fish, coupled with predation and subsistence harvest," one report said, not mentioning the predator control program or the oil spill. I left the meeting even more worried for the Chugach transients.

By the end of the 1996 field season, we'd encountered only six Chugach transients. Not Marie's group. Not Aligo. Not Holgate. Reports from west of the Sound gave us hope. Boat operators from Seward reported large groups of residents using Kenai Fjords. But they also reported a pair of male orcas hunting seals in the ice-filled fjords of Aialik Bay. And sometimes, a group of three shy, difficult-to-approach females appeared, probably transients, they said.

So for the next several years, Craig and I began our field seasons in a new place. Instead of heading straight for the Sound after launching *Lucky Star* in Seward, where it was dry-docked for the winter, we spent the spring season in Kenai Fjords. Strong early king salmon runs attracted fish-eating pods to Resurrection Bay. AD and AK pods took up residence there in May and June, attracting other pods, many of them unfamiliar to us. As we learned to recognize new individuals, as we learned the geography of the fjords—Agnes Bay, Pony Cove, Cheval Narrows, Cape Aialik, Hive Island, Porcupine Cove—we learned the names and personalities of boat captains. Seward, on the road system from Anchorage, and just a short boat ride away from Kenai Fjords National Park, attracted thousands of tourists each summer, and a tour boat industry had slowly built up.

One of the senior operators, a former tugboat captain named Mike Britain, nicknamed "Magic" by his fellow skippers for an uncanny ability to spot whales, became a close friend, and later part of our research team. Like many of the boat operators, he was not just a skipper but also a naturalist. He could tell tourists the difference between a marbled and Kittlitz's murrelet, and explain their distinct nesting and food habits. Magic's round, wire-framed glasses gave him a studious look that belied his workingman's garb of ball cap, cotton shirt, jeans, and XTRAFTUF boots. When he had to, he drove a battered Subaru. Otherwise, he rode a mountain bike around town. The two male transients who hunted in Aialik Bay, Magic told us, were known by the tour operators as "the Bad Boys." He'd watched them kill harbor seals right off his bow. He assumed they were Gulf of Alaska transients, and so did we.

But our first encounter with transients in the fjords wasn't with the Bad Boys. It was, to our relief, with Marie, Ewan, and Paddy, our first encounter with them in two years. As we'd come to expect, no new calf traveled with the whales, despite the fact that both Iktua and Marie were of breeding age. The remaining Chugach transients might be too closely related, or too contaminated—some of the toxins in their blubber are known endocrine disrupters—to reproduce successfully.

It was strange to see those familiar whales transposed, in an unfamiliar place, along the steep, rock-bound coast of Harbor Island. At our approach, they turned and dove, staying under for five minutes. We fixed their direction on our compass, followed that heading, but when they surfaced it was in an unexpected location. After an hour and a half of futile maneuvers, zooming in quickly, or sliding in slowly, or trying to place ourselves in their path, we sat drifting with the hydrophone down, frustrated. As if by accident, the whales surfaced near the skiff, and Craig snapped their photos. Off the cape, they angled southwest, heading for the ocean. Though we hadn't darted Marie's group yet, we knew it would be impossible that day. "Maybe they're hunting porpoises," I said, watching them disappear into the swells.

A few weeks later, we waited for transients at the entrance to Holgate Arm, an ice-choked fjord in Aialik Bay. Tour boats had reported the Bad Boys off the glacier earlier in the day. We hadn't yet identified who they were. We sat on the flying bridge and scanned, our fingertips red from a cold wind off the glacier.

Finally, we spotted blows, off Three-Hole Bay. Marie's group, and with them the Bad Boys, who were not Gulf of Alaska transients after all, but Aligo and Holgate. Even though they were offshore hunting, this time the whales allowed us close, and Craig darted Aligo and Ewan. They hardly reacted, flicking the darts off their skin with a twitch. What was different that day? Perhaps it was simply a matter of mood: some days the whales tolerant, even when hunting, other days intolerant, for reasons unknown.

Two days later, Craig darted Holgate in the protection of Aialik Bay as a storm built in the Gulf. When Holgate and Aligo headed toward the glacier, I longed to follow, but the tour boat radio chatter made us nervous. "She's comin' up," one skipper said. "Green water over the bow." Another operator reported a forty-knot gust at Cape Resurrection. "We came around the cape in twelve-footers," said another. "Better go pelagic." We watched the males swim doggedly into the ice, unperturbed by weather forecasts. We left, following the skipper's advice to "go pelagic," giving Cape Aialik a wide berth, sliding down swells until we tucked into the protection of Agnes Bay.

We wondered if the decline in harbor seals had caused the Chugach transients to spread their hunting efforts between the Sound and Kenai Fjords. But when I studied the nautical chart, I saw that their separation was a misperception. The Sound and Kenai Fjords were indentations in one wide embayment between Cape Saint Elias, to the east, and Nuka Bay, to the west. That water even had a name: Blying Sound. But my heart remained closed to the fjords, as if to love that place would betray another.

One day, a mutual friend who'd accompanied us on a trip in the Sound observed my daily debates with Craig over whether we should stay (orca encounters had been sparse) or head back to the fjords, where surely there were residents. I urged Craig to be patient, to give the Sound a chance. "Look, there's a silver jumping," I'd say. "There are plenty of silvers for the residents here."

Our friend said: "You're much more tied to place, Eva. Craig's much more tied to the whales." Was it true? How could I separate place and whales? Patience was what the Chugach transients exemplified. Patience and fidelity. After a foggy day of futile searching, I considered our friend's words in my journal:

> *Grace eludes me today. All abstractions—peace of mind, calmness—are obscured in the fog of my own desire. The transients are*

out there somewhere, I tell Craig. In fog, nothing is certain. There are only suggestions of things standing for other things. A shadow is actually a shoreline. Ripples on the water are currents, boat wakes, paw-marks of wind. A darkening is an island. Silence on the hydrophone is a transient hunting on the other side of the island.

45

Book of Changes

The geographical split in our study area, the splitting of time between the Sound and Kenai Fjords, the splitting of large resident pods during those years, mirrored our own splits and fractures. My brief marriage to John ended. Craig and Olga separated. I moved from the interior to the coast, Craig and I having come together. Now Craig and Olga traded time with Elli, Lars, and Eve, at home and in the field, two weeks on, two weeks off. They traded sightings during the season, and data at summer's end. Sometimes we met at Whale Camp for a campfire or to pick berries. In the midst of upheaval, the Sound remained constant, Whale Camp a still point, the kids' steadfast love for all of us, for the Sound, bridging our rifts. In 1998, Olga bought a motor sailboat, the new *Whale 1*. Still using *Lucky Star*, though Craig no longer commercially fished for salmon, we needed, as always, another person to drive the boat while we worked with whales in the skiff. Often, that third person was David Grimes.

With only eleven Chugach transients left alive, encounters grew even more sporadic. Olga, from her base at Whale Camp, occasionally found them in the old places. One June morning, in Knight Island Passage, she spotted Eyak and Eccles. *Traveling rapidly north in perfect unison, side by side*, she wrote in her log.

In early July of that year, when resident sightings dropped off in the fjords, Craig, David, Lars, and I, on the heels of a storm, crossed the Gulf to Prince William Sound. Waiting out the weather, I sat at the table drinking tea. It was my thirteenth summer in the Sound. *Terrain that always newly presents itself*, I wrote in my journal, comparing it to my human relationships, especially with Craig. He too was now new terrain. And I was new terrain to myself. David's music and stories grounded me, wove past to present. In a creative fervor, "the songs just coming through," as he put it, he composed every night, his bare feet tapping a beat as he perched on the helm seat like a dark-crowned, blue-eyed bird, head cocked, his guitar tilted at a sharp angle on his lap, the frets at his ear, humming snatches of nascent songs plucked from the air, stopping, considering which chord matched a lyric. Silver strands now threaded through his long, dark hair, but like the Sound, he seemed both old and young at once. "I'm wading in the dappled stream, my feet are cold, my hands are clean," he sang a capella. I'd brought my oboe along, dusted off after years of neglect. Tentatively, I wove in a melody line to that song, played him Irish tunes. "Ain't nobody else ever goes up that hill without any shoes," he sang. "This push of the world is true." Over the winter, he'd grown a goat beard, two long silver chin tufts. Lars lovingly called him "Weird Uncle David." Together they caught fish, meticulously dissected them, examining every part, cooking up the eyes, liver, and heart for us to try. After Lars chanted, "David is good, chocolate pud!" for an entire afternoon, David taught him to make his exotic mousse of cocoa, butter, milk, orange peel, and cinnamon. It was unsettling to see David without *Orca 2*, as though his gnarled bare feet didn't touch the ground when he walked. He'd let her go, was now onto another passionate mission to protect the Copper River, at the Sound's eastern edge. Named for the ore, I liked to think that Copper stood for something else, the hue of millions of red salmon migrating up the river to spawn each year. David and others in Cordova were fighting proposals to connect the town to the road system by paving an old railroad bed along the Copper River corridor. David's methods hadn't changed: he guided trips down the river, regaling clients with stories, music, salmon, and poetry. Like a matchmaker, he set people up to fall in love with the place. Now his platform was a rubber raft, not a wooden boat. His clients were legislators, musicians, agency employees, planners, friends, and activists. "Down the Copper River, mighty happy, the moon is rising up through the trees," he sang to us. "That's my people, they got their arms all around me."

To the soundtrack of David's tunes, I jotted cloud reports as we waited out the storm: *Squalls come and go. Clouds move rapidly from the southeast, fat gray underbellies, like whales overhead. Yesterday, the sky changed from pale blue to gray. Even the islands turned gray as squalls arrived.*

I wrote about change, and David sang about change, and Craig and I talked about change, having both recently taken up Buddhist meditation, so Lars finally asked, looking up from his Calvin and Hobbes cartoon book, "What do you mean, everything is always changing. Maybe there's a new wave. Waves change, but most everything else stays the same." I was surprised and relieved to hear those words from him, considering all the change he'd recently seen. Perhaps the Sound grounded him too. His observation stayed in my mind, like a koan.

The next day, no orcas seen or heard, we headed back across the Gulf to the fjords. The tour boats reported the Bad Boys in Aialik Bay. We found them in the afternoon, Holgate and Aligo, line abreast, in perfect unison, as Olga had described Eyak and Eccles. They foraged along the shoreline from Holgate Head to Aligo Point, and when we left them, they were traveling south, into the Gulf of Alaska.

There is, of course, no perfect unison in nature, human or otherwise. More than a decade after that season of splitting, Craig and I sat at Olga's scarred oak table eating lunch with part of our makeshift family, reshuffled into its new arrangement: Lars, now twenty-one, Olga and her long-term boyfriend, and Olga's first husband Otto, who'd given Craig and Olga the original *Whale 1*. After salmon, rice, and salad, Olga pulled out her laptop to show me the Chugach transients she'd photographed off Whale Camp that summer. In the first encounter, I recognized Chenega, Iktua, and Mike, and in the second, Marie, Ewan, and Paddy. Lars interjected his own Chugach transient story. He'd been crewing on a salmon seine boat the previous summer, and had seen Egagutak "hauling ass" up Valdez Narrows, straight toward the tanker terminal. Egagutak, heading for ground zero. From that terminal, the *Exxon Valdez* had departed on March 23, 1989. The ensuing disaster had changed all our lives. It likely wiped out Egagutak's matriline. He was thirteen at the time of the spill, a sprouting male.

So much changed, but the Sound still calls us back. Every summer, Olga sets up a wall tent at Whale Camp. Every time Craig and I hike on Squire Island, we peer inside the tent flaps, and I remember the seasons it was home for me. Every spring, we hike to King Tree above camp, and wrap our arms around it.

Like the Chugach transients, we're bound to a place—and to one another by a place—in sickness, in health, in our failures, and in our grace.

46

Lament for Eyak

In 1954, when Canadian writer Fred Bodsworth published the book *Last of the Curlews,* it was too late to save the Eskimo curlew. He didn't know that. His book was written as a cry of warning, but it became an elegy. I leaf through the pages of that book, almost too painful to read, and wonder, what purpose does it serve? In the forward to the 1998 edition, the poet W. S. Merwin writes: "From time to time, with a frequency that is hard to assess, the figure of the last representative of some kind of life, some way of being—a palm, a rhinoceros, a sparrow, a fish, a word from a language, a speaker of a language—presents itself to us for a moment like a recurring dream in another form, and then goes out, leaving us to make of it what we can." He calls this last surviving member of a species "a single irreducible warning."

Orca research is fraught with debate about names. Do we call them orcas or killer whales? Is "transient" accurate? Or should we call them hunters, or mammal eaters? No name is sufficient, yet all hold truth. They are killers, hunters, mammal eaters. They are returning to the realm of the dead. They are transient. Like exhalations, they linger against the dark shoreline of our consciousness, drifting as they slowly fade. They are still out there, hunting in Prince William Sound, as real as the mist of whale breath drying on my face. What is their irreducible message?

To talk about Eyak the whale, you first have to talk about the human Eyak. The Eyak people today live mostly in Cordova—where Prince William Sound meets the Copper River Delta—and in Yakutat, farther east in the Gulf of Alaska. To tell the final chapter of Eyak's story, I have to talk about the Eyak people, and how, in the end, the whale's story intertwined with theirs. Just as Eccles's story, in the end, intertwined with that of the Chugachmiut people in Chenega Village.

In some of the oldest indigenous stories from coastal Alaska, it's said that people reincarnate as orcas. Anthropologist Herbert O. Anungazuk, originally of Wales, an Inuqiaq community on St. Lawrence Island in the Bering Sea, writes: "Elderly hunters, refined in the art form of hunting on the northern ice and seas, will say to their crews, 'Someone is already hunting here,' when the *aqlu* is encountered during hunts. The hunters leave in search of other hunting grounds immediately." The Alutiiq people, which include the Chugachmiut, say, "We used to believe in animals. . . . When killer whales come into a bay with a village, the villagers are sad. They think the killer whale is after someone's spirit. They believe that after the killer whales leave, someone is going to die. It won't be long. Sure enough it happens." From that perspective, from the perspective of people who think of an orca as "someone," not "it," the stories of whale and human are so intertwined that they can't be told one without the other. So I have to begin there, under Eyak Mountain, near Cordova, to tell what happened to Eyak the whale.

The Eyak are a distinct cultural group that thousands of years ago migrated from Interior Alaska to settle in scattered villages along the rain forest coast. Devastated by the influx of Europeans to the region, by the late nineteenth century, thirty or so Eyak survived in Cordova, only half of whom still spoke the native language. Some spoke Tlingit, the language of a powerful adjacent culture from Southeast Alaska. Eyak language isn't related to Tlingit, or to Sugcestun, the language spoken by the Chugachmiut. Eyak is related to Interior Athabascan, and also to the Navajo-Apache languages of the desert Southwest. Reporter Elizabeth Kolbert, in an article called "Last Words: A Language Dies," published in the *New Yorker* in 2005, described the Eyak as "a mysterious people" who lived "in close proximity to other, more formidable nations," but who for thousands of years "somehow managed to maintain not only their own culture but also their own language."

How strangely similar this is to the Chugach transients. Perhaps geographical isolation—say, being cut off from other transients during the last ice age—established their distinctness. But for thousands of years since the ice retreated, their isolation from other transients has been maintained culturally, without geographical barriers. Lance's genetic tree, depicting the relationships among orca populations using Prince William Sound, places the Chugach transients on their own lonely branch. An offshoot from some long-lost common ancestor of North Pacific orcas, their "language" is entirely unique. Something kept the Chugach transients faithful to their isolation, even at the cost of survival. They refused to assimilate. It dooms them and at the same time imparts on them dignity.

Lance's genetic study suggested that the Chugach transients exist in a population bottleneck. The animals he sampled had much higher genetic diversity than one would expect in such a small, insular population. That's why, with only twenty-two members before the spill, they could still produce calves. Genetic bottlenecks can result from a sudden decrease in population size. You can live inside a bottleneck for a very long time, but though you look and act robust and vigorous, you are vulnerable. One disaster—one oil spill—leading to the untimely death of key reproductive males or females can be a stopper in the bottle's neck.

Orcas are not like us. At all costs, they hold true to traditions, like whom to mate with and what language to speak. The surviving Eyak people gradually assimilated, aligning with the powerful Tlingit. They adopted new traditions, dropped old ones. Gradually, their language slipped away. Some might say Eyak died as a culture. But others might say it evolved. The culture evolved into a new version of Eyak. In fact, the entity known today as the Native Village of Eyak—a federally recognized tribe—is composed of Native Alaskans of various cultures who occupy the former homeland of the Eyak people.

When Kolbert wrote her article, there was only one full-blooded Eyak person left, the last indigenous speaker of the language, Chief Marie Smith Jones, the namesake of AT2, Marie. Chief Marie told Kolbert that her Eyak name translated as "a sound that calls people from afar." She said, "I got that strong feeling right here that it's going to come back." She put her hand over her heart. "God will send down Eyak to start all over again."

After Marie died, the only Eyak speaker left was the linguist Michael Krauss. He'd compiled an Eyak dictionary during the years Marie and others fought to revive the language and culture. Once, in Cordova, I heard him speak about what it meant for a language to die. A whole way of knowing a place—a home—dies. For example, he said, take rain. The

Eyak word for rain means "something is happening." The layers beneath that word are, like the layers of a poem, or the layers under Eyak's and Eccles's songs, impossible to decipher. What they say about the rain forest coast of the Sound and Copper River Delta has been lost, buried with the last speakers. The language vanishes. But the place remains. Chief Marie told David Grimes that when she died she didn't really believe the language would go extinct, because the language comes from the land, and as long as the land, water, and animals survive, as long as the place survives, the language exists in its elemental form. Like a bulb, like a spore, like a rootstock, it lies dormant, waiting. Perhaps it will take a new kind of listening, of living close to the place, to bring Eyak back, "to start all over again." Marie told David she believed the language would be reborn.

Over the years after the death of Lankard and Gage, Eyak and Eccles's bond endured. When mariners sent orca photographs taken in Icy Bay, invariably Eyak and Eccles were in them. Reports of small groups of orcas, sometimes pairs of males, trickled in from tour boat operators frequenting the glacial fjords in the northern Sound too. And we continued to see Aligo and Holgate in Kenai Fjords. Sometimes we'd receive photos taken near Cordova, also of Aligo and Holgate. Only Egatutak, who seemed most bonded to Marie's group, traveled alone regularly. And once in awhile, the Chugach transients came together to call and socialize in the old way.

And then, after the turn of a new century, things began to change.

The last one of us to see Eyak and Eccles together was Olga. On June 27, 2000, in Montague Strait, she observed them foraging near Grass Island. They milled for a while, and then joined together, and side-by-side, in unison, traveled south toward the Gulf.

On July 8, 2000, I sat on the back deck of our new research boat *Natoa*, recovering from a two-day crossing of the Gulf. We were bringing *Natoa* up to the Sound from Vancouver. A former fishing boat, she was the perfect size for two or three people, and she was seaworthy. That afternoon, enjoying a break anchored in the calm of Jeannie Cove, my stomach settling after forty-eight hours in ocean swells, I wrote in my journal.

Twelve years later, finding that entry again, I am taken aback. I have to read it twice, checking the dates, to be sure:

*After my first five-hour wheel watch during the crossing, I struggled
to maintain equilibrium, to concentrate on one thing and not to
move my eyes too much. I passed from hour to hour, my thoughts in
a kind of mental quicksand. Then, in the bunk, where I retreated
when the seasickness got strong, I imagined finding an orca
grounded on a beach, how I'd pour water over its skin. I imagined
taking a fragment of its skin for a sample. I thought of our friend's
story, how he'd found an orca temporarily grounded by the tide on
a river delta in western Alaska. How he'd walked over to it, and
instinctively, reached out to peel away a strip of its flaking skin. By
mistake, he'd placed his foot on a flipper. His hand outstretched,
he'd locked eyes with the orca, its message unequivocal. He'd stood
frozen, then carefully removed his foot, retracted his hand.*

The next day, unbeknown to me, Eyak grounded on Mummy Island,
near Cordova. Before European contact, the island was a burial site,
where the mummified remains of honored dead were swaddled in sea
grass mats and placed in sea caves. A pair of biologists who saw Eyak
stranded there noticed that his dorsal fin had begun to droop, a sign of
grave stress. But two nights later, Eyak was gone from the island. The tide
swept back and took him in.

At 11:00 a.m. on July 11, 2000, Eyak, his breathing labored, swam in
circles off the Orca Cannery dock, north of Cordova. Witnesses took
photographs. A half hour later, he swam into Hartney Bay, in Orca Inlet,
a few miles south of town. There he beached again. Volunteers arrived an
hour later, dousing him with saltwater, laying moist canvas on his body
to prevent dehydration, hoping he'd swim free during the next high tide.
For three hours, people worked to save him. Someone collected sloughed
skin for a sample. But despite their efforts, at 4:15 p.m. on July 11, Eyak
died. He was thirty-three years old.

That day, Craig and I arrived back in Homer. On Craig's answering
machine was a message from our friend in Cordova: a male orca had
beached there. He called her back, only to learn that it was too late.
He asked her to cut blubber and skin samples from the whale's side, in
case the tide carried the body away. He assumed it was a Gulf of Alaska
transient.

What ensued was a spontaneous coming together of the community
of Cordova: biologists, members of the Native Village of Eyak, teachers,

schoolchildren, volunteers. No one had drawn up a contingency plan for the death of an orca, but the community acted as if they had one. They used an inflatable to tow Eyak's body into shallower water and anchored it there. The next day, Mark King, a local Native fisherman, towed the carcass partway up a creek. Then he and others used a pickup truck to drag Eyak's body above the high tide line, near the road. That night, biologists took measurements and filled out stranding forms. A young woman biologist stayed all night with the body, to protect it from scavengers, human and nonhuman. At five the next morning, everyone returned for the necropsy. Biologists opened the stomach to find it full of harbor seals. Over a week's time, they flensed flesh from bone, dismantling Eyak's body, loading the bones into totes on truck beds. On July 15, a woman at the hospital X-rayed one of Eyak's massive pectoral flippers. The tissue was denser than anything the machine had previously handled. It produced a murky image that would guide the reconstruction of the flipper bones, which resemble the bones of a human hand. The totes were loaded onto a tender, the bones stuffed into crab pots and sunk in the ocean to be cleaned by tiny marine organisms. After months, the pots were retrieved, the bones placed in burlap bags, and with the help of high school students, immersed in crab cookers, to remove the last of the oil and flesh.

By then, the photographs had been developed. By then, we knew it was Eyak. But all that summer, before his identity was confirmed, I kept alive a hope that it had been a Gulf of Alaska transient, lost in unfamiliar waters. In my journal, two weeks after, I wrote: *A whale has died and been dismembered by now, sunk to the sea floor, to be reassembled after sand fleas eat the flesh from its bones. I saw a photograph: the whale wrapped in wet cloth to keep it alive.* I wrote as though I were a stranger to that whale, as though he were anonymous. As if, by turning away, I'd hold the truth at bay: it was a whale I knew by sound, by sight. In late July, in Holgate Arm, near the glacier, we found Aligo and Holgate. So it wasn't one of them, I knew. What I didn't know was this: it would be the last time I'd see Aligo and Holgate together. That year, Aligo was at least forty-one, and Holgate was thirty-six.

One August evening, back in the Sound, after dinner Craig and I hiked with Elli and Eve to a place we called Goose Feather Lake. I'd strung seine twine through yogurt containers to make berry-picking vessels, which we wore dangling from our necks. In muskegs tinged maroon, flecked with tufts of cotton grass, we stopped often to pick blueberries. Near the forest edge, we stumbled upon a bear, also picking. It was a small bear, and it galloped away when we tried edging closer. That night, I tallied evidence of continuities in my journal. *Blueberries. Bear. Olga at Whale Camp with Lars. Resident orcas in Montague Strait.* I'd begun to worry that the residents had permanently abandoned the Sound for Kenai Fjords. But it was only my fear of change, and change was everywhere. That summer, a road to Whittier had opened despite years of protest. It would bring more Anchorage boats into the Sound. We'd written letter after letter—*the Sound is still fragile, slowly recovering, some animals, like AB pod, like the transients, like herring, not recovering—* but it hadn't mattered. Even Elli had written, mourning the loss of the train, a journey to the Sound she'd taken since babyhood. David Grimes said often, "Healing is not possible; it's inevitable," but so is change. Still, every time a storm rolled through the Sound, I was thankful. *Small craft advisory. Gale warning. Storm warning.* No road could temper that force.

A few nights later, I sat up after Craig and the girls went to sleep. It had been another long day with residents. We'd followed AB and AJ pods in the strait. For the first time since the spill, we'd seen the two halves of AB pod together. *Natoa* surrounded by orcas, Eve and Elli had climbed into the boat's rigging after they'd made us dinner—pizza and soda pop—and Eve had called out, "It's the way it used to be!" Even though, before the spill, she'd been just a toddler. We'd followed the whales until it got dark. In that moment, healing knitted us to the whales, to the changing sky as a storm came on, to one another. The approaching weather front slowly, like a shadow, passed across the Sound as we made our way to anchor. Rain began, then wind, at full force, instantly flattening the water, darkening it, tearing at it.

I cracked the window to hear the night sounds of Sleepy Bay, the hum of wind, the splashing of seals chasing fish, the huffing breaths of sea lions, the screaming of gulls, all feeding on salmon gathering in the shallows. If my senses were keen enough, I'd surely hear the sloshing of a bear wading in to nose after a fish. *I feel sick when I think of Eccles alone,* I wrote.

I hope the whale that died near Cordova wasn't Eyak, but I fear it was. And where are Chenega, Ikuta, and Mike? And Marie's group? We've seen only males this summer. Always silent. I haven't

*heard their loud calls in a long time. I read yesterday that some
say animals are not aware of death. Is that true? And how would
someone know? I project my own fear of loneliness onto Eccles.
And onto Eyak: a lonely death on the sand assailed by people with
buckets. But if animals don't think of death—are alive purely in the
moment—does death take them by surprise? Or do they give themselves up to it? Is death already in them, the way building a web is
born inside a spider? And is it in us, too? Do we already know how
to die, but our brains clutter up our knowing with fear?*

That summer, I'd been reading Harold Brodkey's memoir *This Wild
Darkness,* in which he chronicles his dying from AIDS. "I feel the silence
ahead of me as I have all my life felt the silence of God as a given. . . . It
is the shape that life takes toward its end. It is a form of life." I tried to
imagine the shape of the life that met its end on a beach near Cordova.
What would it be like to stand beside him as he took that last breath
and let it go? Would I feel his spirit passing by me, like a sudden wind
gust, or would I feel it travel across my face like refracted light, on its
way into that wild darkness, that great silence? Perhaps his death was the
wildest thing of all.

Maybe I'm not a "real" scientist, I wrote in my journal. *I'm just a small
eye in front of which the story of Eyak unwinds forever. I travel along, peering
through binoculars. My small eye. Within a bigger, deeper eye, an eye with
limitless depth of field and perspective. What I know about Eyak is one facet
of that dragonfly eye.*

In early March 2001, Mike Britain photographed a lone male in Resurrection Bay. It was Holgate, the last time he'd be photographed alive.
Later that summer, a Japanese photographer sent us a photo of a male
breaching in Icy Bay. It was Eccles.

Through May, June, and most of July, we saw only residents. Then
finally, on July 24, we found Marie's group in Aialik Bay, combing a
shoreline with Egagutak. For two days, we watched them hunting for
porpoises, hunting for seals, almost always surrounded by tour boats.
With our help, the tour operators had written viewing guidelines, agree-
ing to give the Chugach transients space, and mostly they abided by that
intention. But when no other orcas appeared, their desire to please their
customers overrode all else. They kept their distance, but the rumbling of

engines and generators under the water never ceased. The following day, Mike and Iktua appeared off Cape Resurrection, hunting for porpoises, spending eight, nine minutes below the surface, impossible to approach. No sign of Chenega. At season's end, we'd photographed only seven Chugach transients. Later, when I looked at Graeme's field summary of identified whales, it seemed that holes had been shot through the fabric of their lives. The next year, the holes were even bigger.

An orca alone seems a strange creature. An orca alone expresses its individuality, its unique voice and personality. Take a human being out of the context of family, even for a short time, and you will see the same phenomenon. There's a glimpse of pure essence, like watching one of Craig and Olga's kids, when they were little, absorbed in solitary play on the beach, or sing-talking to King Tree. In those few encounters, I saw the essence of Eyak, of Egagutak, of Eccles, of Mike. How do you quantify personality? There are only a few gestures, the sound of a voice, the pattern of calls, but I can tell you that those lone males were more than instinct, more than the sum of their behaviors, more than the average length of their dives, more than track lines on a map, more than transient, more than Chugach, more than killer whale or orca or fat-chopper or blackfish or *arlluk*—whatever descriptor you want to apply.

The water around him, murky and greenish below a bowed silver surface, goes greener, goes black. Down into the black he glides, pectoral flippers and fluke still, body propelled by the after-thrust of his dive. Air, in the chambers and passageways of his lungs, the labyrinth of his respiratory tract—he forces one pinched-off increment through an aperture. Air vibrates, energy pulses through the oil encased in his forehead, pierces the water in front of him, a cone of sound, a wail, blasting past salmon, past porpoises who startle and freeze, past plankton, past a feeding shark, fanning out, attenuating, a little of it lost to the water, bit by bit, down the passage, past the Pleiades, part of it deflected off rocks, now just a faint remainder bouncing off icebergs, entering an iceberg, changing its molecular structure, the ice now, like the water, reflecting the passing of that sound, a thread-like tendril, diffused and nearly masked by the sizzling of an enormous raft of melting ice, entering the lower jaw of Eccles, who waits at the entrance to Icy Bay. Eccles

veers around. Dives. The water around him, milky bluish, silty,
turning gray, then black, then blacker. Eccles gliding, pectoral flip-
pers and fluke motionless. Gathering energy, like a contracting heart
just before its beat, blasting it into the ocean, sending it back. I hear
you. I am here.

In 2002, a male orca washed up on Hinchinbrook Island. The carcass badly decomposed, genetic analysis told us it was a Chugach transient, either Aligo or Holgate. Neither male appeared in the Sound or Kenai Fjords that year.

In the spring of 2003, our friends Andy and Kate, from Chenega Village, spotted a floating carcass in Latouche Passage, not far from the village. At first, they thought it was a small humpback or gray whale, because the whale's skin had faded. When they approached the carcass in their skiff, they saw the male dorsal fin. Andy and Kate towed it to a beach near their cabin on Latouche Island. They tied a rope from his caudal peduncle to a tree so he wouldn't float away. A NMFS biologist flew out to help them do a necropsy. The male was twenty-three feet long, his dorsal fin a little over four feet tall. In his stomach, they found the remains of seals, a few seabirds, some kelp, sea otters. DNA was extracted from a scrap of the whale's skin. It was a Chugach transient, though too decomposed to establish identity. But the presence of those sea otters in its stomach suggested a whale hunting alone, resorting to smaller prey. Probably Eccles. At the end of that field season, seven Chugach transients were left alive.

Soon after, NMFS, under pressure from environmental groups including the Eyak Preservation Council and our nonprofit, granted the Chugach transients "depleted" status, but that word offered the whales little in the way of protection. And I question the word itself. To be depleted is, according to *Merriam-Webster's*, to have been deprived "of something essential to existence or potency." Since 2003, seven Chugach transients have roamed the Sound. Those seven, it's true, have been deprived, in the biological sense, of potency, the capacity to reproduce. But they exist, as fully alive as ever, and they pulse with the potency of last ones.

Some day, there will be a last Chugach transient. Like Marie Smith-Jones, that whale will know a language no other being can understand. I dread that day. Anna Nelson Harris, a contemporary of Marie's, another of the last Eyak speakers, expressed her own dread in a poem "Lament for Eyak":

My aunts are dying off on me and alone I'll be living.
Why, I wonder, are these things happening to me?
My uncles also have all died out on me and I can't forget them.

After the last one dies, the last Chugach transient, that dialect, like Eyak, will exist only in recorded form, as an artifact. We'll still be able to listen to it, and like a strange poem, wonder at its meaning. Like a poem, it holds a map and a code, the secrets of a way of living in a place. Like a poem, it will remain untranslatable, until we listen close enough to the place to hear and understand its deep language. Once, in the distant time, humans and animals spoke the same language. *That* language.

Yes,
why is it I alone,
just I alone have survived?
I survive.

In May of 2009, Craig and I heard the distant calls of a Chugach transient male on our hydrophone. A few hours later, we found Marie's group traveling along the shore of Montague Island. They angled into open water and headed toward Cordova, utterly silent. We took ID photos. Paddy's fin had finally developed its adult shape, a broad triangle. Noting their steady compass heading, we settled down for a long evening of waiting to see what would happen. They kept up a regular pattern, eight-minute dives, and then several breaths, hardly making progress against a strong current flowing south out Hinchinbrook Entrance. After the whales dove a quarter mile behind us, I shut down the engine, anticipating that they would appear nearby the next time they surfaced. But they didn't. After eight minutes, nine, Craig and I began glassing. The water was calm, but the sun was setting, casting glare on the sea surface. Ten minutes, twelve. Had we lost them? Though it had happened dozens of times—losing them—we still said it, "How could they disappear like that?" Then I spotted splashes to the north, orcas chasing something. We started the engine and raced toward them. Sure enough, there were three: a male and two females. They splashed and milled, then began traveling in the opposite direction, with much shorter dives. Something didn't seem right.

"From this angle, their fins don't even look transient," I mused, and a few minutes later, I realized that we'd been fooled. The whales weren't Marie's group. They were residents. That's when Craig spotted blows ahead: dozens of residents. In what was the ultimate shape-shifter, trickster maneuver, Marie's group had shaken us off. No calf traveled with them, but that was potency.

I survive.

47

In a Language Lost to Us, Eyak Is Singing

In the far time, nearly
everyone could speak
with salmon,

water, clouds, stars.
every body.

Now no one sees the ocean
though it lives in every tear.

In a language lost to us
god is singing.

—PEGGY SHUMAKER, "MOTHER TONGUE"

Today Craig and I are motoring slowly down Knight Island Passage, trying to intercept the residents we heard this morning on the hydrophone, scanning the flat gray sea for fins. In the night, a bank of low clouds pulled over, as though trying to damp down days of too-bright sun. Under its cover, binding ocean to sky, the orcas remain hidden. We're motivated, though: the weather forecast for tomorrow is grim. Hurricane-force wind is expected.

Now, at the end of the 2011 field season, my twenty-fourth, all seven remaining Chugach transients are accounted for—Chenega, Iktua, Mike, Marie, Ewan, Paddy, and Egagutak. But I haven't seen them with my own eyes in two years. Last year, I didn't see them because I was being treated for cancer in Boston. This summer, I haven't been in the right place at the right time. They've been nowhere to me but in memory, in my recollections as I've written this book. Knowing they are somewhere, alive, is almost enough for me now. As I write these words, I look across Knight Island Passage, hoping to spot a fin. That hope is potency, potential energy enlivening the Sound.

A Chugach transient might still appear in Herring Bay, Long Channel, Copper Bay, Culross Passage, Lucky Bay, Squire Cove, off Tigertail Glacier. Those places pulse with possibility. They pulse with premonition: a day in the future when the last Chugach transient is left, like that last Eskimo curlew of my childhood, calling without a response.

Extinction is a process. Rarely is it sudden. Its impact on the ecology of a place plays out over time. The oil spill taught me this: the net, as it once was, unravels, and at the same time is rebuilt in a new form: the food chain that doesn't contain Eyak is still a food chain. Nature goes on. For years, the Exxon Valdez Oil Spill Trustee Council funded restoration projects. But true restoration is impossible. Today no one can deny that the Sound, over two decades after the oil spill, is a functioning ecosystem. But it's not the same ecosystem it was when I flew to the Esther Island hatchery in 1986. In a dynamic, wild place, local extinction, the disappearance of an endemic population, a group of animals indistinguishable to the untrained eye from hundreds of other orcas still roaming the Sound, can go unnoticed by all but a few people. You'd never guess there'd been an oil spill here, some claim. Millions of shorebirds still migrate between North and South America, and some of them look a lot like Eskimo curlews. Some scientists, like those who called the aftermath of the spill a great research opportunity, might even find the extinction of the Chugach transients interesting, an occasion for study.

Some of the first words I wrote in my journal when beginning this book were these: *I loved the place before I loved the whales. I will still love the place when they're gone. But it will be a different kind of love, and it will be a different place, and I will be a different person.* That was my mindset when I set out to write the story of the Chugach transients. But I see it differently now. When I wrote those words, I hadn't had my final encounter with Eyak.

48

The Spirit Line

The old Navajo weavers used to insert an unmatched thread into each of their rugs, a contrasting color that runs to the outside edge. You can spot an authentic rug by this intentional flaw, which is called a spirit line, meant to release the energy trapped inside the rug and pave the way for the next creation.

—GAIL CALDWELL, *LET'S TAKE THE LONG WAY HOME*

Fine mist falling, fog down to the decks of boats in the harbor. On the breakwater, shags and herons cluster, hunch-shouldered against gusts. I see them through the spaces in his ribs. I stare down into the cradle of his rib cage, basket of bones, hoop of barrel staves, empty frame. The flat flipper-bones—so like hand-bones—splayed wide on either side. The right flipper-bones ossified. He must have slammed that pec down too hard one time—onto a rock, an iceberg, or the block-head of a bull sea lion nipping at his flanks—to crack it. And how it mended, reinforcing itself with foliose growth, like lichen, over the fractured bone. I search for the crack, the spirit line. And then? And now? I want to crawl inside, huddle at his skull's base, a dark, secret place, to listen.

In September of 2011, I traveled to Whittier to board the fast ferry *Chenega* for a three-hour journey to Cordova. Nowadays you don't hoist yourself onto the train in Portage to make that last leg of the trip to the Sound. Now you stay in your car, pay your toll, wait in a line for the one-way tunnel to open, and then drive through the mountain, trying to keep your wheels on either side of the track. The tunnel is dark, ventilated with enormous fans. It's a catacomb, the blasted rock sweating.

After ten minutes in the dark, you're through—and this hasn't changed: the sudden brightness, the shock of being in the Sound. There's Passage Canal on your left, and the same ramshackle grit of Whittier ahead. The brand-new hotel and more tourist shacks on the waterfront haven't changed the grim gestalt. I looked, of course, to the water, remembering that long-ago pair of orcas. The inlet was glassy, opaque with its load of glacial silt, uncut by any dorsal fins.

I was on my way to see Eyak, what was left of him. To finally go to the place where he died. The day was rare for fall, a clearing sky on the heels of a storm. The breath of the next impending storm showed itself above broken overcast: mare's tails, a sun dog, spreading jet contrails. On the ferry I watched familiar landmarks pass all too quickly, and I wished the damn ferry would slow down: Blackstone Glacier, Pigot Point, Port Wells, Lake Bay, Quillian Bay, Esther Passage, and a brief glimpse, far to the south, of Knight Island, its peaks swaddled in cloud. Craig was down there somewhere, on his last research trip of the season. I kept my eyes glued to the window hoping to spot fins, but the only wake disturbing the Sound's ice mirror was the *Itswoot*'s. The ferry dwarfed the old barge. Soon we left it behind, plowing its way toward the hatchery.

That night, while I slept in a friend's attic, the storm descended on Cordova, and I woke to sideways rain. A good day to don rain gear and gum boots, to encounter for the first time Eyak's bones. Cold, windy, shoulder-hunching weather. On September 22, the equinox, coastal Alaska poised between autumn and winter. I walked the block-long business district, stopped in at the Orca Bookstore to say hello to the proprietors, old friends, who scolded me as always for not carrying an umbrella. Then down the steep hill to cannery row, I backtracked along the harbor past the AC Commercial Company store to Ilanka, the Native Village of Eyak's new cultural center, which overlooks the fishermen's memorial and the slip where one fall I lived on *Whale 2*.

My heart beat harder and harder. A familiar sensation arose in my body, a cold inrush of tide. The same feeling I get every time Craig's about to tag or dart an orca. That same ice jam in my chest when I waited by the phone for the breast biopsy result the previous spring. *That* feeling. That "something is happening" moment. The Eyak word for rain.

The cultural center—a converted warehouse—is modern, fronted by a wall of windows. Their surfaces mirrored the gray sky, so it wasn't until I was very close that I began to make out the bones. They solidified behind the glass, like I was watching an orca rise out of deep water, co-alescing into form, the way Eyak had so many times. But this time it was just bones. That was my first thought, the first words to coalesce in my head: *Just bones.* As though an unconscious part of me had believed I'd find the flesh-and-blood Eyak in that room. I stood, becalmed, in front of the glass, rain dripping off my slicker hood, and took in the curve of the vertebral column, a sinuous line, suspended in space. No dorsal fin. No fluke. No saddle patch. No heart. No lung. No eye. I pushed the glass door open.

Part of the strangeness was the hum of business. He had been hung in a foyer, between a staircase to the second floor and that wall of glass. The space was bright, lit by fluorescent bulbs. At the top of the stairs were offices and meeting rooms and dark-haired people walking briskly about in work clothes, sheaves of papers in their hands. I felt out of place in my gum boots and rain gear. To get underneath Eyak's skeleton, you have to walk around a wall to the museum's reception area and foyer. I wasn't ready, so I slowly climbed upstairs, the skeleton so close to the pony wall that I could have reached out and touched the pectoral bones. I was nearer to Eyak than I'd ever been. I slid my eyes along his backbone, each vertebra diminishing in size and complexity toward the tip, an ellipsis of bony oblongs. The larger vertebrae were winged, one cylinder fitting perfectly against the other. A single vertebra, head on, is shaped very like the cross-section of an orca, I realized.

Standing there, halfway up the stairs, I winged back and forth, from scientist to emotional wreck, one minute fighting tears, the next count-ing the vertebrae: there were forty-nine. One for every year of my life if you count zero: birth. I slipped out of my backpack, shrugged off my rain jacket, dug out my journal and pen. I sat on the stairs, scrunching close to the pony wall when someone hurried by. I kept my head down. In my journal, I talked to him. *I'm sorry I wasn't there when you died. I'm sorry it's taken me so long to come here. I miss you in the Sound. Paddy finally has an adult fin. So does Mike.*

In a moment like that, how to act, how to not leave anything out, un-done, unfelt? I stood again, studied the heaviest bones: skull and pectoral flipper. *Remember, once my ancestors walked on land,* they seemed to say. *Once, Eva, your ancestors swam.* In comparison, the rest of the skeleton was delicate as a corset. I imagined the smack of that pectoral onto the water, the sensation resonating in the body's core.

Gazing down into the rib cage, that's when time telescoped. I imagined crawling inside, curling up in the place where there once was a heart. Suddenly seasick, dizzy, as though Eyak had swept me into his perpetual dive, I sensed how weighted, how wrong, his body must have felt on land. I had to straighten, take deep breaths, look away.

I walked downstairs, around the curved wall to the adjacent museum, to take a break, but there was no reprieve. In the small gallery, I found artist Mike Webber's "Shame Pole," carved and painted years after the spill, right before the fishermen's lawsuit against Exxon—for unpaid oil spill damage claims—was considered by the US Supreme Court. By that time, six thousand plaintiffs had already died. Webber, part Alutiiq, part Tlingit, wrote that shame poles were built by the Tlingit for the purpose of "forcing some person of high standing to meet or recognize an obligation."

"We will make you whole," one of Exxon's spokesmen had claimed during a public meeting in Cordova after the spill. Instead, the pole argued, Exxon had left "a hole in the heart of the Native." I thought of the energy trapped inside it, the wrath and shame and grief. I hoped a crack somewhere in the wood—a spirit line—could release it. I thought of the hole in the heart of the Chugach transients, the deathblow of the spill. No love or science or law or ritual could repair it. Into the hole Eyak and Eccles and Aligo and Holgate had descended. One day, the others would follow. Sooner or later, so would I. Perhaps that's why I sensed falling. Down into cradle of ribs, where once Eyak's great heart pounded.

I walked back to the skeleton, stood finally beneath the skull, looked up into the open mouth, took the seals-eye view, and felt afraid. "Every story in life worth holding on to has to have a spirit line," writes Gail Caldwell. "You can call this hope or tomorrow or the 'and then' of narrative itself, but without it—without that bright, dissonant fact of the unknown, of what we cannot control—consciousness and everything with it would tumble and implode." Perhaps that's why I sensed the falling, the tumbling. Just bones. The unknown of Eyak long ago escaped through that spirit line.

A few days later, during another downpour, I gave a reading—of an essay about Eyak's bones—at the Orca Bookstore. As people settled into chairs, a woman with shoulder-length gray hair approached me. She seemed shy. She wanted to know how long the reading would be, and then said, "I was there when Eyak died. It's strange, whenever killer whales show up near town, people die in threes." Her friend, sitting nearby, nodded in assent. "It's happened three times since I've lived here. Once, it was my boy, who was born with a genetic defect. Right after, he died in my arms." I told her about the Chugachmiut belief, that when orcas come near a village, someone will die. They come to call someone home. The women began to cry, and my eyes welled over too. All around us people chatted, waiting for the reading to begin. After the reading, all the questions were scientific. The bones themselves—exquisite, masterful—are, after all, the province of science.

Where is Eyak? And where is the spirit line? I think I know. It's nowhere and everywhere. It was there during the night when a woman sat vigil with his corpse. It was in the re-articulation of his bones. Acting out the heart's one prayer: that what's broken can be mended. That what's shattered can be made whole. That what's damaged can be repaired. That the end of the story is "and then—"

And then there was Eyak. Always and forever, amen.

Acknowledgments

A study—a book—covering twenty-five years owes its life to extraordinary support. Thank you to all who helped midwife this work but especially:

First, foremost, and always, the Chugach transients, for finding me, for being.

My pod, my teachers: Craig, Elli, Lars, Eve, Olga, and David.

The incredible humans of the Sound, who provide whale sightings, showers, saunas, hot tea, tools, tows, rides to town, diversions, moral support, news of the world, airdrops, role models, company, fish, seal meat, fresh lettuce, eggs, local knowledge, yarns, safe harbor, advice, newspapers, weather reports.

My field assistants—along with our guardian angels in the Sound, Harold Kalve, David Grimes, Jim and Nancy Lethcoe, and Roger and Marilyn Stowell—without whom I'd surely be bones at the bottom of Knight Island Passage.

David Grimes, Riki Ott, Rick Steiner, Marybeth Holleman, Jim and Nancy Lethcoe, Dean Rand, Stan Stephens, Kate McLaughlin, Dune Lankard, Nancy Bird, Karl Becker, Dave and Annette Janka, and all those who work their hearts out to protect the heart of Prince William Sound.

Chenega Village and the Exxon Valdez Oil Spill Trustee Council, for protecting Chugach transient habitat in the Sound.

Bud, Graeme, John, Mike, Lance, and Kathy, for all they have taught me about integrity and commitment in science.

Fellow transient orca biologists Alexandra Morton, Volker Deecke,

Christophe Guinet, and Robin Baird for their work and insights, and Lloyd Lowry and Kathy Frost, for insights about harbor seals.

Allen Marquette for sharing his enthusiasm, as well as his photos and stories of Eyak's death and the salvaging of his skeleton. And Ilanka for providing a home for his remains.

The organizations who funded my research: the American Museum of Natural History, Alaska Sea-Grant, National Marine Fisheries Service, the Exxon Valdez Oil Spill Trustee Council, and the American Women's Fishing Association.

The talented members of my community who designed graphics for this book, Carey Restino for the family tree, and Allison Gaylord for the map.

Kathy Smith for scanning the slides, multiple times, which would become this book's cover and interior photos.

My agent Jeff Kleinman, for prodding, cajoling, enthusing, and believing. He helped me finish the book proposal while I was undergoing chemotherapy. What more can I say?

The committed staff at Beacon Press, and especially my editor, Alexis Rizzuto, a kindred spirit from the get-go. Thank you for truly hearing these words, these whales.

Nancy Lord, for the right words at the right time, so many times.

The first readers (and listeners) of very long first drafts: Kyra Wagner, Asia Freeman, Mara Liebling, Jo Going, Kathy Heise, Margaret Baker, David Grimes, Nancy Lord and Craig Matkin.

Wilderness, midwife of woods, words, and soul.

Craig, for allowing me to write through an entire field season, while he did most of the searching. And for his photographs. And his love. And for saying yes so long ago.

Mara, for lifelines over a lifetime.

Further Reading about
the Exxon Valdez Oil Spill

Bushell, Sharon, and Stan Jones. *The Spill: Personal Stories from the Exxon Valdez Disaster*. Kenmore, WA: Epicenter Press, 2009.

Holleman, Marybeth. *The Heart of the Sound: An Alaskan Paradise Found and Nearly Lost*. Salt Lake City: University of Utah Press, 2004.

Keeble, John. *Out of the Channel: The Exxon Valdez Oil Spill in Prince William Sound*. New York: HarperCollins, 1991.

Ott, Riki. *Not One Drop: Betrayal and Courage in the Wake of the Exxon Valdez Oil Spill*. White River Junction, VT: Chelsea Green, 2008.

———. *Sound Truth and Corporate Myths: The Legacy of the Exxon Valdez Oil Spill*. Cordova, AK: Dragonfly Sisters Press, 2005.

Wohlforth, Charles. *The Fate of Nature: Rediscovering Our Ability to Rescue the Earth*. New York: Thomas Dunne Books/St. Martin's Press, 2010.

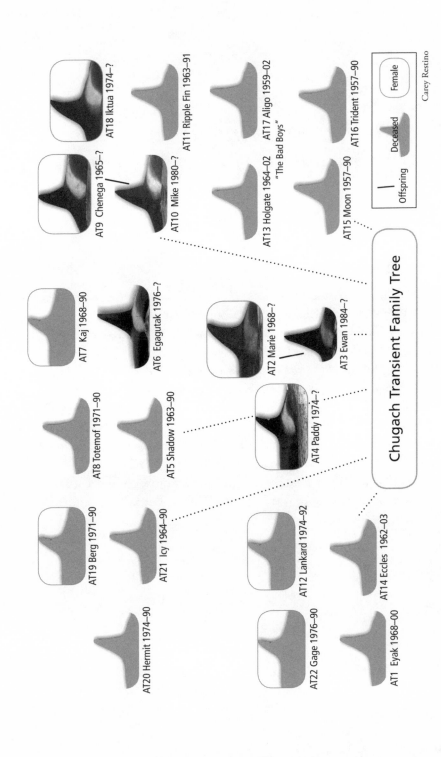

Chugach Transient Family Tree

AT18 Iktua 1974–?
AT11 Ripple Fin 1963–91
AT17 Aligo 1959–02
AT16 Trident 1957–90

AT9 Chenega 1965–?
AT10 Mike 1980–?
AT13 Holgate 1964–02
"The Bad Boys"
AT15 Moon 1957–90

AT7 Kaj 1968–90
AT6 Egagutak 1976–?
AT2 Marie 1968–?
AT3 Ewan 1984–?

AT8 Totemof 1971–90
AT5 Shadow 1963–90
AT4 Paddy 1974–?

AT19 Berg 1971–90
AT21 Icy 1964–90
AT12 Lankard 1974–92
AT14 Eccles 1962–03

AT20 Hermit 1974–90
AT22 Gage 1976–90
AT1 Eyak 1968–00

Offspring
Deceased
Female

Carey Restino